The Mark of **666**

AMERICA
SEAT OF THE BEAST

The Apostle John's New Testament

REVELATION UNFOLDED

Christopher

666, The Mark of America—Seat of the Beast:
The Apostle John's New Testament Revelation Unfolded

LIMITED EDITION (500 in print)
ISBN 13: 978-0-9785264-0-5   ISBN 10: 0-9785264-0-6

HARDBACK FIRST EDITION
ISBN 13: 978-0-9785264-1-2   ISBN 10: 0-9785264-1-4

SOFTCOVER FIRST EDITION
ISBN 13: 978-0-9785264-2-9   ISBN 10: 0-9785264-2-2

Library of Congress Catalog Number: 2006932698

Worldwide United Publishing
A division of the Worldwide United Foundation—http://wwunited.org
2303 Sherwood Drive, Lemon Grove, CA 91945
http://wupublishing.com—1.888.499.9666

Printed in The United States of America

Revelation 13:18

Here is wisdom. Let him that hath understanding count **the number of the beast:** *for it is* **the number of a man;** *and his number is* **Six hundred threescore and six.**

———————————————

I Kings 10:14

Now **the weight of gold** *that came to* **Solomon** *in one year was* **six hundred threescore and six** *talents of gold.*

Revelation 2:13

I know thy works, and where thou dwellest, **even where Satan's seat is***...*

Revelation 13:2

And the beast which I saw was like unto a leopard, and his feet were as the feet of a bear, and his mouth as the mouth of a lion: and **the dragon gave him his power, and his seat, and great authority***.*

Revelation 16:10

And the fifth angel poured out his vial upon the seat of the beast; *and his kingdom was full of darkness; and they gnawed their tongues for pain...*

T ABLE
OF CONTENTS

REVELATION UNFOLDED

FOREWORD

Courage has been defined as the ability to face danger, difficulty, uncertainty, or pain without being overcome by fear of being deflected from a chosen course of action. It was with *courage* that the early explorers set out on oceanic voyages in a world that was determined as being flat, knowing that a possibility existed that they would eventually fall off the end of the earth. It was with *courage* that Galileo stood against the powerful Catholic Church and defended truth, when imprisonment was the consequence. It is with *courage* that the foundations of human intelligence evolve, as those so endowed with its rare strengths and tendencies, stand up against preconceived and established "truths," which fall by the sword of the *real truth* wielded by those so courageous.

It will be with great *courage* that the reader takes this book in hand and endows his or her limited understanding of reality with the *real truth*.

If you do not have the *courage* to face the possibility that your family, friends, community, or church will condemn you and cast you out as a deceived or insane heretic of established thought, imprisoning you in a cell of isolation and rejection, then do not read this book. If you do not have the *courage* to seek for an understanding amidst the falsehoods and dogma established within the esoteric walls of organized religion and the closed doors of politics, then do not read this book.

This book is for the brave, the honest, the seeker of truth and wisdom. It is a disclosure of truth that has been hidden from the minds of scholars, popes, priests, and kings for hundreds of years. It presents an explanation of the foundation of the human condition that is long overdue in a world that is crumbling under the pressure of its own ignorance.

But most fascinating of all, the reader will delve into a mystery that has perplexed the whole of Christianity, and has brought undeserved fear and desperation to millions of people who believe the *Bible* to be the literal and ultimate "word of God." With this same "word," by using the references of the same *Bible*, the author has brought to the world an understanding that is overwhelmingly specific and direct in its interpretation, and unwaveringly exact in its description of the most talked about and studied book in modern religion.

Unlike other works authored with the same purpose (to explain the book of *Revelation*), this book crushes all the uninspired rhetoric put forth in past and present works, which are full of imaginative prose and interpretation that, when contrasted with the truth, will surely fall significantly. Truly, there can be no other source of the explanations presented herein than the mouth of the original author himself, John the Beloved.

This is where *courage* must present itself with definitive and deliberate rationale in the mind of the reader. This is where the claim of the author (that he was taught personally by John) must be weighed in contrast to the threats of excommunication or being deceived by a charlatan. If this work is true, it is the greatest book ever written concerning the true purpose and meaning of the book of *Revelation* and its relevance to the world. Its omens must be heeded, its information disclosed, in order to prepare a world to view itself as it really is, and not how its inhabitants have been deceived into accepting it.

No one who reads this book will walk away as the same person. Its enlightenment will enhance the truth seeker's perception, and confuse the skeptic's arguments. Windows will be fashioned in the walls of darkened boxes in which most people live their lives, from which a light will illuminate the reality that they indeed live in a box.

The masterful way in which John wrote his words is revealed in this book by commentary that supports the truths he expected to disclose (*Apocalypse* in Greek) to the people of the latter days. His truths confound all those who have set themselves up above others as leaders "called of God" to reveal the truth to the world. God cannot be a respecter of persons and maintain the due benevolence given to such a title. If He has something to say, He will say it to one and all the same.

Finally, the *Apocalypse* has come. The truth is revealed. And to the *courageous* who read it from the beginning to the end, this book will promise the realization of the profound statement: The truth will set you free.

Have **courage** and be set free!

PREFACE

Sections One through **Nine** present a philosophical and logical view of the human condition. Besides the title of each Section and its last paragraph, no religious connotation or explanation is given by the author. The purpose for this is to give a different perspective of the meaning behind the Biblical *New Testament* book of *Revelation*.

Some readers have no experience in scriptural text, and can easily become bored and disinterested in reading comments and quotes with which they are not familiar or comfortable. Furthermore, to many people, *the Bible* is a compilation of religious hopes and dreams which have little to do with the reality of everyday life; written, they believe, by men who lived long ago in another culture and time inconsistent with their own.

The author of *Revelation*, the man recognized as John the Beloved, understands the human condition better than any other person alive upon the earth. **Sections One** through **Nine** give his personal perspective in contemporary prose. These have been written so that there is no confusion of what John intended the reader to understand in reading his words. His esoteric and figurative expressions used throughout the book of *Revelation* tend to confuse a reader when not read in context with what was understood in the culture and time period in which it was written.

Sections One through **Nine** provoke thought and contemplation, and must be read with reason and logic—the very essence of their intention. Each Section leads to the next, and culminates in a final statement that relates its meaning with the symbolism used in the book of *Revelation*.

A strong foundational understanding will be gained by careful consideration of these first nine Sections. After reading them, the mind will be prepared to receive an understanding of the greatest REVELATION ever given by a mortal man to his fellow beings.

The CORRUPTION OF MAN

Giving science the due respect it demands from rational thinkers, let's assume that the human race has evolved into *a typical* species in the animal kingdom. How then, through this supposed evolutionary process, did our species evolve so dramatically different than any other species in the natural world and become *atypical*?

Where does there exist another species, genus, family, order, class, or phylum—in which its constituents are, by their own choice, divided into class structures—where one individual dominates and controls another in order to benefit itself exclusively? Outside the human species, where does there exist another animal group that consciously sees its other members as lower class, middle class, or upper class? Where else are there caste types set, wherein by birth alone, a creature is assigned a specific honor that sets it in prominence above others? Where in the animal kingdom do the natural instincts of one member serve *itself* instead of the whole?

A weak argument held by some is that there are some alpha males and females throughout the natural world who are given prominent distinction by nature's law. Others might suppose that the queen bee, for example, by the majestic nature of her birth, warrants the worship and class distinction she is given. In reality, the *queen* bee is a slave to the community. Any others born of the same *royal birth* are immediately killed, because there is only need for *one* to fill the role for which she exists.

The *alpha* of any group has little to do with birthrights, but is instead dependent upon the age and strength of the one given the title. If the human race followed this natural law, then the strong African slave would have had dominance over the smaller white landowner without argument. But as it is, the smaller human is able to subdue the larger and stronger, not because of any law of nature, but because of the manipulation of these laws by man.

The laws of nature have a single purpose. That purpose is to assure the perpetuation of the species. Alpha males and females are supported in order to assure a hierarchy that works well for the sake of the whole, just as queen bees are coddled and protected to ensure offspring. Regardless of these instincts, the natural law of the *animal* kingdom does not implement rules and laws that have the potential of destroying entire species. Each species acts within the well-balanced realm of its own environs to ensure that future generations will exist. Instinctual behavior demands this of all species except one: Homo sapiens.

Homo sapiens means "*wise one.*" The term is taken from the scientific classification given as the genus *homo* and the species *sapiens*. Of course, those who invented this scientific classification system did not see themselves as *stupid* creatures, and thus were so inclined to include their genus in comparison to the rest of the animal kingdom as *intelligent* and *wise* (sapiens).

These *wise ones* of the animal kingdom came up with a theory in which they could, through their self-proclaimed *wisdom*, logically support their classification system. This is the Theory of Evolution. Its premise is based on what is termed, "Natural Selection," which again as they suppose, is *wise* because *they* thought of it.

Natural selection can best be described as an evolutionary mechanism that occurs when some individuals of a population are better able to adapt to their environment, and subsequently produce more offspring. Nature, in effect, selects which members of a population are fit to survive long enough to reproduce. Differential reproductive success between individuals is the key. Those who produce more offspring have a greater influence on the gene frequencies of the next generation. In easier terms for the common *wise ones* to understand: "survival of the fittest."

It would seem, therefore, that if this *wise* theory could be substantiated as a true law of nature, it would apply to all of the animal kingdom. Yet, if science has proven that a species exists to maintain and perpetuate itself, then the Theory of Evolution has no verifiable application in the ant world, for example, in which the strongest (the soldiers) could surely kill every worker and every queen and take over the hill. Likewise, an alpha male could kill all other males, he being the strongest of the group, as well as could an alpha female drive off or kill the other females, thus assuring her prominence and future posterity.

If only the strongest survive, how have insect species existed for millions of years without any indication of evolution or subjection to the theorized law of natural selection? Could it be that Darwin (the so-called father of the Theory of Evolution) was not paying attention to the ants crawling up his pants as he crouched on the ground watching the birds? Furthermore, if *Homo sapiens* evolved from other primates, why aren't other primates evolving?

The more the species *sapiens* learns about itself and its environs, the more it begins to realize that there are more than just two kingdoms on this planet. There are three: the plant kingdom, the animal kingdom, *and* the human kingdom. Because the human kingdom follows none of the instinctual and natural laws that the other two kingdoms follow, it cannot be logically included under their classifications.

The plant kingdom cannot survive without the animal kingdom, and the animal kingdom cannot survive without the plant kingdom; but both can do rather well without the human kingdom. In fact, because of the human kingdom, the plant and animal kingdoms are being destroyed, not by natural law, but by *wise* human law.

The laws of nature create a balance and order (some refer to as a symbiotic state) that perfectly sustain the perpetuation of the creatures for which these laws exist. The lion eats no more than that which satisfies its hunger. When its hunger is satisfied, it does not kill unless it feels its life is threatened. The flower takes no more sun and water than what it needs to grow and flourish.

The laws of nature uphold the design of all creatures to sustain the life of their species, and *also* maintain the environment from which they take this life. Creatures beholden to these natural laws do not have the ability to see themselves as individual and separate parts, but fulfill the measure of their creation in order *to sustain the whole.* No individual buffalo looks at its herd and makes the decision not to mate so that the herd doesn't get any bigger. No plant or animal subjected to the laws of nature worries about tomorrow, nor do they look up at the stars and wonder what those shining lights are.

Humans are not subjected to the laws of nature. Yes, they are *affected* by the natural world, but they stand alone from all other genuses in their ability to consciously rebel against any law they so choose. If a wise one chooses to have sex for pure enjoyment, for example, it can do so by superseding *natural law* with the *human law* of birth control.

This natural earth is not subjected to *human law*, but follows the course it has been following for millions of years. It wasn't until the *wise ones* showed up that natural law began to be violated and disregarded.

Natural law fills the atmosphere with clean, pure air that brings energy to the plants and animals it sustains. It fills pristine streams and rivers with colorful and healthy plants and wildlife. It assures the calm rest of winter brings the refreshing life of spring. In all things, it creates a balance and order for the benefit of all those subjected to it. There is only one thing that keeps nature from doing what it does best: **The Corruption of Man.**

D^{The}RAGON

How can it be the fault of humans, that by consequence of their innate desires, they live contrary to the laws of nature? If they see themselves as the *wise ones*, they can no longer exist in harmony with a perfectly balanced world. This is because they recognize their abilities and their unique intelligence, which allow them to rule and have dominion over other creations that live by instinctual and natural law.

Though some groups of indigenous tribes found that this harmony with nature worked well for them, the majority of the *wise ones* soon assimilated these "less intelligent" (as they were judged) groups into the expanding sea of "civilized" humanity.

A human infant hasn't a chance of survival in the natural world without something distinguishing it from the rest of the self-equipped and instinctually motivated species of the *animal kingdom*. It is incapable of defending itself. Unlike other members of the *animal kingdom*, it has no fight or flight response that lessens the incidence of death as these instinctual protective measures do in other species. This further disproves Darwin's Theory of Evolution and the concept of survival of the fittest.

Humans simply do not properly fit into the balance of nature!

An infant has no fur to protect it from the cold, no camouflage to hide it, no pungent smell to ward off predators, and no overwhelming natural strength possessed by its adult protectors to utilize the fight or flight response to their advantage. Modern scientists speculate and hypothesize how the Homo sapiens were able to exist and flourish for thousands of years amongst ferocious predators; but none of their conclusions make sense or seem logical. Humans, by the weakness of their nature, are an easy source of prey for stronger predatory animals.

There are two simple differences that set the human species apart from the rest of the animal kingdom—*self-awareness* and *the ability to reason*. This ability is not instinctual, and did not come from years of cognitive evolution as some would suggest. From scientific speculations, a few *wise ones* formulated the myth of "cavemen," whose grunts and groans eventually developed into a communal language of cooperation, which aided the success of the species. If this were the case, science would see the same development in other animal species. But it does not, and *will* not, because these other species haven't the ability to reason; nor are they aware of *the self* as an individual part of a greater whole possessing the ability to exercise free will in order to maintain individuality.

This self-awareness and the ability to reason can appropriately be called "selfishness." Humans are the only purely selfish creatures in nature. After their basic needs of food and procreative sex are met, their *self*ishness motivates them to eat for pleasure, have sex for pleasure, and further establish their individuality from the rest of the whole of humanity. Therefore, "selfishness" becomes a natural human tendency by reason of their own existence. Recognizing "selfishness" for what it truly is, establishes a positive definition instead of the negative connotation generally recognized as improper behavior.

The *individual* is the essence of the *wise ones*. To find this "essence," one must experience a lifetime of choices in which actions contrary to the whole are taken in order to maintain a balance of self-awareness and individuality.

Humans divide themselves into family units to develop and maintain individuality. A male and female do not commit to lifelong partnerships to contribute to the whole, but to maintain self-awareness. "Love" is a value placed on something outside of *the self*. "Being in love" is a selfish abstract human creation. One "loves" if he or she contributes to the individuality of the one being loved. When there no longer exists a feeling of support for the *individual*, "love" no longer exists. A woman, for example, will stay "in love" with a man as long as she feels the man sees her as his "one and only," the most beautiful example of womanhood, or any other emotional support that builds her self-perception that she is uniquely distinguished from other women.

Humans may also form partnerships with those of the same sex, with no intent to procreate, but to maintain the essence of their individuality. When a male, for example, senses he is valued by another male, but his individual preference does not fit the accepted "norm," the union is emotionally justified because it appears natural and appropriate to both men whose *individuality* is supported by it.

Children are not consciously desired to guarantee the perpetuation of the species, but to give more credibility and support to the individuals who create them. A father and mother validate themselves by their children.

Most family rules and expectations are set, not to allow the children to become individuals, but to further the selfish desires of the parents to maintain their own individuality. When a child eventually becomes aware that his or her existence is no longer dependent upon the parent, and that his or her *self* is more important than the whole of the family, a rebellion ensues. This ultimately brings heartache and instability to the family unit, which was instituted, not for the sake of the child, but for the parent.

To further maintain the essence for which they exist, humans place values on other abstractions that can more easily establish a state of individuality among them. Material possessions become a distinction of class and prestige. Distinctions of accumulation of knowledge (not intelligence) set one individual apart from another by allowing the opportunity for self-worth to foundationalize individuality. A college degree or employment experience that none other has achieved helps maintain this human "essence." The color and style of hair, the jewelry adorning the body, and other personalized choices, support the *individual* against the *whole*.

Self-awareness creates the individual human experience, and the ability to reason maintains it. These unique human characteristics determine the balance by which we acquire a personal awareness of *the self*. If maintained properly, this balance serves us well, and gives meaning and purpose to our existence.

Individuality is the value placed upon this existence. When this value is compromised, there is no longer balance. Humans recognize balance and imbalance as happiness and unhappiness respectively.

Like "love," "happiness" and "unhappiness" are abstract emotions felt when the individual receives or doesn't receive recognition for its uniqueness. When one is not acknowledged separately from *the whole*, the purpose of existence is breeched, and the *wise one* becomes unbalanced, contrary to its nature. The human either exists in a continual state of unhappiness, or seeks to alleviate the discomfort by setting itself apart from *the whole*, thus fulfilling the measure of its creation.

Since humans seek to fulfill the purpose for which they exist (i.e., to be recognized and valued as individuals), they use their superior intelligence to accomplish this goal. Since the goal is individual and has nothing to do with the whole of humanity, whatever or whoever interferes with reaching this goal becomes a detriment to the happiness (balance) of the human being.

A serpent has long been viewed as a symbol of wisdom and cunningness whose power consumes anything or anyone who stands in the way of its desires. The *dragon* is an abstract serpentine fantasy contrived to exude power and destruction upon any who dare confront it. Though we fear no fantasy, we must be aware of our innate desires, which have become **The Dragon** that threatens our very existence.

B_{EAST} The 3

The individual pursuit of happiness has led to the rapid intellectual and technological evolution of the human species. Though these advances have come from the *wise ones* yearning to fulfill the measure of their creation individually, they have had little effect, if any, on the desired end of their existence—happiness.

When more knowledge is acquired by the whole, it has the potential of creating widespread equality and understanding, but this threatens individuality—the purpose of human existence.

Knowledge is what is agreed upon through mutual experience and perception. It is not synonymous with *real truth,* because it changes as other facts are acquired which negate the *accepted truth* upon which it was based. The accumulation of knowledge does little to bring happiness to a person, except as a distinction that protects or promotes individuality.

To protect this self-perception and set a distinction between themselves and others, some seek to acquire superior knowledge that sets them above the masses. When these are accepted as being more knowledgeable, they take advantage of the perception. These gain power over the need of their followers to maintain individuality and feel set apart from others. These become leaders.

Some are not convinced of a leader's superior knowledge and understanding, because in doing so, they will lose their own individuality by succumbing to the direction in which the leader has pointed the followers. These rebel against the leader and become enemies of the leader's self-image and power.

The first leader recognized in the human experience is the parent who forms a family unit. Through no choice of its own, in its early years, the child becomes an inculcated follower of the traditions, beliefs, and customs (knowledge) of its parents. The parents base *their* knowledge on time-honored respect for what has been taught to them. To protect these traditions, parents unite with other "followers." They form communities of families that are led in the same direction by whomever or whatever they have chosen as their leader.

These leaders protect the knowledge upon which the followers have agreed. These communities form cities and nations based on shared perceptions of individuality. The nations are led by the leaders who have convinced their followers of their superior knowledge and ability to protect the core of their power—the family unit established through individuality.

Leaders answer to themselves or to the images and illusions they have created that support their personal agendas. If the leader has the support of the nation, then the people have been convinced that whomever or whatever guides and gives direction to the leader is truth.

In ancient times, humans honored and worshipped their leaders because they were convinced that unseen and powerful gods led and directed them. As knowledge increased and spread to the masses, these unseen gods were replaced with other intangible gods, which had just as much power over the minds and motives of the people as did their mortal leaders. Whatever god is chosen, the leaders maintain control over the people by perpetuating and promoting the god in which the people believe.

Unseen gods religiously motivate humans to revere the whole to which the individual belongs, subjecting all to the will of these mysterious forces. These gods are known and accepted because people have placed their faith and support in mortal leaders who have convinced them of the supernatural essence in which they *should* believe.

It can be profoundly stated that a "god" is the equivalent of a *Powerful Human Motivator.* By utilizing this knowledge, leaders establish themselves above others, fulfilling *their* true nature of individual self-awareness; but are never able to satisfy their followers' desires to arrive at the same awareness.

Being the *wise ones* that they are, humans soon developed a *Powerful Human Motivator* (a god) that would allow them, whether leader or follower, to maintain the illusion that their existence was indeed leading to a full self-awareness of their individuality. They created specific values placed on each other and the resources of the natural earth. These values would always sustain a continual state of distinction and division, assuring individuality—the balance of human happiness.

These values began something like this:

The Story of Ug and Thug

A long time ago, long before the discovery of silver and gold, there lived a man named Ug. Ug lived in a community of people who prospered well for that time, herding sheep, raising cows, and growing grain.

One day while Ug was fishing in a stream near his home, he noticed a shiny rock exhibiting its countenance through the crystal clear water.

"That's a nice looking stone," Ug thought as he retrieved it from its resting place.

As Ug pondered on the discovery he had made, he wondered what use this pretty rock could have. He decided that although the rock was beautiful, it served him no real purpose; so he threw it back. Now that he had discovered the existence of the rock, he began to notice that the streambed where he was fishing was full of the peculiar looking stone.

Ug's neighbor, Thug, was a lazy sort, and spent many a day down by the stream idly dreaming up ways he could get out of the responsibilities of work that were required of him by the community of people where he lived.

One day, Thug noticed the shiny rock that his friend, Ug, had discarded.

"Hey!" thought Thug, "I bet I could convince Ug's wife that this pretty stone is worth a mammoth meat pie." (Something Thug loved to eat, but was too lazy to make himself.)

Thug took the stone and fashioned it into a trinket and gave it to Ug's wife, who upon seeing it, immediately fell in love with its shiny attributes. She made Thug his pie, and couldn't wait to show off her new trinket to her friends.

"Wow!" thought Thug. "If Ug's wife liked the stone, maybe all the other women will like one too. I'll never have to make another mammoth pie again!"

Thug went down to the streambed and gathered up all the shiny rocks he could find. When the other men's wives wanted a shiny trinket like Ug's wife, their husbands searched in vain for the rocks Thug had already taken.

The other women were distraught that they could not have a trinket like Mrs. Ug. These women began to pester their husbands until the pestering became unbearable. The men went to Thug and asked him for some of his shiny rocks for their wives.

"What will you give me for one of these rocks?" Thug asked.

"I will build you a fence," said one man.

"And I will give you three cows to put inside the fence," said another.

Soon Thug, the laziest man in town, had the best house, barn, fence, and animals in all the community. Thug spent most of his time looking and digging for the now "precious" stones. The more he found, the less there were for others to find.

It wasn't long before Thug made a list of the things for which he could trade his stones. He divided his stones up into groups according to size. The littlest stones he traded for a cow, a sheep, or an ox. A bigger stone he gave in exchange for a new shed to be built on his land. And the biggest stones—well, these he kept for himself because he knew he could break them into littler stones that he could trade for practically anything he wanted.

Ug's cow died and he didn't have any way to procure milk for his growing children. He asked his wife if she would let him have her trinket so he could trade it to his brother (whose wife had one but wanted two) for one of his cows. Reluctantly, Ug's wife gave up her trinket so that her children could have milk. Ug traded the stone for one of his brother's cows. Ug's brother, Shrug, took the stone, which was way too big for just one cow, and traded it to another neighbor for six sheep and five bushels of wheat.

Ug's brother never told him that his wife's stone was worth more than just one cow. He knew his brother needed a cow more than he needed a stone that he couldn't eat, wear, or sleep in; so he decided he had done his brother a favor. And for the favor; he would get more for the stone than what he gave for it.

This situation went on for some time. Before long, the stones were worth much more to the people of the community than any of their other possessions.

One wise man set up a little business by the bank of the stream where the stones had first been found. His wise premise was to help people save their stones and get more stones by lending them out to others in return for a bigger stone than what they had borrowed in the first place. When this man lent out a stone that was the size of a walnut, he told the borrowers that they would have to pay him back a stone the size of an apple. When the bigger stone was paid back as agreed, the man would then chip off a little bit of the *apple-sized* stone for himself and give the person who had deposited his stone in the business a stone which was bigger than what he had originally deposited.

"What an easy way to get more stones without finding any, or trading anything for them," boasted the man.

Since his business seemed to be successful by the bank of the stream, he called his business, *The Bank*.

Soon the people of the community were spending far more time figuring out ways to get and trade stones than they were raising things to eat, making things to wear, or building houses. It wasn't long before there were lots of stones lying around that no one could eat, wear, or live in. The people began to die from hunger and the cold outside, or they were killed by someone wanting their stones.

Ug analyzed what had happened to his community, and called the people together and told them what Thug had done. He explained that Thug had taken advantage of all of them because he didn't want to work like the rest of the community. He made Thug's name known throughout the land as a lazy con artist who took advantage of the peoples' industry for his own good. His name has been infamous ever since.

It wasn't long before Thug killed his brother for speaking against him; and because of Thug's riches and power, no one cared.

Our true natures consistently motivate us to maintain our individuality due to our unique awareness that we are different and independent from everything else in the Universe. As explained, we are aware of our *self*, and we use our ability to reason to experience things that validate our existence, or this individuality. Therefore, we naturally seek out those things that confirm this uniqueness. From our honest perspective, everything in the Universe exists for us to use in our experiences to arrive at happiness, which is the balance that we seek.

In the above story, Ug's wife was aware that wearing a trinket set her apart from others. When the other women noticed this difference that set Ug's wife apart from them, they recognized her uniqueness, and believed that they too could become different in the same way. Once all of them possessed the same bracelet, their individualism was diminished. To separate themselves further from each other, and reach a state of independent awareness that would bring them balance (happiness), each sought out other things—maybe two bracelets or three bracelets instead of one—to recover their distinctiveness.

This natural tendency is why humans establish borders, nations, communities, and families, and seek for personal riches and emotional securities such as patriotism or religious or group affiliations that separate them from others. Though these things are abstract, and are as varied as each particular mind interprets their meaning and value, they have become an important constant, and the utmost desire of a *wise one* in search of his or her natural balance.

Even those who do not want borders, nations, communities or families, and who do not seek material wealth or depend on the emotional securities that distinguish one human from another, still protect their individuality by not belonging to the group of those who *do* seek after these things. Inevitably, it is impossible for humans not to crave their selfish desires—no matter what they might be.

The leaders we choose to lead us are determined by their ability to protect and allow our individuality. The democracies of the world are premised on the ability of the people to choose for themselves the laws and governments that promote their selfish desires.

Governments that allow a person the liberty to exist and determine what brings balance to *the self*, and which guarantee this pursuit of happiness, are unquestionably supported by human nature. These types of governments encourage the perpetual quest for individuality. They promise their supporters the ability to achieve the realization of their selfish dreams.

Humans exist on a planet whose natural laws will never satisfy their free-willed intrinsic character. They are not like other creatures of the animal kingdom that have no concept of self-awareness, and maintain balance by working with natural law to perpetuate the whole. Working against the laws of nature, human self-awareness supports the individual, and sets a unique standard of balance (happiness) for which it continually seeks. Human intelligence and reason has created a powerful entity of motivation that helps maintain this balance. This *Powerful Human Motivator* is a *great beast* that has no part of the normal order of the animal world.

In other words, the **corruption of man** has created **the dragon**, which has given birth to a beast upon whose back the whole of humanity rides. Nothing stands in the way of this dragon and its desires. The beast receives its power from the dragon, and reigns throughout the whole earth. Who would want (or dare) to make war with or attempt to overthrow **The Beast** that fulfills the very essence of human desire?

I The MAGE

Because of their intelligence and ability to reason, the *wise ones* have progressed and evolved in their ability to protect *the self* and its desires. Standards of living have been created that determine the measure of happiness associated with human behavior. It might be argued that one who spends many days traveling hundreds of miles by foot to reach a desired destination, pales in comparative balance (happiness) to one who can travel the same distance in a matter of minutes in an airplane. If presented with both options of travel, one who has the ability to reason, measures each option by the standard that brings the most balance.

The innate realm of personal choice that supports each individual creates variables, which cannot be ignored when a standard of balance is being sought. One who travels by foot might enjoy the fresh air and the exercise, while the one who travels by airplane might enjoy the time saved. The purpose for the trip must be considered, as well as the desired destination.

As the *wise ones* reason their way to continual advancements in technology and science, they convince themselves that the standard of living necessary to maintain the quintessential balance must remain the purpose and end of these advancements.

Their ability to reason supports the idea, for example, that if a person wants to travel from point A to point B, that it would seem logical that whatever can be done to expedite the trip would lend to a more perfect balance. Ignoring the laws of nature, which mandate that a 50 ton mass cannot disregard the law of gravity, these *wise ones* use their superior intellect and free will to find a better way to make the trip in less time. Once they arrive at what they believe to be a more balanced end (in this example, the fastest means of travel), they set a standard by which they measure happiness (balance).

Once the standard is set, most humans are convinced that they must measure themselves by this standard—surely one who walks 300 miles by foot is perceived as foolish if an airplane is available to offer an alternative means of transportation.

The *end* becomes more important than the *means* to reach it. The *end* is happiness, and whatever the *wise ones* must do to reach this *end* they will do, no matter what natural law they must circumvent or violate in order to accomplish their goal. The consequences of ignoring the natural laws of the earth have little importance to the *wise ones* once their fundamental needs are satisfied. These needs are the same as those of the animal kingdom, i.e., food, sex, and survival.

The fulfillment of these needs, or better, the subjection to and compliance with the natural laws that mandate them, *does not* achieve the realization of human existence, which is the awareness of *the self*. In pursuit of individualism and uniqueness, the *wise ones* violate and ignore natural law, subjecting themselves to the resultant penalties and consequences.

In the example above, sitting on an airplane without exercising the functions of the body will cause muscle and joint atrophy; whereas a leisurely walk of many miles, without time restraints, would add to the health and vitality of the individual. The desired end is the destination. The human cost is the means that is not reasoned or calculated into the scenario, because it is not given the same value as is given to the satisfaction experienced at the *end*.

Free-willed beings have no laws they *must* obey, no instincts that guide them, and even less natural ability to accomplish their desires—

which have little or nothing to do with natural law. There is no law of nature that presupposes or mandates happiness and the smile it produces in a human being. The uniqueness of the smile is the emotional end result of a preconceived desire being fulfilled.

When no results are experienced which end in a smile, people refer to the natural laws to which they are beholden in an attempt to feel satisfied—which they perceive as balance and happiness. They know that eating satisfies the pangs of hunger, thus proving that there is always one end that can be satisfied through free agency. Therefore, as one example, when a human is sad because of the inability to reach the desired end of a preconception, they eat and eat and eat; something they can control by circumventing natural law (whereas animals eat to live, not live to eat).

Some couples stay together, not because they necessarily like each other, but because they know through experience that the natural law that mandates sexual urges can be satisfied; and a semblance of balance and happiness can be achieved in doing so. Humans will always find ways to satisfy themselves temporarily, but rarely attain lasting happiness.

The long-term effects of circumventing the laws of nature, which have been followed by all other animals for millions of years, are not measured when the expected standard is the end fulifillment of human behavior—happiness. Once a standard is set and accepted by the whole of humanity, it isn't long before exercising free will motivates an individual to set him or her self apart from, or above, the whole by attempting to change the established standard. The reason for continual scientific and technological advancement has little to do with what is best for the whole, but all to do with what will help promote individuality.

To be the one who discovers the next great step in the standardization of human happiness, lends to the constant desire to be recognized apart from the whole. Inventors, explorers, scientists, actors, musicians, athletes, business icons, or whoever differentiates and distinguishes themselves from others, all have one common goal: to become the one who sets *the self* apart from the rest.

However, these personal goals are not shared by everyone. There are many, many *wise ones* who have no interest in setting themselves apart from others in this way, but have found their own happiness in other ways.

They have no desire to outdo their peers, and consequently, contribute little to the advancements of technologies that ostensibly support human happiness. Yet even so, they too, in their own way, seek individuality.

Ironically, through their efforts to establish a universal standard of living by which all can benefit, the *wise ones* have created their own opposition and challenges, which diametrically oppose the balance (happiness) they seek. From technological advancements, cities are developed and concentrated on small tracts of land where happiness is hardly experienced by their citizens. To escape urban sprawl and the crowding effects of these advancements, humans escape to the mountains, deserts, and other natural environs left unaffected by the standard of living effectuated by the *wise ones* and forced upon the masses. Humankind circumvents natural law and its environs in search of happiness, and then ironically, returns to these same environs in their natural state to recapture and experience what they lost through their own actions.

All humans want to experience happiness. Nothing is more soothing and provides more comfort than an unforced smile that comes as the result of a preconceived notion or desired goal being fulfilled.

Goals are based on what is conjured up in the mind. They are images created by the desire to experience happiness, which are directly associated with the need to sustain individuality in a vast sea of humanity. From the moment a little girl, for example, is able to distinguish herself from others, she begins to establish fundamental concepts of her world and what she must do to maintain who and what she is, and what she *should* be when she becomes an adult.

Human aspirations lead to miraculous discoveries intended to promote the concept of self-realization. Television, books, magazines, and predominately, the examples of the adults around her (who appear to a child as those who have a stable and secure *self*-image), create images for the little girl. From these images, she formulates her desire to become someone or something that either fits securely within the standardized images, or puts her above them.

Her balance in life becomes dependent on her ability to reach the desired end of her preconceptions. She competes with thousands of her peers who also imagine themselves as the next great actress, model, musician, businesswoman, or president; each living her life hoping to experience the end result of fulfilling *her* dream.

For the majority of little girls, it will always be just a dream. Their lives will be spent in misery and stress as they attempt to realize a persistent but virtually hopeless illusion. These dreams are based on an image formed in their minds when they first entered a world shared by billions of others with the same quest—attempting to find out who and what they are as individuals. These young women are tragically convinced that they do not fit in properly, nor do they fulfill the purpose of their existence and find happiness, *unless* their preconceived image becomes a reality.

The Image takes precedence over the natural laws that have been violated by the ***corruption of man***. ***The dragon*** and ***the beast*** give life to this image, causing all upon the earth to worship and desire it above all else. A hope of a life of happiness has become dependent upon *this image*. Those who fail to live up to its expectations and standards, lose this life. In essence, they are killed. Those who relentlessly pursue and worship *this image* have no rest day or night. Well has it been said of those placed above others as successful, rich, and living the "Dream": it is not in what is real, but it has all to do with ***The Image.***

The Mark 5

As humans attempt to exert themselves in discovering self-worth, they experience feelings, then develop attitudes, and then make choices of action. These actions, gestures, and other outward signs are how they define themselves as individuals in comparison to others. Likewise, humans define each other based on their own feelings and attitudes, whether or not the definition lends to a positive or negative impression. The overwhelming evidence of who a person is, or what one has become, remains long after he or she no longer exists among those who were affected by his or her existence.

When a standard of human prominence or excellence is conceived or envisioned, and accepted by a group of individuals, all others are measured by this standard. The group with the greatest physical strength and power sets the standard by which it expects all others to abide. If others do not live up to this level of quality accepted as the norm, they are branded as "sub-standard," and perceived as a threat to the view of the strongest.

The strongest group is not necessarily the largest or majority; it is merely the one that has the means of force available to subjugate all others to its standard. Humans create and raise flags as symbols of their standards, and by means of war, protect the flag upon which their standard is based. Judicial systems of law are created to protect the level of human behavior expected when one lives under the auspices of these flags and the governments that protect them. Force is used to take away the free will of the individual who lives contrary or substandard to the measure set by those who have the physical means to take away life or liberty.

These systems of law generally do more to protect the *image* of the established measure, than they do to protect the citizens' individual rights to become who and what they desire to become by use of their own free choice. When this is the precedent and purpose of law, and these laws are enforced by the threat of loss of life or liberty, the natural human is in a constant state of rebellion. This is because it is predisposed to set itself apart from others as an individual. When this standard is forced upon them, humans are thrown out of balance—experiencing unhappiness because they do not feel their self-worth is validated by those attempting to force them to be someone or something they are not.

When a standard has been set, a person must both support the standard and conform personal desires, attitudes, feelings, and gestures to the standard or *mark* set; or else be known as a non-conformist or criminal outside of the law. People are either known and remembered for how well they conform to the accepted standards, or for rebelling against them.

Therefore, by our actions, gestures, and outward signs, we fulfill the need to be valued as an individual by leaving our *mark* upon the society in which we live. Yet, when a human is not being true to *the self*, as is its natural tendency, a lasting happiness can never be achieved.

Humans experience temporary satisfaction until they realize they are no longer individuals, but *only* a part of *the whole*. If one cannot gain a sense of self-worth by conforming to the laws of *the whole* and the accepted standard upon which they are predicated, then the natural tendency is to develop this self-recognition and worth by becoming an outlaw, or a revolutionist determined to promote change or set a different standard. If the revolutionary movement develops strength and becomes physically stronger than the group that set the old standard, then the former flag is thrown down and another is raised in its place—setting a new standard to be enforced.

Most people would rather conform than rebel. Behaving acceptably fulfills a human's desire to be valued as "worthy" based on compliance with the set standard. When there exists no hope for a revolutionary force of substantial strength to overthrow the powers that be, most will relegate and surrender in agreement with the old adage: "If you can't beat 'em, join 'em." This submission may promise security and liberty, but does not guarantee peace and happiness.

A temporary personal satisfaction occurs when a set goal is reached. But when attainment leads to a "higher" standard being set because someone has already reached and surpassed the original goal, complacency becomes the norm, and personal fulfillment the illusion. Unless one sees *the self* as an individual of value, he or she will constantly crave to assert *the self* as acceptable by set standards, or will desire to surpass these norms.

At some point in human history, people were convinced that *education* was the appropriate standard. Obtaining some form of a distinguishing outward gesture allows a person to feel up to par with the set expectation of being educated. Degrees, titles, and honors were developed as outward symbols of conformity. Ironically, those who set the standard for education are the same ones who benefit from it.

Professors do not disseminate "education" for free. Therefore, to leave their personal *mark*, and set themselves apart from the rest of humanity, they convince others that their knowledge is, first, worth knowing, and secondly, worth another's time and money to find out about it. These are similar to the "Thugs" who did not like to work in the fields doing menial labor that produced the basic needs for human survival. Instead of finding glittering gold in a stream to produce captivating pieces of jewelry, they invented the sparkle of an academic "degree," which they then used to convince others of their self-worth and assert their individuality.

Originally, farmers saw no benefit from sending their children to school when there were crops to harvest. However, seeing the leisurely life an educated "Professor" enjoyed, they hoped their children would not have to work as hard as they did to survive and live up to the standard set by society. Hardworking parents sacrifice for their children, and want them to conform to society in ways that they cannot, thus vicariously affecting their own individuality and self-worth by the *mark* left on society by their children.

It was not long before farmers saw their children as valuable assets to the future of the human race, and more importantly, their own self-worth. Therefore, they became convinced that their children were in need of "education." But if their children received this education, how would they continue to grow and harvest their crops? This dilemma was solved by finding other creatures who did not fit the standard set for their own children. Their darkened skin naturally classified them as "substandard."

In their natural state, these "substandard" creatures lived a lower quality of life with few organized and mandated laws. In comparison, their tribes were certainly "uncivilized" to those cultures established by the more "civilized" *wise ones.* According to the farmer, if these did not live like a "normal" human being, then they were not considered human, but were viewed as animals that could be domesticated and harnessed as beasts of burden.

To leave *his mark* on the world, a rich farmer or merchant, for example, recognizes himself as "wealthy" or successful based on the amount of money or product he produces. His self-worth is then determined by the comparison made to other farmers and merchants of like trades who share the same personal goals. If he can convince others (as in the story of Ug and Thug) that his products and services are beneficial to the whole, then he has made himself valuable, and has set a *mark* for which others aim to reach or exceed. If he is powerful, because his club is bigger than another's, or his finger sits on a button that can launch a missile to take away life, he is in a position to protect this standard from any who disagree.

At another time in history, a few rich farmers and merchants lived under a crown that set a royal standard expected of all citizens protected under the reigning king's criteria. They decided, that in order to establish their self-worth and leave *their mark* upon society, they had to individually produce more abundantly and possess more than any other. Their standard was set just above the standard of their neighbor. Since each had the same goals, competition began to change the accepted measure until it became an unreachable illusion based on the desire of each to own the land next to his.

To maintain his *own* standard, the King demanded by royal decree the payment of taxes on all that was produced by the rich merchants. The monarchial justification for a tax came from the expense of protecting the sovereignty of the set standard. Yet in his attempt to leave his own *mark* written in the annals of human history, the king's standard threatened the *mark* desired to be left by the "rulers" of some isolated colonial states. These rich "colonial kings" set their own standard under a new flag, which they presented to the world as the quintessential "standard of freedom."

At the time of this revolution, the wealthy colonists enjoyed most of the freedoms included in their *declaratory* and *independent* standard; except for one: they had to pay taxes to the king. The new "kings" (some refer to them as *"Founding Fathers"*) decided it would be more advantageous for them to have the people pay taxes to support *their* standard of living. Their "standard" included the ownership of land, slaves (those *creatures* who did not fit their "standard"), the payment of $300 each to avoid conscription for them and their children, AND the exclusion of women (and anyone else who didn't fit their measure) in the right to vote for these "standards."

With bravado and patriotic rhetoric, these "new kings" (these wealthy farmers and merchants) have left their *mark* upon a world that has set them up individually and apart from others as some of the most courageous and intelligent *wise ones* the world has ever known. This *mark* has influenced a work ethic and level of "excellence" that is written upon the hands of all those who indulge in its pursuit. The *mark* has now become the primary thoughts and desires in the foreheads of their slaves—slaves who do not consider themselves as such. This is because their "new kings" have convinced them that they are not *forced* to labor, therefore they are not slaves; yet in reality, they *are* forced to labor in order to survive.

With intelligent manipulation, these pseudoslaves have been convinced by their masters that they too can leave their own *mark* upon the world by working hard in the various fields, so that one day they can be crowned a "King" too! However, as these slaves toil and labor for these "kings," hoping to leave their *own mark* one day, they begin to see that the closer they get to arriving at the majestic standard, the further away it appears. This is because the "kings'" level must be continuously set a little higher than the rest.

Humans desire to be acknowledged and valued for who they are and what they do. The *mark* that is left by a human in pursuit of its individuality and self-worth is the *name* by which one person will be distinguished from all others in mortality, and remembered after death. The vast extent and importance of the *mark* is substantiated by the works of the hands and the thoughts in the forehead of each individual. All have received this *mark*, and are enticed to pursue a standard of excellence set by the illusion of human achievement. No one is immune from the innate desire to be of value and leave some symbol of a life lived with purpose and meaning; whether that life is lived according to the standards set by others, or by the individual.

Humans are deceived by the miracles and ***the image*** presented by ***the beast***, who receives its power from ***the dragon***, which is supported by ***the corruption of man***. Prominent in the right hand or upon the forehead of every free-willed *wise one* is the essence of the individual— ***The Mark*** of the beast.

The WRATH OF GOD

The consequences of human behavior are as natural and self-evident as the behavior itself. Free-willed in their ability and capacity to experience life without predetermined functions and instincts to mandate action, humans are directly affected by the decisions they make. In other words, they are right where they have decided to be.

Though the effects of nature can force unexpected experience and circumstance upon all biological life subjected to its laws, humans are also independently affected by what *they* choose to do individually with their free agency. Besides being eaten by an animal higher up the food chain, no other life form has the secondary responsibility of suffering retribution for its actions. Conversely, neither does any other possess the ability to experience a sense of fulfillment when an individual choice reaches the desired end for which it was intended.

If the laws of nature determine for the human being what actions need to be taken in order to maintain a consistent balance, without allowing consequences (like all other life), humans would exist for the sake of nature alone. Therefore, they would not be able to distinguish themselves separately from the whole. With their ability to reason and choose their actions without an inborn pattern of perfunctory behaviors, humans are able to experience a life full of consequences of their own choosing.

Figuratively expressed, it's as if a human has been presented a table upon which are two bowls—one is filled with fruit that tastes good, and the other is filled with bitter-tasting fruit. Because the fruits look the same on the outside, the determination of whether or not one tastes better than the other can only be experienced by sampling each fruit. If the good fruit came from the same tree at the same season, the laws of nature would have already predetermined that all the fruit of the tree would taste exactly the same. Therefore, the bitter fruit either came from a different tree, or at another time of season when the fruit was not quite ripe.

The good fruit will always be chosen over the bad fruit. But in order to know the difference (when the outward appearance gives no apparent clue to its sweetness), one must be given the opportunity to choose from *both* bowls, and determine for oneself which tastes better. If one is presented with a table upon which is placed *only* good fruit, there could be no comparison, and the degree of goodness could not be determined. If one continually ate from the bowl of sweet fruit, he or she would miss the opportunity to fully enjoy and appreciate the benefits that the opposition of the comparative experience would provide.

Put another way:

A father wanted his children to experience the great joy of eating a piece of good fruit. His children lived with him and ate effortlessly from his garden in which there was every tree that was pleasant to the sight and good to the taste. He taught his children that they could eat of every tree in his garden except for one. The one from which they were not allowed to eat was a tree of good *and* bad fruit. The fruit on this particular tree was indeed pleasant to the eyes and most desirous to the soul, but eating the bad fruit would cause a lingering bitter taste in one's mouth. There was no way, however, to tell whether it was sweet or bitter unless it was partaken of and tasted.

The father knew his children were becoming unappreciative of his garden, and the effort he put in to making sure there was always good fruit to eat. He knew his children would eventually take for granted the wonderful fruit available to them, unless they also tasted the bitter.

A kind father would never allow his children to do something he would never do himself. However, he had already tasted the bad fruit and knew the difference. He knew his children would always wonder for themselves what could be so bad about a fruit that looked so good. So that he would not be blamed for the bad taste that would linger in their mouths, the father never told the children that it was *permissible* to eat the bad fruit so that they could appreciate the good. To allow them the opportunity to make the choice, if they wanted, the father went away, and told his children to dress and keep the garden by themselves.

Enticed by their individuality and a desire to encounter new things they had not yet experienced, some of the children began to dare others to partake of the fruit of the tree of the good and bitter fruit. To establish themselves as individuals (which is the character of their true nature), some of the children ate the fruit of the forbidden tree and discovered it was wonderful to the taste. They took the fruit to others and told them it was good, and that they should eat it too. It wasn't long before they began to suffer from the lingering bad taste of which their father had warned them. But it was too late. They had tasted the fruit, and couldn't get the terrible aftertaste out of their mouths. They would never distrust their father and partake of the fruit of that tree again.

Humans have the instinctual ability to know what makes them happy and what does not. This knowledge allows them to make choices, the consequences for which they *alone* are responsible. With this ability to reason, which has been termed "common sense," they are able to determine for themselves those things that perpetuate happiness, and those that take away their happiness. In order to fully appreciate and completely understand the difference, no force, no unseen entity, and no advanced being from another galaxy, intervenes to curtail the use of their free agency.

As they experience the retribution for their actions, *wise ones* learn to value the actions that bring happiness, and depreciate the actions that take away from their happiness. These constant experiences propel the human condition towards a universal acceptance of values and circumstances that perpetuate and sustain the end desire of human existence—happiness. With each step taken backwards in experiencing retribution for their actions, humankind takes two steps forward. The steps backwards do slow the progress and process of arriving at a consistent state of balance and happiness, but nonetheless, these negative experiences also continue it forward.

If natural laws and forces (instincts) mandated eternal progression towards human development and learning, there would be depreciation in the value of the intended experience. However, the subsequent ramifications of this progression are the price that must be paid to satisfy the demands of the laws that guarantee happiness.

These ramifications are the penalties, punishments, woes, and consequences of opposing goodness and happiness. Though many humans believe that these consequences are part of the essence and penalties of a just God; a righteous Creator cannot violate the very purpose for which He exists—to provide happiness for His creations.

Therefore, it can be said that the *"wrath of God"* is nothing more than the *non-intervention* of more advanced and intelligent Beings (who could help, but choose not to), which allows the actions of free-willed beings, who are learning by their own experience about *the hell* they are creating for themselves.

The corruption of man supports ***the dragon*** that breathes fire within and gives power to and keeps alive ***the beast***, which has created ***the image*** that has left ***the mark*** upon all humankind, which suffers deservingly from ***The Wrath of God***.

P ATIE NCE
The
OF THE SAINTS

Human existence is a continual battle to establish and maintain individuality. This innate struggle is the natural effect of self-awareness. The battle lines are drawn by the ability to reason logically and defend the desired position of self-worth and separation from others. Confronted with a daily realization that everyone else is fighting for the same end only adds to the human condition.

This ever-present human conflict is intrinsic and exists within the conscious thoughts of *the self*. When one feels powerless over the armies of outward circumstance and the influences that clash with self-awareness, the natural tendency is to relieve the ensuing battle within by joining others outside *the self* and engaging an enemy that does not threaten individuality.

When the individual becomes part of a whole, the deliberate or immediate need to reach self-realization no longer exists because the values of self-worth are defined as generalizations, which exclude personal preference in favor of accepted norms. Lost on this battlefield is the conscious ability to maintain uniqueness and independence.

Thus, to ease and ignore the inner conflicts that humans engage in to assert *the self*, and find the balance to which they are naturally inclined, they look for battles outside of themselves. When others are found who have likewise given up the pursuit of individualism because of the outward pressures that fight against it, peer groups of equality are formed.

Peer pressure has little to do with the demands that others have on an individual, but more to do with the desire to replace the losing battle of *one* with the concerted effort of several. A battle shout of *many* transforms the unheard cry of one into an emotional array of substance that brings perceived unity and fulfills the wish of being counted of worth.

The first form of this unity comes when humans separate themselves from others into family units in which the parents' inability to realize self-worth is substantially decreased by the hope that the child will one day be of a greater value than them. No sacrifice is too great to assure the parents' self-worth by the success of the child. Parents spend their entire life savings to send their children to school for a college education to become, either what they did not, or to meet or exceed what they have. The need to demonstrate a purpose for their lives forces poor peasants to sacrifice their safety for a better life for their children. Hence, the losing battle within is forgotten by the hope of their children's victory.

Sibling rivalry threatens the unity desired by the parent. Each child, through its own effort to fulfill its true nature and become separate from the whole, jockeys for a position of individuality within the family. The fight within the child becomes a battle within the home. To relieve the pressures of the family: communities, cities, and nations become the battleground on which a continual effort to suppress the conflict within is supported.

Nations rise up against other nations, creating wars of death and destruction supported by the soldier whose individuality is forced into submission to the whole. In the pocket of each soldier is found a picture that justifies the killing of another human being—a photo of the family. Upon the mantle within the home is found another picture that supports the same justification—the photo of "Our Hero." Both the solider and the family use the *wise ones'* ability to reason to excuse the death of another in defense of their own self-awareness and individuality.

Even when a war of death is not being waged to alleviate or replace the battle within, the constant yearning to establish *the self* continues. Competition in business, sports, and opinion becomes the arena in which the conflict persists. Humans try to assert *the self* in order to be recognized and singled out from the whole. The competition and drive to win by a favorite sports team replaces the patriotic allegiance to a nation that fights by war to conquer. Losing oneself in the pursuit of *the Pennant*, the possession of *the Cup*, or the relish of "First Place," detracts from the emotionally depressive awareness that "*I am nobody*;" because when one's home team is *Number One*, then "*I am somebody*."

Wars of opinion and words create religions, political parties, and other groups that assert themselves as clusters of lost and insecure people seeking to find themselves by uniting with others who are in search of the same. Once dissolved into a molten mixture of humanity, people are cast into prefabricated forms that produce the opposite of human desire—individualize. Thus, the desire to stop the war within creates a greater war without.

To promote and create peace without, peace must first be experienced within. Feeling secure is the first step in finding peace. Giving no heed or attention to what goes on outside *the self* promotes the ability to establish self-confidence within, and leads to security. When there is no comparison to what is outside, what is inside takes precedence over everything else. A "kingdom" setup within an individual is governed by its own crowned ruler—*the self*. Fortified with high walls and secure gates, it becomes a city of refuge and peace, in which only those allowed therein are able to take advantage of its protection. When threatened by those without its walls, the gates are shut, and fortified with a confidence that the king within is the greatest of all the kings of the earth.

Humans who truly see themselves as distinct and unique individuals have reached self-awareness, and have no need to look outside *the self* for recognition or worth. There is no inward battle taking place, nor constant yearning to know oneself or be known of others. They see others as they see themselves—unique and distinct individuals fulfilling the measure of their creation.

This self-awareness creates a calmness that is not affected by anything outside of *the self*. In patience, they wait for others to stop fighting, end the wars, and see what *they* have seen all along—we are all so different, which makes us all the same.

Patience is best defined as the ability to tolerate being provoked or annoyed without complaint or loss of temper, and the ability to endure waiting or delay without becoming upset—persevering calmly when faced with difficulties. No matter what state of emotional duress is encountered by the enemy without, because of *the corruption of man* that supports *the dragon*, *the beast*, *the image*, or *the mark* left upon the field of battle, the armor worn during the final battle that protects against *the wrath of God* is made of *The Patience of the Saints*.

S A HARP
TWO-EDGED SWORD

The insistent determination of the *wise ones* to assert their individuality has propelled the human kingdom into a chaotic state of affairs that threatens its very existence. Under the auspices and power of but a few *wise ones*, the survival of the majority hangs precariously thin by a small thread unwoven from the tapestry of humanity. One end of the thread is held by a small percentage of human beings. At the other dangles the masses, who unknowingly are bound by a delicate link, which if severed, would precipitate their downfall *or* their liberation.

There is a sword that can cut both ways and sever the thread with one mighty blow. It can release the weight dangling from its unsteady point of attachment, giving solid ground to maintain its mass with stability. As it cuts, the thread is left dangling without purpose, held by those who are no longer needed to hold it up.

The sword is truth.

There are more than six billion human beings upon the earth at this time. Less than one percent (sixty million) of these hold the rest in chains of slavery and inequality from which there is no escape. The promise of becoming one of the elite—one of this *blessed* one percent, assures the efficacy of the rationale for the chains—work hard enough in the fields of slavery, and one day, you *might* become a master.

Upon the wall in plain view of the enslaved, hangs *the key* to their chains. It is not a tangible key, because there is no actual lock. It is the *writing upon the wall* that resonates in words that the chained cannot interpret for themselves: The truth shall set you free!

Someone must boldly step forward without agenda and personal expectation, wielding the sword of truth in defense of the yoked. The sword will cut for the benefit of the poor, the meek, the downtrodden, and the exploited of the world. But for the exalted, who are those who live deliciously and fare sumptuously from the woes of others, the sword only cuts one way:

> "The lofty looks of man must be humbled, and the haughtiness of men bowed down. The sword of truth and justice must fall upon every one who is proud and lofty, and upon every one who is lifted up, and they must be brought low. Like glorious trees of both cedar and oak that are high and lifted up, the truth must fall them into splintered wood. It must fall upon the high mountains, and upon all the hills that are lifted up, and upon every high tower, and upon every fenced wall, which are the borders that keep the lofty isolated like islands of the sea. These mountains will flee at the truth and the islands will be removed out of their place.

> It must fall upon all the ships which sail upon the sea of humanity carrying treasures of silver and gold—the idols of man—from one port of merchandise to another. The truth must fall upon all the pleasant pictures painted by the brushes of selfish artists who have colored beauty which they alone behold. The sword of truth will cause the loftiness of man to bow down, and the haughtiness of men to become low; for the truth alone must be exalted for freedom to reign.

When the truth is revealed, a man will cast his idols of silver, and his idols of gold, which were made each one for himself to worship, to the moles and to the bats which live in the clefts of rocks, and on the tops of ragged stones. Who are these *wise ones* and wherein are they to be accounted of? The mighty man, and the man of war, the judge, and the prophet, and the prudent, and the ancient, the captain of fifty, and the honorable man, and the counselor, and the cunning artificer, and the eloquent orator, these shall all cease because their breath is in their nostrils and the truth they have not known. The truth will exalt the children to be their princes, and babes shall rule over them."

Here is that truth:

For every **one** person who can claim success in reaching the standard of accepted self-awareness and prosperity, **ninety-nine** others suffer from the means used to achieve this prosperity without the ability to attain it for themselves. In the race to be counted of worth in a world of values and standards set to benefit those who set them, no notice is given to the devastating effects of the contest.

"Freedom" is an abstract idea perpetuated by those in power over others. Evident forced slavery has simply been replaced with tacit slavery. Rising to the sound of a rooster's crow to harness the mule to the plow has been replaced with the obtrusive sound of an alarm clock that signals the beginning of another enslaved day. In both types of slavery, the *wise ones* are forced to work or they will die. The former was provided food, clothing, and shelter; the latter is given a piece of paper that must be exchanged for commodities owned by another slave owner.

The slave's desire to live enriches the landowner for whom he or she works, and also the merchant from whom he or she must purchase life. The former was forced into chains if work and rules were not completed as established by the master; the latter is locked in a jail cell for the same reasons. Neither chose to be born into slavery; each would have *rather* been born the child of a slave owner: one who never saw the butt end of a mule pulling a harrow, or the other who will never hear the sound of a time punch-clock.

Though modern owners do not outwardly display their employees as personal human property, the slave trade has transformed itself into a shared commodity of the corporations and wealthy of the world. Within the commercial organizations that buy and sell goods, make products, and provide services, there exists a proprietary implication that if a slave refuses to work for one business, in order to remain alive, the rebellious runaway must submit to another. By running away from one plantation, the need to eat, and be clothed and housed necessitates the acceptance of another.

Chained ignorantly without lock or key, the *writing on the wall* has little affect on the minds of the *wise ones* who see themselves as individual and equal human beings instead of slaves. Thus, have they been convinced and deceived. The very essence of their innate human nature disallows the possibility that they can be controlled. They are convinced that it is possible that one day they, too, might own a business and have others work for them, forgetting their immediate state of enslavement by the illusory daydream of financial freedom and wealth.

Day after day, their minds are gratified and lulled into a tempered calm as they toil in the fields, cubicles, or other employment they do not enjoy but have chosen by force. The "Dream" satisfies their inner conflict by convincing them that it is possible to become a landowner; hence, they are indeed equal to their masters who were once enslaved like them.

The *wise ones* are not isolated to being slaves to the rich and powerful, but have also become indentured to their own desire to become a master. "Getting ahead in the world" has become the model of individuality. It becomes easier for them to alienate their minds from the conditions of poverty and destitution required at the bottom of the corporate chain, because of the image in their minds of future success and the opportunity to jump from the **ninety-nine** percent to the **one** percent.

The *wise ones* have become desensitized, and pay no attention to human history that has paved a path of awareness to the place where the thin thread hangs, and demonstrates that the set percentages have never changed, and never will—**one** *wise one* on top needs **ninety-nine** others below in order to keep them buoyed up on the sea of humanity.

Many of the **ninety-nine** die with little notice or fanfare, and are soon replaced by other unknown faces, struggling to stay alive, and hoping to one day reach the top. The *ones* pay no attention to the loss of faceless individuals they knew nothing about. Clothed in robes of excess and prosperity, they find no relevance in any matter outside the walls of their personal kingdom of gratification and family. The robes by which they are clothed came at a price—the cost of other human beings whose every breath stitched the woven threads of their contrived tapestries.

In the torrid sun, the stones of the fields are removed by calloused hands. Sweat stings the eyes of those who work tirelessly; laboring until the sun gives way to a reprieve of darkness—TEN.

Each day the field is plowed, furrowed, and prepared for seed, which requires more sweat, more toil, and more death to produce the billowing soft fibers—TWENTY.

When nature takes it course, and the mortality of verdant leaves becomes evident by the colors of harvest, more souls are tasked with the burden of collecting the crop. Nature's product is delivered to others—THIRTY.

Day after day, night after night, broken hearts and souls sit in the same position, separating and spinning the delicate fibers into thread—FORTY.

Passed on to others who stand at the loom, or the machines that have replaced it, the threads are woven into cloth using the same process, every minute of every day of every year, expressing the apparition of a human shadow cast upon the loom, until no distinction can be made between the two—FIFTY.

The cloth is cut and sewn by bent backs and fingers, sitting undaunted in dungeons of production overseen by task masters who peer intrusively, assuring that no move is made that is not expected—the same moves expected yesterday, today, and tomorrow—SIXTY.

Checked for quality and packaged appropriately, the product is ready to be transported by redundant hands and hearts—SEVENTY.

Transportation provides the means up the chain by following roads of boredom and melancholy, finally arriving to unload the cargo—EIGHTY.

Received with pride and hope of profit, the changed and fabricated natural seed is proudly displayed with a learned sense of fashion by those whose hope resides in its marketable placement—NINETY.

Unaware of the **ninety-nine** people who brought it into being, the **one** out shopping sees the beautiful robe that is envisioned hanging next to the many others in the wardrobe of the **one** who will turn off the closet light, never giving a second thought from where each robe came.

Money has become the determining value by which others are appreciated or depreciated among the *wise ones*. A brain surgeon spends his time studying and gaining experience to save lives. These doctors allow slaves to remain well enough to continue working in the fields where they pick the strawberries and milk the cows from which the scarlet fruits are covered with white delight to satisfy the surgeon's palate.

Without something to eat, from where would the doctor get the energy to save lives? How many lives does he save in comparison to how many are saved by the produce of the hardworking fieldworkers? It takes only **one** doctor to operate on a brain, but **ninety-nine** migrant workers to assure the harvest doesn't spoil in the countryside fields.

The **one's** worth is augmented, not only by the values they have placed upon their own abilities, but also by the prospect that by the sweat of the brows of unseen others of lesser means, their worth can be increased. Appalling to human decency, corporations and capitalistic business enterprises offer stock in their companies to the **ones**, promising that by paying low wages, few benefits, and keeping the **ninety-nine** percent in slavery, a healthy dividend will be paid for doing absolutely nothing! These stocks are more precious to the holder than the lives of the oppressed needed to create their value.

To avoid personal accountability for actions deemed necessary in pursuing profit, the *wise ones* found a way to detach themselves from the stigma of greed and merchant despotism. The introduction of "corporations" and "charitable foundations" created entities as abstract as the values placed upon them.

Corporations are groups of *wise ones* acting as a single entity with one purpose only—profit. Charitable organizations are set up to bring value to the **ones** who set them up, or donate to them, with attempts to hide profits and deceive themselves and the rest of the **ninety-nine**, that by what they are doing, they are solving the world's problems. Without taking away the purpose for which they are established, corporations and charitable foundations cannot acknowledge that the *real* problem is slavery—and they do absolutely nothing about this!

Profit is the monetary worth that remains after the value of the **ninety-nine** has been subtracted from the value of the **one**. To increase the sum of this insensitive equation, the value of either the **one** or the **ninety-nine** must be decreased proportionally to obtain the desired amount of profit. Since corporations and foundations have replaced the **one**, or better, the **ones** have *become* the corporations and foundations (and most business laws protect and secure the value of the person founding these entities), **only one** determinant is left to be lowered to increase the overall profit. The equation is: (corporate/foundation value) – (human value) = (profit). These entities will not, by choice, devalue themselves; therefore, the only determinant left to be reduced is human value.

At length, there are those who awaken from the deep sleep into which they have been lulled by the carnal security provided by their master. By the light of day, they see the hopelessness in reaching the top of the chain. They witness others clamoring over each other, dragging each other down in their attempt to reach the top. They realize they have been deceived by the master, and that there is no lock on their chain. Cast aside, the chain no longer has significance to their individual state of existence. Yet, without it, they will die. So they fight the masters, determined to proclaim their independence from the chains by which they were bound. But their sticks and stones are no match for their masters' whips and weapons. They either submit or are killed.

These are seen as rebellious criminals, terrorists, or insurgents who have no hope of being valued by others for what they *refuse* to do. So they gain value in their own eyes by what *they decide* to do for themselves. They did not set the standard and values by which they have been judged by others. They had no part of the decision made between two *wise ones* insistent on perpetuating their own value by creating the standards. Hitherto forced into existence, they must submit the identifying nature of their souls to the will of others' expectations.

"Submit or die" is a far cry from the liberty inalienably guaranteed by free will and the ability to recognize *the self*.

Submit to what? To the self-evident realization that one *wise one* is not considered as good as another? Can this submission transcend the feeling of knowing that *the self* exists independently because of its ability to think and recognize itself? Claiming one is better than another prioritizes the worth of existence, thus giving credence to the imposed reality that supremacy negates the lives of those considered inferior—the **ninety-nine** do not exist to the **one**.

Many years might pass before the **ninety-nine** percent finally realizes they are not valued by the **one** percent as equals. But as they do, a revolution of thought replaces their inner struggles with wars and rumor of wars, demanding that they are recognized and valued as equal human beings.

Unfortunately for the masses (even if the majority possess powerful hand-held weapons and the physical strength to wield them against the minority), technological superiority allows just **one** to be at the controls of a warplane or nuclear weapon and quash any revolution of the greater number. The **one** will always rule and set the measures, the values, and the standard to which the **ninety-nine** must submit or be killed.

What is needed is for the **ninety-nine** to appoint **one** to represent them, who becomes the **Anointed One**, having the power and knowledge to represent all equally. This chosen one must possess the gentle nature of a lamb to assure equality and fairness to all, but brandish a sword from which none are immune from the strength of its blow.

This "**Anointed One**" is truth and justice for **all** equally.

The patience of the saints await the triumphant day when *the corruption of man,* which supports *the dragon*, *the beast*, *the image*, and *the mark*, all which caused *the wrath of God*, are subdued by *The Sharp Two-Edged Sword* of truth and justice.

The END OF TIMES

Faced with a continual battle in order to maintain, assert, and protect individuality, humankind finds itself precariously close to being destroyed from within. Complete annihilation appears to be the destination humans are headed for along a path of self-protection and defense of the human ego. This "ego" is the *wise one's* idea of his or her own importance and worth compared to others. Some have an exaggerated sense of their own importance, and a feeling of superiority over other people. This minority threatens and exploits the majority of humankind.

Nevertheless, *all* struggle incessantly with the universal reality of existence, empirically expressed in *the self* by the adage: "*I think, therefore I am.*"

It is in how an individual *thinks* that threatens the very essence of the "*am*" *therefore* established. How a person thinks about *the self* determines how one is treated, and also how others are treated. Self-deprecating thoughts can destroy an individual, whether by drugs, alcohol, overeating, or allowing the natural urges of sex to overwhelm normal *thinking* patterns. This destruction occurs when the physical body and its needs become the main focus of existence. When this focal point has been established within the mind of the individual, the point of *thinking* is missed, and therefore, the point of *existence* also.

Thinking has absolutely nothing to do with the physical body. If it did, then those with the greatest minds would have the greatest physical attributes. As human egos go, those who spend their existence in pursuit of improving the physical nature of the body, can lack in the ability and exercise of *thinking*. Conversely, those *wise ones* who are distinguished by others as "being full of wisdom," are not generally considered as physically "beautiful" to the preconceived standards of the human eye.

The human world has become inundated with the idea of beauty, thus perpetuating an image of *the self* based on the outward physical body. It has done this in hopes of establishing a value and worth to individuality. Beauty magazines promote low self-esteem when the models (who are paid generously to become the image of human perfection) are seen and revered by those whose natural physical body will never be worthy of the measure that has been set. Natural aging brings depression and hopelessness, adding to the invented belief that an individual does not exist unless *the self* stands out in the eyes of others.

Physical goals of asserting and defending *the self* are perfectly in line when dealing with the reality of individual existence; but they have created a new adage: *"I am, therefore I don't need to think."* The *thinking* has already been done for humans in the standards and measures set by the society into which they have come into existence. These have replaced individuality (the essence of free will) with forced submission to the whole; thereby negating existence by not allowing the expression of the individual. Those who do not meet the standards and measures established are removed from the whole.

Ironically, it is this imagined reality that will eventually lead to the extinction of the human race. When the more physically powerful groups of *wise ones* destroy the weaker ones, all that will be left is a group of beings continually fixated on asserting, maintaining, and protecting *the self* in spite of the group—the bacteria of human ego will destroy the whole from within.

Natural law cannot be superseded and replaced with inventions that work against it. Free-willed entities must be allowed to be who and what they are; or by their free will, the natural course of their existence will end. New ways are found to improve the outward physical body in order to get closer to the set standard of perfection. Disregarding inward needs, faster and more efficient ways are discovered to destroy human life through warfare. These advancements in technology have the potential of destroying humankind from within and without.

Human salvation can only come in respecting *the self*, and supporting its right to exist separately from others. We must learn to do unto others what we would have them do unto us. Or better, we must allow others to exist and pursue who they are as they desire, as we would want them to allow *us* to exist and pursue who we are. We cannot establish standards of beauty, education, monetary success, and other measures in order to define the value and worth of an individual. We cannot set expectations for human existence if we want to allow others to exist as we do.

When a free-willed *wise one* is born into a world that has already determined what must be done in order to establish oneself as a viable human being, it becomes unstable and unhappy. This is because it cannot maintain the natural balance that makes it a *wise one* and not an animal. It cannot be forced into submission against its free will and its ability to use its reason (*thinking*) to determine who and what it is as an individual, and still maintain balance. It *must* be allowed free agency, and the right to exercise this agency, in order to fulfill the measure of its creation—individuality.

The *wise one* cannot be told what beauty is, but must be allowed to use its reasoning capabilities to determine its *own* perception. It must defend its individuality when it does not meet the expectation and standard of beauty others have instituted. The balance of peace and happiness comes from being amongst others who see each individual as beautiful no matter if the appearance of another is different from their own—seeing the beauty in others, as they would like others to see theirs.

A free-willed being cannot be forced to survive as a slave, becoming part of a worldwide conglomerate of corporate greed and profit. The planet does not exist by the laws of nature just to maintain the individuality of only one, but of *all* life thereupon. The natural resources of the earth cannot be controlled by one individual's assertion of *self* without regard to everyone else's natural prerogative to claim the same right.

Imaginary lines (borders) cannot be established making one group's pursuit and support of individuality of more worth than another's; nor can the resources of earth be owned and controlled within these pretended boundaries. If the laws of nature create a life, then these same laws must support it.

All *wise ones* are equally endowed with the inalienable rights to life, liberty, and the pursuit of happiness as each desires by exercising his or her own free agency. Only when laws, statutes, expectations, and standards are instituted to guarantee this, will there be established a foundation of peace and happiness that will bring balance to human existence.

Groups of some cannot be allowed to create their own standards and force these standards upon others whom do not agree with them. Those groups, who create illusory lines (borders) that separate one human from another, also invent imaginary entities that transcend the ability to be controlled by the logic of human reason. This creates emotional borders that are enforced with the same hate and prejudice as physical borders.

Any religion or god that does not support the law of allowing the free will of another, and does not teach its followers to do the same, does not support the essence or reality of existence. If it does not teach one to react, or to *not* react, in a way that supports an individual's right (as long as theirs is not being influenced), then it does not exist itself, or cannot be allowed to exist and destroy the peace of humankind.

Abstract material value (money) cannot create a measuring stick by which individuality is calculated, nor can it be a requirement for existence when life itself is free. In order to establish peace and happiness, **all** *wise ones* must be freely provided with the means to exist: food, shelter, clothing, and health care. These things structure the "*guarantee*" of life, liberty, and the pursuit of happiness. Without this assurance, the true essence of life (self-awareness) loses its meaning. Liberty is counteracted by servitude to those who place their own "life" above that of others. Happiness becomes a hope and ambition instead of the natural balance of life.

The *wise ones* must utilize their free will and unique ability to reason in order to stop inventing things that *protect* individuality; and instead, use this intelligence and dominion over the natural world to *support* it. Protecting one's *own* life and individuality without regard for the protection of others, creates fear, war, and destruction, while supporting life and guaranteeing *equality* in the pursuit of individuality lays a foundation of peace that leads to lasting happiness.

This foundation must come from a worldwide effort that transcends nationality, race, religion, pride, and personal ego, in order to address the human problem of inequality, hopelessness, and unhappiness. The **ninety-nine** percent majority must unite and demonstrate to the powerful **one** percent (that controls their destinies and has disregarded the *guarantee of life*), a solidarity of strength and resolve. They must demand the premise of human decency—all humans are created equal!

However, the powerful minority cannot be denied what the majority is demanding of them either. They also have a right to wealth, pride, prestige, and distinction, and anything else their egos require of their free will. What *can* be insisted upon is that the powerful use their might and authority to support the individualism of *all* people by turning the effectiveness of their ability to make war and conquer, into eliminating the struggle of human existence—turning their swords into plowshares. If a *wise one* is allowed to exist in freedom, his or her natural course will fulfill the reason for human existence (happiness) and allow it to be properly experienced.

Religious prophets and social pundits have made various attempts throughout human history to eliminate poverty and inequality. There is only one human organization that has ever been founded on the premise of worldwide equality and the guarantee of food, shelter, clothing, and health care to **all** *wise ones*. This organization has the proper formula needed to succeed: It is ***The Worldwide United Foundation*** (www.wwunited.org).

This united effort is the last chance for the species of *wise ones* to stop their decline and spiral into chaos, turmoil, and emotional and physical destruction. United, the people of the earth *can* solve their own problems and reinstate the preamble of their existence: We are free-willed beings with the ability to reason and use our free agency to establish our own individuality.

If we cannot do it for ourselves, the only hope is that a *wise one* who lives on another planet where peace and happiness is the norm (and who has much more wisdom, power, and knowledge than us), will come to this earth and save us from ourselves. This will be done by establishing supreme law and order based on the proven universal principle: Value others as you value yourself.

The end of times of war, inequality, and unhappiness must cease, or *The End of Times* of the human race will come.

In the words of a *wise one* who knows: ***"Even so, come!"***

REVELATION UNFOLDED

AUTHOR'S NOTE:

After reading this section, the reader will be left with no doubt that the **Great Beast** presented in the *New Testament* book of *Revelation* **is** the **United States of America**. It will be known that *all* human beings have the **mark of the beast** in their **right hand** and/or *forehead*. There will be no doubt what has caused the human condition upon this earth and the problems that are associated with it. And there will be no excuse to not do what must be done to solve these problems.

The book of *Revelation* holds up a mirror in which the world can view its own reflection. Lost from our memories are our childlike reflections, and the remembrance of anything beyond the first light that warmed our eyes in a strange new world. Our birth signaled the beginning of a journey in which our travels would lead us each down a different path. While traveling on these paths, we become lost. We join others on their paths, only to find that theirs is not our own. Once we realize that only our own path can take us where we want to go, we struggle continually to stay on it.

But exactly what are we looking for? Are we not searching to find our true *self* within? Do we not seek to see, once again, the reflection of who we truly are individually—not as the rest of the world sees us, but as we saw ourselves before the definitions and expectations of the world consumed our minds and made us into someone we are not? We deeply long to see ourselves the way we saw the carefree child smiling back at us, when we first noticed our image in a mirror.

As we grow and continue down our chosen paths, the lines of experience begin to crisscross our face like a road map—not showing us where to go, but only showing us where we have been. We begin to see the reflection in the mirror as something we are not. Our reality is affected by the illusory image staring back at us, and we become convinced that what we see is who we truly are.

These wrinkles are well worn into our face. We see these creases as flaws in our *real self*, not realizing they were created from the natural course we have followed in becoming what we have become. We have created the wrinkled roadmap by following the path we have chosen for ourselves. In essence, we have caused our own suffering.

The causes of human suffering become overwhelmingly real and inexcusable as we look at the face staring back at us, expecting to see the serenity and balance we once knew as a child. The mirror reflects the image of a being created from the passions and propensities of human nature that devour anything in their way. At the same time, our natures motivate us to search for happiness and a confident self-realization that we are equal to everyone else. In this way, we feel secure in what we see in the mirror.

No one doubts that the world at large is deteriorating as fast as it is progressing. As we discover new technology, strive for freedom, and connect via the Internet, television, and other advanced communication processes, we are uniting unlike any other time in recorded world history. But uniting for what purpose? Never has there been such rampant disregard for human life or the earth's environs. Life and survival have created a delicate balance between the natural world and the emotional world we have imagined to find our happiness.

The book of *Revelation* is a masterpiece painted by John the Beloved that reveals the causes and effects of human nature. As with any masterpiece, the artistic expression and medium used by the painter is unique, and can only be understood completely by the artist himself. Some of us look at contemporary "masterpieces" with contempt by comparing them to a child's work. Others look in awe at the colors, contours, lines, shades, and patterns; speculating and imagining the real intent of the artist, thus creating an illusory masterpiece in their own minds.

In a similar manner, some see the book of *Revelation* as a montage of illusionary creatures and situations created from the imagination of a religious "Van Gogh." While others, who are unimaginative and uninspired fearmongers, see it as a literal prophecy of future world events because of what they interpret as the world's wickedness.

John the Beloved wrote *Revelation* in the early part of the 4th Century. By then, he had witnessed human nature from a perspective that could only be drawn from many years of experience living among the different peoples of the earth. John's 2000-plus years of longevity is implied by Christ's words in the following verses:

> *Then Peter, turning about, seeth the disciple whom Jesus loved following; which also leaned on his breast at supper, and said, Lord, which is he that betrayeth thee? Peter seeing him saith to Jesus, Lord, and what shall this man do? Jesus saith unto him, **If I will that he tarry till I come, what is that to thee?** follow thou me. Then went this saying abroad among the brethren, that that disciple should not die: yet Jesus said not unto him, He shall not die; but, If I will that he tarry till I come, what is that to thee? This is the disciple which testifieth of these things, and wrote these things: and we know that his testimony is true. And there are also many other things which Jesus did, the which, if they should be written every one, I suppose that even the world itself could not contain the books that should be written. Amen.* (John 21:20–25)

Only two means of proof would satisfy both skeptics and believers. One would be John's revealing himself to the public, and allowing science to verify that Advanced Beings manipulated his genetic patterns—Beings who knew how to use *Their* knowledge of genetic engineering to change the course of human flesh and eliminate aging. The other means would be for a complete and comprehensive explanation to be given of the master-piece he penned, which is precisely what transpired to produce this book! How else could it be possible to unfold these mysteries, since only John knows why he wrote what he did? Only he knows what each metaphor and figurative expression represents.

For as long as the book of *Revelation* has been studied by apocalyptic and eschatological students and teachers, there have been numerous attempts to unlock the mystery of *Revelation*. Though many would like to take credit for attempting to reveal its mysteries and John's original intent, all have failed miserably, because *John* was not the source of their information. In contrast, the integrity of this work is maintained, and the claim that the author was taught personally by John himself is substantiated, as this book realizes the purpose for which it was written: *to explain exactly what John intended, and to unfold all of the symbolism he used in the presentation of his message*.

John's intent was to hold up a mirror in which we could each view the image of the creature that we call a *human being*.

John presents *the image* as a compendium of natural, or fleshly desires. These desires are continually burning with fear, hate, discord, strife, and all that fights against the essence of our true inner longings for peace and happiness. The rising smoke from the fires of our fleshly desires stings our eyes, filling them with tears that distort our vision of reality, and blinding us to the truth that we, alone, are responsible for providing the fuel for the fire that consumes us.

The rising smoke also creates clouds and mists of darkness, which shield us from the light of truth. These clouds and mists of darkness have spread throughout the entire earth. No light can be found anywhere. No religions, no spiritualists, no learned ones, no psychics, no popes, bishops, priests, leaders, no gurus or self-proclaimed experts have lit a candle with sufficient illumination to reflect the image.

We stare blankly into the mirror. In darkness, self-appointed prophets and teachers have invented religions, theories, philosophies, and illusory imaginations of what *the image* should look like; soothing the eyes and ears of those who hold them up as torches by which to see.

In spite of the clouds and mists of darkness, there has always been a source of light. The sun has never stopped fulfilling the purpose of its creation. It warms and gives life to the earth. But when clouds of darkness prevail, the light of the sun is hidden. However, the earth is not left alone. The moon majestically reflects the light of the sun, casting its light upon those who sit in darkness. Only by the light of the moon can people in darkness begin to see their true reflection.

Alas, people of the world sit comfortably in houses they have fashioned for themselves—houses built upon sandy foundations with no hope of surviving the slightest tremor of a living earth. Inside these houses the people sit in repose, uninterested in the light of the moon. People utilize artificial lights they have invented for themselves to illuminate their darkened state. They have been convinced that they do not need the natural light given by the sun, the moon, and the stars. Nevertheless, the moon is always there reflecting the light of yesterday and portending the light of tomorrow. Though eclipsed by the earth during its different stages, there has always been a moon set in the darkened sky to illuminate a path for those who choose to follow it.

The Apostle John was alive when Jesus Christ was upon the earth. Carrying a lamp as he journeyed with Jesus in a darkened land, John filled it with the oil he received from this *natural vine*. For hundreds of years, he covered his lamp as he lived among the earth's inhabitants. Like a golden candlestick on which a flame still burns after hundreds of years, John's lamp remains lit. It would light the world, if it were not hidden among a group of writings accepted by the masses as a source of all truth. It has become known as the book of *Revelation*. His lamp is unable to give its light and warmth because of the dark robes and dark suits worn by the religious leaders who stand in front of it, keeping the people from seeing its light.

The books of the *New Testament* were not selected, edited, and collated until hundreds of years after the death of Jesus. John was still alive then, and in disguise, visited those responsible for its canonization. His writings were profound. They gave the editors a different view of Jesus' ministry than that which had been passed down from one generation to the next. John also delivered his manuscript for his *Revelation* to the editors, knowing they would never comprehend its meaning because of the symbolic and metaphorical way in which it was written. In this way, John maintained the integrity of the manuscript for hundreds of years.

To truly understand *Revelation*, we must recognize and acknowledge that with our fleshly desires, WE have created the beast—the monetary system that perpetuates and assures inequality, poverty, and human misery. We have its mark in our right hands and in our foreheads. We worship its image, we possess the number of its name, and we have created the hell from whence it came.

It is time to stand aside, those of you who are dressed in cloaks of darkness, and allow the flame from John's lamp to give its light unto all who are in the house.

–Christopher

REVELATION
UNFOLDED

INTRODUCTION:

The *Revelation* of John has never been taken lightly by those who profess Christianity. However, there has never been a clear indication that what was included in the *New Testament* canon as the book of *Revelation* is what John actually intended to write. Not only did he write in a different language than that in which the text has been modernly translated, but there is no way to make an absolute verification of his translated words unless a person has access to the original manuscript written by John's own hand.

The author of this book has taken the time, done the research, and has the means whereby he is able to translate John's words as they were intended and came forth from his pen. With this accurate translation, John's words presented in the book of *Revelation* come alive with clarity, which allows for a more concise rendering of what was truly meant.

Upon reading John's message with the plain and precious meanings properly revealed, it truly becomes the greatest and most important given prophecy ever written for the end of times. It is necessary to understand that John prepared his words knowing they would be fulfilled in the latter days. Keeping this in mind will help one come to a better understanding of John's *Revelation*.

To fully and properly comprehend his message, one must approach it from John's point of reference. John has two main points of reference from which he formulated his thoughts and words into the presentation of his message: 1) The truth, or reality, and 2) The *Old Testament*. From these two points of reference came John's entire message, as all the symbolism and figurative expressions used by him can be found in *Old Testament* writings, which were the only form of written scripture available in his day.

Revelation is divided into three purposeful and intended sections, which as a whole, give a figurative presentation of the salvation offered by God to the human race. The first section (chapters 1 through 4) describes the general state of human nature, calling upon humankind to overcome this nature and repent of its corrupted state. The second section (chapters 5 through 13) shows the effects of human nature on the physical world, and most importantly, on each other. The last section (chapters 14 through 22) comprises the solution to the problems caused by human nature.

The commentary provided allows the reader access to insight and information needed to easily and completely understand the book of *Revelation*. **A complete understanding cannot be attained unless the reader begins at the first part of John's message and continues to the end. Skipping parts or jumping from section to section will lead to confusion and misunderstanding, which is the way in which *Revelation* is currently understood by religion, and learned by students of *New Testament* writings**.

The easiest way to understand what John has presented, both figuratively and symbolically in his writings, is to have the secrets and mysteries of God explained. This knowledge and understanding has been revealed throughout time to true prophets of God; but each has been laid under a strict command to only reveal those things allowed and relevant to his particular day and age.

> *Surely the Lord GOD will do nothing, but he revealeth his secret unto his servants the prophets.* (Amos 3:7)

There has never been a time in the history of this world when the minds of humans have been more prepared to have the mysteries of God revealed in plainness. With the advancements in technology, and the access to information currently available to the human race, it is no longer necessary to keep the many mysteries of God "sealed" from the understanding of His creations.

Had these same mysteries been revealed in the days of the ancient prophets, the people would have killed them for blasphemy and gross heresy spoken against the accepted religious doctrines and precepts accepted as truth in their day.

Even though the prophets kept the truth "sealed" in the symbolism of their writings, they were still killed, because they spoke against the religious leaders and false prophets to whom the people looked for guidance and direction, and who received money and adoration for their deception. All prophets of God were misfits of society, who the majority of people despised and cast out because they preached repentance and doctrines that opposed what their accepted leaders taught.

Modern times are not much different. The mysteries of God are "unsealed" and revealed in these writings. This understanding and plainness deflates and upends the authority and claims of all religious leaders and spiritual gurus, who have set themselves up above the people (for material or social gain) as a *"light on a candlestick."*

It is expected that the masses thus blinded will rise up in rebellion and anger against this message of truth, as it explains the book of *Revelation* in a plainness and simplicity never before known. Though organized religions of the world and self-proclaimed experts might rise up, fight, and reject these truths and unfolded revelations, their disagreement does not negate the truthfulness and wondrous glory of the mysteries of God presented in the book of *Revelation.*

Now, for the very first time in the history of the world, and as an introduction to the continued explanation of John's *Revelation,* here is a mystery of God all prophets have known since the beginning of time:

In our Universe, there exists an infinite amount of dark space and dark matter in which there are an infinite number of galaxies. "Dark matter" can be best described as matter that is composed of elements scientists have not yet discovered and do not understand. There is no part of the Universe in which there is not some form of matter, as there is no such thing as *emptiness*; for even when a clear glass stands empty to the human eye, it is still filled to its brim with the matter that makes up air, i.e., oxygen, nitrogen, argon, and other trace minerals named by the primitive understandings of modern human scientists.

Each galaxy is comprised of a finite, yet enormous number of solar systems. Each solar system is comprised of a finite number of planets. Dark matter and dark space have always been. The Universe has always been. Though continually being created throughout the endless Universe, galaxies have always been; solar systems have always been; eternal laws have always been; life has always been. Eternal means just that—eternal—no beginning and no end.

Eternal laws ensure a course of balance called happiness. All element, all matter, and all things obey eternal laws. The greatest source of happiness is experienced by free-willed beings who can consciously, and through their own agency, utilize eternal law for their individual happiness. Therefore, the eternal purpose of all things is to arrive at a state of eternal happiness, which can only be achieved by arriving at a state of eternal existence—currently expressed for our understanding as "resurrection and eternal life." Human beings who have progressed and advanced to the ultimate level of potential to experience happiness can be referred to as "Gods."

If we are children (creations) of God, then it follows that the course of our nature is to become like our Creator, thus all becoming Godlike in nature; or according to eternal law, all achieving eternal happiness according to our individual desires of happiness. This state of happiness occurs through both physical and mental progression when we view God from the perspective that He is a profoundly advanced human being and represents the end of our own eventual eternal state of being:

> *And God said, Let us make man in our image, after our*
> *likeness: and let them have dominion over the fish of the*
> *sea, and over the fowl of the air, and over the cattle, and*
> *over all the earth, and over every creeping thing that*
> *creepeth upon the earth. So God created man in his own*

image, in the image of God created he him; male and female created he them. (Genesis 1:26–27)

If humans are created in the image of God, and males and females are this image, then this appropriately implies that "becoming as Gods" is NOT restricted to male beings only, but also includes female deities.

*For God doth know that in the day ye eat thereof, then your eyes shall be opened, and **ye shall be as gods**, knowing good and evil.* (Genesis 3:5)

*Then the Jews took up stones again to stone him. Jesus answered them, Many good works have I showed you from my Father; for which of those works do ye stone me? The Jews answered him, saying, For a good work we stone thee not; but for blasphemy; and because that **thou, being a man, makest thyself God**. Jesus answered them, Is it not written in your law, I said, **Ye are gods**? If he called them gods, unto whom the word of God came, and the scripture cannot be broken; Say ye of him, whom the Father hath sanctified, and sent into the world, Thou blasphemest; because I said, I am the Son of God? If I do not the works of my Father, believe me not. But if I do, though ye believe not me, believe the works: that ye may know, and believe, that the Father is in me, and I in him.*" (John 10:31–38)

*For though there be that are called gods, whether in heaven or in earth, as there be **gods many, and lords many**; But to us there is but one God, the Father, of whom are all things, and we in him; and one Lord Jesus Christ, by whom are all things, and we by him.* (I Corinthians 8:5–6)

*Wherefore thou art no more a servant, but a son; and **if a son, then an heir of God** through Christ. Howbeit then, when ye knew not God, ye did service unto them which by* *nature are no gods. But now, after that ye have known God, or rather are known of God, how turn ye again to the weak and beggarly elements, whereunto ye desire again to be in bondage?* (Galatians 4:7–9)

God is a highly advanced and eternal being who uses the eternal laws of nature to do His work. His work is to bring about the eternal happiness of all those whom He creates. He has a body comparable to our human body that does not age or sicken, nor is otherwise corruptible. When Jesus Christ appeared to his disciples as a resurrected Being, he demonstrated the type of body an Eternal God has. His disciples testified of this mystery:

So then after the Lord had spoken unto them, he was received up into heaven, and sat on the right hand of God. (Mark 16:19)

And it came to pass, while he blessed them, he was parted from them, and was carried up into heaven. (Luke 24:51)

Jesus saith unto her, Touch me not; for I am not yet ascended to my Father, but go to my brethren, and say unto them, I ascend unto my Father, and your Father; and to my God, and your God. (John 20:17)

And when he had spoken these things, while they beheld, he was taken up; and a cloud received him out of their sight. And while they looked stedfastly toward heaven as he went up, behold, two men stood by them in white apparel; Which also said, Ye men of Galilee, why stand ye gazing up into heaven? this same Jesus, which is taken up from you into heaven, shall so come in like manner as ye have seen him go into heaven. (Acts 1:9–11)

Common sense would tell us that Christ is not sitting behind a cloud, nor is he on any planet in our solar system. He was transported to another planet in another solar system relatively close to our own, but far more progressed and advanced than ours. There, he waits the day of his return to the earth to usher in the last phase of our mortal existence, known as the Millennium.

Christ is not the creator of our spirits or solar system, but was created by our "Father" to be the overseer of our solar system; therefore he can be appropriately called our God—being One who acts as God would act.

Each solar system has its own Anointed One—a Christ—who was prepared and put into authority by God to make sure the eternal laws are followed in all things in the small section of the Universe placed under his direction. He was appointed, or better, created by our Creator to serve us by teaching us the things we need to know and do to find happiness—which comes in the way we associate with each other. The role of a Christ is to teach us how to treat each other so that we can live eternally in peace and happiness; in other words, so the use of our free will brings us happiness, and also happiness to those around us.

There is nothing mysterious to God, but only to man in his veiled infancy. His plan follows logic, reason, and all the natural laws to which we are all subject; and His understanding of these laws gives Him a power that we are only beginning to understand. Humans have the knowledge to create a nuclear weapon so powerful it can *take the life* of every living person. God has the knowledge and power to create a sun that *gives life* to every single organism upon this planet.

John's message given in the book of *Revelation* and sealed from the knowledge of humankind until now, is an unveiling of this great mystery of God pertaining to our Universe and the eternal design of our happiness.

Presented herein for the first time in recorded history, are John's words as he intended them, with commentary from this author, who received the commission and understanding from none other than John himself.

(NOTE: The universally accepted *King James* translation of *the New Testament* can be used as a guideline. Hereafter, the correct translation of John's original writings is interspersed throughout the *King James* translation in ***bold italics***.)

Chapter

REVELATION
UNFOLDED

1:1 The Revelation of **_John, a servant of God_**, which **_was given_** unto him of Jesus Christ, to show unto **_those who believe on his name_** things which must shortly come to pass; and **_God_** sent and signified it by **_His Son_** unto John:

The correct translation of this verse indicates that the revelation was given to John by Jesus Christ, himself; whereas the original editors of the *New Testament* changed this verse to signify it was a revelation given by an *angel*. This was because of their orthodox belief at the time, that Jesus Christ should be worshipped, thus contradicting Revelation 22:8–9, in which Jesus Christ insists that John *not* worship him. The editors also changed the title in 22:8 to "*the angel*" for the same reason. A proper reading of 22:7 and 12–13 leaves no doubt that the Being who is delivering this message to John, is indeed Jesus Christ.

1:2 Who bare record of the word of God, and **_who bareth_** testimony of Jesus Christ, **_who gave unto him the word_**. And **_John, a witness in the flesh of Christ, testifieth_** of all things that he saw.

Compare these words to the *Gospel of John*, in which proof is substantiated that the author of these writings is the same John, who is ecumenically known as *John, the Beloved*, the closest apostle and friend to Jesus Christ, and the one who "tarries" still upon the earth:

> *In the beginning was the Word, and the Word was with God, and the Word was God.* (John 1:1)

1:3 Blessed *are they who read and understand* the words of this prophecy, and keep *the commandments of God; for these shall understand* those things which are written therein; for the time *of the coming of the Lord draweth nigh*.

1:4 *Now this is the testimony of* John to *the servants of* the seven churches which are in Asia, *or in other words, to all the servants of God upon the earth*: Grace be unto you, and peace, from him *who* is, and *who* was, and *who* is to come; and *who hath been sent forth from* before *the* throne *of God to testify unto those who are the servants of the* seven *churches* which are *in the world*;

"*Servants*" represent all those who choose to properly *serve* and worship Jesus Christ by following his example and adhering to the principles and counsels he taught. These are also referred to as "*the elect*," distinguishing one who *elects* (or chooses) to worship and serve Christ by keeping his commandments from those who do not.

John was well aware of the seven main continents of the earth, and gave the term "*churches*" as those who gather and belong to a group of people of the same belief and faith. By using the terms of his day relative to Asia and some of its cities, John hid (with divine purpose) the knowledge he had of the other continents outside of the known world in his time. The symbolism of "*seven*" represents the seven main continents of the entire earth, and throughout *Revelation* continually symbolizes *all* the people of the earth.

The *New Testament* editors knew little to nothing of any continents other than the region they occupied or legends of more distant places; therefore, they transcribed John's allegory and presented it as a revelation relevant to the Christian churches known by them at that time, having no idea that the revelation was meant for the latter days when world geography would include seven main continents. The intent of John's message is for everyone upon all the continents and isles, and all peoples of the earth in the latter days.

1:5 *Therefore, I, John, a* faithful witness, ***bear record of the things which were delivered me of the angel of God, who is*** Jesus Christ, the first begotten of ***the Father in the flesh, and he who was risen first from*** the dead, and ***who shall overcome Lucifer***, the prince of the kings of the earth.

"*Lucifer*" is mentioned only once in the biblical text of the *Old Testament*. The name is a translation of "*the Son of the Morning*," and is again mentioned here by John. Interestingly, Christ is likewise referred to as the "*bright and morning star*" (see Revelation 22:16).

Jesus became mortal and received a body of *flesh*, which "flesh," or human nature, when revealed according to its true meaning, is synonymous with *Lucifer*, often referred to as "the devil" or "Satan." In the symbolic relation given in which Jesus is tempted by the devil, he was contemplating the vast powers passed on to him from the DNA patterns of God, when his human side began to tempt him:

> *And when he had fasted forty days and forty nights, he was afterward an hungered. And when **the tempter came to him**, he said, If thou be the Son of God, command that these stones be made bread. But he answered and said, It is written, Man shall not live by bread alone, but by every word that proceedeth out of the mouth of God. Then the devil taketh him up into the holy city, and setteth him on a pinnacle of the temple, And saith unto him, If thou be the Son of God, cast thyself down: for it is written, He shall give his angels charge concerning thee: and in their hands they shall bear thee up, lest at any time thou dash thy foot against a stone. Jesus said unto him, It is*

written again, Thou shalt not tempt the Lord thy God. Again, the devil taketh him up into an exceeding high mountain, and showeth him all the kingdoms of the world, and the glory of them; And saith unto him, All these things will I give thee, if thou wilt fall down and worship me. Then saith Jesus unto him, **Get thee hence, Satan**: *for it is written, Thou shalt worship the Lord thy God, and him only shalt thou serve. Then the devil leaveth him, and, behold, angels came and ministered unto him.* (Matthew 4:2–11)

If Lucifer were an actual personage, why would Jesus allow him to *"take him up into the holy city"* or *"take him up into an exceeding high mountain"*? The conversation took place in Jesus' mind. The experience was shared with his disciples to teach them that serving God is more important than giving in to human nature and its desires. In essence, John is saying that Jesus was born into the same mortal flesh as the rest of us, but overcame the flesh. He was born into the world to teach us by his example and laws how to overcome our own flesh (Lucifer), which in reality is our human nature—*"the prince of the kings of the earth."*

1:6 And unto him **who** loved us, **giving us of the glory of the Father by providing the way whereby we might be** washed from our sins, **because of** his own blood, **which was shed as an example to us that we might have his spirit to be with us always;** and **who** hath **power to make** us kings and priests unto God, his Father; **and to the Father** be glory and dominion for ever and ever. Amen.

The literal blood of Christ saves no one. The *blood* that filled his body signifies the things He taught, and the spirit and attitude by which he did all things. As we follow him by doing the things we see him do, with the attitude by which he did them, his *"blood"* (teachings and manner) saves us, or atones for our sins. In no way does the murder and shedding of Christ's *blood* do anything for us. John further verifies this throughout his *Revelation*.

"*Kings and priests*" are titles given to those who belong to a kingdom. If we follow the example and words of Christ, we become heirs of the kingdom of God; thus the titles appropriately signifying those who have *elected* to follow God's plan. However, at no time did Jesus ever teach that one should be put above another in title or deed. (See Galatians 4:7–9 referenced in the introductory commentary to John's *Revelation* above.)

1:7 Behold, he cometh *in the* clouds *with tens of thousands of his saints from the kingdom of God, clothed with the glory of his Father*. And every eye shall see him, and they also *who* pierced him *and rejected the word that he gave unto them by his own mouth and by the mouths of his seven servants, which he hath sent unto the seven churches*; and all kindreds of the earth *who worship the prince of the kings of the earth* shall wail because of him. Even so, Amen.

There is no set number of those who will return to the earth with Christ during the Millennium. The "*tens of thousands*" referred to by John, simply means "quite a few." The reference to "*seven servants*" and "*seven churches*" refers to the gospel of Jesus Christ brought to *all parts* of the earth. This does NOT insinuate Christianity only, but any doctrine of any religion that teaches the precept of doing unto others as you would have others do unto you.

John tells us that "*all kindreds of the earth...shall wail because of him,*" which portends an unpleasant experience for the earth's inhabitants because of their rejection of his gospel.

1:8 *For he saith*, I am Alpha and Omega, the beginning and the ending. *And thus* saith the Lord, *who* is, and *who* was, and *who* is to come, *the Anointed One of* the Almighty, *called by Him to save the world*.

Christ, the "Anointed One," was appointed in the beginning to oversee this solar system, which is the eternal kingdom of God pertaining to our world. He is referred to as "*Alpha and Omega, the beginning and the ending,*" because he was the *only one* created by God for this purpose. And he will reign forever in this part of the Universe, assuring that the eternal laws are always obeyed. He saves us in this eternal kingdom by teaching the laws designed to help us get along with each other, so that we will experience peace and happiness forever in our associations with one another.

We have been given free will to act according to our own desires. Christ was created and given certain innate characteristics and instructions (much like the instincts given to animals), which allow him to fulfill the measure of his creation without fail. The Creator cannot take a chance that His *appointed* Administrator of truth and righteousness in this solar system can fail. The rest of humanity can fail, but Christ cannot; because he has been preprogrammed, through his very nature, to succeed in the role for which he was created from the beginning.

1:9 I John, who also am your brother, and companion in tribulation, and *who also belongeth to the church of the Lamb of God, which is* the kingdom and patience of Jesus Christ, was in the isle that is called Patmos, *having been exiled from the world* for the word of God *which I have given to the world*, and *also* for the testimony *which I have given* of Jesus Christ, *he who gave the word unto me*.

Here again, John is determined to help us understand that he is equal to us, and also that all of us are equal to Christ. (Compare Revelation 22:9.)

1:10 I was in the Spirit *pondering upon the word of the Lord*, and heard behind me a great voice, as of a trumpet,

Notice that the "*great voice, as of a trumpet*" is always reported as being heard from "*behind*" the one receiving the revelation. Ezekiel puts it this way:

> *Then the spirit took me up, and **I heard behind me** a voice of a great rushing, saying, Blessed be the glory of the LORD from his place.* (Ezekiel 3:12)

The symbolism of this coincides with the way battles were waged in ancient times. The chosen leaders would lead the soldiers into battle, and the strength and power of the leaders were demonstrated in the lines of troops *behind* them. All prophets are called to lead the battle against unrighteousness, having the truth (the revelation they receive) behind them to support and fight their battles.

Many prophets have referred to the revelation they received as a *"voice like a trumpet."* Trumpets are blown to warn of impending danger or herald the announcement of important events:

> *Cry aloud, spare not, lift up thy **voice like a trumpet**, and show my people their transgression, and the house of Jacob their sins.* (Isaiah 58:1)

> *Declare ye in Judah, and publish in Jerusalem; and say, **Blow ye the trumpet** in the land: cry, gather together, and say, Assemble yourselves, and let us go into the defenced cities.* (Jeremiah 4:5)

> *Then whosoever **heareth the sound of the trumpet, and taketh not warning**; if the sword come, and take him away, his blood shall be upon his own head. He heard the sound of the trumpet, and took not warning; his blood shall be upon him. But he that taketh warning shall deliver his soul. But if the watchman see the sword come, **and blow not the trumpet**, and the people be not warned; if the sword come, and take any person from among them, he is taken away in his iniquity; but his blood will I require at the watchman's hand. So thou, O son of man, I have set thee a watchman unto the house of Israel; therefore thou shalt hear the word at my mouth, and warn them from me.* (Ezekiel 33:4–7)

John uses the word *"trumpet"* throughout his writings to emphasize the heralding of new information or important events.

1:11 Saying, I am Alpha and Omega, the first and the last, ***the beginning***

and the ending, the Lord who is, and who was, and who is to come, the Almighty. Greetings, my friend. Unto thee shall be given that which none other of thy brethren hath known, even those things which shall come to pass before I come again upon the earth to take the throne which my Father hath given me; and, What thou seest, write in a book *as the Spirit shall command thee, writing that which hath been sealed, so that it shall remain sealed unto all those who are not called by my name. Behold, thou shalt* send it unto the seven churches which are in Asia; unto Ephesus, and unto Smyrna, and unto Pergamos, and unto Thyatira, and unto Sardis, and unto Philadelphia, and unto Laodicea; *For behold, these are the churches of men who have strayed from my ordinances and broken mine everlasting covenant. Therefore, they shall not have these things given unto them in plainness, that they might be tried in their faith concerning me*.

John is commanded to write what he sees in the vision of the future, but to keep it "*sealed*" from those "*who are not called by [his] name*," or who do not do the works of Christ and follow his example. Throughout *Revelation*, John uses many of the metaphors and allegories that were used by some of the *Old Testament* prophets to keep "*eyes that do not see*" from seeing. John is commanded to send what he writes out into all the earth, so that those who have "*eyes that see*," will. The same was commanded of other prophets who preceded John. Isaiah was commanded:

> *Go, and tell this people, Hear ye indeed, but understand not; and see ye indeed, but perceive not. Make the heart of this people fat, and make their ears heavy, and shut their eyes; lest they see with their eyes, and hear with their ears, and understand with their heart, and convert, and be healed.* (Isaiah 6:9–10)

When people hear or read things they do not understand, the things they hear "make their ears heavy" with superfluity and incomprehensible prose. Yet humans thrive on the unknown and mysterious, just as an audience enjoys the illusions and tricks of a magician of which they have no understanding. Their "hearts are fat" because of the emotional state the mysterious unknown stirs up in them. If they knew the truth, there would be no emotional buildup (*fat*) in their feelings (*heart*).

It is not that God does not want His creations to understand the truth. But for our own sakes these things are withheld when we rebel, so that we can experience what it is like *not* to follow God's plan, thus reinforcing the necessity to do so. Also refer to Revelation 10:4, in which John is told to seal up the things which he knows (this being at a time of great wickedness upon the earth in his day), and compare this with 22:10, in which he is commanded to *not* seal them any longer from those who are "the elect," who *choose* righteousness (following the words of Christ) over wickedness (not following his words).

The *Revelation* is being unfolded in the last days so that the truth will be fully known, and the world will be judged by this truth without having an excuse that it didn't have the opportunity to understand because of "sealed" revelation.

As previously mentioned, John is using these "*churches*" only figuratively to represent the seven continents of the world, of which he (but not many others in his day) was aware. The "plain and precious parts" now restored in a proper translation, inform us as to why the book of *Revelation* is so difficult for people to understand; i.e., because they do not follow the mandates of Christ, and instead reject his truth.

1:12 And *as* I turned *again* to see the voice that spake with me, *I beheld a vision; and in the vision* I saw seven golden candlesticks;

Just before sharing the Beatitudes with the Jews, teaching them all they needed to do to find salvation and happiness, Jesus turned to his disciples and said:

> *Ye are the light of the world. A city that is set on an hill cannot be hid. Neither do men light a candle, and put it under a bushel, but on a candlestick; and it giveth light unto all that are in the house. Let your light so shine before men, that they may see your good works, and glorify your*

Father which is in heaven. (Matthew 5:14–16)

Jesus calls his disciples the *"light of the world."* According to the Mosaic Law in setting up the tabernacle, *"golden candlesticks"* were placed before the altar. He could have said, appropriately, *"Ye are the light upon the candlesticks."* The *"candlesticks"* represent the nations of the world as implied properly by those who understood the symbolism, purpose, and function of the preparations and presentations of the ordinances in the Mosaic Law. Paul understood these things and wrote to the Hebrews:

> *Then verily the first covenant had also ordinances of divine service, and a **worldly sanctuary**. For there was a tabernacle made; the first, wherein was **the candlestick**, and the table, and the showbread; **which is called the sanctuary**.* (Hebrews 9:1–2)

1:13 And in the midst of the seven candlesticks **was** the Son of man, **of whom I bore record of to the world, being one of his eyewitnesses in the flesh. And he was** clothed with a garment down to the foot, and girt about the paps with a golden girdle.

Christ was born into the world in the area of Palestine, which for all intents and purposes, was located in the *"midst"* of all other nations of the earth known at that time.

A girdle is an accessory belt or cord that surrounds or encircles loose-fitting clothing. Our flesh is symbolically represented by *loose-fitting* clothing or robes, demonstrating the *temporary* state (loose-fitting) of the flesh in clothing our eternal spirit. The *"girdle"* represents our actions, deeds, and thoughts (works) that encircle or surround all we do in the flesh. Being placed *"about the paps,"* demonstrates what nourishes our souls; as *"paps"* is short for "papillae" which means "nipples," from which all mortals receive their first nutrition.

Our works tie our flesh and spirit together and are a demonstration of who we really are. Many of the articles and items used by the Levite priests in the exercising of the Law of Moses were made of gold (*golden girdle*), which is considered within scripture as the purest element, and used to describe pure works:

> And righteousness shall be the **girdle** of his loins, and faithfulness the **girdle** of his reins. (Isaiah 11:5)

1:14 His head and his hairs were white like wool, as white as snow; and his eyes were as a flame of fire; *for any who looked upon them in unrighteousness would burn from within*.

1:15 And his **arms and his** feet like unto fine brass, as if they **were** burned in a furnace; and his voice as the sound of many waters.

John borrows the description of Christ from the book of *Daniel*:

> I beheld till the thrones were cast down, and the Ancient of days did sit, whose garment was white as snow, and the hair of his head like the pure wool: his throne was like the fiery flame, and his wheels as burning fire. (Daniel 7:9)

Notice that John elaborates more than Daniel's vague description of Christ's power of motion. Daniel used *"wheels as burning fire"* instead of John's more subtle *"feet...burned in a furnace."* Both prophets used these terms to express the work of Christ as he moves forth in his glory—figuratively *burning* up the works of the wicked. Everywhere he walks and everywhere he goes, people will burn inside because of their pride and wickedness.

Daniel did not pull the expression *"wheels as burning fire"* out of nowhere. The same expression is used by Ezekiel, who likewise describes the works and wonders of God as *"wheels,"* describing their color as John does the *"feet"* (means of motion) of Christ:

> The **appearance of the wheels and their work was like unto the colour of a beryl**: and they four had one likeness: and their appearance and their work was as it were **a wheel in the middle of a wheel**. (Ezekiel 1:16)

Each saw the same vision of truth.

With modern technology, we can take pictures of any part of our vast Universe. Upon viewing it from any angle, we see galaxies which look very much like a pinwheel formation of countless solar systems, which systems can appear as a wheel as the planets rotate in formation as spokes around the center hub—the sun (*"burning fire"*).

The prophets saw the Universe in their vision and presented the work of God in the way they were allowed to without revealing the mysteries they were given to know and understand. Ezekiel would have been quite correct characterizing our solar system in the confines of our galaxy as "*a wheel in the middle of a wheel.*"

John introduces the *"voice as the sound of many waters"* as the inhabitants that belong to this solar system agreeing with the commission of Christ. What Christ speaks is confirmed and supported by the rest of God's human creations, who are the *"many waters"* mentioned later in Revelation 14:2, 17:1, and especially in 19:5–7, which says:

> *And the voice of the Lamb came out of the throne, saying, Praise our God, all ye his servants, and ye that fear him not, both small and great. And I heard* **the voice of a great multitude, and as the voice of many waters, and also as the voice of mighty thunderings,** *saying, Alleluia and Amen: for the Lord God omnipotent reigneth. Let us be glad and rejoice, and give honour to him: for the marriage of the Lamb is come, and his wife hath made herself ready. Behold, I am the bridegroom prepared for my wife.* (Revelation 19:5–7)

1:16 And he had in his right hand seven stars **which he kept always before him**; and out of his mouth went a sharp two-edged sword **that slew all those who came forth except those who he held in his right hand**; and his countenance was as the sun **which** shineth in **its** strength.

This "*sword*" refers to the words of Christ, his gospel, and what he will say from his mouth, which defends the truth and fights against the opinions, perceptions, and desires of the world (or "*the beast*" as they are later referred to in *Revelation*).

A "*two-edge sword*" is something that has, or can have, both favorable and unfavorable consequences. When Christ comes to the earth, his presence and teachings will be well received and uplifting to those who treat others good, and bad for those who do not.

The "*stars*" are symbolic of all people. Those who are righteous (those "*held in his right hand*") will not be ashamed at his countenance. This first reference to "*stars*" being people was understood by some of the early American leaders who followed the esotericism of Masonry, and who eventually incorporated the symbol into the American flag as a representation of the colonies of people. Little did they realize that placing the stars on a dark background in contrast to the blood stains (red stripes) on an all white flag (the standard of righteousness humans should follow), prophetically expresses the darkness under which the people of the United States exist.

1:17 And when I saw him, I fell at his feet as *if I were* dead. *And I dared not look upon him, knowing the wickedness of my ways*. And he laid his right hand upon me, saying unto me, Fear not; I am the first and the last:

1:18 I am he that liveth, and was dead; and, behold, I am alive for evermore, Amen; and have the keys of hell and of death, *which is the sword that thou sawest proceeding forth from my mouth. And thy sins are forgiven thee*.

John's humility is apparent in acknowledging the sins of the flesh (Lucifer) that so easily sway one to act contrary to the precepts and commands of God.

Here we have an explanation making it clear that the "*keys of hell and of death*" are a knowledge of the gospel of Jesus Christ, or the way that we treat and love each other as he taught us. The opposite of being happy is being in hell. The key to happiness and the way out of hell, is in the way we treat each other. As we treat each other equally and as we would want to be treated, we eliminate hell, and prepare to live forever (the opposite of death) without causing any unhappiness to ourselves or to others—this is the "*key*" to overcoming "*hell and death.*"

His gospel is the "*sword*" that he uses to bring all things in order and balance in our Universe and protects and guarantees our personal free agency and eternal happiness.

1:19 Write the things which thou hast seen, ***and also the things which thou shalt see, which are*** the things which are, and the things which shall be hereafter, ***even that which shall befall the people of the latter days***;

John is commanded to write what he will witness befall the earth, or the patterns of human behavior that cause certain events in the latter days. As his *Revelation* is unfolded and understood in truth, it is easy to see the fulfillment of the vision he was given, and Christ's reason for giving him a command to write it.

1:20 ***Behold***, the mystery of the seven stars which thou sawest in my right hand, and the seven golden candlesticks. The seven stars are the ***servants of God*** of the seven churches, ***which are the righteous of the world***; and the seven candlesticks which thou sawest are the seven ***nations of the world wherein the servants shall dwell and shine and give their light unto the world***.

Throughout John's *Revelation* he uses "*seven stars*" (in contrast to just mentioning "*stars*" or "*servants*") to represent the righteous people found on the seven continents of the earth; and though their numbers will be few, they will be armed with righteousness and with the power of God to overcome the sins of the world.

Chapter

R EVELATION 2 UNFOLDED

2:1 Unto the *servant* of the church of Ephesus write; These things saith he that holdeth the seven stars in his right hand, who walketh in the midst of the seven golden candlesticks;

Here is where John begins to use actual names of certain churches of his time to represent varying degrees of righteousness and wickedness that existed in his day, paralleling them with the wickedness and righteousness of the human race in the last days. These are the same sins that have always existed when human societies have been present, and which John saw in his vision. Each of the churches described by John illustrates symbolically one of the *Seven Deadly Sins*, or the human vices that corrupt the soul and cause unhappiness in the world:

Anger (Ephesus), *Gluttony* (Smyrna), *Pride* (Pergamos), *Lust* (Thyatira), *Slothfulness* (Sardis), *Envy* (Philadelphia), and *Greed* (Laodiceans). In each case, John gives the name of a known *church* in his day as a figurative expression, and offers the corresponding vice followed by an expression of the virtue needed to overcome it:

Ephesus is *angry* with false prophets and those who set themselves above others, but is commanded to return to the *"first works,"* or the words of Christ which teach us to love our enemies and do good to those who hate and persecute us.

Smyrna is given the example of Daniel and his friends who would not partake of the King's food for *ten days*; proving that the appetites offered in the world (*gluttony*) should never supersede an appetite for keeping the commandments of God.

Pergamos has many who are full of *pride* and set themselves above others. The example of the martyr Antipas is used, who was a church leader who never put himself above another and who was killed because he refused to.

Thyatira relates the example of Jezebel, a woman who was given to the *lusts* of the world. Those who sleep with her are figuratively giving in to the lusts of the flesh and are condemned.

Sardis is given as an example of those who take upon them the name of Christ, but are *slothful* in doing the works that should support the name to which they make claim.

Philadelphia shows an example of those who seek for knowledge (which are the "keys" to open doors of understanding), but who can't find it; and who *envy* those who appear to have great knowledge, but actually do not. This church represents many who are deceived by those who claim to know and understand God. These *envy* the supposed knowledge of their leaders and others, but are, instead, led away from God, causing them to worship and give reverence to those whom they envy.

Finally, *Laodiceans* represents those who seek for the fine things of the earth and are filled with material *greed*.

2:2 I know thy works, and thy labour, and thy patience, and how thou canst not bear them which are evil, **and how thou hatest them who belong to the church of the devil**; and thou hast tried them which say they are apostles **of the Lamb**, and are not, and hast found them liars **because of their works, which are evil**;

2:3 And **thou** hast borne, and hast patience, and for my name's sake hast laboured, and hast not fainted.

John describes those who have elected ("the elect") to follow the tenets of his gospel. These "elect" are judges only in the sense of how others (especially those who *claim* to be servants of Christ) keep the commandments and follow the example of Christ—"*by their works ye shall know them.*" Someone who keeps the commandments in a certain environment and situation, literally judges those who, in the exact same situation, do not. The judgment is made by the example and proof that it can be done. John specifically mentions those "*which say they are apostles of the Lamb, and are not*" because of the many leaders in the latter days who claim authority from God, yet do not follow the example of Christ or teach his commandments. These include all latter-day religious leaders.

2:4 Nevertheless I have somewhat against ***those whom thou servest***, because ***they have*** left ***their*** first love ***because of the anger they have for their enemies***, ***who are not of thee***.

In the *King James* translation, it appears that the Lord is first praising the church of Ephesus and then in Revelation 2:4 is condemning it in his next breath. These seemingly contradictory statements are resolved when the correct translation is given.

The Lord is referring to those who are called the "*servant(s) of the church*," who follow him faithfully. These *others* are those who "*have left their first love*," or who were baptized and accepted Christ only to go back to their former ways "*because of the anger they have for their enemies.*" No matter how wicked a person may be, or whom one might choose to worship, Christ commands us not to become angry with them, but to love and do good to them always.

2:5 ***Preach repentance unto them***, ***saying***: Remember therefore from whence thou art fallen, and repent, and do the first works ***which were given thee by thy first love***; or else I will come unto thee quickly, and will remove ***my servants*** out of ***their*** place. ***And I will remove the light from upon*** thy candlestick, except thou repent.

Because of free agency, the Lord will never interfere in the desires of humans. But he *will* remove those inspired ones who understand truth, but who fail, or refuse, to properly lead those willing to receive truth and righteousness. Without righteous leaders, there is no "*light from upon thy candlestick*" given to a darkened world.

2:6 But this thou hast *in thy favor, the hate* that thou *hast is for* the deeds of the Nicolaitians, which I also hate. *For they take that which is good and make it evil; and that which is evil, they make good.*

The best definition of the Nicolaitians is to say that they represent a hierarchy or ruling class that takes authority and presumes superiority over the rest of the people, developing a bureaucracy of human leadership. They were given to sensual appetites as were most Roman citizens who lived in the time of John. Although there was not a separated group who called themselves by this name, the moniker was contrived as a descriptive title used by those who were abused by the Nicolaitians because of social and class differences.

The main tenet of the gospel of Christ is that all are equal, none above the other; and those who lead should be the least among men and the servants of all. Modern-day world and religious leaders are the equivalent of the Nicolaitians.

Though God is incapable of *hate* (the word is used to express His condemnation of evil works), John reiterates the *human trait* most disturbing to One who is no respecter of persons, and who loves all the same—**pride**.

2:7 He that hath an ear, let him hear what the Spirit saith unto the churches; To him that overcometh *the works of this world* will I give to eat of the tree of life, which is in the midst of the paradise of God; *and the paradise of God is the eternal happiness of His kingdom.*

John uses the phrase, "*He that hath an ear, let him hear,*" throughout his *Revelation.* This is a reference to any who understands the truth (rejecting the opinions and doctrines of men) as whispered in authority by the Spirit or explained by a true prophet of God. This phrase is used symbolically, and follows the way the Jews performed services on the Sabbath day.

After service was done in the synagogue, the Jews would go to dinner. After dinner, they would go to what was known as a school (sometimes referred to as "*school of the prophets*"), or a lecture of divinity. Here, a chosen minister would read and expound on doctrine. He that read did not use an audible voice, but muttered it with a small whisper in the ear of another; and the person to whom it was whispered announced it aloud to all the people. This custom is referenced in the *New Testament* where Christ taught, but did not follow, the customary rites to teach the people:

> *And he taught in their synagogues, being glorified of all. And he came to Nazareth, where he had been brought up: and, as his custom was, he went into the synagogue on the sabbath day, and stood up for to read. And there was delivered unto him the book of the prophet Esaias. And when he had opened the book, he found the place where it was written, The Spirit of the Lord is upon me, because he hath anointed me to preach the gospel to the poor; he hath sent me to heal the brokenhearted, to preach deliverance to the captives, and recovering of sight to the blind, to set at liberty them that are bruised, To preach the acceptable year of the Lord. And he closed the book, and he gave it again to the minister, and sat down. And the eyes of all them that were in the synagogue were fastened on him. And he began to say unto them, This day is this scripture fulfilled in your ears.* (Luke 4:15–21)

What astounded the Jews about Christ was his understanding of the prophecies and doctrine, and the way he expounded them to the people without having anyone of authority whispering in his ear, or by whispering in anyone else's ear their meaning—this upset the Jews:

> *And all they in the synagogue, when they heard these things, were filled with wrath, And rose up, and thrust him out of the city, and led him unto the brow of the hill whereon their city was built, that they might cast him down headlong.* (Luke 4:28–29)

John uses this same relation to exemplify those who understand his prophecies, (which no human in the latter days does, except those who have received the proper explanation from a true prophet of God), following in symbolism the custom established by the Jews. Because Christ was a true prophet of God, he circumvented the Jewish custom and taught his disciples, *"what ye hear in the ear, that preach ye upon the housetops"* (Matthew 10:27).

2:8 And unto the **servant** of the church in Smyrna write: These things saith **he who teacheth his will to** the first and the last, **even he who** was dead, and is **now** alive;

John points out that the gospel taught by Christ while he was upon the earth is the same gospel he will always teach the people, and will be the same words he teaches when he comes in glory. This gospel is given in its fullness in Matthew, chapters 5, 6, and 7. This is the doctrine and *"will"* of God, and the *only* thing Christ will ever teach.

2:9 I know thy works, and tribulation, and poverty, (but thou art rich **as to the things of God**) and I know the blasphemy of them which say they are Jews, and are not, but are **of** the **church of the devil whose desires are the appetites of the flesh**.

There are only *two* churches: one is a group of people who are living the commandments and ways of Christ, known as the church of the Lamb, and the other is a group of people who are living contrary to the gospel of Jesus Christ, known as the church of the devil. There are *none* in-between. A person belongs to one of the two churches regardless of whether he or she claims allegiance to *any* man-made organized religion. Revelation 3:16 substantiates this truth.

2:10 Fear none of those things which thou shalt suffer **in the flesh**; behold, the **servants of the** devil shall cast some of you into prison, that ye may be tried **and tested in your faith**; and ye shall have tribulation, **but be ye steadfast as they who restrain from eating the food and wine of the king for** ten days; **and ye shall become strong in the Spirit as**

they did who received the crown of life. *And if* thou *art* faithful unto death, I will give thee *also* a crown of life.

Here, the figurative expression is given in parallel to the experience of Daniel and his friends (Hananiah, Mishael, and Azariah):

> *Prove thy servants, I beseech thee, **ten days**; and let them give us pulse to eat, and water to drink.* (Daniel 1:12)

These four refused the food offered and eaten by the king and his servants (figuratively expressed as the knowledge and ways of the world—"*the king/crown*" of the earth) and chose instead to have "*pulse to eat, and water to drink*" (the knowledge and ways of God—"*the king/crown*" *of life*).

The commentary on this verse further substantiates the fact that this author received his authority to explain the meaning of *Revelation* from John. Until now, none has made the connection between Revelation 2:10 and Daniel's writings. The book of *Daniel* is a favorite of John, as he borrows much of the symbolism from it to describe his vision.

2:11 He that hath an ear, let him hear what the Spirit saith unto the churches; He that overcometh *the things of this world* shall not be hurt of the second death *which shall come upon all those who eat the food of the kings of this world*.

Again, John points out that only those who listen to the true spirit and to a true prophet of God would understand these things. Any man or woman authoring books or presenting discourses or explanations of *Revelation* who does not give the correct interpretation and explanation of Revelation 2:10–11, does NOT have the proper spirit, and misleads those who study their works.

The "*second death*" is when one does not receive a resurrected body, and is not placed on one of the eternal planets, because he or she refuses to live the eternal laws and commandments of God, which are essentially: Do unto others what you would have them do unto you. The way of the world ("*food of the kings of this world*") is: Do unto others only as it benefits you. If this type of "food" was served on eternal planets, or better, if this type of attitude was allowed to exist in the eternal worlds, the same problems we experience in our associations with each other here, would exist there. Therefore, only those who have overcome this selfish and self-serving attitude will be allowed to exist in the eternal worlds.

2:12 And to the ***servant*** of the church in Pergamos write; These things saith he ***who*** hath the sharp sword with two edges ***that proceedeth forth from his mouth and cuts asunder those who deny him and do not the works of God***:

See the commentary on Revelation 1:16.

2:13 I know thy works, and where ***thy heart*** dwellest, even ***when thou dwellest*** where Satan's seat is, ***thou hearest me***, and thou holdest fast my name, and hast not denied ***me in thy*** faith, even ***as*** in those days wherein Antipas was my faithful martyr, who was slain among you, where Satan dwelleth ***and exerciseth his power***; ***yea***, ***even then thou didst not betray me***.

Antipas was John's personal friend and was called by the apostle to be a leader of the church in Pergamos. John uses his name (Antipas literally means "to stand against all") as a symbolic representation of standing up against the world and its governments. Antipas stood up against the powers that ruled "*Satan's seat.*" He preached that the leaders were changing the pure gospel of Jesus Christ into doctrines and precepts of men. He angered the governor and the Greeks after refusing to pinch some incense in the red-hot copper bull-shaped altar of Caesar, so they threw him into the same brazen altar burning him alive. The saint fervently prayed to God, glorifying His great power and thanking Him for being worthy to suffer for His love. Not once did Antipas curse his enemies.

This symbolism is important to the "saints" of the latter days who must stand up against the governments and rulers of the world in order to live the gospel of Jesus Christ.

2:14 But I have a few things against thee, because thou hast there them that hold the doctrine of Balaam *and envy those things he offered unto* Balac to cast a stumblingblock before the children of Israel, *commanding them* to eat things sacrificed unto idols, and to commit fornication *with unbelievers*.

John uses the example of the false prophet Balaam and the influence he had over King Balac to relate how politicians are influenced by their religious beliefs, which cause them to live contrary to Christ's law. Being leaders of the people, they become "stumbling blocks," because the people look to their leaders for an example of how they should live and what they might become. The people envy the riches and prominence of their leaders, and are led according to the whims and ways of the politicians and religious leaders who the people allow to rule over them.

2:15 So hast thou also them that hold the doctrine of the Nicolaitians, which thing I hate. *For thou knowest that I esteem all flesh the same, and no man is above another, for I am no respecter of persons*.

See the commentary on Revelation 2:6.

2:16 Repent; or else I will come unto thee quickly, and will fight against them *that are of the Nicolaitians* with the sword of my mouth.

When Christ comes again, he will overthrow all the governments and leaders of the world. This will not be done by force, but by what he teaches the people, who will, at that day, recognize Christ for who he is. Once the people hear the truth from the mouth of Christ ("*sword of my mouth*"), they will no longer respect or recognize the authority of any political or religious leader.

2:17 He that hath an ear, let him hear what the Spirit saith unto the churches; To him that overcometh *the flesh of this world* will I give to eat of the hidden manna, *which is that which shall save them, not as it did their fathers in the wilderness, for they are dead; but unto him* *who receiveth this manna, I shall give eternal life*. And I will give him a white stone, *which shall be a light unto perfection to those who receive it*; and in the stone a new name *shall be* written, which no man knoweth saving he that receiveth it.

Here, John is expounding on what he wrote in his own relation of what Christ taught:

> *Whoso eateth my flesh, and drinketh my blood, hath eternal life; and I will raise him up at the last day. For my flesh is meat indeed, and my blood is drink indeed. He that eateth my flesh, and drinketh my blood, dwelleth in me, and I in him. As the living Father hath sent me, and I live by the Father: so he that eateth me, even he shall live by me. This is that bread which came down from heaven: not as your fathers did eat manna, and are dead: he that eateth of this bread shall live for ever.* (John 6:54–58)

Christ's flesh is figurative of his works; and his blood is figurative of his intentions. Though some do what appear to be good works, if their intent is not Christ-like, their works are done in vain. Christ-like intent means that one acts for the sake of another and not for one's own sake. For example, if one gives to the poor so that one feels better about oneself (the warm and fuzzy feeling), and does not take into consideration the real needs of the recipient, the act is done with a selfish intent, and is vain. "Charity" is usually referred to as Christ-like intent and understanding (*his blood*). Therefore, Paul wrote:

> *And though I bestow all my goods to feed the poor, and though I give my body to be burned, and have not charity, it profiteth me nothing.* (I Corinthians 13:3)

Christ gave his body as a figurative representation of the "*hidden manna*" because most did not understand the symbolism of the manna that fed the Israelites in the wilderness.

We live in this world (a virtual wilderness bereft of the food and drink of life—the truth), and are fed manna from heaven symbolically. If a person does the works of Christ (*eats his flesh*) with Christ-like intent (*drinks his blood*), that person will be a candidate for eternal life.

The "*stone*" is the same reference as Christ gave in his teachings when he referred to a "*rock*." He used the reference when he taught:

> *Therefore whosoever heareth these sayings of mine, and doeth them, I will liken him unto a wise man, which built his house upon* **a rock***: And the rain descended, and the floods came, and the winds blew, and beat upon that house; and it fell not: for it was* **founded upon a rock***.* (Matthew 7:24–25)

A *name* is always representative of our works; or better, we make a name for ourselves by our works. The "*new name*" is the new person one becomes as he or she "*heareth these sayings of mine, and doeth them.*" Only those who have experienced becoming a new person (receiving a new name) by doing the works of Christ, with the proper intent, will understand how this change has transformed their life. Thus, "*no man knoweth saving he that receiveth it.*" (Compare to Revelation 3:12.)

2:18 And unto the **servant** of the church in Thyatira write; These things saith the Son of God, who hath eyes like unto a flame of fire, and his feet are like fine brass;

See the commentary on Revelation 1:14–15.

2:19 I know thy works; **yea, I know that they are full of** charity, and service, and faith; and thy patience **I have seen**, and thy works **I have also seen**; and the last to be more than the first; **and this because thy works are many.**

Many people are properly engaged in good works in hopes that their works will save them, believing that the more good they can do, the better they will fare in heaven. However, being constantly engaged this way can wear on a person, and cause one's works to become selfish desires of an accumulation of "good points," instead of doing these works because one is truly a genuinely good person. For this reason, *patience* in doing good works for the right reason (for the sake of others and not for the personal accumulation of points) is important in the true light of righteous living.

2:20 Notwithstanding I have a few things against thee, because thou sufferest that woman **dressed in scarlet, even the whore of all the earth, who is as** Jezebel **who killed the prophets**; **who** called herself a prophetess, **so that she could** teach and seduce my servants to commit fornication **with her**, and to eat things sacrificed unto **the** idols **who are her gods**.

Here, John introduces the works of the world represented as a "*woman*," comparing her to Jezebel who is mentioned in the *Old Testament*. Jezebel represents the wicked nature of this world that casts out and kills the true prophets of God, just as Jezebel did in *Old Testament* times. When Jezebel's actions towards the true prophets of God are studied and considered, it becomes quite apparent why John chose her as an example. Casting out and killing the prophets is symbolic of casting the words of Christ to the side and not paying attention to them. The symbolism of the "*woman*" is used throughout *Revelation* to describe the ways of the world:

> *So he carried me away in the spirit into the wilderness:*
> *and I saw a **woman** sit upon a scarlet coloured beast, full*
> *of names of blasphemy, having seven heads and ten horns.*
> (Revelation 17:3)

2:21 And I **shall give her and those who sleep in** her **bed** space to repent of **their** fornication; and **if they do not repent**;

The world will be given every opportunity to repent of its misdeeds so that humans learn to do unto others what they would have done unto them (the fullness of the gospel of Christ) before Christ comes in his glory.

2:22 Behold, *those who are in* her bed, and them *who* commit adultery with her, I will cast into great tribulation, except they repent of their deeds.

2:23 And I will kill her children with death; *yea, they shall be cut asunder by the sword of my mouth*; and all the churches shall know that I am he *who* searcheth the reins and *desires of the* heart; and I will give unto every one of you according to your works *and the desires of your hearts*.

All those who choose the desires of the world, its glory, its pomp, its desires, its riches, its power, and its image over the gospel of Christ (doing unto others), will reap the destruction of their egos when Christ comes again. Nothing is more frustrating and deadening to the soul than being told one has been wrong and deceived all of one's life. Nothing cuts as deeply as the sword of truth.

By the words of Christ, we will judge ourselves. We, alone, know the true intents of how we live our lives. Because the churches of humankind (organized religion) teach doctrines and precepts that specify that a person must perform certain mandated ordinances and practices of the respective church, the Lord specifically mentions that "*all the churches shall know*" that a person is judged, not by how they obey a church, but by how they obey the words of Christ.

2:24 But unto *those of* you *who are righteous* I say, and *also* unto the rest in Thyatira, *even* as many as have not *followed* this doctrine *and committed fornication with this woman dressed in scarlet*, and which have not known the depths of *the ways of* Satan, *even* as *she speaks as if his ways are good to seduce you, but they are not*; *behold*, I will put upon you none other burden *except that which I have already commanded you*.

2:25 But that which ye have already *from me*, hold fast till I come.

Those who do not partake of the world's ways and have not been seduced by its enticing offerings—many of these being things the world thinks are good, but are actually contrary to the words of Christ—need only follow the gospel as Christ taught it to the Jews when he was among them: "*that which ye have already from me*" (Matthew 5, 6, and 7). Nothing else is needed to gain salvation.

2:26 And *to him* that overcometh, and keepeth my ***commandments*** unto the end, to him will I give ***the*** power ***to live in my kingdoms***;

2:27 And *I* shall rule ***over him*** with ***the word of God***; ***and he shall be in my hands*** as the vessels of ***clay in the hands of*** a potter; ***and he shall receive this power by faith, given with equity and justice*** even as I received of my Father ***and do His will. But those who do not overcome, their vessels*** shall be broken to shivers:

Christ's words shall set the precedent for all law and order. As he teaches the people and sets up his government, the people will be "*clay in the hands*," as he forms them into the type of people who can live in peace and harmony with each other forever in the kingdom of God. Those who refuse to live according to his law and order will not be allowed to corrupt the rest of the people by causing turmoil and contention, which would negate the peace and happiness promised in the kingdom of God.

2:28 And I will give ***those who have overcome, all that I have, even all that the Father hath given me***, the ***bright and*** morning star.

This "*bright and morning star*" is also used in Revelation 22:16, signifying the resurrection unto eternal life exemplified by Christ—he being the first "*bright and morning star*" to rise from the darkness of night (death).

2:29 He that hath an ear, let him hear what the Spirit saith unto the churches.

Again, John reiterates that only those who choose to listen will understand what he is trying to say in his writings.

Chapter

REVELATION
UNFOLDED

3:1 And unto the ***servant*** of the church in Sardis write; These things saith he ***who*** hath the seven stars, ***which are the seven servants*** of God; I know thy works, that thou hast ***declared*** a name ***by which thou livest*** that ***can give thee eternal life, but thou*** art dead.

Here the Lord takes issue with those who are hypocrites, who claim they are Christian and follow Christ, but who do nothing that he taught them to do. Their faith, without works, is dead; because *"declaring a name,"* or taking upon ourselves the *name of Christ,* are expressions which refer to the way we live (our works), and have nothing to do with vain professions of belief:

> *Thou believest that there is one God; thou doest well: the devils also believe, and tremble. But wilt thou know, O vain man, that faith without works is dead?* (James 2:19–20)

3:2 Be watchful ***therefore***, and strengthen ***those who*** remain ***with thee,***

who are ready to die *because they know not the name by which they are called, and whose works* I have not found perfect before God.

Speaking of death spiritually instead of literally, the Lord admonishes those who proclaim his name to live what he taught, and teach by their works (their righteous example) those who do not know him or the example he gave while in the flesh as Jesus. Living an exemplary life filled with the tenets of love, acceptance, tolerance, forgiveness, and other Christ-like attributes, is much more important than preaching words to others by claiming one's ways are more righteous and correct than another's.

3:3 Remember therefore how thou hast received and heard *the name thou hast been given*, and hold fast *to the rod of truth I have given you*, and repent *of thy slothful ways. Watch and prepare for my coming; but* if therefore thou shalt not watch, I will come on thee as a thief, *for* thou shalt not know what hour I will come upon thee.

When one comes to know the word of God and begins to treat others according to this word, this gives evidence that the person has received, appropriately, the "name" of Christ. Further evidence is given from within as the person begins to feel peace, love, and harmony with his or her spiritual and physical surroundings. Remaining receptive to these feelings is a constant challenge which *"the rod of truth"* (the *"name,"* i.e., doing unto others) helps us to achieve.

In letting down the guard of proper conduct, our personal judgments come quickly, and when we least expect them, cause us to feel the opposite of the peace we once knew. Christ referred to this as a *"thief"* coming in the night when we are asleep and unaware of the intrusion. If we do not watch how we treat others, we will be lulled to sleep, figuratively speaking. Surprised by the "thief," we will be ashamed of how easily flesh (Lucifer) overcomes the *"name"* of Christ.

3:4 Thou hast a few *who remember their* names, even in Sardis, *who* have not defiled their garments; and they shall walk with me in white *raiment*; for they are worthy *and are called by my name*.

There are a very few who truly live righteously, but there are many, many more, who *believe* in their hearts that they do, but are actually deceiving themselves. This personal deception has always defiled the person who claims to be Christian but disregards the words of Christ.

One of the greatest stumbling blocks ever placed in front of the words of Christ are the canon of "scriptures" presented by the early Catholic (worldwide) Church as the letters and words of Paul. Not only is there no verification that Paul actually wrote these words, but in many instances, what is presented as Paul's counsel to various nations contradicts the words of Christ.

An honest investigation into most of what the *New Testament* canon attributes to Paul, reveals they were letters and doctrines made up by the early leaders of the Catholic Church in an effort to present its corrupted doctrine the way the leaders wanted the people to understand it. When the modern Catholic Church is presented with inquiries from historians researching the roots and formation of Christianity, and requesting visual evidence of the original manuscripts from which the *New Testament* was constructed, the Church remains illusive and prohibitory, because it knows these documents do not exist.

The teachings and counsels of Jesus Christ are the words that he spoke to the multitude, known ecumenically as the Beatitudes (i.e., in which **attitude** we should **be**), or better, *The Sermon on the Mount*. The words of Christ—the fullness of his gospel—are the only commandments and requirements ever given to the human race. They are contained in their completeness in book of Matthew, chapters 5, 6 and 7—This is the work of Christ that he was given to do by his Father, and which he accomplished before he was killed by the Romans upon the cross. Here are the words of Christ given many months **before** he was crucified and died on the cross:

> *I have glorified thee on the earth:* **I have finished the work which thou gavest me to do**. (See John 17:4.)

The Lord finished his work when he had taught the people how to get along with each other properly—the *only* thing he was sent by God to do.

3:5 He that overcometh *the world*, the same shall be clothed in white raiment; and I will not blot out his name out of the Book of Life, but I will confess his name before my Father, and before his angels.

Throughout his *Revelation*, John presents *"raiment"* as a representation of the mortal works accomplished during our mortality. Each person enters the world without clothing and proceeds to clothe oneself according to one's individuality and personal choices. There are many different clothing styles worn by humans, but John specifically uses *"white"* as the color of the raiment worn by those who are righteous. The only time John uses another adjective besides *"white"* to describe the actions and desires of humans (their *"raiment"*), is when he references worldly desires and appetites in verse 17, in which he chooses *"fine raiment"* as the representation.

Throughout the scriptures, "nakedness" is always used as a reference to unrighteous works. If we do not overcome our human nature (Lucifer), which causes us to treat others poorly, we will not be allowed to live on the planets that will be prepared for our eternal existence—which privilege and final state is referred to in the expression: *"I will not blot out his name out of the Book of Life."* The work of God and all the angels is to help sustain us in this pursuit of eternal life (happiness) and to reach this end.

3:6 He that hath an ear, let him hear what the Spirit saith unto the churches.

3:7 And to the *servant* of the church in Philadelphia write; These things saith he that is holy, he that *speaketh truth*, he that hath the key *to the house of* David, *which* openeth, and no man shutteth; and shutteth, and no man openeth;

A *"key"* is always symbolic of knowledge otherwise locked away and hidden from mortals. In order to open the door that leads to truth, one must have the proper key. In order to unlock and open the door to understanding what John has stated here, or find the *"key"* to do so, we must take a look at an earlier prophet's writings in which he used vague symbolism to hide the truth from those who weren't worthy to have this *"key"* to understanding. Thus spoke the Lord to Isaiah:

Go, and tell this people, Hear ye indeed, but understand not; and see ye indeed, but perceive not. Make the heart of this people fat, and make their ears heavy, and shut their eyes; lest they see with their eyes, and hear with their ears, and understand with their heart, and convert, and be healed. (Isaiah 6:9–10)

In his day, Isaiah received the same vision that John did. Like John, Isaiah uses his own symbolism, with names known in his own time, to represent certain future events of which he is prophesying. Isaiah chapters 1 to 35 are the beginning of Isaiah's vision. Because the *Old Testament* editors were confused by the symbolism of Isaiah's vision, they interpolated chapters 36 to 39 in an attempt to make sense out of what Isaiah was prophesying.

These editors did not have the "*key*" to unlock the mystery of Isaiah's words; but not wanting others to know they didn't understand, they plagiarized an earlier part of the *Old Testament* text in hopes of making sense of something they couldn't figure out for themselves. Just as the Christians of John's day (as well as all modern-day Christians) could not understand his symbolism, the Jews could not understand Isaiah's.

Herein is recorded a good example of how the authors and editors of the *Old Testament* borrowed text in an attempt to bring some logical consistency to Isaiah's prophecies, which were purposefully given in such a way to keep the "*key*" from the unrighteous:

And when they had called to the king, there came out to them Eliakim the son of Hilkiah, which was over the household, and Shebna the scribe, and Joah the son of Asaph the recorder. (II Kings 18:18)

Then came forth unto him Eliakim, Hilkiah's son, which was over the house, and Shebna the scribe, and Joah, Asaph's son, the recorder. (Isaiah 36:3)

Then said Eliakim the son of Hilkiah, and Shebna, and Joah, unto Rabshakeh, Speak, I pray thee, to thy servants in the Syrian language; for we understand it: and talk not with us in the Jews' language in the ears of the people that are on the wall. (II Kings 18:26)

Then said Eliakim and Shebna and Joah unto Rabshakeh, Speak, I pray thee, unto thy servants in the Syrian language; for we understand it; and speak not to us in the Jews' language, in the ears of the people that are on the wall. (Isaiah 36:11)

Then came Eliakim the son of Hilkiah, which was over the household, and Shebna the scribe, and Joah the son of Asaph the recorder, to Hezekiah with their clothes rent, and told him the words of Rabshakeh. (II Kings 18:37)

Then came Eliakim, the son of Hilkiah, that was over the household, and Shebna the scribe, and Joah, the son of Asaph, the recorder, to Hezekiah with their clothes rent, and told him the words of Rabshakeh. (Isaiah 36:22)

And it came to pass, when king Hezekiah heard it, that he rent his clothes, and covered himself with sackcloth, and went into the house of the LORD. And he sent Eliakim, which was over the household, and Shebna the scribe, and the elders of the priests, covered with sackcloth, to Isaiah the prophet the son of Amoz. (II Kings 19:1–2)

And it came to pass, when king Hezekiah heard it, that he rent his clothes, and covered himself with sackcloth, and went into the house of the LORD. And he sent Eliakim, who was over the household, and Shebna the scribe, and the elders of the priests covered with sackcloth, unto Isaiah the prophet the son of Amoz. (Isaiah 37:1–2)

Isaiah made use of these contemporary names to represent Christ in his revelation. John knew this, and borrowed the *"key of David"* from his predecessor:

*And it shall come to pass in that day, that I will call my servant Eliakim the son of Hilkiah: And I will clothe him with thy robe, and strengthen him with thy girdle, and I will commit thy government into his hand: and he shall be a father to the inhabitants of Jerusalem, and to the house of Judah. And the **key of the house of David** will I lay upon his shoulder; so he shall open, and none shall shut; and he shall shut, and none shall open. And **I will fasten him as a nail in a sure place**; and he shall be for a glorious throne to his father's house. And they shall hang upon him all the glory of his father's house, the offspring and the issue, all vessels of small quantity, from the vessels of cups, even to all the vessels of flagons. In that day, saith the LORD of hosts, shall the nail that is fastened in the sure place be removed, and be cut down, and fall; and the burden that was upon it shall be cut off: for the LORD hath spoken it.* (Isaiah 22:20–25)

The Jews had no idea what Isaiah was trying to say, not realizing that Isaiah had plagiarized his own predecessor, the prophet Ezra:

*And now for a little space grace hath been shewed from the LORD our God, to leave us a remnant to escape, and to give us a **nail in his holy place**, that our God may lighten our eyes, and give us a little reviving in our bondage.* (Ezra 9:8)

The *"key of the house of David"* is the gospel of Jesus Christ that gives the knowledge needed to understand the simple truths of all things which truly can "revive (us) in our bondage," assuring us "a sure place" in the kingdom of God, *"fastened securely by a nail."* Unfortunately, we live in a day that, "the nail that is fastened in the sure place" has been removed, thus none understand the words of the prophets. (Note: the *nail* in this instance has nothing to do with the crucifixion of Christ.)

3:8 I know thy works. Behold, I have set before thee an open door *which I have unlocked with the key*, and no man can shut it. *I have unlocked it and opened it up for thee*; for thou hast a little strength, *but* hast kept my word, and hast not denied my name. *Nevertheless, there are those among you who envy the key which I have given unto thee, and they pretend to be with thee, but they are not.*

3:9 Behold, I will make them of the synagogue of Satan, which say they are *of the house of Israel, but* are not, but do lie; behold, I will *not give them the key, but I shall give unto thee a crown and* make them to come and worship before thy feet, and to know that I have loved thee.

The whole of the religious and secular world envies an understanding of the mysteries of God. The learned look too deeply into understanding, thereby missing the simplicity of it all. In trying to come up with explanations that support the precepts, opinions, theories, and doctrines they have learned since birth, few ever come to a knowledge of the truth.

> *Ever learning, and never able to come to the knowledge of the truth.* (II Timothy 3:7)

Those who obey the gospel of Jesus Christ will have an understanding of the truth (this proper understanding is referred to as *charity*) because they become like a little child, throwing out all the "old wine" (old beliefs/thinking) so they can receive the "new." And in the day of the Lord these will be greatly respected and envied by those who could never discover the *"key"* to the mysteries of God.

3:10 Because thou hast kept *my* word *with* patience, I also will keep thee from the hour of temptation, which shall come upon all the world, to try them that dwell upon the earth. *For Satan shall be loosed and a key given unto those who follow him that they may unlock the chains by which he has been bound.*

In the latter days, technological advances and secular knowledge will grow beyond any previous level experienced by the human race. Because of the power and knowledge they will acquire, those who are involved in this worldly knowledge will believe that humans are more intelligent than they have ever been, convincing themselves that there is no God. Also, there will be those who believe that God has blessed them with this knowledge, not knowing it is really *Satan* who has given them the *"key"* and is whom they truly worship.

"Satan being bound" simply means that certain *"keys"* (knowledge) have been kept away from the *fleshly* brains of humankind so that they could not understand a technology that would have destroyed them. Imagine what would have happened to the earth had humans come up with the atomic bomb thousands of years ago!

The *chains of Satan* (which need a *"key"* to be unlocked) are chains of ignorance. John's reference to *"chains"* simply means that God has not allowed humans to have certain information regarding natural law for their own sake. For thousands of years, *Satan* was bound; which is to say *he* was not allowed to introduce certain aspects of technology, which *he* has finally been permitted to release in the latter days.

With the proliferation of this technological knowledge (*key*), modern humans have been allowed to experience distractions and temptations which have taken them away from living the fullness of the gospel of Jesus Christ. The Lord promises to uphold those who obey his gospel, keeping them from the effects of this *"hour of temptation."*

3:11 Behold, I come quickly: hold that fast which thou hast *been given of me*, that no man take thy crown.

A "*crown*" is symbolic of certain powers and rights given to the bearer. Each of us has the power and the right to know the mysteries of God for ourselves and run our own lives, working out our own salvation according to the plan of happiness guaranteed to all without respect of persons. When we listen to others, whether they are religious leaders or those to whom we look for wisdom, we have given away our "*crown*"; or in other words, they have taken it from us.

3:12 *For* him that overcometh will I make a pillar in the temple of my God, and he shall ***dwell in this sanctuary and*** go no more out: and I will write upon him the name of my God, and ***he shall dwell in*** the city of my God, which is ***the*** new Jerusalem, which cometh down out of heaven from my God; and I will write upon him ***the*** new name, ***which no man shall know saving he that receiveth it***.

The ancient Greeks were known to place a pillar in a temple to honor a dignitary. However, John takes his symbolism from the Jews, who also practiced this act as reported in II Samuel 18:18:

> *Now Absalom in his lifetime had taken and reared up for himself **a pillar**, which is in the king's dale: for he said, I have no son to keep my name in remembrance: and he called **the pillar after his own name**: and it is called unto this day, Absalom's place.* (II Samuel 18:18)

A "*name*" is symbolic of the works one does—our actions, deeds, and thoughts. If a person overcomes the temptations of the world, his or her actions and thoughts will be those exemplified and taught by Christ, the Son of God. That person will then be at peace, knowing and understanding that his or her actions, deeds, and thoughts "*write upon him the name of my God.*"

An emotional stability, calm, and peace will radiate from within those who dwell in the kingdom of God ("*city of my God*" also referred to as the "*New Jerusalem*") that Christ taught is within each of us (see Luke 17:21). Once we are affected by the peace and happiness the teachings of

Christ bring to us, we will act, do, and think differently (*"write upon him the new name"*); much differently from the rest of the human race who has not received the promised peace and joy of the gospel, which is why *"no man shall know saving he that receiveth it."* (See commentary of Revelation 2:17.)

3:13 He that hath an ear, let him hear what the Spirit saith unto the churches.

3:14 And unto the *servant* of the church of the Laodiceans write; These things saith *he who hath the final word, who is* the faithful and true witness *of this word, which word was in* the beginning of the creation of God;

John uses the term *"the word"* in writing his testimony of the mission and works of Jesus Christ (see John 1:1–14). This "word" has been, is, and will always be: *Do unto others what you would have them do unto you.* We were created as social beings that need each other to experience happiness. We gain this happiness in the associations we have with each other. The Creator Himself would say:

> *I have created you in my image, therefore ye are my children whom I love. And even as I have eternal joy, I have created you that ye might also have this joy. And for no other purpose have I created you except that ye might have joy. Behold, ye shall have joy as ye associate one with another according to the free will that I have given to each of you, even according to my image in which ye were created. And this joy ye shall receive when ye have become perfected in me and have received a body of flesh and bone as ye see that I have. For this is my work and my glory: to bring to pass your eternal lives that ye might forever experience this joy as I experience it.* (Source withheld)

3:15 I know thy works, *and from thy cup I cannot drink because* thou *offerest a* drink *unto me that is* neither cold nor hot; I would *that* thou *would bring forth a drink offering of* cold or hot.

Referencing this figurative description of a person's works (*offerings*) to the "*drink offering*" commanded in the Mosaic Law as described in *Old Testament* writings, John places emphasis on the difference between works that are acceptable to God and works which are not. Drinks are either offered "cold," to cool and refresh the body, or "hot" to soothe and warm it. Any drink that is lukewarm serves no purpose.

3:16 So then because thou *offerest that which is* lukewarm, and neither cold nor hot, I will spue *it* out of my mouth.

Jesus said it this way:

Not every one that saith unto me, Lord, Lord, shall enter the kingdom of heaven; but he that doeth the will of my Father which is in heaven. (Matthew 7:21)

When Christ comes again, there will be many who have convinced themselves that they have led righteous Christian lives, only to find out upon listening to what the Lord teaches as real truth (that which is "*spued out of my mouth*"), that they have done none of the works consistent with the *Royal Law* of the Father:

If ye fulfill the royal law according to the scripture, Thou shalt love thy neighbour as thyself, ye do well. (James 2:8)

3:17 *For* thou sayest, *because of the blessings of the Lord I am rich with gold and fine raiment*, and increased with goods, and have need of nothing; *but thou* knowest not that thou art wretched, and miserable *because thou art* poor, and blind, and naked:

3:18 I counsel thee to buy of me *that* gold *which is* tried in the fire, that thou mayest be rich; and *purchase of me without price* white raiment, that thou mayest be clothed *so* that the shame of thy nakedness *does* not appear; and anoint thine eyes with *my* eyesalve, that thou mayest see.

Verse 17 describes three figurative reasons for being miserable: being "*poor*," "*naked*" and "*blind*." Verse 18 takes each reason and offers the Lord's remedy for each: "*refined gold*," "*white rainment*," and "*eyesalve*" respectively. These three descriptions offer the figurative expression of our natures, which should be righteous works ("*refined gold*"), righteous desires ("*white raiment*"), and righteous judgment ("*eyesalve*"). If one works for raw gold (in contrast to *refined*) to *clothe* oneself in fine clothing, because in one's eyes one perceives oneself as being better than others, this person is diametrically opposed to the commandments of God. However, if we do the works of God ("*refined gold*") by doing unto others what we would have them do unto us, our desires become pure ("*white raiment*") and our eyes see with correct perception (the purpose of "*eyesalve*" is to heal the eyes).

3:19 *And behold, thus saith the Lord unto all the churches*, As many as I love, I rebuke and chasten: be zealous therefore, and repent.

It is given to understand that each of the churches in this first section of John's *Revelation* is presented with a loving accolade of what it does which is right, followed by a rebuke or that of which it should repent. John demonstrates the love and patience of God, our Father, in dealing with His children.

3:20 Behold, I stand at the door, and knock: if any man **upon hearing** my voice **shall** open the door, I will come in to him, and will sup with him, and he with me.

John's description of the Laodicean church (Revelation 3:14–18), in which the final of the *Seven Deadly Sins* ("greed") is presented, follows the figurative expression given in chapter 5 of *Solomon's Song* as given in the *Old Testament*. This part of *the Song* is a dialogue between a woman (*the people of the world* as has been expressed in John's figurative presentation of his vision—see Revelation 2:20) and her *beloved* (the Lord). John's figurative description starts out with reference to drink, continues with a reference to worldly concerns, and ends with the Lord making an attempt to enter into the heart and mind of a person (*knocking*):

(The Lord) **5:1** *I am come into my garden, my sister, my spouse: I have gathered my myrrh with my spice; I have eaten my honeycomb with my honey; I have drunk my wine with my milk: eat, O friends; drink, yea, drink abundantly, O beloved.*

In *the Song*, the Lord does not distinguish between filial (sister) and personal bonds (spouse), considering all equal. Where it could have been written without a repeated first person reference, the Song composer has the Lord specifically stating, "*I have gathered **my** myrrh with **my** spice...eaten **my** honeycomb with **my** honey...drunk **my** wine with **my** milk*," all signifying the Lord has done it ***his way***, living *his* own life, and teaching *his* gospel through word and example and now presents it to *us* that we might "*drink abundantly.*"

(The Woman) **5:2** *I sleep, but my heart waketh: it is the voice of my beloved that knocketh, saying,* (The Lord) *Open to me, my sister, my love, my dove, my undefiled: for my head is filled with dew, and my locks with the drops of the night.*

The Lord is cold and wet, and wishes to come in out of the darkness, having performed his work and having eaten and drunk of the fruits thereof, as expressed in verse one. The Lord has finished his work, and is going through the darkened world attempting to find those who will listen to him and let him into their hearts. "*Rain*" has long symbolized revelation or knowledge coming from "*above*," thus the Lord specifically states his head is wet from the revelation and knowledge received in a darkened world.

(The Woman) **5:3** *I have put off my coat; how shall I put it on? I have washed my feet; how shall I defile them?*

The woman does not want to open the door and go out into the cold night to meet the Lord because she is comfortable in the warm house she has built for herself. In other words, the people will not open up to God because of their worldly ways and comforts.

(The Woman) **5:4** *My beloved put in his hand by the hole of the door, and my bowels were moved for him.*

The Lord was desirous to let himself in, and the woman was desirous to greet him, yet her worldly concerns prevented her immediate response to his efforts to get into the house.

(The Woman) **5:5** *I rose up to open to my beloved; and my hands dropped with myrrh, and my fingers with sweet smelling myrrh, upon the handles of the lock.*

Because her hands were dripping with myrrh (a very expensive spice), she fumbled with the lock and the latch to open the door. Symbolic of one pursuing the wealth and fine things of the world, this narrative describes what occurs when the Lord has taught us his gospel which will bring us peace and happiness. Because of our constant desire to gain worldly treasures and honor, we cannot "open the door to understanding" because we are pursuing material wealth and worldly gain, though our hearts might desire to be close to God.

(The Woman) **5:6** *I opened to my beloved; but my beloved had withdrawn himself, and was gone: my soul failed when he spake: I sought him, but I could not find him; I called him, but he gave me no answer.*

Those who miss the opportunity to know the Lord and his ways in this life because of their selfish, worldly concerns will not receive the peace and happiness promised to all those who obey his gospel.

(The Woman) **5:7** *The watchmen that went about the city found me, they smote me, they wounded me; the keepers of the walls took away my veil from me.*

These "*watchmen*" are the religious leaders, philosophers, and comparable self-help gurus which exist in all human societies. Here, the woman laments that their teachings and counsel have caused her more misery than good, taking away the pure knowledge she once received when she was "veiled" properly for her beloved.

> (The Woman) **5:8** *I charge you, O daughters of Jerusalem, if ye find my beloved, that ye tell him, that I am sick of love.*

The woman laments to others, charging them to listen to the Lord if they ever find him, counseling them not to do what she has done when she could not let him in the door when he knocked the first time.

> (The Watchmen) **5:9** *What is thy beloved more than another beloved, O thou fairest among women? What is thy beloved more than another beloved, that thou dost so charge us?*

The false teachers who do not know Christ (though they think they do), are perplexed by a person's unwillingness to accept their understanding and perceptions of truth. Human beings who have placed themselves above others, believing that they know God better than anyone else, make zealous attempts to get others to believe in them. However, a person who has known the Lord (as the woman who has slept with her beloved), will never be able to accept a substitute for what they experienced in real truth. To illustrate this figuratively, the woman goes on in the next few verses of *the Song* describing her beloved, who is incomparable to the other men who desire her.

> **5:10** *My beloved is white and ruddy, the chiefest among ten thousand.*

> **5:11** *His head is as the most fine gold, his locks are bushy, and black as a raven.*

> **5:12** *His eyes are as the eyes of doves by the rivers of waters, washed with milk, and fitly set.*

5:13 *His cheeks are as a bed of spices, as sweet flowers: his lips like lilies, dropping sweet smelling myrrh.*

5:14 *His hands are as gold rings set with the beryl: his belly is as bright ivory overlaid with sapphires.*

5:15 *His legs are as pillars of marble, set upon sockets of fine gold: his countenance is as Lebanon, excellent as the cedars.* (Compare Revelation 10:1 *"And his feet as pillars of fire."*)

5:16 *His mouth is most sweet: yea, he is altogether lovely. This is my beloved, and this is my friend, O daughters of Jerusalem.*

The crux of John's message is: If you hear a knock at your door and you know it is the Lord, you had better not hesitate to open up to him; and your hands better not be so busy in worldly affairs and comforts that you are unable to open the door, fearing you might get a little cold and wet.

3:21 To him that overcometh *the sins of this world* will I grant to sit with me in my *kingdom*, even *so it shall be* as I also overcame and am set down with my Father in His *kingdom*.

Christ's life gave us a sure example that we can exist in this world and keep the commandments of God, doing good to each other always. To have the peace and happiness he has promised, which is what the kingdom of God offers, we must follow his example and do as he did and taught. Simply put, we must do unto others what we would have them do unto us, or we will not be allowed to live in the kingdom of God forever.

3:22 He that hath an ear, let him hear what the Spirit saith unto the churches.

John wraps up this part of his figurative explanation of the world (*the seven churches*) and the sins that cause the most problems in our world (or the seven sins insinuated against the seven different churches).

His purpose was to give a general overview of the state of human affairs upon this earth and give encouragement to those who attempt to overcome **Anger, Gluttony, Pride, Lust, Slothfulness, Envy,** and **Greed**—the basic struggles of human nature that are the cause of the unhappiness of humankind. He encourages us to replace human nature with the fruits of the Spirit (*"what the Spirit saith unto the churches"*), which are **Love, Temperance, Meekness, Goodness, Longsuffering, Peace,** and **Joy.**

Chapter

Revelation
Unfolded

In the preceding chapter, an example was given in which John, as a matter of literary style and for his purposes, borrowed much of his symbolism from prophets who preceded him. His prophetic predecessors, likewise, borrowed from each other. The reason these prophets and seers could do this and maintain the propriety and integrity of their individual messages, is found in the absolute literary license each held in common over the exact same vision of the mysteries of God. Each received their authority to do so from the same God, and each was under strict command not to reveal with plainness the vision to anyone else, except those prepared to receive the truth.

Consequently, each used symbolic and figurative expressions (often borrowed or copied from earlier prophets), to assure that his narrative kept secret any literal exposition of the vision of the mysteries of God until the latter times—when the prophesied events would begin to unfold. (See Revelation 1:11 and 10:4.)

Much of John's symbolism comes from the book of Ezekiel. He also uses numerical and mathematical symbolism, taking much of this from the book of *Daniel.* Almost all of John's symbolism was borrowed from the only source of scripture he had in his day—the *Old Testament.*

With this insight, it is much easier to arrive at an understanding of the message of truth John has buried in his writings and "*sealed*" away from the understanding of those who would never have accepted it in his day. Could a person living hundreds of years ago have believed that there were galaxies and solar systems with inhabited planets in the mysterious sky, not to mention the truths and technologies to which *we* have been exposed, which not even the most learned among them could have ever imagined?

4:1 After this I looked, ***and still in the vision, I beheld, and it appeared as if*** a door was opened in heaven: and I heard ***again*** the first voice which was as it were of a trumpet talking with me; which said, Come up hither, and I will show thee things which must be hereafter.

John relates how his understanding of the Universe began to open up for him. In other words, the eyes of his understanding were opened. Throughout *Revelation,* "*eyes*" are figuratively expressed as knowledge and understanding. The reference to "*a door*" is the same figurative expression used previously by John. (See commentary on Revelation 3:7–8, 20). At this point, John assures us that Christ is continuing as his guide during this vision. (Refer to Revelation 1:10–11.)

4:2 And immediately I was ***taken*** in the spirit; and ***beheld*** a throne set ***high*** in heaven, and one sat on the throne.

Being "*taken in the spirit*" has the same significance as one's eyes being opened so that one sees, or having a "*door opened*" to an understanding. Spirit entities have many experiences and great knowledge recorded in the molecules that make up the ethereal reality we religiously refer to as "*the spirit.*" Our mortal bodies do not have the capacity to allow our spirits to react with our brains in such a way that will allow us to remember all that is recorded. Jesus told his disciples that after he was gone, he would send the Holy Ghost (Spirit) who would help them remember the things their spirits already knew, but which their flesh did not allow them to remember:

But the Comforter, which is the Holy Ghost, whom the Father will send in my name, he shall teach you all things, and bring all things to your remembrance, whatsoever I have said unto you. (John 14:26)

Throughout Jesus' ministry, he taught the people that if they listened to him and kept his commandments, they would have the Holy Ghost to be with them. All of Christ's counsels and commandments (if followed) bring peace, serenity, and comfort to a person. When one is at peace, is serene, and has no worries, the ability of the spirit entity to use the brain to bring memories and understanding to a conscious level increases proportionately to the brain's capacity to allow it.

A computer works much the same way. If a computer's memory chip is filled to capacity, it can only recall and work with what is stored in its memory chip. Therefore, the computer (or "the chip") becomes incapable of using certain programs which require more memory. Our mortal bodies are like the computer's hardware, its memory card and processor, etc. Our spirits are like a software program, such as a highly advanced computer game we desire to play. When we try to download the game's software on our computer, we find that our computer cannot support the software because it lacks sufficient memory; therefore, we cannot play the game. If we free up sufficient memory by erasing portions that have already been recorded and used by the computer, we will be able to play the game.

By analogy, if we do what Christ taught, we erase feelings of pride and vanity, bad feelings for others, worries about the past, present, and future, and many other things that are taking up space in our limited brains. Upon doing so, our minds are open and ready to receive and remember what our spirit has to offer, even though our mortal brain lacks the capacity to remember all things. Eternal, resurrected, advanced bodies will have the ability to remember *all* things recorded in the spiritual element.

John was "*taken in the spirit*" because he had no other worries or emotions which were *taking him* away from the door of understanding that had been opened up for him.

Where verse 2 says, "*and one sat on the throne,*" the "*one*" here represents God, the Father, a highly advanced human who dwells on a planet in another galaxy. Sitting on a throne is symbolic of power and authority, and has nothing to do with the way worldly kings are dignified and worshipped. The fact that John is writing of the Father is verified in Revelation 5:1–6, in which John again figuratively presents the Father sitting upon the throne, and in possession of a *book* which only Christ is worthy to open.

4:3 And *I looked and saw, near unto the throne, another who* sat, *and* was to look upon like a sardine and jasper stone, *and also* like unto an emerald; and *I saw as it were the appearance of fire, and it shown in brightness as* a rainbow round about the throne.

For his figurative expression of the visage of Christ, the Anointed One of God, John uses three of the names of the stones taken from the "Breastplate of Judgment" described in Exodus 28:15–21.

Moses was commanded to make certain articles of clothing and vestments for Aaron, who symbolically represented the source of wisdom and authority among the children of Israel. The **sardius** stone was the first stone placed on the breastplate representing Reuben, the *"firstborn Son."* The fourth stone placed in the breastplate was the **emerald**, representing Judah, from whose loins came forth Jesus Christ, the *Firstborn Son of God.* **Jasper**, which was the last stone placed, represented Benjamin, whose Hebrew name literally means, *"Son of my right hand."* Christ, who will judge the world, is consistently described as being on the right hand of God, thus the symbolism of the stones coming from the "Breastplate of Judgment."

It is appropriate here to note that a *Urim and Thummim* (see Exodus 28:30) was attached and carried by Aaron, whose assignment was to teach the Israelites the word of God. All true prophets of God possess a *Urim and Thummim* from which they receive direction from God. This device is similar to a highly advanced cell phone that receives text messages from the planets where God and Christ dwell.

When activated properly and with authority, a *Urim and Thummim* emits light. John represents this figuratively by describing how the light of the sun (which in prophetic prose is often described as *"fire"*) shines through the *twelve gems* set in the *breastplate*, and creates a *"rainbow"* effect. This illustrates that the truth and the word of God are being given to the different peoples of the earth, who are figuratively represented throughout *Revelation* as the twelve tribes of Israel. The "light" of God illuminates the world from the throne on which He sits, given symbolically by John as the light passing through the prisms of the twelve gems and appearing "*as a rainbow.*"

Ezekiel describes the vision of the same scene in this way:

And above the firmament that was over their heads was the likeness of a throne, as the **appearance of a sapphire stone***: and upon the likeness of the throne was the likeness as the appearance of a man above upon it.*

And I saw as the colour of amber, as the appearance of fire round about within it, from the appearance of his loins even upward, and from the appearance of his loins even downward, I saw as it were **the appearance of fire, and it had brightness round about.**

As the appearance of the bow *that is in the cloud in the day of rain, so was the appearance of the brightness round about. This was the appearance of the likeness of the glory of the Lord. And when I saw it, I fell upon my face, and I heard a voice of one that spake.* (Ezekiel 1:26–28)

4:4 And **in the midst of** the throne were four and twenty seats: and upon the seats I saw four and twenty elders sitting, clothed in white raiment; and they had on their heads crowns of gold.

These "*four and twenty elders*" represent the righteous prophets called to serve the people of the earth during the first 6000 years. The seventh thousand years are reserved for the final prophet, Christ. These are called by God through the ministrations of exalted beings sent from other planets to this earth, to offer the calling to certain individuals, who are then sent to the different nations of the earth. This number is figurative, and has nothing to do with the actual number of prophets who have been sent with the proper authority of God.

John uses *twenty-four* in his symbolic presentation to coincide with the other numbers he uses to represent the people of the earth. Throughout the 6000 years (which number is used by John to describe the years of human existence up until the beginning of the seven thousandth year) John utilizes the number *twenty-four* to represent those who have taught the people of the earth the true principles and commandments of God.

The people who accept the prophets' message are those who are symbolically represented as receiving the "*seal of God in their foreheads*"; or in other words, their intentions and thoughts are turned toward God.

If one **multiplies** the efforts of the prophets (represented by the number **24**) **by** the number of years of human existence (**6000**) leading up to the Millennium, the equation produces the product given by John in Revelation 7:4: **144,000**.

John uses these mathematical truths to represent those who have lived upon the earth and listened to the prophets, and who have accepted the "*elders*'" message and turned their hearts and minds (foreheads) toward God. The numbers are purely figurative, and are not meant to give an exact number of people; as there have been many more than twenty-four prophets of God upon the earth during the 6000 years of human existence, and many more than just 144,000 who have accepted their message. However, the symbolism stands with clarity: during the 6000 years of human existence, whoever listens to the true prophets of God and turns their mind toward Him receives His "*seal in their forehead*," and is considered one of "the elect."

4:5 And out of the throne proceeded *four beasts*. *And* lightnings and thunderings and voices *came out of* seven lamps of fire burning before the throne *in the midst of the four beasts*, which *each gives its light to* the seven *servants* of God.

John gives a relation of the "*four beasts*," and compares their faces ("*every one had four faces apiece*"—from Ezekiel below) to certain species in the animal kingdom. These are figurative expressions that describe all creatures that live by instinct (or by the command of God) and are created and programmed for specific purposes to maintain the order and balance of nature upon the earth.

The *"beasts"* represent the angels of God, and their purpose and actions in fulfilling the commands they receive from God for the benefit of the human race upon this earth. The angels are responsible for what is done upon this earth. They are highly advanced and exalted human beings who, like God, gain their eternal happiness being in service to others forever. They create and destroy by their command, in order to maintain a proper order upon this earth. However, they cannot take away the free agency of a human being.

Though the prophet Ezekiel uses the word *"creature"* instead of *"beast"* to describe the angels, he eventually reveals their true identity as *"cherubim"*:

> And **the cherubims** *lifted up their wings, and mounted up from the earth in my sight: when they went out, the wheels also were beside them, and every one stood at the door of the east gate of the Lord's house; and the glory of the God of Israel was over them above.* **This is the living creature** *that I saw under the God of Israel by the river of Chebar;* [as described in Ezekiel 1:5] *and I knew that* **they were the cherubims.** *Every one had four faces apiece, and every one four wings; and the likeness of the hands of a man was under their wings. And the likeness of their faces was the same faces which I saw by the river of Chebar, their appearances and themselves: they went every one straight forward.* (Ezekiel 10:19–22)

These cherubim (*"beasts/angels"*) and their actions and powers, are described and outlined more specifically in Ezekiel's writings than in John's (see Ezekiel 1:5–12):

> **1:5** *Also out of the midst thereof came the likeness of four living creatures. And this was their appearance; they had the likeness of a man....*

Angels of God are exalted and eternal humans who have reached a level of power and authority given only to those who have proven themselves worthy to use it properly.

Continuing with Ezekiel's figurative expressions:

1:6 *And every one had four faces, and every one had four wings.*

The number "four" was chosen to be used in a figurative description, but is not intended to be specific as to the number of angels assigned to perform work on this earth. *"Four"* represents the fact that angels have influence and power, which covers the **four** corners of the earth, from East to West and North to South.

1:7 *And their feet were straight feet; and the sole of their feet was like the sole of a calf's foot: and they sparkled like the colour of burnished brass.* (Compare Revelation 1:15.)

The angels go forth and do exactly as they are told (*"straight feet"*), and when they do their work on earth, they leave no empirical evidence of what they have done; thus the comparison *"like the sole of a calf's foot,"* which leaves little, if any, footprint in comparison with adult cattle.

1:8 *And they had the hands of a man under their wings on their four sides;*

The works of angels are always for the benefit of humankind (*"man"*). Prophets use the word *"hand(s)"* to symbolize the works or actions of a person. Thus, angels' works are all to do with mankind.

1:8–9 *And they four had their faces and their wings. Their wings were joined one to another; they turned not when they went; they went every one straight forward.*

Wings show power of movement and balance. Angels keep all things in precise natural balance throughout the earth.

> **1:10** *As for the likeness of their faces, they four had the face of a man, and the face of a lion, on the right side: and they four had the face of an ox on the left side; they four also had the face of an eagle.*

The symbolism of the faces is revealed below.

> **1:11–12** *Thus were their faces; and their wings were stretched upwards two wings of every one were joined one to another, and two covered their bodies. And they went every one straight forward; whither the spirit was to go, they went; and they turned not when they went.*

This signifies angels using their power in a united effort always in obedience and honor to the will of God, and having their intentions being one with God's.

Ezekiel continues his description of these angels:

> **1:13–14** *As for the likeness of the living creatures, their appearance was like burning coals of fire, and like the appearance of lamps: it went up and down among the living creatures; and the fire was bright, and out of the fire went forth lightning. And the living creatures ran and returned as the appearance of a flash of lightning.*

Returning again to the commentary on Revelation 4:5:

God's power and will is metaphorically described as "*lightning and thunder*" coming from His throne, as all His creations agree to support His eternal plan. Later in *Revelation*, the multitude of people created for this solar system will give their unified consent, and be referred to by John as:

"the voice of a great multitude, and as the voice of many waters, and also as the voice of mighty thunderings, saying, Alleluia and Amen: for the Lord God omnipotent reigneth." (See Revelation 19:6.)

The angels deliver the word and will of God to His prophets (*"four and twenty servants"*) upon the earth. They travel within an advanced transportation system that can transport them between planets and solar systems, *"as the appearance of a flash of lightning."* To a human living in the 16th Century, our modern means of transportation would seem as if we were traveling miraculously and very fast. Imagine what the means of transportation is like for humans who are thousands of years more advanced than we are today!

The mention of the *"seven lamps of fire burning"* expresses the accessibility to knowledge and the understanding of the mysteries (truths) of God available to all humankind equally. All prophets have access to the understanding of truth. However, having knowledge does not necessarily mean one has an understanding of truth. *Real* truth *"burns"* with reality, and leaves no confusion; whereas *most* knowledge is dependent on the understanding of the recipient and the teacher presenting the knowledge. Mortal knowledge is not truth, but a perception developed from the experience of the person. As the individual gains more experience, the knowledge changes. It was an accepted knowledge that the world was flat, until through experience, the truth was finally known.

The burning that will take place when a prophet refers to the *fires of hell and damnation,* is the consternation and embarrassment that one will feel when the truth is revealed, and destroys all the knowledge once embraced as truth. Those who have exalted themselves above others will suffer the most (*weeping, wailing, and gnashing their teeth*). This is because not only will they be embarrassed by their own foolishness, but those who they had once convinced that they were "knowledgeable," will see them for the fools they really are. *"And whosoever shall exalt himself shall be abased; and he that shall humble himself shall be exalted.* (See Matthew 23:12.)

The *"lamps"* are the vessels that contain the oil (knowledge of real truth), which when ignited, provide the light by which one sees in the darkness. Jesus gave a parable of ten virgins who each had a lamp.

Five kept their lamps filled and trimmed with a true understanding of the mysteries of God; and when the hour of midnight's darkness fell upon them, they were able to trim and light their lamps, and find their way to the *marriage* ceremony. This marriage was given symbolically to represent the *unification* of the five virgins with the real truth and understanding of the One anointed (Christ) as the overseer of this solar system.

The foolish ones didn't have any oil in their lamps, and when they asked for an explanation of the mysteries of God (oil), the wise virgins told them to *"go to them that sell."* Those who *sell* are the organized religions, the spiritual advisers, and the religious promoters and sellers, who offer their wares in church meetings, books, television shows, radio programs, and the likes. The wise need none of their wares, because their lamps are filled and properly trimmed.

> *The lord of that servant shall come in a day when he looketh not for him, and in an hour that he is not aware of, and shall cut him asunder, and appoint him his portion with the hypocrites: there shall be weeping and gnashing of teeth. Then shall the kingdom of heaven be likened unto ten virgins, which took their lamps, and went forth to meet the bridegroom. And five of them were wise, and five were foolish. They that were foolish took their lamps, and took no oil with them: But the wise took oil in their vessels with their lamps. While the bridegroom tarried, they all slumbered and slept. And at midnight there was a cry made, Behold, the bridegroom cometh; go ye out to meet him. Then all those virgins arose, and trimmed their lamps. And the foolish said unto the wise, Give us of your oil; for our lamps are gone out. But the wise answered, saying, Not so; lest there be not enough for us and you: but go ye rather to them that sell, and buy for yourselves. And while they went to buy, the bridegroom came; and they that were ready went in with him to the marriage: and the door was shut. Afterward came also the other virgins, saying, Lord, Lord,*

open to us. But he answered and said, Verily I say unto you, I know you not. Watch therefore, for ye know neither the day nor the hour wherein the Son of man cometh. (Matthew 24:50–51; 25:1–13)

By the time the foolish ones figure things out, it becomes too late, and the door to understanding is closed. And when these stand outside the door and proclaim with a loud voice, *"Lord, have we not prophesied in thy name? and in thy name have cast out devils? and in thy name done many wonderful works?* Please! Look at the oil we have purchased from those who sell! Our lamps are now full, are they not?" Then will the answer be given that will cause their weeping and gnashing of teeth: *"I never knew you: depart from me ye that work iniquity."* (See Matthew 7:22–23.)

4:6 And before the throne there **appeared** a sea **like unto a looking** glass **of** crystal: and **it was** in the midst of the throne **where the four and twenty elders sat**, and round about the throne, were *the* four beasts full of eyes before and behind.

John describes the ability of exalted beings to see everything that *has* happened, that *is* happening, and that *will* happen. Human imagination has used this verse as a means of obtaining truth through a crystal ball. From this reference comes the practice of pretended mystics, who supposedly see throughout time by looking into a crystal ball. The symbolism comes from another *Old Testament* writing found in Job 37:15–18:

> *"Dost thou know when God disposed them, and caused the light of his cloud to shine? Dost thou know the balancings of the clouds, the wondrous works of him which is perfect in knowledge? How thy garments are warm, when he quieteth the earth by the south wind? Hast thou with him spread out the sky, which is strong, and **as a molten looking glass**?"*

The *Urim and Thummim* have an appearance like glass, and give all prophets ("*four and twenty elders*") the ability to see the past and the future as is needed for them to fulfill their calling. The angels of God ("*four beasts*") know all things of the future and the past ("*eyes before and behind.*")

4:7 And ***each beast had the likeness of four faces: the*** first was like a lion, and the second like a calf, and the third **like** a face as a man, and the fourth was like a flying eagle.

With the proper translation, John uses the same symbolism as Ezekiel to describe the angels of God:

> *As for the likeness of their faces, they four had the face of a man, and the face of a lion, on the right side: and they four had the face of an ox on the left side; they four also had the face of an eagle.* (Ezekiel 1:10)

Angels travel from other planets to the earth to do what they are commanded to do for our sakes. Throughout the *Old Testament*, the phrase "*I will set my face*" is used to describe an action taken by one with an intention to perform a deed. This phrase was generally used to explain a course of action God was going to take to intercede in the lives of the people. However, even in modern times it can be said that when a person is intent on doing something, he has *set his face* to do it.

In the following *Old Testament* verses, one can replace the words "**set my face**" with "**send my angels**," and it will give the meaning that John chose when he describes angels, figuratively, as having "*four faces,*" because they do the work of God:

> *And I will **set my face** against that man, and will cut him off from among his people; because he hath given of his seed unto Molech, to defile my sanctuary, and to profane my holy name.* (Leviticus 20:3)

> *For I have **set my face** against this city for evil, and not for good, saith the LORD: it shall be given into the hand of*

the king of Babylon, and he shall burn it with fire.
(Jeremiah 21:10)

*And I will **set my face** against that man, and will make
him a sign and a proverb, and I will cut him off from the
midst of my people; and ye shall know that I am the
LORD.* (Ezekiel 14:8)

In the following verse, Ezekiel describes how men have turned
their works and intentions towards idols instead of God by putting *"the
stumblingblock of their iniquity before **their face**"*:

*Son of man, these men have set up their idols in their heart,
and put the stumblingblock of their iniquity before **their
face**: should I be inquired of at all by them?* (Ezekiel 14:3)

Daniel uses the phrase to demonstrate his intent to serve God
through righteous works:

*And I **set my face** unto the Lord God, to seek by prayer
and supplications, with fasting, and sackcloth, and ashes:*
(Daniel 9:3)

The *"four faces"* (the intentions/works) of these four cherubim
represent the work and purpose expected of certain natural orders of the
creatures that God has placed upon this earth, of which our mortal flesh is
also a part. The *"calf"* or the "ox" represents those animals that eat plants,
which were first placed upon the earth to provide the necessary elements
needed for other life to exist. Plants receive their power and life from the
sun, which is the great fire that gives its life-giving power to all of the earth.

Another face, the *"lion,"* represents those animals that were placed
on the earth to eat the flesh of the plant eaters for their sustenance; thus
maintaining a proper balance within the order of nature to which all things
are subjected.

The *"eagle"* represents the nature of the fowls of the air, which are seemingly unrestricted in certain laws of nature, making their conveyance (through the air) unlike all other creatures. Most birds live in the air *and* on earth, and are dependent on both. They enable plants to grow by spreading seeds, and also keep small, plant-eating rodents in check.

The final face is that of a "*man*," which represents the primate species, or those animals that are like humans.

Part of our predestined purpose for being upon the earth is to learn opposition in all things. In order that we may properly experience the opposite of an eternal body that does not die or sicken, the angels oversaw the evolution of the *Homo sapiens*, a primate species from which most of our mortal bodies evolved over time, and in which we can experience the effects of death and sickness. All of these natural orders work as *one* in the hands of the angels assigned to this planet, each order working according to the commandments that each has received of the Father. Without any one of the *four* natural orders, none of the others could exist and fulfill the measure of its creation.

4:8 And the four beasts had each of them *four* wings about him; and they were full of eyes within: and they rest not day and night, saying, Holy, holy, holy, Lord God Almighty, which was, and is, and is to come.

The great mystery of God is that there have always been Gods. There has never been a time when there wasn't a Creator whose position and role in the eternities was to prepare solar systems for life to exist. If there had been a *First* God, then it would be logical to believe there would be a *Last* God. John describes this eternal role as "*Lord God Almighty, which was, is, and is to come.*" (See verse 11 below.)

4:9 And when those beasts give **this** glory and honour and thanks to him that sat on the throne, who liveth for ever and ever,

4:10 The four and twenty elders fall down before him that sat on the throne, and worship him that liveth for ever and ever, and cast their crowns before the throne, saying,

4:11 Thou art worthy, O Lord, to receive glory and honour and power: for thou hast created all things, and for thy pleasure they are and were created.

True prophets of God (*"four and twenty elders"*) understand their roles as tools in the hands of the angels (who do the work and will of God, the Eternal Father, day and night.) These mortal servants of God realize from whom they receive their callings (from angels). Those from whom they do, have great knowledge and understanding (*"full of eyes within"*) and great power (*"four wings"*). Prophets realize whose work it is that the angels actually do. Upon their realization that the angels *only* do the work of the Father, prophets feel a deep humility and take no glory or honor to themselves; knowing full well that without the intercession of the angels of God, they would not know the mysteries of God, nor could they do His work upon the earth.

Chapter

REVELATION 5 UNFOLDED

5:1 And I saw in the right hand of him *who* sat on the throne *the* Book of Life. *And it was full of words* written within and on the backside, *and* sealed with seven seals.

The *"Book of Life"* is the figurative expression of the blueprints, keys, commands, and instructions to create life and to assure that all things arrive at the eternal purpose for which they are created—i.e., happiness. This handbook, a kind of *Cookbook of Life And Happiness* is followed by all Creators in preparing solar systems and planets for human habitation. It provides instructions and power needed by these Celestial Beings to bring those created through the three stages or "estates" of eternal development.

Our *first estate* of existence (the beginning) is an individual spirit state. It is one composed of elements of matter that can record experience on a molecular level, but which cannot be seen by the natural eyes of those in their second estate. The *second estate* is the mortal and corruptible body to which the spirit body of element is assigned to inhabit for testing, proba-tion, and determination of that which brings happiness to the individual.

The *third estate* is the physical, incorruptible body prepared through the advanced technology and blueprints found in the "*Book of Life*," rendering death of the body impossible—this is the resurrection.

The purpose and end of all life and creation is to exist forever in happiness, a state otherwise referred to by prophets as "salvation" or "eternal life." It is not in God's plan to allow us to have eternal bodies and live on eternal planets unless we can do so without causing problems for each other. Therefore, it is not possible to obtain an eternal body until *we* can prove by the way we live in mortality that we can be trusted not to be a problem to our fellow beings in the third estate.

To be able to understand happiness, we must first experience what happiness is like outside of the influence of our Creator while cloaked in the flesh of mortality. Therefore, the purpose of mortal life is for us to learn how to live with each other in peace, harmony, and happiness, while freely experiencing the effects of unhappiness caused by our personal relationships and environs in mortality. (This is what is figuratively expressed as partaking of the *Tree of Knowledge of Good and Evil*.) As we experience the opposite of happiness, we learn to fully understand misery, tribulation, wickedness (personal and otherwise), and the multitude of experiences that bring unhappiness.

"Happiness" is the balance which comes as the result of attaining a proper realization of what *truly* makes each one of us happy in how we view *ourselves*, and in how we interact with our fellow beings in the environment and circumstances in which we are placed.

Christ is the One appointed by God to show us how to associate with each other and to assure that we do so properly, so that we will always experience happiness. Thus, it can be said that eternal life is only through this one being, Jesus Christ. It comes because of his message and example; and *not* because his blood was shed at the hands of evil men who rejected his simple message (as they did to many of the prophets like him). Just as his body (like ours) required blood to exist mortally, so also in this fleshly body he showed us the way to live. This is the power and significance of the body and blood of Christ.

Unless we learn how to properly respond to his message by the way we live, we cannot be resurrected into a physical body that does not die. In other words, if we do not learn to do unto each other what we would have done unto us, then we will not be in compliance with Christ's teachings; therefore, we cannot be saved (live forever) in one of the mansions of God.

This is God's plan of salvation for those whom He has created in His own image, i.e., His children. His works always follow the eternal laws of nature in the *Creator's Handbook*, which for want of a better name, John calls the "*Book of Life.*"

These instructions and laws cannot be added to or taken away from. Thus, the book is "*full of words written within and on the backside,*" leaving no space for any additions. These instructions must be followed the same way in this solar system as they were in all other solar systems in which life has been created. Those who have the power to create, and who possess the *handbook* and blueprints of creation, are *only* those who have proven themselves worthy enough to handle this great knowledge and power in righteousness. These use their power *only* to serve others and not for their own personal gain.

This test of worthiness is given during mortal life in which an individual acts with a physical body according to the desires given by the spiritual entity within this body; which has recorded in it the person's personality and desires of happiness.

The book is in the "*right hand*" of God. The *right hand* is symbolic of righteous works—one's actions being figuratively expressed as what is done with the hands. Conversely, whatever is done on the left is considered unrighteous.

Throughout *the Bible*, the right and left hands are used to represent proper and improper choices:

> *Thy **right hand**, O LORD, is become glorious in power: thy **right hand**, O LORD, hath dashed in pieces the enemy.* (Exodus 15:6)

> *Then shalt thou kill the ram, and take of his blood, and put it upon the tip of the **right** ear (that they may hear only righteousness) of Aaron, and upon the tip of the **right** ear of his sons, and upon the thumb of their **right** hand (that they*

may do only righteousness), and upon the great toe of their **right** *foot (that they may follow and lead others in the path of righteousness, as the "great toe" leads all the rest), and sprinkle the blood upon the altar round about.* (Exodus 29:20)

I have set the Lord always before me: because he is at my **right hand**, *I shall not be moved.* (Psalms 16:8)

Mine hand also hath laid the foundation of the earth, and my **right hand** *hath spanned the heavens: when I call unto them, they stand up together.* (Isaiah 48:13)

That led them by the **right hand** *of Moses with his glorious arm, dividing the water before them, to make himself an everlasting name?* (Isaiah 63:12)

Go thee one way or other, either on the **right hand**, *or on the* **left**, *whithersoever thy face is set.* (Ezekiel 21:16)

But when thou doest alms, let not thy **left hand** *know what thy* **right hand** *doeth:* (Matthew 6:3)

And he shall set the sheep on his **right hand**, *but the goats on the* **left**. *Then shall the King say unto them on his* **right hand**, *Come, ye blessed of my Father, inherit the kingdom prepared for you from the foundation of the world: For I was an hungered, and ye gave me meat: I was thirsty, and ye gave me drink: I was a stranger, and ye took me in:* (Matthew 25:33–35)

Then shall he say also unto them on the **left hand**, *Depart from me, ye cursed, into everlasting fire, prepared for the devil and his angels: For I was an hungered, and ye gave me no meat: I was thirsty, and ye gave me no drink:* (Matthew 25:41–42)

By using the term "*seven seals*," John figuratively expresses that there are seven different stages of human development that naturally occur when free-willed beings are allowed to act on their own accord. Life experience must allow for these seven stages to occur in order for the being to arrive at the final stage of human development—Divine Enlightenment, or recognizing and accepting who we really are.

To come to this conclusive seventh stage, we must pass through all of the other six stages in mortality; therefore, by our own experience, attaining a proper realization of what truly makes us happy. As human societies go through each stage, certain effects are experienced. These effects are illustrated figuratively by John as he describes each *seal* being opened, or loosed, and then relates what happens during each particular stage.

In his metaphoric writings, John gives each stage 1000 years of time in which to take place, allowing enough time for successful experience so that we learn from one stage before going on to the next.

Those chosen to oversee the completion of each stage are given the knowledge and power to do so. This knowledge and power is described and written in "*the book*" and sealed away from any who are not worthy to use it properly. To oversee God's plan of salvation for His creations in this particular solar system, one must have the capability to do so, just as God would do it Himself. Christ is the one prepared to do this, which John beautifully expresses figuratively in the verses that follow.

5:2 And I saw ***the four beasts, who are the angels of God in their power***, proclaiming with a loud voice ***as if it were a trumpet***, Who is worthy to open the book, and to loose the seals thereof?

In other words, the angels of God are ready to help out in this part of the Universe by doing what they do—overseeing the balance of this solar system by keeping all things in their proper order according to the eternal laws of nature. However, they work for the Creator, who is the Father. Angels choose not to create children themselves; they work unseen to serve the purposes of the eternal plan of salvation in other ways. One of their jobs is to make sure no unworthy soul discovers the power and knowledge of God; knowing that if an unrighteous soul did, a possibility might arise which could disrupt the delicate balance that exists in nature to perpetuate happiness. The angels are "*trumpeting*" a rally to action, standing ready to do the work of God when the free-willed beings have accepted and sustained *the* one to be their overseer, Lord, and servant.

5:3 And no man in heaven above the earth, neither **below** the earth, was able to open the book, neither to look thereon.

John describes these things as he sees them from a perspective of looking at our entire solar system created for the children of God who are destined to inhabit its planets. What he presents here is that there is no one worthy enough to oversee the work of the Father in any part of our solar system (*above the earth or below the earth*). Imagine any human mortal being trusted with that kind of power and knowledge.

Since "*no man…was able to open the book,*" we know that none of the seals had been opened yet (the "*first seal*" being the start of mortal life upon this earth). Therefore, John is expressing the events of premortality.

5:4 And I wept much, because no man was found worthy to open and to read the book, neither to look thereon.

Weeping is an effect of unhappiness. Here, John relates how happiness cannot be experienced unless someone oversees the *eternal plan of happiness* God is attempting to complete in this part of the Universe. None of us wants an unrighteous leader, who, instead of serving us, serves himself. Unfortunately, however, all mortal leaders are in this unrighteous state. They have either set themselves up, or have been set up by others, above everyone else. They have power because we allow them to have power over us.

Because all of us have the curse of human nature, and *inherently* possess the possibility of failing by using our free will, none who has free will can be completely trusted to lead the rest of us in righteousness. Throughout almost 6000 years, we have experienced what happens when we allow other free-willed beings to lead us.

A righteous leader does not lead. He or she shows by example how truly happy and at peace he or she is, and then teaches us how to arrive at this same level of happiness. There are no leadership positions prescribed or allowed in the blueprints found in the *"Book of Life"*; only positions of servitude held by those whose joy is dependent on helping others experience happiness. For this reason, John never refers to one in authority as a leader, but always as a *"servant."*

Jesus had problems teaching this important lesson to his disciples who were accustomed to the doctrines and traditions of men:

> *And there was also a strife among them, which of them should be accounted the greatest. And he said unto them, The kings of the Gentiles exercise lordship over them; and they that exercise authority upon them are called benefactors. But ye shall not be so: but he that is greatest among you, let him be as the younger; and he that is chief, as he that doth serve. For whether is greater, he that sitteth at meat, or he that serveth? is not he that sitteth at meat? but I am among you as he that serveth.*
> (Luke 22:24–27)

5:5 And one of the elders saith unto me, Weep not: behold, the Lion of the tribe of Juda, the Root of David, hath ***been prepared*** to open the book, and to loose the seven seals thereof.

The original translators of John's *Revelation* did not understand the mysteries of God. Therefore, their translations did not follow the truth as John intended. The proper translation presents the truth that Christ *"the Lion of the tribe of Juda, the Root of David,"* was *"prepared"* and created to perform the work as the overseer of God's work in this solar system. At this point, he had not yet *"prevailed"* over anything, as none of the seals had yet been opened. So that the laws of nature would be followed, and so that the house of God, or mansions of God, (which is this particular solar system and its planets for those assigned to this earth) could be established, Christ was chosen, *"prepared,"* and sent, and became the chief cornerstone upon which the foundation of the kingdom of God would stand.

Wherefore also it is contained in the scripture, **Behold, I lay in Sion a chief corner stone, elect, precious: and he that believeth on him shall not be confounded.** *Unto you therefore which believe he is precious: but unto them which be disobedient, the stone which the builders disallowed, the same is made the head of the corner, and a stone of stumbling, and a rock of offence, even to them which stumble at the word, being disobedient: whereunto also they were appointed.* (I Peter 2:6–8)

Where wast thou when I laid the foundations of the earth? declare, if thou hast understanding. Who hath laid the measures thereof, if thou knowest? or who hath stretched the line upon it? Whereupon are the foundations thereof fastened? or who laid the corner stone thereof; When the morning stars sang together, and all the sons of God shouted for joy? (Job 38:4–7)

Christ does not have free will, as do the rest of us, including the prophets. He alone was created and programmed to carry out specific instructions, ensuring that he would never fail. Just as animals have been programmed (given instincts) to fulfill the measure of their creation, so was the Anointed One prepared in such a way that he could not fail. Creators would not put someone in charge of a perfect work who is not perfect himself. John, who knew him best, shares many of the things Jesus Christ said pertaining to his relationship with God and to the mission he was created to perform:

But Jesus answered them, My Father worketh hitherto, and I work. (John 5:17)

Then Jesus said unto them, Verily, verily, I say unto you, Moses gave you not that bread from heaven; but my Father giveth you the true bread from heaven. For the bread of God is he which cometh down from heaven, and giveth life unto the world. Then said they unto him, Lord, evermore give us this bread. And Jesus said unto them, I am the bread of life: he that cometh to me shall never hunger; and he that believeth on me shall never thirst. (John 6:32–35)

Then said they unto him, Where is thy Father? Jesus answered, Ye neither know me, nor my Father: if ye had known me, ye should have known my Father also. ...Then said Jesus unto them, When ye have lifted up the Son of man, then shall ye know that I am he, and that I do nothing of myself; but as my Father hath taught me, I speak these things. And he that sent me is with me: the Father hath not left me alone; for I do always those things that please him. ...I speak that which I have seen with my Father: and ye do that which ye have seen with your father. (John 8:19, 28–29, 38)

No man taketh it from me, but I lay it down of myself. I have power to lay it down, and I have power to take it again. This commandment have I received of my Father. (John 10:18)

In my Father's house are many mansions: if it were not so, I would have told you. I go to prepare a place for you. And if I go and prepare a place for you, I will come again, and receive you unto myself; that where I am there ye may be also...If ye had known me, ye should have known my Father also: and from henceforth ye know him, and have seen him. Philip saith unto him, Lord, shew us the Father, and it sufficeth us. Jesus saith unto him, Have I been so long time with you, and yet hast thou not known me, Philip? he that hath seen me hath seen the Father; and how sayest thou then, Shew us the Father? Believest thou not that I am in the Father, and the Father in me? the words that I speak unto you I speak not of myself: but the Father that dwelleth in me, he doeth the works. Believe me that I am in the Father, and the Father in me: or else believe me for the very works' sake. Verily, verily, I say unto you, He that believeth on me, the works that I do shall he do also; and greater works than these shall he do; because I go unto my Father. (John 14:2–3, 7–12)

As the Father hath loved me, so have I loved you: continue ye in my love. If ye keep my commandments, ye shall abide in my love; even as I have kept my Father's commandments, and abide in his love. These things have I spoken unto you, that my joy might remain in you, and that your joy might be full. This is my commandment, That ye love one another, as I have loved you. (John 15:9–12)

Christ's purpose is to oversee the progression of the plan of salvation pertaining to this part of the Universe, where the purpose of mortality (human development) will take at least 7000 years. His assignment pertaining to this earth (our *second estate*) is to make sure these 7000 years pass according to the plan and laws which have always been followed by the universal organizers, or Creators, of life.

Overseeing this progression is what is meant by "*opening the seals*"; Christ being the one found worthy to assure that this development takes place, and that we learn how to get along with each other. This all, so we can live together in peace and happiness on the planets (the eternal kingdoms of God) of this solar system that will one day be made inhabitable by the advanced technology and knowledge of Those who are worthy to possess "*the Book of Life.*"

When he tried to declare the truth of who he was and the reality of God, the people either would not listen, or were unable to shift their thinking from what they had been taught by their leaders. When he explained that it was not necessary to subscribe to or comply with the tenets of any organized religion, or to participate in their ordinances and sacrifices, their leaders, who were *not servants* of the people, but instead those who had been placed above the people, were greatly offended, and had him crucified for speaking such blasphemy.

5:6 And I beheld, and, lo, in the midst of the throne and the four beasts, stood the elders *and* a Lamb as *if* it *were to be* slain, having *twelve* horns and *twelve* eyes, which are the *twelve servants* of God sent forth into all the earth.

Here John sees the angels (represented as "*the four beasts*") waiting for the preordained mission of Christ to be given and acknowledged by all those who were created by God and given free will to choose for themselves whom they would follow. Many of the "*elders,*" who were among the free-willed spirits, and who had proven themselves worthy to serve in a position of authority, waited also for Christ to be appointed by God and given power over our planets.

A lamb is the gentlest of all creatures. Though gentle in nature, in this instance, it is given horns to protect itself. Christ's presence, teachings, and countenance are as gentle as a lamb:

> *Come unto me, all ye that labour and are heavy laden, and I will give you rest. Take my yoke upon you, and learn of me; for I am meek and lowly in heart: and ye shall find rest unto your souls. For my yoke is easy, and my burden is light.* (Matthew 11:28–30)

Nevertheless, he stands as a protector ("*twelve horns*") of the people under his authority, and knows and understands ("*twelve eyes*") the people's desires, and what is needed to bring them happiness. The prophets ("*twelve servants*") to whom Christ gives knowledge and authority ("*twelve eyes*"), go throughout the earth and teach the people, and become, in essence, his mouth, his ears, and his eyes.

> *The **eyes of the LORD** preserve knowledge, and he over-throweth the words of the transgressor.* (Proverbs 22:12)

> *For the **eyes of the LORD** run to and fro throughout the whole earth, to shew himself strong in the behalf of them whose heart is perfect toward him. Herein thou hast done*

foolishly: therefore from henceforth thou shalt have wars.
(II Chronicles 16:9)

*For who hath despised the day of small things? for they shall rejoice, and shall see the plummet in the hand of Zerubbabel with those seven; they are the **eyes of the LORD**, which run to and fro through the whole earth.*
(Zechariah 4:10)

5:7 And he **who was prepared** came and took the book out of the right hand of him that sat upon the throne.

Christ was given all the necessary tools to know what the Father knows, do what the Father does, think like the Father thinks, and act in the position of a God in our solar system. His mission as the anointed and chosen One (a Christ) and all that he is required to do, is outlined in the "*Book of Life.*" He will only use this knowledge and power to do as all Gods have done before him—to bring to pass the immortality and eternal life of humankind. Christ cannot fail in his mission any more than the earth can fail to rotate each day, or the sun can fail to give light and warmth; all three having been programmed and instructed by the Creator to fulfill the measure of their particular creation.

5:8 And when he had taken the book, the four beasts **rejoiced**, and **the** four and twenty elders fell down before the Lamb, having every one of them harps, and golden vials full of **the smoke of incense**, which are the prayers of saints.

When Christ was presented by the Creator as the one to serve as the overseer of this solar system, he had to be acknowledged and accepted by all free-willed beings. This was to fulfill the law of free agency that assures each of us a right to choose without being forced into any action or decision we make. We did not have to accept Christ as our Supreme Servant of God, but we knew that the only way our desires of happiness (balance) would ever be realized, was if we abided by the eternal laws that we could see pleased our Creators and other Exalted Beings. Each of these Beings had to pass through a mortality at one time and accept a Christ too, so that the process of human evolution could play out for Them as it must for us. They also arrived at the state of existence in which They found Themselves the most fulfilled.

John figuratively expresses this scene by portraying the Exalted Ones (the "*angels/beasts*") in the attitude of rejoicing for us, because we accepted Christ and the Father's eternal plan of salvation. John shows our acknowledgement and acceptance figuratively, by our spiritual representatives ("*four and twenty elders*") bowing down (always a symbol of honor and acceptance) before Christ. As our representatives and our servants, they know our deepest desires and expectations of happiness.

A *harp* is a musical instrument invented by artistic-minded humans. They use it to express themselves in a way that others may enjoy the expression of delight from the music, without actually being able to play the instrument themselves. These "*four and twenty elders*" express the beauty and truth of God's plan with a rhythm and harmony that is pleasant to our ears and soothing to our souls—they play their "*harps*" for us.

John figuratively expresses each of us as "*golden vials full of the smoke of incense.*" (In Revelation 17:4, the same expression was translated as "*golden cup*," symbolic of each of us.) Each of us is considered "*gold*" to our Creators. Though it always shows forth the beauty of its natural tendencies, gold is hard to find, as it is hidden among the other elements of the earth. But when it is found and refined, it becomes easily malleable and can create spectacular arrays of beautiful works pleasing to the eye of the beholder.

> *And he shall sit as a refiner and purifier of silver: and he shall purify the sons of Levi, and purge them as gold and silver, that they may offer unto the LORD an offering in righteousness.* (Malachi 3:3)

Our prayers are the desires and expectations of our hearts. We pray that we might be given the desires of our hearts. Throughout the *Old Testament*, and more specifically as the Jews set up their ordinances and rituals according to the Law of Moses, *gold* and silver cups and vessels were used to burn incense. As the incense burned, the smoke would rise into the air. These streams of smoke were symbolic of the prayers of the people making their way to God for consideration and fulfillment.

Our expectation ("*golden vial full of the smoke of incense*") of God is that He will fulfill His promise to us of eternal happiness. The only reason why we accept Christ and those chosen to serve us, is because we trust they will bring us the happiness we were promised; and that they will help us fulfill the end for which we were created. As we listen to their song ("*harps*"), we trust that our prayers will be answered.

5:9 And they sung a new song, saying, Thou art worthy to take the book, and to open the seals thereof: for thou wast **prepared as a lamb to be** slain, **to redeem** us to God out of every kindred, and tongue, and people, and nation by thy **sweat and** blood;

The *old song* which we heard our servants singing presented us with the eternal plan of salvation and is as *old* as the Universe itself, which of course, is ageless and eternal. The "*new song*," however, is the creation of a *new* solar system specifically for us; one we can call our own home in which we can partake of the plan of salvation. Christ is he whom we accepted as the one who would work for God ("*by thy sweat and blood*") in this part of the Universe, and who would make sure the eternal plan of happiness was followed.

He oversees this work. If we follow his counsel and abide by the laws we are given (which all culminate into the one *Royal Law*—love others as you want them to love you), we will one day be given eternal life, and live upon one of the planets of this solar system according to our individual desires of happiness.

It is obvious that we do not all have the same desires of happiness. Therefore, it is logical that there are more planets than just one in this solar system on which humankind in our exalted state may be placed, according to the various desires of happiness each of us has.

To the chagrin of those who have misunderstood the mission of Jesus Christ and mistranslated the scriptures to support their misunder-standings, Jesus' blood does not atone for anyone's sins. This is one of the many stumbling blocks of modern Christians, and is the same reason why the Jews would not accept Jesus Christ when he tried to teach them that no sacrificial animal's blood was going to atone for *their* transgressions.

To understand the true nature of the atonement, one must first understand the many metaphors given throughout the scriptures when talking about or describing the atonement of Christ. Metaphors are a figure of speech in which a word or phrase, literally denoting one kind of object or idea, is used in place of another to suggest a likeness or analogy between them. Figurative language is how the prophets of God teach the mysteries of God *without* plainness, so that people who are not worthy and ready might stumble in their understanding of God's mysteries.

Thus again, Isaiah was commanded to:

Go, and tell this people, Hear ye indeed, but understand not; and see ye indeed, but perceive not. Make the heart of this people fat, and make their ears heavy, and shut their eyes; lest they see with their eyes, and hear with their ears, and understand with their heart, and convert, and be healed. (Isaiah 6:9–10)

This is a good example of the metaphors that are used by the prophets of God who wrote scripture. Isaiah was told to preach in such a way so that the people could *not* understand in their wickedness.

How can Isaiah make the heart of the people fat, or their ears heavy? When people feel emotions that overwhelm them, this is what it means to make their "hearts fat." These emotions come from the esoteric and mysterious things that they hear ("make their ears heavy") concerning things that they do not understand—which are generally, all the truths of God.

When a magician performs his magic, and it remains a mystery to the audience how the trick is performed, the audience is overwhelmed (*their hearts are fat*) with awe and intrigue. But when the revelation is given of exactly how the trick is performed, there is no more "awe" and "intrigue," thus eliminating the emotion that comes from seeing a spectacular trick. Many times, the audience would rather *not* know how the trick is performed so that they can enjoy the emotions that are excited by the awe-inspiring performance. The magician makes the people's heart fat by making their ears (in this case their eyes) heavy with tricks they do not understand.

Isaiah was a master at using metaphors to make the *heart of the people fat* and *their ears heavy*. The book of *Revelation* is also filled with a lot of "heavy" reading that produces a lot of "fat."

That "the blood of Christ atones for the sins of the world" is one of these metaphors, and has been one of the greatest stumbling blocks that has kept many from seeing with their eyes and hearing with their ears that they might understand truth. It is a conceptual doctrine that causes great emotion in people (*hearts fat*) upon hearing it time and time again (*ears heavy*) from every Christian pulpit and platform throughout the world.

To simplify the understanding of this metaphor, one needs to look at modern-day quotes that expressly imply the true meaning of the term "blood" as used by the prophets in their metaphorical writings (the scriptures):

How many times has it been said of a person's work that he has done this thing by his "*blood, toil, tears,* and *sweat*"—his blood given to mean the intensity of the work he has done?

Sir Winston Churchill said:

*I would say to the House, as I said to those who have joined the Government: 'I have nothing to **offer** but **blood, toil, tears, and sweat**.'*

Dwight D. Eisenhower offered:

*Humility must always be the portion of any man who receives acclaim earned **in the blood** of his followers and the sacrifices of his friends.*

Theodore Roosevelt concurred:

It is not the critic who counts; not the man who points out how the strong man stumbles, or where the doer of deeds

*could have done them better. The credit belongs to the man
who is actually in the arena, whose face is marred by **dust
and sweat and blood**, who strives valiantly, who errs
and comes short again and again, because there is not
effort without error and shortcoming, but who knows the
great enthusiasm, the great devotion, who spends himself
in a worthy cause; who at the best, knows, in the end, the
triumph of high achievement, and who, at the worst, if he
fails, at least he fails while daring greatly, so that his place
shall never be with those cold and timid souls who knew
neither victory nor defeat.*

The quotes of these worldly leaders easily could have been used as
metaphors that referred to Christ and the *blood, sweat*, and *tears* that he
shed for us. His *blood, sweat*, and *tears* are *the result and expression of
his works*; i.e., the things that he was taught by the Father and sacrificed
his life for in teaching us. Thus, the metaphor of Christ suffering to such a
degree that he bled from every pore begins to make sense. It has the same
metaphoric meaning (as intended by the prophet who used it to describe
what Christ went through) as the use of the words, "*blood, toil, tears*, and
sweat" used above by leaders in modern times.

Isaiah used the metaphor of "blood" when he referred to the
unrighteous works of the Israelites:

*And when ye spread forth your hands, I will hide mine
eyes from you: yea, when ye make many prayers, I will not
hear: your hands are full of **blood**. Wash you, make you
clean; put away the evil of your doings from before mine
eyes; cease to do evil; Learn to do well; seek judgment,
relieve the oppressed, judge the fatherless, plead for the
widow. Come now, and let us reason together, saith the
Lord: though your sins be as scarlet, they shall be as white
as snow; though they be red like crimson, they shall be as
wool. If ye be willing and obedient, ye shall eat the good*

of the land: But if ye refuse and rebel, ye shall be devoured with the sword: for the mouth of the Lord hath spoken it. (Isaiah 1:15–20)

Isaiah was not telling these people to wash their hands of the *literal blood* of others, but to wash their hands of their own unrighteous works. He then describes their sins as being "*scarlet*" (the color of blood); and tells them that if they are willing and obedient in doing good (and the good is described as taking care of the needy, which is the true purpose of religion and the commandments of the Father), then they shall become as "*white as snow*" through these good works.

Isaiah further prophesies concerning the second coming of Christ:

*Who is this that cometh from Edom, with dyed garments from Bozrah? this that is glorious in his apparel, traveling in the greatness of his strength? I that speak in righteousness, mighty to save. Wherefore art thou red in thine apparel, and thy garments like him that treadeth in the winefat? I have trodden the winepress alone; and of the people there was none with me: for I will tread them in mine anger, and trample them in my fury; and their **blood** shall be sprinkled upon my garments, and I will stain all my raiment. For the day of vengeance is in mine heart, and the year of my redeemed is come. And I looked, and there was none to help; and I wondered that there was none to uphold: therefore mine own arm brought salvation unto me; and my fury, it upheld me. And I will tread down the people in mine anger, and make them drunk in my fury, and I will bring down their strength to the earth.* (Isaiah 63:1–6)

Obviously, the prophet is not referring to the *literal blood* of the people, or he would be insinuating that the Lord is a bloodthirsty man who enjoys destroying instead of saving. The unrighteous works of the people cause the righteousness of the Lord's work (his *white garments*) to be stained in red.

In every instance throughout the Holy Scriptures where a prophet of God has written concerning the "***blood of Christ atones for our sins***," or "***through the atonement of Christ***," or "***through his blood are we saved***," it has been given as a metaphoric expression of the life, mission, and the works of Jesus Christ—these metaphors mean nothing more, nothing less. However, this understanding is only given to those with *eyes that see and ears that hear and understand*, and are reserved only for those with the true spirit of prophesy. This being the case, false teachers and the misguided are clearly in abundance in the Christian world.

The purpose of the life, mission, and works of Jesus Christ is to teach us the will and commandments of the Father which we must do in order to change the *natural* man (who is an enemy of the plan of the Father), into a saint who loves his neighbor as himself. Upon learning by experience to comply with this *Royal Law*, we can all abide in the eternal kingdom of the Father and not cause each other problems, thus assuring eternal life and happiness forever. There was *no* other purpose for which Jesus Christ came in the flesh; and it was the *only* mission given him of the Father.

5:10 And ***thou*** hast ***the power to exalt us and make*** us kings and priests unto our God, and we shall ***inherit the kingdom of God upon*** earth.

The scriptures refer to humans as the heirs of the kingdom, simply meaning, that if we learn to love each other as we would want to be loved (accepting and being one—atonement— with Christ), we will be ready to live upon the respective planet best suited for each of us in this solar system forever:

> *The Spirit itself beareth witness with our spirit, that we are the children of God: And if children, then heirs; heirs of God, and joint-heirs with Christ; if so be that we suffer with him, that we may be also glorified together.* (Romans 8:16–17)

There is neither Jew nor Greek, there is neither bond nor free, there is neither male nor female: for ye are all one in Christ Jesus. And if ye be Christ's, then are ye Abraham's seed, and heirs according to the promise. Now I say, That the heir, as long as he is a child, differeth nothing from a servant, though he be lord of all; But is under tutors and governors until the time appointed of the father. Even so we, when we were children, were in bondage under the elements of the world: But when the fulness of the time was come, God sent forth his Son, made of a woman, made under the law, To redeem them that were under the law, that we might receive the adoption of sons. And because ye are sons, God hath sent forth the Spirit of his Son into your hearts, crying, Abba, Father. Wherefore thou art no more a servant, but a son; and if a son, then an heir of God through Christ. (Galatians 3:28–29; 4:1–7)

5:11 And I beheld, and I heard the voice of many ***spirits*** round about the throne ***where*** the beasts ***were*** and ***where*** the elders ***stood***; and the number of them was ten thousand times ten thousand, and thousands of thousands;

All of us who were created and given cognitive capabilities to exercise free will in this solar system, were present in the beginning. This is when the plan was presented to us for our yea or nay in following its course. The creation of our spirits is no more or less different than the production of devices used to store information (memory chips). However, our creation was done on a molecular level by advanced Beings who have the technology and ability to create what we call "our spirits," which give us the ability to think, reason, and act of our own accord.

5:12 Saying with a loud voice, Worthy is the Lamb that ***is to be*** slain to receive ***this*** power ***from God, to give unto us the*** riches ***of life in*** wisdom, and strength. And ***we will for ever give him*** honour and glory ***for this*** blessing.

This represents the then-future human race of this earth and solar system (as this visionary scene is pre-mortal), rejoicing and accepting the plan of happiness outlined and presented by its Creator; and accepting Christ as the God and Supreme Authority of this solar system. In ancient times, an animal was prepared to be slain by performing certain rituals and ordinances to assure that the sacrifice was accepted by God. These preparations were the symbolic equivalent of Christ being prepared by God for us. Of this Law of Sacrifice Jesus said:

> *Think not that I am come to destroy the law, or the prophets: I am not come to destroy, but to fulfil. For verily I say unto you, Till heaven and earth pass, one jot or one tittle shall in no wise pass from the law, till all be fulfilled.* (Matthew 5:17–18)

Christ said the above words just before he began to teach the people the true commandments and expectations of God, which encompassed in one sentence, the command for us to do unto others what we would want them to do unto us. By teaching us these things, he fulfilled the measure of his creation—and was killed because of his works—"*slain*" upon the altar.

5:13 And every creature which is *above the earth*, and on the earth, and under the earth, and such as are in the sea, and all that are *with* them, heard I saying, Honour and glory be unto Him *who hath blessed us, and who in* power sitteth upon the throne, and *hath given* unto *us* the Lamb, *glory to Him* for ever and ever.

All of nature, the birds that fly above the earth, the animals and insects that live upon and underneath the earth, and the creatures of the sea—(all which have been created for the benefit and happiness of humankind in this solar system)—serve the will and follow the plan of the Eternal God. This is our Creator, who has prepared everything—including Christ (the Lamb), to bring us happiness.

5:14 And the four beasts said, Amen. And the four and twenty elders *with the golden vials* fell down and worshipped him that liveth for ever and ever.

The angels are already exalted beings and are equal to God in their eternal place of happiness; therefore, their acknowledgment and agreement concerning the creation of our earth is affirmed by a simple: "*Amen.*" The rest of us ("*golden vials*"—see commentary on verse 8) who are led by the prophets ("*four and twenty elders*"), bowed before the Creator in gratitude for what He had prepared for our happiness.

Chapter

R**EVELATION**

UNFOLDED

6:1 And when the Lamb opened one of the seals, I saw and heard, as it were the noise of thunder, and one of the four beasts saying, Come and see.

    As mentioned in the commentary of Revelation 4:5, the *"noise of thunder"* is the instruction and power coming from God. The angels (*"four beasts"* or cherubim) speak and do the will of the Father in all things. Therefore, their voices are also described as *"the noise of thunder."*

    For the first four thousand years, while abiding by the laws of nature which govern the earth, the angels of God allow the human race to do whatever it is inclined to do according to the desires of the people. It is important to note again that the seals represent *general* time frames of human progression and do *not* specifically occur in 1000 year intervals. However, the advanced Beings who control the course of this solar system know, by their experience, that it usually takes about 1000 years of mortal life for the transitions from one stage to another to take place.

    When discussing the events that occur during the opening of the *sixth seal*, for example, it is better to relate the time frame as *near the end of time* in which we have no contact with extraterrestrial Beings. If we knew of them, we would gain a greater understanding of who, why, and what we are doing on this planet; thus taking away our free will to govern ourselves according to our own knowledge.

During the opening of the first four seals, the angels ("*the beasts*") direct John to: "*Come and see* what the people of the world do to themselves." What John sees is a "*horse*" and a "*rider*," which figuratively represent the actions and interactions of humankind in its environs upon the earth. Each horse is different in color, and each rider appears unique in his actions, figuratively representing what human nature has *led* people to do according to their free will.

Horses are wild until tamed and forced into submission by the commands of the rider. The free will of the horse (the natural world) is directed and controlled by the free will of the rider (humankind).

When the fifth and sixth seals are opened, John receives *no* invitation to "*come and see*," and there are no *horses* with *riders* mentioned. During the time of the fifth and sixth seals, the angels ("*the beasts*"), who during the first *four seals* were speaking to John figuratively in heaven, and not upon the earth, are now very much involved in the state of the world, and at times, control nature and its course beyond the free will of humankind.

Throughout the latter times, the angels must be available to curtail the technological and scientific understanding of the elements of the natural world, such as electricity and electronics, chemical, biological and nuclear energy that humans begin to come up with on their own. If they do not maintain some control, the people would destroy themselves and the earth. The angels ("*beasts*") are not present in heaven in the vision John has of the opening of the *fifth* and *sixth seals*, because they are needed upon the earth doing their work and directing the course of humankind for its sake and protection.

Human nature is what it is, and what it has always been when free-willed beings are allowed to exist. There has never been a time when there have not been humans in some part of the Universe. The makeup of the human body consists of billions of independent molecular entities all seeking a level of balance. This balance causes different atoms to bond together to form molecules, cells, organs, bone, and tissue. The final end of all molecular and quantum creation and interaction is to arrive at the balance they seek naturally; which balance always conforms to eternal natural laws have always existed. Humans recognize and identify this balance as *happiness*.

To arrive at this optimum state, a set plan has been outlined, an evolution followed, and a progression set in motion that has never changed, nor ever will. This is the eternal plan of salvation attributed to God, the Creator of all things, whose mysterious persona is revealed with the knowledge that there have always been Gods to oversee the eternal plan of life.

Because of Their eternal experience, the Gods know exactly how free-willed beings act in certain situations and under certain conditions. In modern science labs, truths are established by experimentation which includes the observation of how certain substances act and react in different environmental situations. Once the conditions have been re-created, and the outcome observed long enough, and the conditions produce the exact same reactions and results, science then resolves itself to calling the conclusive outcome: a law of nature, laws of mathematics, etc. Science arrives at this conclusion because the outcome becomes consistent, and its behavior is replicated under the same set of circumstances.

Gods are simply omnipotent, omniscient, and advanced scientists who have been observing the exact same conditions and outcomes forever; thus making the conclusions of Their observations, the *"Eternal Laws of Heaven and Earth."* Gods do not experiment, having no need to increase Their knowledge. They use these eternal laws to produce the end result of Their desires, which in every case, is to reach the final outcome all laws produce, i.e., *balance*. This balance is always experienced and recognized by the advanced and eternal human being as *happiness*.

Modern science has proven on a molecular level that all atoms continue in a state of imbalance and act "radically" until they find their balance. When placed on an earth and given free will to act according to their natures, humans (radicals) seek happiness (balance) and act according to their free will (radically) until they find it. It takes about 7000 years of mortality to find this balance.

The "human experiment," per se, follows the eternal laws of nature, and will eventually produce the desired result. However, before it does, it must go through the same procedural and customary steps it has always followed to arrive at the same end.

The "*seven seals*" symbolize the seven necessary steps outlined in the "*Book of Life*" (thus the book being sealed with *seven seals*) necessary to graduate through the stages of the "human experiment" on this earth. This in essence becomes a trial or probationary period in which those who do not understand the full effects of happiness, *will*, after experiencing what doesn't make them happy. John's figurative horses and riders demonstrate the different stages of this wonderful scientific exploration of happiness called mortality.

6:2 And I saw, and ***beheld*** a white horse ***upon the earth***: and he that sat on him had a crown given unto him, ***and around and about the crown appeared a rainbow***; and he went forth conquering, and to ***be conquered***.

It is no secret from where John borrowed his presentation of four different colored horses. However, the secret is hidden sufficiently enough so that "eyes that do not see" will remain blind:

> *And I turned, and lifted up mine eyes, and looked, and, behold, there came four chariots out from between two mountains; and the mountains were mountains of brass. In the first chariot were **red horses**; and in the second chariot **black horses**; And in the third chariot **white horses**; and in the fourth chariot **grisled and bay horses**. Then I answered and said unto the angel that talked with me, What are these, my lord? And the angel answered and said unto me, These are the four spirits of the heavens, which go forth from standing before the Lord of all the earth. The black horses which are therein go forth into the north country; and the white go forth after them; and the grisled go forth toward the south country. And the bay went forth, and sought to go that they might walk to and fro through the earth: and he said, Get you hence, walk to and fro through the earth. So they walked to and fro through the earth.* (Zechariah 6:1–7)

When humans were first introduced into the natural world, they were innocent and pure in nature (*"white horse"*), having been taught the laws by which they should abide to be happy. This truth is figuratively expressed in the stories of Adam and Eve, who walked, conversed with, and were taught by God in the metaphoric Garden of Eden. According to the figurative story, once expelled from His presence, they continued for some time to live righteously as they had been commanded.

Throughout scripture, a *"crown"* represents certain rights and powers given to an individual. Innocent and pure humans (the *"rider"* upon the *"white horse"*) were given the right and power to act and be acted upon (*"conquering, and to be conquered"*) according to the natural laws of the earth:

> And God blessed them, and God said unto them, Be fruitful, and multiply, and replenish the earth, **and subdue it** [conquer it]: and have dominion over the fish of the sea, and over the fowl of the air, and over every living thing that moveth upon the earth. (Genesis 1:28)

In John's figurative expressions of the human race, he uses the descriptive symbol of the twelve tribes of Israel and the stones respective to each (See the commentary on Revelation 4:3.) The *"crown"* is made up of twelve stones, which, when light passes through, creates a *"rainbow"* effect (This same reference to the number *"twelve"* being the people of the earth is used in Revelation 10:1 and in 12:1.) Humans, who were given the right and power to act and to be acted upon according to their own free will, received their first instructions (*light*) from the Gods who placed them upon the earth.

6:3 And when he had opened the second seal, I heard the second beast say, Come and see.

6:4 And there went out **upon the earth** another horse that was red; and **a crown of** power was given to him that sat thereon to take peace from the earth, and there was given unto him a great sword, **because it was allowed** that they should kill one another.

During the first years of human existence, there was widespread peace and harmony until the people of the earth began to divide themselves into families, communities, cities, and nations of the world. With these divisions, each group/nation bolstered its manifest right to exist by going forth and overrunning other lands, bringing the weakest among them under the subjection of the strongest.

"Peace was taken from the earth" when humans began to kill each other during their quest to subjugate others under their man-made laws and ordinances. And so it happened, by the course of human nature (*Satan/Lucifer*), that war began to destroy them and take away their peace and happiness. During the opening of the *"second seal,"* the horse and its rider are presented as *"red,"* symbolizing the *blood* spilt from the people of the earth.

6:5 And when he had opened the third seal, I heard the third beast say, Come and see. And I beheld, and lo a black horse **went forth upon the earth**; and he that sat on him had a pair of balances in his hand.

6:6 And I heard a voice **that came from the throne which was** in the midst of the four beasts say, **Let them sell** a measure of wheat for a penny, and three measures of barley for a penny; **for** thou **seest that they** hurt not the oil and the wine.

With the opening of the *"third seal,"* another aspect of human nature began to be manifested as humans placed value upon the material things of the earth and their worth according to their own judgments. This is symbolized by the *"pair of balances"* in the rider's hand.

Humans began to use money—buying and selling those things that were necessary for life (*"wheat and barley,"* figuratively)—and hoard for themselves those things which they valued the most (*"oil and wine"*). They ascribed one person's value within their societies as greater than another simply by the nature of work each performed.

During this time, the great trading nations of the earth became established, and their elite classes and leaders began to accumulate riches and strength at the expense of the poor and oppressed, thus becoming accomplished in the acquisition of personal and national wealth.

Worldly commerce and economy is established by the wealthy and powerful who hold the "*balances*" in their hands, determining the worth of products and of human life. Slavery is forced upon the weakened and power-less masses by the strong, who rely on them to satisfy their *bottomless* appetite for material gain. This is what Daniel refers to as "*the abomination that maketh desolate*," and which John later refers to as "*the beast*." (See Revelation 17:3–5.) It is the methods and means used to acquire the riches that make one person's house full, while leaving the other's house *desolate* and empty:

> *And arms shall stand on his part, and they shall pollute the sanctuary of strength, and shall take away the daily sacrifice, and they shall place* **the abomination that maketh desolate***.* (Daniel 11:31)

Furthermore, this great "*abomination that maketh desolate*" is descriptive of the economic policies of the world, which make humans completely desolate of the Spirit of God. Their hearts become so set upon the things of the world, and its honors and glories, that their spirits are left *desolate* and barren as to things pertaining to righteousness (doing unto others what they would have others do unto them). Because of this abomination, *few* are able to become rich, but by the course of acquiring riches followed by those who do, the majority of humans are left *desolate* of equality and happiness.

This inequality is a great abomination to the happiness promised by a God, who is not a respecter of persons, and has created the earth to be shared equally by all. This is, and shall always be, *the abomination* that brings the most misery and unhappiness to the earth and human existence. The horse and rider that represent this aspect of human nature are presented as black (*darkness*), signifying the great wickedness of humankind because of the commerce and values set up among them.

6:7 And when he had opened the fourth seal, I heard the voice of the fourth beast say, Come and see.

6:8 And I looked, and **beheld** a pale horse **upon the earth**: and his name that sat on him was Death, and Hell followed with him. And power was given unto them over the fourth part of the earth, to kill with sword, and with hunger, and with death, and with the beasts of the earth.

Civilization advanced and progressed upon the earth until it had discovered, as it supposed, the ultimate innovation in politics, business, social welfare, and national warfare. This particular *rider* (human action) was the only one given a name by John as he leads the reader of his *Revelation* metaphorically through the stages of human development. This "*name—Death and Hell*") is a result of the greatest civilization ever established in the pre-modern world, and which (according to the understanding of the world at that time), covered "*the fourth part*" of the known earth.

The world had never known a united group of people like this great empire. Its decadence, leisure, and world dominance permeated every aspect of life. Its soldiers meted out death to any individual, or any nation, that stood against it. Its sporting events included barbaric acts of competition and brutal human sacrifices; delivering thousands to death at the fangs and claws of *the beasts of the earth*. It literally created *hell* on earth for any who stood in its way.

Its political policies created a very wealthy class of relatively few individuals with great power. This consequently created a middle class, which buffered the impact that absolute wealth and power had on the majority of people. This majority included the poor laboring class that always suffered in poverty. Throughout history, the poor majority had been able to rise up and overthrow the few in power when the situation called sufficiently for reformation. But during the historical period this *horse and rider* represent, the middle class stood in their way.

Teetering on the edge of wealth and believing that they could become just as the wealthy, the middle class stood between the rich and poor: coveting one, while fearing a return to the other; validating the actions of the rich, while pacifying the cries of the poor.

The military strength of this type of human civilization overpowers weaker nations and leaves many desolate; causing thousands of deaths from the effects of war, hunger, disease, and poverty left over from its military conquests and occupations. There is *no* part of this type of civilization that promotes equality, or the *Royal Law*—do unto others what you would have them do unto you.

Until modern times, there has not been another nation rise to such world prominence (according to the principles and desires founded in its *name*—works), until this type of society's modern fraternal twin "*came up out of the earth.*" (See Revelation 13:11.)

People use their free will to become what they desire, and by these actions make a *name* for themselves. Given time in following their innate natures, the human race seeks self-validation through unification. The name—given anciently: the *Great Roman Empire*, and in modern times: the *United States of America*—represents the works of the "*pale horse*" and its "*rider.*"

These *man-made names* can well be described as *Death* (both physical and spiritual), with its effects creating a literal *Hell* on earth. When desires are set upon materialism and the honors of pride, the world loses its spiritual roots—*the blood* that gives life to its body. For our own sake, we are allowed ("*power was given unto them*") to form these societies. In these societies, the sacrifice of *the blood* of Jesus Christ (which is his teaching us how to love one another) is nowhere to be found. Thus, John presents it as a "*pale horse*"—strong in might and purpose and able to bear its rider, but barren of the blood (of Christ) that brings color to its skin.

6:9 And when he had opened the fifth seal, I saw the souls of them **upon the earth who** were slain **upon the altar** for the word of God, and for the testimony which they held:

An altar is something built by mortal hands for the purpose of making an offering upon it, usually dedicated to a Deity. When one obeys the commands of God, one is effectually dedicating his or her works "*upon the altar*" before God, figuratively exclaiming, "Here, O my God, are my works that I have fulfilled and dedicated to Thee!" Therefore, being "*slain upon the altar*" means that one has sacrificed one's life "*for the word of God*" by keeping His commandments.

In the same spirit Jesus said:

He that findeth his life shall lose it: and he that loseth his life for my sake shall find it. (Matthew 10:39)

John is referring to all those upon the earth who have "*lost their lives*" in dedication to obeying the commands of God. It is truly a great sacrifice to live the gospel of Jesus Christ in a world that rejects it. The gentle and reassuring spirit of Psalms explains:

*I will say unto God my rock, Why hast thou forgotten me? why go I mourning because of the oppression of the enemy? As with a sword in my bones [**i.e., being slain**], mine enemies reproach me; while they say daily unto me, Where is thy God? Why art thou cast down, O my soul? And why art thou disquieted within me? hope thou in God: for I shall yet praise him, who is the health of my countenance, and my God. Judge me, O God, and plead my cause against an ungodly nation: O deliver me from the deceitful and unjust man. For thou art the God of my strength: why dost thou cast me off? why go I mourning because of the oppression of the enemy? O send out thy light and thy truth: let them lead me; let them bring me unto thy holy hill, and to thy tabernacles. Then will I go **unto the altar of God**, unto God my exceeding joy: yea, upon the harp will I praise thee, O God my God. Why art thou cast down, O my soul? and why art thou disquieted within me? hope in God: for I shall yet praise him, who is the health of my countenance, and my God.* (Psalms 42:9–11; 43:1–5)

Isaiah reiterates the purpose and symbolism of altars:

At that day shall a man look to his Maker, and his eyes shall have respect to the Holy One of Israel. And he shall *not look to **the altars, the work of his hands**, neither shall respect that which his fingers have made, either the groves, or the images.* (Isaiah 17:7–8)

Moses was commanded to construct an altar to specified dimensions. This is symbolic of the commandments of God being specific in their purpose, which Jesus gives as the greatest law and commandment of all the prophets—do unto others what you would have them do unto you.

Ezekiel borrows the symbolism to reiterate that the law of God is exact, and thus should our works be exact as we offer them upon an altar *before the Lord*:

The altar of wood was three cubits high, and the length thereof two cubits; and the corners thereof, and the length thereof, and the walls thereof, were of wood: and he said unto me, This is the table that is before the LORD. (Ezekiel 41:22)

Ezekiel continued in his teachings by figuratively expressing that we should purge ourselves of sin (which is anything we do to another that we wouldn't want done to us) and purify our lives throughout mortality (*seven days*), which is our symbolic offering upon the altar to God:

Seven days shall they purge the altar and purify it; and they shall consecrate themselves. (Ezekiel 43:26)

6:10 And ***the four and twenty elders*** cried with a loud voice, saying, How long, O Lord, holy and true, dost thou not judge them that dwell on the earth and avenge ***their*** blood, ***which has been spilt upon the altar***?

In other words, the prophets who have been sent to teach the people what they should do to serve God properly, are asking how long the Lord will allow the earth to remain in a state where living the word of God is such a tremendous sacrifice.

6:11 And white robes were given unto every one of them *who were sacrificed upon the altar*; and it was said unto them, that they should rest yet for a little season until their fellowservants and their brethren *who would also* be killed *upon the altar* as they were should fulfill *their works*.

Uninspired teachers would interpret the above passage as referring to those called of God, or in this case, who have *called themselves* to be missionaries, pastors, bishops, or administrators of God's word. They assume in a pious attitude of sacrifice and self-glorification, that these leaders must also be killed before the Lord comes again. Inasmuch as the true nature of "*slain* or *sacrificed upon the altar*" has now been properly revealed, John's later description of those given "*white robes*" puts the truth in proper perspective:

> *After this I beheld, and, lo, this great multitude, which no man could number, of all nations, and kindreds, and people, and tongues, stood before the throne, and before the Lamb,* **clothed with white robes**, *and palms in their hands; And one of the elders spake unto me saying, Who are these who are arrayed in* **white robes**? *and from whence did they come? And I said unto him, Sir, thou knowest. And he said to me, These are they who came out of great tribulation, and have washed their own robes, and made them white in the blood of the Lamb.* (Revelation 7:9, 13–14)

Clothing has always symbolized one's actions, deeds, and thoughts. Notice John was *not* told that Christ washed the blood out of the robes, but "*These...have washed their own robes and made them white in the blood of the Lamb.*" The works of Christ cannot save us unless we learn to do the same works he did, apply the principles he taught, and follow the example he set, and for which he lost his life, and lose ours in the same way.

Here John is telling us that those who follow the teachings and precepts of Christ will *rest* from all worldly trials and adversity that cause tribulation in one's life, supporting what he heard Jesus teach the people:

Come unto me, all ye that labour and are heavy laden, and I will give you rest. Take my yoke upon you, and learn of me; for I am meek and lowly in heart: and ye shall find rest unto your souls. For my yoke is easy, and my burden is light. (Matthew 11:28–30)

All must be allowed to live in mortality and prove themselves worthy to live in eternal worlds where they will not cause problems. Until one learns to always do unto another that which they would want done unto them, they will not be allowed to possess an exalted body that never dies and live on a planet which supports this type of body.

Those who learn and apply the gospel of Jesus Christ (given a *white robe*) will rest from tribulations and hell that others are experiencing in life. Nevertheless, mortality must be allowed to continue "*yet for a little season*" until *all* have been given ample opportunity to "*fulfill their works.*"

6:12 And I beheld when he had opened the sixth seal, and, lo, there was a great earthquake *and the earth reeled to and fro like a drunkard*; and the sun became black, *clothed in a* sackcloth *made* of hair, *because* the moon *was turned into* blood;

One of the most significant rules in understanding the writings of prophets is this: **When a prophet is expressing himself figuratively, *everything* he writes is given as a figurative expression. The reader cannot pick or choose which parts of the prophecy are literal, and which parts are symbolic.**

Common sense tells us that the sun cannot become "*black as sackcloth of hair*" and the moon cannot turn into "*blood.*" Therefore, those who are waiting for the literal "*great earthquake*" of this otherwise figurative portrayal, are going to be waiting a long, long time. False teachers and leaders have misinterpreted what is going to happen in fulfillment of this verse, when in fact, the "*great earthquake*" is occurring even as they read these words. They simply do not know or understand the metaphoric way in which it is presented to them in John's writings.

To understand these things, one must take into consideration the source from which John took his symbolism. Throughout the *Old Testament*, clues are given to help reveal the proper origin and understanding of John's mysterious metaphors:

> *For the stars of heaven and the constellations thereof shall not give their light: the sun shall be darkened in his going forth, and the moon shall not cause her light to shine. And I will punish the world for their evil, and the wicked for their iniquity; and I will cause the arrogancy of the proud to cease, and will lay low the haughtiness of the terrible. I will make a man more precious than fine gold; even a man than the golden wedge of Ophir. Therefore I will shake the heavens, and the earth shall remove out of her place, in the wrath of the LORD of hosts, and in the day of his fierce anger.* (Isaiah 13:10–13)

Isaiah is saying that people are not allowing the light from within to shine forth in good works (*stars...shall not give their light*). Therefore, they receive none of the light from God (*sun shall be darkened*). The prophets are those who teach and preach to the people who live in darkness, reflecting the light they receive from God to the people who are in need of harsh reminding to return to the commandments of God.

The moon has no light of its own, but reflects the light of the sun that shown yesterday and the sun that will shine tomorrow, giving this light to a darkened world. The prophets of God are metaphorically presented as *the moon*. When the people choose wickedness over righteousness, God withdraws His prophets from among the people (*the moon shall not cause her light to shine*). When the people reject, cast out, and kill the prophets, "*the moon becomes as blood.*"

The "*earthquakes*" represent the great wickedness of the human race upon the earth, signifying that the world as a whole is not doing what it was naturally commanded to do—stand with balance and firmness in keeping the commandments of God.

Isaiah's writings give further explanation:

*And it shall come to pass, that he who fleeth from the noise of the fear shall fall into the pit; and he that cometh up out of the midst of the pit shall be taken in the snare: for the windows from on high are open, and the foundations of the earth do shake. The earth is utterly broken down, the earth is clean dissolved, the earth is moved exceedingly. The earth **shall reel to and fro like a drunkard, and shall be removed like a cottage; and the transgression thereof shall be heavy upon it; and it shall fall, and not rise again.** And it shall come to pass in that day, that the LORD shall punish the host of the high ones that are on high, and the kings of the earth upon the earth. And they shall be gathered together, as prisoners are gathered in the pit, and shall be shut up in the prison, and after many days shall they be visited. Then the moon shall be confounded, and the sun ashamed, when the Lord of hosts shall reign in mount Zion, and in Jerusalem, and before his ancients gloriously.* (Isaiah 24:18–23)

Those in mourning wear sackcloth. John suggests that God is in mourning when people live wickedly. God figuratively blackens the sky with "*a sackcloth made of hair,*" thereby keeping the light of the sun from shining through to give warmth to the earth. In other words, because of the wickedness of the people, God does not send revelation or inspiration.

The first part of the human body that receives warmth from the sun, when a person is standing erect, is the head, which is covered with hair. Here John presents the hair as black, signifying that the head is receiving no sunlight, which would have lightened the hair with more exposure. Similarly, we have the vision of Christ in which he is seen as one with hair as *white as snow.*

Other *Old Testament* writings reiterate John's theme:

How then can man be justified with God? or how can he be clean that is born of a woman? **Behold even to the moon, and it shineth not***; yea, the stars are not pure in his sight.* (Job 25:4–5)

Wherefore, when I came, was there no man? when I called, was there none to answer? Is my hand shortened at all, that it cannot redeem? or have I no power to deliver? behold, at my rebuke I dry up the sea, I make the rivers a wilderness: their fish stinketh, because there is no water, and dieth for thirst. **I clothe the heavens with blackness, and I make sackcloth their covering***.* (Isaiah 50:2–3)

And when I shall put thee out, I will cover the heaven, and make the stars thereof dark; I will **cover the sun with a cloud, and the moon shall not give her light***. All the bright lights of heaven will I make dark over thee, and set darkness upon thy land, saith the Lord GOD.* (Ezekiel 32:7–8)

The earth shall quake before them; the heavens shall tremble: **the sun and the moon shall be dark***, and the stars shall withdraw their shining:* (Joel 2:10)

6:13 And the stars of heaven fell unto the earth **because of the great earthquake**, even as a fig tree casteth her untimely figs, when she is shaken of a mighty wind.

We now know that the "*great earthquake*" is figurative of the wickedness of humankind. We know also that John uses "*stars*" to represent the inhabitants of the earth. Therefore, why do the "*stars of heaven fall to the earth*" as the "*untimely fig*"? Because the unbalanced people are shaken by the "*earthquake*" (wickedness) which causes them to fall into transgression.

John borrowed Isaiah's figurative expressions:

And all the host of heaven shall be dissolved, and the heavens shall be rolled together as a scroll: and all their host shall fall down, as the leaf falleth off from the vine, and as a falling fig from the fig tree. (Isaiah 34:4)

Throughout scripture, prophets have referred to people and their works as fig or olive trees. The tree itself represents humankind; its *branches*, the differing peoples of the earth. The *fruit* of the tree represents the actions, deeds, and thoughts of the people. The *word of God* is the sunshine and the rain that comes from heaven which nourishes the tree. The *roots* take in the nutrition from the earth, representing the work of the prophets upon the earth, which include the greatest prophet of all, Jesus Christ, who said:

A certain man had a fig tree planted in his vineyard; and he came and sought fruit thereon, and found none. Then said he unto the dresser of his vineyard, Behold, these three years I come seeking fruit on this fig tree, and find none: cut it down; why cumbereth it the ground? And he answering said unto him, Lord, let it alone this year also, till I shall dig about it, and dung it: And if it bear fruit, well: and if not, then after that thou shalt cut it down. (Luke 13:6–9)

When a fig tree receives proper nutrition and pruning, it thrives, and its branches and fruit stand strong and firm against all winds. When it has *not* been nourished properly, its branches and fruit are weak, and unable to hang on, and are cast to the earth before they are fully ripened. This means that before humankind learns the proper way to live with each other (being *ripened*), in preparation to receive eternal bodies and live on eternal planets, they will most certainly fall because of the *winds* (which will later be revealed as the false doctrines and precepts of the world) that blow upon the earth.

All true prophets knew this secret:

*I found Israel like grapes in the wilderness; I saw your fathers as the firstripe in the **fig tree** at her first time: but they went to Baal-peor, and separated themselves unto that shame; and their abominations were according as they loved.* (Hosea 9:10)

*All thy strong holds shall be like **fig trees** with the firstripe figs: if they be shaken, they shall even fall into the mouth of the eater.* (Nahum 3:12)

*The vine is dried up, and the **fig tree** languisheth; the pomegranate tree, the palm tree also, and the apple tree, even all the trees of the field, are withered: because joy is withered away from the sons of men.* (Joel 1:12)

*But they shall sit every man under his vine and under his **fig tree**; and none shall make them afraid: for the mouth of the LORD of hosts hath spoken it.* (Micah 4:4)

*Although the **fig tree** shall not blossom, neither shall fruit be in the vines; the labour of the olive shall fail, and the fields shall yield no meat; the flock shall be cut off from the fold, and there shall be no herd in the stalls:* (Habakkuk 3:17)

6:14 *And it came to pass that* the heavens ***opened*** as a scroll ***is opened*** when it is rolled together; and every mountain and island ***was*** moved out of ***its*** place ***because of that which was written therein***.

Figuratively, every action, every deed, and every thought are *symbolically* written in a book ("*scroll*") kept in heaven. In other words, the works of humankind are recorded through the technological advancement of Beings which reach far beyond our current capabilities of making a video documentary of someone's life. The mystery is, that the recording devices are incorporated into *our own spiritual makeup*, which elements have the ability to record everything we think and do.

Not permitted to explain this mystery in its fullness in their day, the ancient prophets made reference to what John has hinted:

> **Take thee a roll of a book, and write therein all the words that I have spoken unto thee against Israel, and against Judah, and against all the nations,** *from the day I spake unto thee, from the days of Josiah, even unto this day. It may be that the house of Judah will hear all the evil which I purpose to do unto them; that they may return every man from his evil way; that I may forgive their iniquity and their sin.* (Jeremiah 36:2–3)

> *And when I looked, behold, an hand was sent unto me; and, lo,* ***a roll of a book was therein****; And he spread it before me; and it was written within and without: and there was written therein lamentations, and mourning, and woe.* (Ezekiel 2:9–10)

Of all the attributes of humankind that draw us away from doing unto others what we would expect to have done unto us, none is as devastating and corruptive to peace and happiness as **pride**. Pride causes many to put themselves above others or to separate themselves, believing they are superior. The prophets figuratively characterized those who put themselves above others as "*mountains.*" Those who isolate themselves from the rest of the world, believing they are more righteous than others, are expressed as "*islands.*"

When the truth is finally revealed, when "*the scroll* (containing the memories of what they have done) *is opened up,*" the *exalted* and *isolated* will learn of their great wickedness, and will be brought down. This is because they will realize that they are no different, no better, or no more right, than any other person upon the earth.

John's continued prophecy, "*And every island fled away, and the mountains were not found*" (see Revelation 16:20), reinforces what his ancient mentors proclaimed:

*Keep silence before me, **O islands**; and let the people renew their strength: let them come near; then let them speak: let us come near together to judgment.* (Isaiah 41:1)

*According to their deeds, accordingly he will repay, fury to his adversaries, recompense to his enemies; **to the islands** he will repay recompense.* (Isaiah 59:18)

*And the word of the Lord came unto me, saying, Son of man, set thy face toward **the mountains of Israel**, and prophesy against them, And say, Ye mountains of Israel, hear the word of the Lord GOD; Thus saith the Lord GOD to the mountains, and to the hills, to the rivers, and to the valleys; Behold, I, even I, will bring a sword upon you, and **I will destroy your high places**.* (Ezekiel 6:1–3)

6:15 And the kings of the earth, and the great men, and the rich men, and the chief captains, and the mighty men, **yea even** every **man who bringeth bondage upon another who is not** free, hid themselves in the dens and in the rocks of the mountains;

6:16 And **these** said to the mountains and rocks, Fall on us, and hide us from the face of him that sitteth on the throne, and from the wrath of the Lamb, w**hose countenance we cannot bear**.

6:17 For the great day of his wrath is come; and who **among us** shall be able to stand?

John has shown us the stages and effects of human development when we are left to our own devices with complete control over our environment and actions. Our Father and Creator does not get angry as we prefer to think, or have been taught by false leaders and teachers. John has led us to quite a different understanding of what is meant when we speak of the "*the wrath of God*," which refers to His *non-intervention* in the affairs of humankind.

When we are undeserving, we are left to suffer the full effects of our self-imposed situations. He has taught us that when we do not live by the *Royal Law*, we do not receive the intervention or divine instruction from above through righteous and true prophets—the sun is darkened (no light or revelation is given) because of our wickedness. As a result of rejecting the prophets and killing them, the moon is turned into blood. This is the "*wrath of God*." It is happening now, and will continue until Christ himself comes to the earth to teach what he has always taught: Do unto others what you would have them do unto you.

Our pride, our families, our nations, our desire for material gain and honor, and all of our works due to our human natures, lead us away from this *Royal Law* upon which all other laws and all the prophets are predicated:

> *Therefore all things whatsoever ye would that men should do to you, do ye even so to them: for this is the law and the prophets.* (Matthew 7:12)

John is warning us, as did those before him:

> *But they that escape of them shall escape, and shall be on the mountains like doves of the valleys, all of them mourning, every one for his iniquity. All hands shall be feeble, and all knees shall be weak as water. They shall also gird themselves with sackcloth, and horror shall cover them; and shame shall be upon all faces, and baldness upon all their heads. They shall cast their silver in the streets, and their gold shall be removed: their silver and their gold shall not be able to deliver them in the day of the wrath of the LORD: they shall not satisfy their souls, neither fill their bowels: because it is the stumblingblock of their iniquity.* (Ezekiel 7:16–19)

*But who may abide the day of his coming? And who shall stand **before him with clean hands** when he appeareth? For he is like a refiner's fire, **which is used to remove the impurities of element**, and like fullers' soap, **which is used to clean the works of his** hands. And he shall sit as a refiner and purifier of silver **and of gold. And with a fervent heat shall the elements of this earth be refined, even the gold and silver filled with dross**. And he shall purify the sons of Levi, **who have corrupted the people and led them astray, filling them with dross. And he shall** purge them as gold and silver, that they may offer unto the Lord an offering in righteousness. **For behold, all their offerings they have polluted, and there are none who are pure. But they shall know good at that day, that they might cast out the evil from among them.*** (Malachi 3:2–3)

Chapter

R EVELATION
UNFOLDED

7:1 And after these things I saw four angels ***ascending from the east*** standing on the four corners of the earth, holding the four winds of the earth, that the wind should not blow on the earth, nor on the sea, nor on any tree.

John is telling us here that the truth (*"the four winds"*) is being withheld from the people of the earth. The *"trees"* represent humankind (see Revelation 6:13 commentary). John also writes that the wind does not blow *"on the sea."* The *"sea"* translates throughout *Revelation* as *"waters"*: *And he saith unto me, The waters which thou sawest...are peoples, and multitudes, and nations, and tongues."* (See Revelation 17:15.) This verse is given to refer to a condition on earth when the spirit of God (truth/*"wind"*) is withheld.

The *"wind"* represents an understanding of truth, regardless of whether that understanding comes from an outside source, such as when a prophet speaks, or from within, as when one has an epiphany of realization and understanding. In some verses of scripture, *"wind"* has represented the workings of the Spirit, which Jesus also named or referred to as the

Holy Ghost. The term *"Holy Ghost"* was not used by *Old Testament* prophets, and when the term *"Holy Spirit"* is used, it is *only* in reference to the Lord's spirit, which can be replaced in all instances with "truth":

> *Behold, I was shapen in iniquity, and in sin did my mother conceive me. Behold, thou desirest truth in the inward parts: and in the hidden part thou shalt make me to know wisdom. Purge me with hyssop, and I shall be clean: wash me, and I shall be whiter than snow. Make me to hear joy and gladness; that the bones which thou hast broken may rejoice. Hide thy face from my sins, and blot out all mine iniquities. Create in me a clean heart, O God; and renew a right spirit within me. Cast me not away from thy presence; and take not **thy holy spirit** from me. Restore unto me the joy of thy salvation; and uphold me with thy **free spirit**.* (Psalms 51:5–12)

> *In all their affliction he was afflicted, and the angel of his presence saved them: in his love and in his pity he redeemed them; and he bare them, and carried them all the days of old. But they rebelled, and vexed his **holy Spirit**: therefore he was turned to be their enemy, and he fought against them. Then he remembered the days of old, Moses, and his people, saying, Where is he that brought them up out of the sea with the shepherd of his flock? where is he that put his **holy Spirit** within him? That led them by the right hand of Moses with his glorious arm, dividing the water before them, to make himself an everlasting name?* (Isaiah 63:9–12)

According to *Old Testament* stories, Moses spoke to the Lord face to face, and received from his mouth the commandments by which the people should live. These words from the mount are what Isaiah was speaking of when he wrote, "put his holy Spirit within him." This signifies *"the wind"* that passes from the Lord's mouth, and which John gives as the *"four winds"* of truth that *"the angels"* have power to give to the world:

*He sendeth out his word, and melteth them: he **causeth his wind to blow**, and the waters flow. He **sheweth his word** unto Jacob, his statutes and his judgments unto Israel.* (Psalms 147:18–19)

When Christ was living among mortals, "*the wind*" was given directly from his own mouth. But when he died and was no longer among them, "*the wind*" came from a direction no one could understand:

*And when the day of Pentecost was fully come, they were all with one accord in one place. And suddenly there came a sound from heaven as of a rushing **mighty wind**, and it filled all the house where they were sitting. And there appeared unto them cloven tongues like as of fire, and it sat upon each of them. And they were all filled with the Holy Ghost, and began to speak with other tongues, as **the Spirit** gave them utterance.* (Acts 2:1–4)

A contemporary musical group sang a popular song, seemingly understanding that truth (*whispering wind*) would be the steps, or stairway, to heaven:

*Your head is humming and it won't go because you don't know...the pipers calling you to join him. Dear lady can't you hear the **wind blow** and did you know: Your stairway lies on the whispering wind.* (Stairway To Heaven, Led Zeppelin)

7:2 And I saw another angel ascending from the east, having the seal of the living God **to give to those who overcome the world**; And he cried with a loud voice to the **other** four angels, to whom it was given to hurt the earth and the sea **by the winds which they held**,

Throughout the *Old Testament*, the "*east wind*" has always represented the destruction which comes upon the wicked:

And the seven thin and ill favoured kine that came up after them are seven years; and the seven empty ears blasted with the east wind shall be seven years of famine. (Genesis 41:27)

And Moses stretched forth his rod over the land of Egypt, and the Lord brought an east wind upon the land all that day, and all that night; and when it was morning, the east wind brought the locusts. (Exodus 10:13)

Just as in nature (in which hurricane winds generally come from the east bringing their gusty turmoil), the metaphoric representation of the "*east wind*" has reference, not to the physical destruction of the people, but rather to the spiritual carnage that occurs when true prophets confound the false doctrines and precepts of men. Prophets lay bare before the eyes of the people the vanity of hope in their false beliefs. John reiterates the figurative destructive power of the angels by writing, "*to the other four angels, to whom it was given to **hurt** the earth and the sea by the winds which they held.*"

When we speak, we create *wind* and "blow" out, as it were, our words. *Wind* is symbolic of the words we speak, wherein a person attempts to communicate thoughts to those whom he or she wishes to *feel* the "*wind*" of the mind. The "*wind*" these angels are holding is the true knowledge and understanding of God that will destroy the false doctrine and precepts of men.

Falsehoods have also been referred to throughout scripture as *wind* coming forth to destroy righteousness:

*And every one that heareth these sayings of mine, and doeth them not, shall be likened unto a foolish man, which built his house upon the sand: And the rain descended, and the floods came, and the **winds blew**, and beat upon that house; and it fell: and great was the fall of it.* (Matthew 7:26–27)

*That we henceforth be no more children, tossed to and fro, and carried about with every **wind of doctrine**, by the sleight of men, and cunning craftiness, whereby they lie in wait to deceive;* (Ephesians 4:14)

*Should a wise man utter vain knowledge, and fill his belly with the **east wind**? Should he reason with unprofitable talk? Or with speeches wherewith he can do no good?* (Job 15:2–3)

***Ephraim compasseth me about with lies**, and the house of Israel with deceit: but Judah yet ruleth with God, and is faithful with the saints. **Ephraim feedeth on wind, and followeth after the east wind**: he daily increaseth lies and desolation; and they do make a covenant with the Assyrians, and oil is carried into Egypt.* (Hosea 11:12; 12:1)

Jesus asked the Jews if they considered John the Baptist one who was easily swayed by the doctrines of men, then proclaimed forcefully that he certainly was *not*:

*And as they departed, Jesus began to say unto the multitudes concerning John, What went ye out into the wilderness to see? **A reed shaken with the wind**? But what went ye out for to see? A man clothed in soft raiment? behold, they that wear soft clothing are in kings' houses. But what went ye out for to see? A prophet? yea, I say unto you, and more than a prophet.* (Matthew 11:7–9)

Also, the Lord is represented as coming from the "*east*": "*For as the lightning cometh **out of the east**, and shineth even unto the west; so shall also the coming of the Son of man be.*" (Matthew 24:27)

And the "*wind*" from his mouth (the truth) will destroy all wickedness: "*Thou breakest the ships of Tarshish with an **east wind**.*" (Psalms

48:7) ; "*I will scatter them as with an **east wind** before the enemy: I will shew them the back, and not the face, in the day of their calamity.*" (Jeremiah 18:17)

Ezekiel explains that though the people are taught the truth, they (the *trees* and the *sea*) are shriveling spiritually for lack of proper nutrition (knowledge), because the influence of false doctrines which permeates most of their thoughts will cause them to *wither* away from the truth: (See verse 3 below.)

> *It was planted in a good soil by great waters, that it might bring forth branches, and that it might bear fruit, that it might be a goodly vine. Say thou, Thus saith the Lord GOD; Shall it prosper? shall he not pull up the roots thereof, and cut off the fruit thereof, that it wither? it shall wither in all the leaves of her spring, even without great power or many people to pluck it up by the roots thereof. Yea, behold, being planted, shall it prosper?* ***shall it not utterly wither, when the east wind toucheth it?*** *it shall wither in the furrows where it grew.* (Ezekiel 17:8–10)

7:3 Saying, Hurt not the earth, neither the sea, nor the trees, till we have sealed the servants of our God in their foreheads.

Before the "*great earthquake*" and the "*east winds*" of truth blow upon the people of the earth to destroy (*hurt*) their pride, arrogance, and vanity, those who serve God in righteousness by keeping His command-ments are able to come to a knowledge and understanding of the truth. By understanding truth and the mysteries of God, they will not be *hurt* like the rest of the inhabitants (who, though they think they have the truth, are far from it).

Figuratively speaking, we think and understand in our "*foreheads*." When people receive the "*seal of God in their foreheads*," they are thinking, perceiving, and understanding the truths ("*four winds*") of God properly, thus reacting to their cognitive processes with righteous works.

Jesus tells his disciples the same thing in a slightly different way:

*And he shall send his angels with a great sound of a trumpet,
and they **shall gather together his elect from the four
winds**, from one end of heaven to the other.* (Matthew 24:31)

Isaiah also states it this way:

*Or let him take hold of my strength, that he may make
peace with me; and he shall make peace with me. He shall
cause them that come of Jacob to take root: Israel shall
blossom and bud, and fill the face of the world with fruit.
Hath he smitten him, as he smote those that smote him?
or is he slain according to the slaughter of them that are
slain by him? In measure, when it shooteth forth, thou
wilt debate with it: **he stayeth his rough wind in the
day of the east wind**.* (Isaiah 27:5–8)

There are some people who sincerely seek for truth and understanding, who nevertheless, follow the false doctrine and precepts given by
organized religions and those who have put themselves up as their spiritual
guides. If the Lord came to the earth today, many sincere seekers of truth
would be devastated and *hurt*, realizing they were both the deceived and the
deceivers as members of an organized church or as a self-proclaimed guru
who provided counsel and teachings for those with itching ears:

*For the time will come when they will not endure sound
doctrine; but after their own lusts shall they heap to themselves teachers, having itching ears; And they shall turn
away their ears from the truth, and shall be turned unto
fables.* (II Timothy 4:3–4)

These people trust their religious and spiritual leaders, and believe
them to be inspired and ordained by God. But to their dismay and chagrin,
they will find out they have been living and following a lie, thus *"hurt"* by

the "*wind*" of truth held in the mouths of the true servants (*angels*) of God.

In fairness and mercy, the truth will not be revealed as the "*east wind*" to the world until those who "elect" to do unto others as they would have done unto them (those who receive the "*seal of God in their foreheads*") have it revealed to them first. When the truth is finally revealed to the rest of the inhabitants of the earth, those choosing to follow the words of Christ will not be tormented or suffer as those electing not to.

7:4 And I heard the number of them which were sealed *in their foreheads with the name of the Father*; and *they were among all the nations of the earth, and* there were sealed an hundred and forty and four thousand of all the *scattered* tribes of the children of Israel.

A correct translation of John's words gives the reader the impression that those who think ("*foreheads*") as God would have them think, will do the same works ("*name of the Father*") as He would. This is confirmed in Revelation 14:1.

> *And I looked, and, lo, a Lamb stood on the mount Sion, and with him an hundred forty and four thousand, having his Father's name written in their foreheads.* (Revelation 14:1)

As mentioned in the commentary of Revelation 4:4, in which a description is given of those who have the "*seal of God in their foreheads*," those who accept the message of the prophets ("*the twenty and four elders*") and abide by the *Royal Law*, will think the same thoughts ("*forehead*") as Christ, and will follow his example.

Because God is no respecter of persons and has not chosen any one group of people over another, John presents those who accept the gospel of Christ by receiving the "*seal of the Father in their foreheads*" as an *equal number* of each particular tribe of Israel. Many of the Jews in John's time used their family's ancestry as a way of putting themselves above others.

For example, there were groups from the tribe of Judah and Levi who thought themselves more worthy and chosen than those whose ancestry linked them to the tribe of Rueben, or the tribe of Simeon. Even in modern times, religious groups set themselves above others by claiming lines of ancestry either directly or through adoption to one group of the sons of Israel or another. This mentality, and the obsession of one's genealogy, are contrary to the gospel of Jesus Christ, in which one's lineage means absolutely nothing. John exemplifies this in his narration by presenting all tribes as equal in relation to the righteous people of the world. (See commentary on Revelation 4:4.)

7:5 Of the tribe of Juda were sealed twelve thousand. Of the tribe of Reuben were sealed twelve thousand. Of the tribe of Gad were sealed twelve thousand.

7:6 Of the tribe of Aser were sealed twelve thousand. Of the tribe of Nephthalim were sealed twelve thousand. Of the tribe of Manasses were sealed twelve thousand.

7:7 Of the tribe of Simeon were sealed twelve thousand. Of the tribe of Levi were sealed twelve thousand. Of the tribe of Issachar were sealed twelve thousand.

7:8 Of the tribe of Zabulon were sealed twelve thousand. Of the tribe of Joseph were sealed twelve thousand. Of the tribe of Benjamin were sealed twelve thousand.

As explained above, the preceding verses relate that there are an *equal number* of people from each tribe of Israel. This number is *figurative only*, representing the attitude of absolute equality God has towards all mankind; and showing that He is *not* a respecter of persons in bringing the truth to *all* peoples of the earth who "elect" to follow His guidance and commandments. This truth is further verified in verse 9.

7:9 After this I beheld, and, lo, **this** great multitude, which no man could number, of all nations, and kindreds, and people, and tongues, stood before the throne, and before the Lamb, clothed with white robes, and palms in their hands;

These are those who know and understand the truth, and who have been set free of the earth's tribulations, which are the product of the falsehoods and ways of the world. (See verses 13–17.) Their state of being ("*white robes*" as explained above in the commentary on Revelation 6:11) reflects the purity of the work of their hands, and is further represented by the "*palms*" they hold, having overcome the world. The *palm* leaf has always symbolized victory or success. Roman citizens would wave palm leaves in the street when their armies returned from a successful military campaign.

7:10 And cried with a loud voice, saying, Salvation to our God *who* sitteth upon the throne, and unto the Lamb *whom He hath given to us*.

7:11 And *this great multitude* stood *with the elders and the Lamb* round about the throne, and about the four beasts, *who were the angels of God*; and *they* fell before the throne on their faces, and worshipped God,

7:12 Saying, Glory, and thanksgiving, and honour *we give* unto our God for ever and ever *for his* blessings, and wisdom, and power, and might. Amen.

The Creator and the angels that serve in the capacity of overseeing the eternal work of God in this solar system, came from another galaxy; whereas the "*multitudes*," the "*elders*," and Christ ("*the Lamb*") are specific to *this* solar system.

The attitude of giving proper honor along with the acceptance of authority, has always been indicated through the act of prostration. All of those assigned to this solar system sustain the works of these Beings and confirm their acceptance, as ratified in this verse ending in "*Amen*." The angels come from another solar system to help with this one, and do not worship our God in the same manner as we do; therefore, their presence is presented by John in the same way he presents "*the throne*" of God.

With the corrected translation and presentation of John's words in this verse, the truth of this visionary scene is restored to its proper perspective ("*about* the throne, and *about* the four beasts").

7:13 And one of the elders *spake* unto me, saying, *Who* are these *who* are arrayed in white robes? and *from* whence *did* they *come*?

In other words, the prophets are positing an hypothetical question: "How does one become saved in the kingdom of God, or better, become eternally happy?" The "*white robes*" are the righteous works of those who are ready to live forever with other beings in peace and happiness because they have learned to do unto another what they would want done unto them—the overall premise of the gospel of Jesus Christ. Through his figurative expressions, John asks, "*How did they do this?*"

In the next verse the explanation of "*how*" is given.

7:14 And I said unto him, Sir, thou knowest. And he said to me, These are they *who* came out of great tribulation, and have washed their *own* robes, and made them white in the blood of the Lamb.

John is referring to the prophets ("*one of the elders*") who know and understand the mysteries and truths of God. John figuratively presents—as if he doesn't understand but is in the attitude of seeking the enlightenment from one who knows—a true prophet of God. He directs those who are sincere seekers of truth to get it from these "*elders*" rather than by trusting in one's own wisdom or the wisdom of others.

The prophets made reference to this concept when they warned against "*trusting in the arm of flesh*":

> *Thus saith the LORD; Cursed be the man that trusteth in man, and maketh **flesh his arm**, and whose heart departeth from the LORD.* (Jeremiah 17:5)

Whether we trust in our own foolishness or the foolishness of others, we still trust in the "*arm of flesh*" when we don't listen to those properly called and chosen to teach us the will of God. From John's allegoric lesson here, it is quite obvious that he is one of the "*elders*" and understood the mysteries of God.

Washing "*their own robes*" and making them "*white in the blood of the Lamb*" was explained previously in the commentary of Revelation 6:11.

7:15 Therefore they are before the throne of God, and serve him day and night in his **kingdom**; and He that sitteth on the throne shall dwell **with** them.

Jesus taught that the Father was with Him and he was with the Father, and that all of us could dwell with him and the Father in God's kingdom. What the people didn't understand, was what the mystery of the kingdom of God actually is:

> *And he said unto them, Unto you it is given to know the mystery of the kingdom of God: but unto them that are without, all these things are done in parables:* (Mark 4:11)

The *kingdom of God* is a figurative expression meaning nothing more nor less than living in peace, love, and harmony (balance) in our environs, and is that for which we are preparing ourselves in this solar system. The *word of God* is nothing more than that which leads us to this "*kingdom*" or place of peace, love, and harmony:

> *The word which God sent unto the children of Israel,* ***preaching peace by Jesus Christ.*** (Acts 10:36)

> *Suffer the little children to come unto me, and forbid them not: for of such is the kingdom of God.* (Mark 10:14)

> *And he said unto them, I must preach the kingdom of God to other cities also: for therefore am I sent. ...And it came to pass afterward, that he went throughout every city and village, preaching and showing the glad tidings of the kingdom of God: ...And when he was demanded of the Pharisees, when the kingdom of God should come, he answered them and said, The kingdom of God cometh not with observation: Neither shall they say, Lo here! or, lo*

*there! for, behold, **the kingdom of God is within you**.* (Luke 4:43; 8:1; 17:20–21)

Therefore, those who are in the metaphoric (*cometh not with observation*) "*kingdom of God*," and serve Him "*day and night*," are those who do unto others what they would want done unto them; thus promoting peace, love, and harmony always.

7:16 They shall hunger no more, neither thirst any more; neither shall **they need** the sun **to give them** light, nor any heat, and God shall wipe away all tears from their eyes.

Once the gospel is invoked within, the external, less reliable, sources not only become unnecessary, but counterproductive to our well-being. We thus become a new person, self-sustaining, and our "*tears*" being "*wiped away*" as the result of knowledge and proper action. Before Jesus Christ taught the gospel ("Do Unto Others"/the kingdom of God) he said:

> *Blessed are they that mourn: for they shall be comforted.*
> *Blessed are the meek: for they shall inherit the earth.*
> *Blessed are they which do hunger and thirst after right-*
> *eousness: for they shall be filled.* (Matthew 5:4–6)
>
> *Blessed are ye that hunger now: for ye shall be filled.*
> *Blessed are ye that weep now: for ye shall laugh.* (Luke 6:21)
>
> *I am the bread of life: he that cometh to me shall never*
> *hunger; and he that believeth on me shall never thirst.*
> (John 6:35)

7:17 For the Lamb which is in **their** midst **and before** the throne shall feed them, and shall lead them unto living fountains of waters.

Jesus traveled throughout the land and came to a city of Samarians, who were held in disdain by the Jews. He spoke to a Samarian woman who offered him a drink of water:

> But whosoever drinketh of the water that I shall give him shall never thirst; but the water that I shall give him shall be in him a well of water springing up into everlasting life. (John 4:14)

Christ proceeded to teach the Samarians the same things he taught the Jews—the basis of all his teachings (the gospel of Jesus Christ) which is: Do unto others what you would have them do unto you. Thus, Jesus brought the kingdom of God to the Samarians, giving them all they needed to know to find peace, love, and harmony—both in this world, and in the world to come.

To those who can't accept the simplicity of Christ's message, and insist they know their own truth by *trusting in the arm of flesh*, Jesus proclaimed:

> Woe unto you that are full! for ye shall hunger. Woe unto you that laugh now! for ye shall mourn and weep. Woe unto you, when all men shall speak well of you! for so did their fathers to the false prophets. (Luke 6:25–26)

The only commandments of any worth to our salvation (happiness) are the ones Jesus Christ gave in Matthew, chapters 5, 6, and 7. All other actions, thoughts, beliefs, doctrines, or precepts that do not teach a person to do unto another what one would want done unto them, are not, nor have they *ever been* part of, the kingdom of God. This is the gospel of Jesus Christ—*"the living fountain of water."*

Chapter

REVELATION
UNFOLDED

8:1 And **before** he had opened the seventh seal, there was silence in heaven about the space of half an hour.

Christ does not open the seventh seal until later (as described in Revelation 10:3) according to the proper translation of John's endowment:

> *And **he opened the seventh seal and** cried with a loud voice, as when a lion roareth **and maketh all afraid**; and when he had cried, **it was as if** seven thunders uttered their voices.*

In order to understand the hidden meaning of John's words, one must be endowed with the gift and power of prophecy. To expose the unworthiness of those who have tried to teach and explain his words, John uses the riddle of various literary forms, and excerpts of scriptures familiar to him, in ways only known to those given the proper authority to teach the people. In this way, when the clear, simple, and literal common sense explanation is given to the people, allowing them to understand as a child would, they will recognize the authenticity of the true prophet of God chosen to bring John's words to light.

Along with the use of literary forms, John also employs the use of numerology to illustrate (figuratively) occurrences which take place upon the earth. As did many before him, John expresses the timetable of God as 1000 years for each day reckoned by God:

> *For a **thousand years in thy sight are but as yesterday** when it is past, and as a watch in the night.* (Psalms 90:4)

> *But the heavens and the earth, which are now, by the same word are kept in store, reserved unto fire against the day of judgment and perdition of ungodly men. But, beloved, be not ignorant of this one thing, that one day is with the Lord as a thousand years, and **a thousand years as one day**. The Lord is not slack concerning his promise, as some men count slackness; but is longsuffering to us-ward, not willing that any should perish, but that all should come to repentance.* (II Peter 3:7–9)

It is crucial for the reader to understand here, that John further used such terms as "day" and "year" interchangeably, as if they were an algebraic expression to which *he* retains the right to assign appropriate values as he sees fit, after the manner in which God reckons time. These references to God's time being one day to every 1000 years of mortal time, presents the truth that there is no equation of time in heaven, or better, that time is only significant to a mortal understanding, and is insignificant to God. However, because mortals measure time in precise measurements, according to their limited ability to understand the mysteries of God, some prophets use timetables and mathematics to make their point.

The significance of *"about the space of half an hour,"* is to be understood and reckoned according to the timetable used figuratively by God *"in heaven."* With mathematical equations, a half an hour of God's time is about 21 years of our mortal time, or to be mathematically precise: 20.833 years, or ***about*** *the space of half an hour.*

Throughout *Revelation*, John uses the term *"days"* to represent actual earth years; and therefore, he properly uses *"years"* to represent *"days"* interchangeably, in order to lead the reader to an understanding of a specific time period.

In this instance, John has borrowed from the book of *Daniel* to figuratively express, as a specific time frame, that which Daniel experienced in order to prepare *himself* to receive the exact same vision given to both prophets by the same Being:

> *And I Daniel alone saw the vision: for the men that were with me saw not the vision; but a great quaking fell upon them, so that they fled to hide themselves. Therefore I was left alone, and saw this great vision, and there remained no strength in me: for my comeliness was turned in me into corruption, and I retained no strength. Yet heard I the voice of his words: and when I heard the voice of his words, then was I in a deep sleep on my face, and my face toward the ground. And, behold, an hand touched me, which set me upon my knees and upon the palms of my hands. And he said unto me, O Daniel, a man greatly beloved, understand the words that I speak unto thee, and stand upright: for unto thee am I now sent. And when he had spoken this word unto me, I stood trembling. Then said he unto me, Fear not, Daniel: for from the first day that thou didst set thine heart to understand, and to chasten thyself before thy God, thy words were heard, and I am come for thy words. But the prince of the kingdom of Persia [Lucifer] withstood me **one and twenty days**: but, lo, Michael, one of the chief princes, came to help me; and I remained there with the kings of Persia. Now I am come to make thee understand what shall befall thy people in the latter days: for yet the vision is for many days.*
> (Daniel 10:7–14)

Instead of using the term "the prince of the kingdom of Persia" as Daniel did, John wrote it this way: *"**who shall** overcome **Lucifer**, the prince of the kings of the earth."* (See Revelation 1:5 and commentary.)

A careful study of Daniel's presentation of his vision will demonstrate a parallel description of John's *Revelation*. Each man uses contemporary names to hide the true meaning of the vision until the time of the latter days, in which all things would be revealed. In this way, Daniel and John both *"sealed up"* their visions as they were commanded:

> *But thou, O Daniel, **shut up the words, and seal the book, even to the time of the end**: many shall run to and fro, and knowledge shall be increased.* (Daniel 12:4)

> *And when the seven thunders had uttered their voices, I was about to write that which they spoke; and I heard a voice from heaven saying unto me, seal up those things which the seven thunders uttered, **and write them not, for these things shall not come forth unto the children of men until the end of times**.* (Revelation 10:4)

Daniel uses the name *"Michael"* in this verse, as the one who saves the day; throwing secular historians off the mark (*many shall run to and fro, and knowledge shall be increased*) because there is no mention of a "Michael" in the history of the downfall of the Persian kingdom.

The "prince of the kingdom of Persia" represents our own flesh (*Lucifer*), which in reality is our human nature—*"the prince of the kings of the earth."*

For *twenty-one days*, Daniel struggled in agony to understand the mysteries of God. His quest for truth ended on the *twenty-first* day, when he was finally able to overcome his sins (the desires of the flesh):

> *In those days I Daniel was mourning three full weeks. I ate no pleasant bread, neither came flesh nor wine in my mouth, neither did I anoint myself at all, till three whole weeks were fulfilled.* (Daniel 10:2–3)

After this "*silence in heaven about the space of half an hour,*" Daniel received a vision in which the Lord told him that he was aware of his desire to know and understand the truth: "*Fear not, Daniel: for from the first day that thou didst set thine heart to understand, and to chasten thyself before thy God, thy words were heard, and I am come for thy words.*"

The Lord told Daniel that he was always there to give him the knowledge and understanding he desired, but because of his human nature (*and I remained there with the kings of Persia*), the Lord was unable to teach him for his "*three full weeks*" of mourning. This is the length of time that he was depressed and under the bondage of his own sins: "*But the prince of the kingdom of Persia withstood me one and twenty days.*"

It wasn't until the Holy Ghost effectually aided Daniel in overcoming his personal emotional state, that the Lord was allowed to come and teach him the truths he desired: "*but, lo, Michael, one of the chief princes, came to help me.*"

While he was with them, Jesus also taught his disciples the things they needed to do to overcome the flesh (Lucifer) and further explained that when he was no longer with them, the Holy Ghost (*Michael*) would be sent to help bring to their remembrance all the things he had taught them.

*Now is the judgment of this world: now shall **the prince of this world be cast out**.* (John 12:31)

*If ye shall ask any thing in my name, I will do it. If ye love me, keep my commandments. And I will pray the Father, and he shall give you another Comforter, that he may abide with you for ever; Even the Spirit of truth; whom the world cannot receive, because it seeth him not, neither knoweth him: **but ye know him; for he dwelleth with you**, and shall be in you…But the Comforter, which is the Holy Ghost, whom the Father will send in my name, he shall teach you all things, and bring all things to your remembrance, whatsoever I have said unto you.* (John 14:14–17, 26)

John is telling us that after the sixth seal was opened, but before Christ comes again, there will be no revelation given from heaven (*"silence in heaven"*) unless a person does what Daniel did to receive his vision of understanding (*"about the space of half an hour"*). One must seek to know and understand truth, mourn because of one's wickedness (broken heart and contrite spirit), and overcome Lucifer in order to receive an understanding of the mysteries of heaven. This may take us our own *"half an hour of silence,"* which is the figurative representation of however much time it takes for us to follow the path of Christ and learn the mysteries as John and Daniel did.

8:2 And *during the silence* I saw seven angels **who** stood before God; and to them were given seven trumpets *to sound*.

John expresses this period of silence in his *Revelation* as the time in which warnings are given of what will happen to the human race if it continues to disregard the commandments of God. Trumpets are symbolically given as announcements or warnings, and each of the *"seven angels"* has one *"trumpet"* that sounds a warning pertaining to a specific effect caused by wickedness. These warnings pertain to things that are spiritual, or those things which turn our hearts away from peace, harmony, and the love we should have one for another.

Later, in chapter 16, the servants have *vials* in their hands, which they are commanded to pour out upon the earth. Each vial represents the actual spiritual and physical effects of humankind's wickedness, and corresponds to the spiritual warnings given by each of *the angels* with *the trumpets* that sound when humans act contrary to the *Royal Law* of God. The pouring out of the vials spoken of later in John's *Revelation*, cause much tribulation to come upon the earth after humankind has been warned by the trumpeting angels and has ignored the warnings.

John uses similar expressions in this chapter, which is comprised of the warnings given from heaven to the inhabitants of the earth, and what will happen to them *spiritually* when they learn the truth and ignore it. Though he sees in vision what takes place throughout the history of the world, he must present it in a way that it stays hidden from the world until the latter days. This is the reason he calls on the writings of his predecessors, and takes his figurative expressions from *Old Testament* writings.

To understand John's intent, the reader must keep in mind that John is using the *same* set of figurative expressions throughout his *Revelation* to relate the effects of wickedness *both* spiritually and physically when we do not do unto others what we would have them do unto us.

8:3 And another angel came *from upon the earth* and stood at the altar, having a golden censer *filled with* much incense, that he should offer it with the prayers of all saints upon the golden altar which was before the throne.

During the period in which there is no revelation (except to those "*saints*" who do as John figuratively represented in the example of Daniel), the people of the world are praying, worshipping, and piously expressing their desires towards God. These vain prayers and pious acts are represented as the "*golden censer filled with much incense.*" (See commentary on Revelation 5:8, where John figuratively expresses each of us as "*golden vials full of the smoke of incense.*") The "*golden censer filled with much incense*" is figuratively represented separate and distinct from "*the prayers of all saints.*" This is according to an angel who had been upon the earth observing the people, and metaphorically gathered the vain works of the people and filled the "*golden censer,*" to be presented to God along with the "*prayers*" or works "*of the saints.*"

8:4 And the smoke of the incense *from the golden censer*, which came with the prayers of the saints, ascended up before God out of the angel's hand. *And he who sat upon the throne turned away because of the burnt incense before Him*.

Repelled by the pungent aroma of incense in the angel's hand, God instructs the angel to pour out the stinking incense and fill up the censer with the fire of His indignation. God's symbolic response here to the many pious acts of the people on earth demonstrates the unacceptability of their works to Him; worshipping Him with their mouths and lips but their hearts and works are far from Him. Though they profess religion and belief in *their*

God, they fail to keep the one law upon which all others are predicated: *Do unto others what you would have them do unto you.*

8:5   And the angel took the censer, and filled it with fire *from* the altar, and cast it into the earth; and *it was filled with* voices, and thunderings, and lightnings, and *these caused* a *great* earthquake.

The *"fire from the altar"* is the word of God, or the *voice* of the Lord speaking to the people through his prophets. The prophets preach repentance to the people, illuminating their wickedness with plainness, and causing *the earth* on which they stand (the emotional stability within them) to quake as mentioned. (See commentary on Revelation 4:5 and 6:12.)

8:6 And *when the censer was emptied upon the earth* the seven angels which had the seven trumpets prepared themselves to sound.

John, having prefaced his explanation of the coming spiritual destruction with the preceding verses, has shown that no knowledge of truth is given (*"silence in heaven"*) to the people, and that they are offering unrighteous offerings upon the altar set before God. Once he has established that the earth's inhabitants are spiritually corrupt, John gives his figurative expressions of the causes and effects of this corruption in the following verses.

8:7 The first angel sounded, and there followed hail, and fire mingled with *the hail which appeared as* blood, and they were cast upon the earth: and the third part of trees was burnt up, and all green grass was burnt up.

In the story of the Exodus, Moses *warns* Pharaoh of the impending judgments of God if his people are not freed. John borrows from this event:

> *Behold, to morrow about this time I will cause it to rain a very grievous hail, such as hath not been in Egypt since the foundation thereof even until now...And Moses stretched forth his rod toward heaven: and the LORD sent*

thunder and hail, and the fire ran along upon the ground;
and the LORD rained hail upon the land of Egypt. So
*there was hail, and **fire mingled with the hail**, very*
grievous, such as there was none like it in all the land of
Egypt since it became a nation. (Exodus 9:18, 23–24)

The figurative expression of "*hail*" and "*fire*" being the word of God
was taken from Psalms 18:13: "*The LORD also thundered in the heavens,*
*and **the Highest gave his voice; hail stones and coals of fire.**"

The "*trees*" are the people of the world as explained in the commentary
of Revelation 6:13, and the "*green grass*" is representative of the doctrines
and precepts in which they believe and take stock.

Green grass grows into much larger stocks of mature grass that
eventually become the main stem of the plant. Comparitively, the expression
"to take stock in what he says" simply means you can trust you are getting
good information. In this case though, that in which humans take stock (the
doctrines and precepts of men) is "*burnt up*" by the truth:

That bringeth the princes to nothing; he maketh the judges
of the earth as vanity. Yea, they shall not be planted; yea,
*they shall not be sown: yea, **their stock shall not take***
***root in the earth**: and he shall also blow upon them, and*
they shall wither, and the whirlwind shall take them away
as stubble. (Isaiah 40:23–24)

*But they are altogether brutish and foolish: **the stock is a***
***doctrine of vanities**.* (Jeremiah 10:8)

Therefore their inhabitants were of small power, they
were dismayed and confounded: they were as the grass of
the field, and as the green herb, as the grass on the house-
tops, and as corn blasted before it be grown up...The voice
*said, Cry. And he said, What shall I cry? **All flesh is***
***grass**, and all the goodliness thereof is as the flower of the*
field: The grass withereth, the flower fadeth: because the

spirit of the LORD bloweth upon it: surely the people is grass. The grass withereth, the flower fadeth: but the word of our God shall stand for ever. (Isaiah 37:27; 40:6–8)

*And the light of Israel shall be for a fire, and his Holy One for a flame: and **it shall burn and devour his thorns and his briers in one day**; And shall consume the glory of his forest, and of his fruitful field, both soul and body: and they shall be as when a standardbearer fainteth. And the rest of the trees of his forest shall be few, that a child may write them.* (Isaiah 10:17–19)

John writes that a "*third part of the trees…and all green grass was burnt*," which means that "*all* of humanity" is under condemnation. This is because of its works caused by the false doctrines and precepts in which it believes. When people hear the truth, they will be "*tormented with fire and brimstone in the presence of the holy angels, and in the presence of the Lamb*" (see Revelation 14:10). In other words, they will be extremely embarrassed by how they have chosen to live, and by what they have allowed themselves to believe.

Many of the *Old Testament* prophets used the term "*third*" to exemplify three distinct expressions of the *whole* of humankind from which corruption usually occurs: there are those who serve, those who do not, and those who are served. The symbolic use of "*thirds*" expresses that *all* people, no matter in which "*third*" they are found, will be judged and treated equally according to the *Royal Law* of Christ.

This is represented in Jewish custom and exemplified in scripture:

*And all the congregation made a covenant with the king in the house of God. And he said unto them, Behold, the king's son shall reign, as the Lord hath said of the sons of David. This is the thing that ye shall do; **A third part** of you entering on the sabbath, of the priests and of the Levites, shall be porters of the doors; And **a third part** shall be at*

*the king's house; and **a third part** at the gate of the foun-*
dation: and all the people shall be in the courts of the house
of the LORD.   But let none come into the house of the
LORD, save the priests, and they that minister of the
Levites; they shall go in, for they are holy: but all the peo-
ple shall keep the watch of the LORD. (II Chronicles 23:3–6)

Thus saith the Lord GOD; This is Jerusalem: I have set it
in the midst of the nations and countries that are round
about her.   And she hath changed my judgments into
wickedness more than the nations, and my statutes more
than the countries that are round about her: for they have
refused my judgments and my statutes, they have not
walked in them.   Therefore thus saith the Lord GOD;
Because ye multiplied more than the nations that are
round about you, and have not walked in my statutes,
neither have kept my judgments, neither have done
according to the judgments of the nations that are round
about you;   Therefore thus saith the Lord GOD; Behold, I,
even I, am against thee, and will execute judgments in the
midst of thee in the sight of the nations.   ...Wherefore, as
I live, saith the Lord GOD; Surely, because thou hast
defiled my sanctuary with all thy detestable things, and
with all thine abominations, therefore will I also dimin-
ish thee; neither shall mine eye spare, neither will I have
*any pity.   **A third part** of thee shall die with the pesti-*
lence, and with famine shall they be consumed in the
*midst of thee: and **a third part** shall fall by the sword*
*round about thee; and I will scatter **a third part** into all*
the winds, and I will draw out a sword after them.
(Ezekiel 5:5–8, 11–12)

And it shall come to pass, that in all the land, saith the
*LORD, **two parts** therein shall be cut off and die; but **the***
***third** shall be left therein.   And I will bring the third part*

through the fire, and will refine them as silver is refined, and will try them as gold is tried: they shall call on my name, and I will hear them: I will say, It is my people: and they shall say, The LORD is my God. (Zechariah 13:8–9)

*And David sent forth **a third part** of the people under the hand of Joab, and **a third part** under the hand of Abishai the son of Zeruiah, Joab's brother, and **a third part** under the hand of Ittai the Gittite. And the king said unto the people, I will surely go forth with you myself also.* (II Samuel 18:2)

In addition to the metaphor presented by the *Old Testament* prophets above, John further utilizes the expression "*third*" to represent conditions of the flesh. All humans enjoy equality because of the uniformity of natural materials from which we are taken and formed from the earth; no *one* person's materials being any more important or valuable than another's.

Our bodies are made up of *two-thirds* water and *one-third* of other elements. Together, these constitute the flesh by which our spirits are able to *have dominion over* the earth, which elements are the very material from which we are figuratively taken (*created from the dust of the earth*). (Interestingly, the earth itself is made up of about the same ratio of land to water as man is; therefore, we are *as* the earth.)

Whenever John mentions a "*third*" throughout the *Revelation*, he does so figuratively to represent the portion of man that is flesh, and our intrinsic equality in this *earthen state*. It is a *third* (the flesh) that is always destroyed, and a *third* (the flesh) that is always deceived. In other words, it is because of our flesh that we are deceived and will be destroyed, being taken in some way by a figurative "*death*."

Further, we suffer torment and tribulation because of the reaction of our flesh (*the third*) to our environs on this earth, and also by the way we treat and are treated by others. When we do not do unto others as we would have them do unto us, or others do not do unto us as we would want done unto us, our flesh feels the effects through emotional strains of anxiety and depression. Hence, it will always make perfect sense throughout John's writings that our flesh (*a third*) always takes the brunt of the prophesied tribulations.

8:8 And the second angel sounded, and as it were a great mountain burning with fire was cast into the sea: and the third part of the sea became blood;

Again John uses "*the third*" to symbolize the principle of the equality of the flesh as given to the *whole* of humanity as previously mentioned above. The "*sea*" represents the societies of humankind, the "*creatures*" represent the people; and the "*ships*" represent the different ways in which humans navigate throughout life. (See the next verse.) Some choose religion as their "*ship*" and some choose business or other "*ships*"; all boarding the *vessel* of their own choice. Whatever allows a person to journey upon the "high seas" of the world's societies is looked upon by many of the prophets as "*ships*."

All of Ezekiel chapter 27 refers to these figurative expressions of the sea. Here Ezekiel uses Tyrus, a famous seaport, as the figurative backdrop for the situation of the world, which the Lord is very much displeased with:

> *And in their wailing they shall take up a lamentation for thee, and lament over thee, saying, What city is like Tyrus, like the destroyed in the midst of the sea?* (Ezekiel 27:32)

The "*great mountain burning*" is the truth coming from the mouth of the Lord, which will bring down the societies of earth and change them into one of equality, where all are treated as every one would want to be treated:

> *Behold, the name of the LORD cometh from far, burning with his anger, and the burden thereof is heavy: his lips are full of indignation, and his tongue as a devouring fire:* (Isaiah 30:27)

Moses used the terminology first in symbolizing the word and commandments of God:

Specially the day that thou stoodest before the LORD thy God in Horeb, when the LORD said unto me, Gather me the people together, and I will make them hear my words, that they may learn to fear me all the days that they shall live upon the earth, and that they may teach their children. And ye came near and stood under the mountain; and **the mountain burned with fire** *unto the midst of heaven, with darkness, clouds, and thick darkness. And the LORD spake unto you out of the midst of the fire: ye heard the voice of the words, but saw no similitude; only ye heard a voice. And he declared unto you his covenant, which he commanded you to perform, even ten commandments; and he wrote them upon two tables of stone.* (Deuteronomy 4:10–13)

8:9 And the third part of the creatures which were in the sea **that** had life, died; and the third part of the ships were destroyed.

The people (*"creatures"*) believe they are *living* a fulfilling life (*"that had life"*), but will realize when they hear the truth that all their worldly pursuits, goals, and desires meant nothing. As they are waiting for their proverbial "ship to come in," all the *"ships"* of worldly desires and expectations for which they await will be destroyed.

Thus prophesied the prophets:

Thou breakest the ships of Tarshish with an east wind. (Psalms 48:7)

Howl, ye ships of Tarshish: for your strength is laid waste. (Isaiah 23:14)

8:10 And the third angel sounded, and there **had fallen** a great star from heaven, burning as it were a lamp, and it fell upon the third part of the rivers, and upon the fountains of waters;

This *"great star...burning as it were a lamp"* represents all those who put themselves up as one who receives instruction and knowledge *"from heaven."* Throughout *Revelation*, John uses *"stars"* to describe the people; therefore, this *"great star"* symbolizes those who appear superior in knowledge and power to the rest, and who set themselves up as a light to the world (*"burning as it were a lamp"*).

8:11 And the name of the star is called Wormwood: and the third part of the waters *from the rivers and the fountains* became wormwood; and many men died of the waters, because they were made bitter.

This attitude of superiority and wisdom is common among those who teach the word of God (religious and spiritual leaders), or the wisdom of the world (secular teachers). These are *"the rivers"* and the *"fountains of waters"* from which the people quench their thirst for knowledge. John describes these fountains of knowledge as being corrupted by their pride, and using their supposed education and knowledge to obtain personal gain, both monetarily, *and* with titles, honors, and worldly glory. All these he appropriately names *"Wormwood."*

Anyone who listens to the doctrines and precepts given by the leaders and teachers of the world will be led down a path of destruction as to things of the spirit. The prophets of old express very eloquently what John meant:

> *And ye have seen their abominations, and their idols, wood and stone, silver and gold, which were among them; Lest there should be among you man, or woman, or family, or tribe, whose heart turneth away this day from the LORD our God, to go and serve the gods of these nations; lest there should be among you a root that **beareth gall and wormwood**;* (Deuteronomy 29:17–18)

> *My son, attend unto my wisdom, and bow thine ear to my understanding: That thou mayest regard discretion, and that thy lips may keep knowledge. For the lips of a strange woman drop as an honeycomb, and her mouth is*

*smoother than oil: But her end is **bitter as wormwood**, sharp as a twoedged sword. Her feet go down to death; her steps take hold on hell. Lest thou shouldest ponder the path of life, her ways are moveable, that thou canst not know them. Hear me now therefore, O ye children, and depart not from the words of my mouth. Remove thy way far from her, and come not nigh the door of her house: Lest thou give thine honour unto others, and thy years unto the cruel: Lest strangers be filled with thy wealth; and thy labours be in the house of a stranger; And thou mourn at the last, when thy flesh and thy body are consumed, And say, How have I hated instruction, and my heart despised reproof; And have not obeyed the voice of my teachers, nor inclined mine ear to them that instructed me! I was almost in all evil in the midst of the congregation and assembly.* (Proverbs 5:1–14)

*And the LORD saith, Because they have forsaken my law which I set before them, and have not obeyed my voice, neither walked therein; But have walked after the imagination of their own heart, and after Baalim, which their fathers taught them: Therefore thus saith the LORD of hosts, the God of Israel; Behold, I will feed them, even this people, **with wormwood, and give them water of gall to drink**. I will scatter them also among the heathen, whom neither they nor their fathers have known: and I will send a sword after them, till I have consumed them. Thus saith the LORD of hosts, Consider ye, and call for the mourning women, that they may come; and send for cunning women, that they may come:* (Jeremiah 9:13–17)

And I have seen folly in the prophets of Samaria; they prophesied in Baal, and caused my people Israel to err. I have seen also in the prophets of Jerusalem an horrible thing: they commit adultery, and walk in lies: they strengthen also *the hands of evildoers, that none doth return from his wickedness: they are all of them unto me as Sodom, and the inhabitants thereof as Gomorrah. Therefore thus saith the LORD of hosts concerning the prophets; Behold, I will feed them with **wormwood, and make them drink the water of gall**: for from the prophets of Jerusalem is profaneness gone forth into all the land. Thus saith the LORD of hosts, Hearken not unto the words of the prophets that prophesy unto you: they make you vain: they speak a vision of their own heart, and not out of the mouth of the LORD. They say still unto them that despise me, The LORD hath said, Ye shall have peace; and they say unto every one that walketh after the imagination of his own heart, No evil shall come upon you.* (Jeremiah 23:13–17)

*Seek the LORD, and ye shall live; lest he break out like fire in the house of Joseph, and devour it, and there be none to quench it in Beth-el. Ye who **turn judgment to wormwood, and leave off righteousness** in the earth, Seek him that maketh the seven stars and Orion, and turneth the shadow of death into the morning, and maketh the day dark with night: that calleth for the waters of the sea, and poureth them out upon the face of the earth: The LORD is his name:* (Amos 5:6–8)

8:12 And the fourth angel sounded, and the third part of the sun was smitten, and the third part of the moon, and the third part of the stars; *and because a* third part of them was darkened, the day shone not for a third part of it, and the night likewise *received no light*.

Again, John uses the idea of the *equality of the whole world of flesh*, or "*the third*" (see commentary Revelation 8:7), and of the situation mankind shares in common (all being made *of the dust of the earth*), to relate the great amount of darkness that covers all people of the world ("*a third part of them was darkened*").

The natural equality of each and every person could well be contrasted with the *inequality* which exists among them in the way they treat each other on account of inappropriate factors such as race, nationality, social status, or religion; thereby bringing themselves, by virtue of their works, under the bondage of *darkness*.

John's reference to the *sun, moon, and stars* not giving their light to the world, has been previously explained in the commentary on Revelation 6:12. Darkness is the result of the *sun, moon, and stars* not giving off light: mankind ("*the stars*") on account of their works; the prophets ("*the moon*") because of the hardness of the hearts of the people against hearing their words; and God ("*the sun*") because of the unworthiness of the world to receive His administrations. The ancient prophets expounded more upon the cause of darkness:

> *Therefore remove sorrow from thy heart, and put away evil from thy flesh: for childhood and youth are vanity. Remember now thy Creator in the days of thy youth, while the evil days come not, nor the years draw nigh, when thou shalt say, I have no pleasure in them;* **While the sun, or the light, or the moon, or the stars, be not darkened,** *nor the clouds return after the rain:* (Ecclesiastes 11:10; 12:1–2)

> *Behold, the day of the LORD cometh, cruel both with wrath and fierce anger, to lay the land desolate: and he shall destroy the sinners thereof out of it.* **For the stars of heaven and the constellations thereof shall not give their light: the sun shall be darkened in his going forth, and the moon shall not cause her light to shine.** *And I will punish the world for their evil, and the wicked for their iniquity; and I will cause the arrogancy of the proud to cease, and will lay low the haughtiness of the terrible. I will make a man more precious than fine gold; even a man than the golden wedge of Ophir.* (Isaiah 13:9–12)

I will also water with thy blood the land wherein thou swimmest, even to the mountains; and the rivers shall be full of thee. And when I shall put thee out, I will cover the heaven, **and make the stars thereof dark; I will cover the sun with a cloud, and the moon shall not give her light.** *All the bright lights of heaven will I make dark over thee, and set darkness upon thy land, saith the Lord GOD. I will also vex the hearts of many people, when I shall bring thy destruction among the nations, into the countries which thou hast not known.* (Ezekiel 32:6–9)

8:13 And I beheld, and heard an angel flying through the midst of heaven, saying with a loud voice, Woe, woe, woe, to the inhabiters of the earth by reason of the other voices of the *trumpets* of the three angels, which are yet to sound!

The first four angels (verses 7, 8, 10, and 12) have warned the world by the "*sound of their trumpets*" what occurs when we lose our spiritual connection within ourselves, and with each other, because of the desires of the flesh which overcome us. The next three warnings are given such importance, that John presents a *specific* angel to announce each of them.

The first two of these warnings that follow, will show what has caused the vast spiritual demise, and to which John expects us to pay particularly close attention; as these two "*woes,*" or warnings, if heeded and understood, will solve all of our human problems. The final trumpet warns humankind that they are about to meet their maker; and when humans meet their maker, and finally find out the truth of all things, "*Woe, woe, woe*" unto them!

Chapter

REVELATION
UNFOLDED

9:1 And the fifth angel sounded, and I saw *as it were* a star fall from heaven unto the earth: and to him was given *great power and* the key *to* the bottomless pit *which was dug by those upon the earth*.

To understand this part correctly, it is important to remember that human beings in mortality are presented as the *"stars in heaven"* throughout all of *Revelation*. Keeping this in mind, we now have John alluding to Lucifer as a *"fallen star,"* which name he also uses to express the enticements and lusts of the flesh. Jesus Christ taught John personally; therefore he was well aware of the true meaning of *Lucifer, Satan,* and the *devil*. This part of *Revelation* was inspired by what John heard from Christ:

> *And he said unto them, I beheld Satan as **lightning fall from heaven**. Behold, I give unto you power to tread on **serpents** and **scorpions**, and over all the power of the enemy: and nothing shall by any means hurt you.* (Luke 10:18–19)

The ancient prophets also knew the secret:

*How art thou fallen from heaven, **O Lucifer, son of the morning!** how art thou cut down to the ground, which didst weaken the nations! For thou hast said in thine heart, I will ascend into heaven, I will exalt my throne above the stars of God: I will sit also upon the mount of the congregation, in the sides of the north: I will ascend above the heights of the clouds; I will be like the most High. Yet thou shalt be brought down to **hell, to the sides of the pit.*** (Isaiah 14:12–15)

*But thou, O God, shalt bring them down into the **pit of destruction**: bloody and deceitful men shall not live out half their days; but I will trust in thee.* (Psalms 55:23)

*My soul is among lions: and I lie even among them that are set on fire, even the sons of men, whose teeth are spears and arrows, and their tongue a sharp sword. Be thou exalted, O God, above the heavens; let thy glory be above all the earth. They have prepared a net for my steps; my soul is bowed down: **they have digged a pit before me, into the midst whereof they are fallen themselves.** Selah.* (Psalms 57:4–6)

*From the uttermost part of the earth have we heard songs, even glory to the righteous. But I said, My leanness, my leanness, woe unto me! the treacherous dealers have dealt treacherously; yea, the treacherous dealers have dealt very treacherously. **Fear, and the pit, and the snare, are upon thee**, O inhabitant of the earth.* (Isaiah 24:16–17)

*And Moab shall be destroyed from being a people, because he hath magnified himself against the LORD. **Fear, and the pit, and the snare, shall be upon thee**, O inhabitant of Moab, saith the LORD. He that fleeth from the fear shall fall*

*into the pit; and he that getteth up out of the pit shall be taken
in the snare: for I will bring upon it, even upon Moab, the
year of their visitation, saith the LORD.* (Jeremiah 48:42–44)

*Behold, for peace I had great bitterness: but thou hast in
love to my soul delivered it from* **the pit of corruption:** *for
thou hast cast all my sins behind thy back.* (Isaiah 38:17)

Using his mentors' description of the desires and lusts of the
flesh—the innate enticements of human nature (*the pit*)—John describes
this "*pit*" as "*bottomless*." A better translation that would have expressed
John's true intent would have been "*endless*" instead of "*bottomless*," as in
the "*endless torment*" those feel who are thrust into a hell often referred to
as the "*bottomless pit*."

Our human natures create *hell* on earth by digging this great *pit*.
Our desires of worldly riches, glory, power, superiority, and seclusion in our
human groups of race, family, communities, cities, and nations, cause a
never-ending situation of conflict, inequality, argument, war, and competition. No matter how rich we become, our human natures entice us to lust
for *more*. No matter how powerful we might become, we seek to become
more powerful.

In our efforts to become *Number One* in any given situation,
whether that be the best at our job, in the academia world, in artistic theater,
in the athletic arena, or in any other personal pursuit, our desire to excel
above others is *endless*.

This desire to be special and above others is as a *pit* which has no
set bottom as to how low we would go to put ourselves above others in some
way or another. The most destructive cause of our emotional hell is our
desire to be this *Number One* (the best) in our relationships with each other.
As siblings, we strive to exert ourselves to prove our superiority over our
brothers and sisters. As spouses, we expect our partners to put us, alone,
up above all others. As parents, we put our children first before others, and
as friends, we desire to be that *One* and *Only* BEST friend.

In protecting our selfish interests, the flesh propels us into a protec-
tionist state of existence where our instincts to survive and be recognized as

special cause us to forget all aspects of doing unto others what we would want done unto us. Thus in mortality, we are in an *endless* state (*bottomless pit*) of trying to satisfy our human natures.

9:2 And **when** he **had unlocked** the bottomless pit and opened **it**, there arose a smoke out of the pit; and the sun and the air were darkened by reason of the smoke **made by** a great furnace **in** the pit.

Smoke is the by-product of burning, which is a process that occurs after something is done to start a fire. The "*great furnace*" is the works of humankind, its societies, its cultures, and everything that occurs by the exercising of free will as the mortal race progresses and learns. As humans advance and progress, they begin to acquire certain knowledge and understanding (*the key*) which unlocks further technological and societal developments. This "*furnace*" is deep within a "*pit*" dug by the people of the world. The "*smoke*" is the by-product of human interactions. As the people of the earth continue in wickedness, their works are represented as smoke coming out of the "*pit*" they have dug for themselves.

While people involve themselves in families, communities, cities, nations, societies, cultures, and in pursuing worldly things and desiring worldly honor and glory, their actions, deeds, and thoughts ("*the smoke*") continue to "*darken*" the air, not allowing the sun*light* of heaven to get through and give direction, revelation, or inspiration to them.

9:3 And there came out of the smoke locusts **and they went out** upon the earth; and unto them was given power, **and their power was in their tails**, as the scorpions of the earth have power.

John has chosen another of Moses' plagues to illustrate a very destructive force of human nature (Notice that an *east wind* brings in the locusts):

> *Else, if thou refuse to let my people go, behold, to morrow will I bring the locusts into thy coast: And they shall cover the face of the earth, that one cannot be able to see the earth: and they shall eat the residue of that which is escaped,*

which remaineth unto you from the hail, and shall eat
every tree which groweth for you out of the field: …And
Moses stretched forth his rod over the land of Egypt, and
the Lord brought an east wind upon the land all that day,
*and all that night; and when it was morning, **the east***
***wind brought the locusts**. (Exodus 10:4–5, 13)*

These "*locusts*" are the kings, presidents, popes, priests, general authorities, worldly leaders, and any other humans who control the actions of their followers and subjects, either by teaching or by command. They are "*given power*" by those who follow ("*tail*") them whether by devotion or decree. A tail always follows the commands of the creature, and in the case of "*scorpions*," it has a devastating sting. With the power given them, and their proficiency in manipulating those who follow or who are otherwise compelled to execute their commands, these leaders have caused incredible sorrows and torments upon the earth by using their "*tails*" to hurt and torment others.

Past prophets used the same symbolisms:

And say unto him, Take heed, and be quiet; fear not,
*neither be fainthearted for **the two tails of these***
***smoking firebrands**, for the fierce anger of Rezin with*
Syria, and of the son of Remaliah. (Isaiah 7:4)

And they, whether they will hear, or whether they will for-
bear, for they are a rebellious house, yet shall know that
there hath been a prophet among them. And thou, son of
man, be not afraid of them, neither be afraid of their
*words, though briers and thorns be with thee, and **thou***
***dost dwell among scorpions**: be not afraid of their*
words, nor be dismayed at their looks, though they be a
rebellious house. And thou shalt speak my words unto
them, whether they will hear, or whether they will forbear:
for they are most rebellious. (Ezekiel 2:5–7)

9:4 And it was commanded them that they should not hurt the grass of the earth, neither any green thing, neither any tree; but only those men which have not the seal of God in their foreheads.

John alludes to the same scenario in which he described the angels who were commanded not to "*hurt*" or disturb the "*grass of the earth*" (the doctrines and precepts of men) or the "*trees*" (humankind) as was previously explained in the commentary of Revelation 7:2–3. The world is not given an understanding of the truth so that it continues to experience the effects of its actions and learn from them. The only ones who will not be "*hurt*" are those few who have an understanding of God and His mysteries and do His works— doing unto others. The rest will suffer from the effects of their works and those of their leaders ("*the locusts*").

Again the words of Jesus:

> *Behold, I give unto you power to tread on* **serpents and scorpions**, *and over all the power of the enemy: and nothing shall by any means hurt you.* (Luke 10:19)

9:5 And to **the locusts** it was given that they should not kill them, but that they should be tormented five months **until they are healed from their hurt**: and their torment was as the torment **from the tail** of a scorpion when he striketh a man.

Society has reached a point where the majority is lead by a few ("*locusts*") who control every aspect of life. They draw the borders of the land, issue and determine the value of money as well as the value of human life, and also decide what laws should and shouldn't be established to control those whose values they have set. The societies are set up in such a way, that in order to survive, every person must look out for him or herself—completely ignoring an environment of peace and joy guaranteed by following the *Royal Law* of Christ.

The emotional torment caused by the way humans are led by their leaders has truly "*hurt*" them. The leaders know they need those who follow them and give them power; thus (without killing them), they make the people dependent upon them (*"given that they should not kill them"*). People *"hurt"* others to stay alive in pursuit of their own personal desires in life as well as in consequence of serving their leaders. Because of their leaders and the way societies are set up, humans torment each other, they being the *"tail"* that John describes that *"striketh a man."*

John sets a time frame (*"five months"*) in which this *"torment"* would take place. Through the tribulation and *"torment"* that mortals experience, they will obtain knowledge of good and evil; in other words, what works for them and brings them peace and happiness and what does not—mostly experiencing what does not. This is a period in which we learn right from wrong by experiencing both, after which we are redeemed of our tribulation—relieved of our *"torment"*—after all the learning has taken place.

"Five months" is the figurative time frame John uses to describe this period of learning and suffering (*"torment"*). Based on the Jewish calendar of thirty days per month, this equates to *an hundred and fifty days*, after which an *angel* will come *"clothed...with a cloud...and a rainbow upon his head"* to relieve these torments (see Revelation 10:1).

John takes his symbolism from the story of Noah:

> *And GOD saw that the wickedness of man was great in the earth, and that every imagination of the thoughts of his heart was only evil continually. ...And God looked upon the earth, and, behold, it was corrupt; for all flesh had corrupted his way upon the earth.* (Genesis 6:5, 12)

> *And the waters prevailed upon the earth an **hundred and fifty days**. ...The fountains also of the deep and the windows of heaven were stopped, and the rain from heaven was restrained, And the waters returned from off the earth continually: and after the end of the **hundred and fifty days** the waters were abated.* (Genesis 7:24; 8:2–3)

*I do set my **bow in the cloud**, and it shall be for a token
of a covenant between me and the earth.* (Genesis 9:13)

Interestingly, the "*green grass and the trees*" were not "*hurt*" or "*killed*"
during the "*hundred and fifty days*" of the symbolic *Great Flood*, in which all
flesh was destroyed. (See commentary on Revelation 8:7.) During this time of
torment and tribulation, the false doctrines and precepts of men are not confounded, and are allowed to coexist with truth and flourish at the will of the
people, causing even more "*torment*" for those upon the earth, except for those
who know and understand the truth ("*the seal of God in their foreheads*").

9:6 And in those days shall men seek **relief from their torment**, and shall
not find it; and **because of the torment**, **they** shall desire to die, **but they
shall find no relief**, and death shall flee from them.

Depression and anxiety follow the pressures and stress of existence,
and have become a worldwide problem. The cause of this emotional state is
the deprivation of happiness and peace that all people seek, but cannot find,
in a world of constant wars and rumors of wars, political, economic, and
religious slavery in order to survive, abject poverty, and the effects of crime.
Legal and illegal drugs, both natural and synthetic, become the refuge of both
young and old, rich and poor, bond and free, relieving them of a never-ending
"*torment*" that only ends upon death. The "*locusts/scorpions*" (the world's
leaders, teachers, and guides), though they torment the people, do not want
their "*tail*" (followers) dead, otherwise their kingdoms, income, and power
would come to naught.

9:7 And the shapes of the locusts were like unto horses **and their riders
were** prepared unto battle; and on **the** heads **of the riders** were as it were
crowns like gold, and their faces were as the faces of men.

John has already introduced the use of "*horses*" and "*riders*" to
illustrate the actions and effects of the human race on the natural world
(see commentary on Revelation 6). Here John further describes the
"*locusts*" by taking his figurative expressions from the prophet Nahum:

There shall the fire devour thee; the sword shall cut thee off, it shall eat thee up like the cankerworm: make thyself many as the cankerworm, **make thyself many as the locusts.** **Thou hast multiplied thy merchants above the stars of heaven:** *the cankerworm spoileth, and flieth away. Thy crowned are as the locusts, and thy captains as the great grasshoppers, which camp in the hedges in the cold day, but when the sun ariseth they flee away, and their place is not known where they are. Thy shepherds slumber, O king of Assyria: thy nobles shall dwell in the dust: thy people is scattered upon the mountains, and no man gathereth them. There is no healing of thy bruise; thy wound is grievous: all that hear the bruit of thee shall clap the hands over thee: for upon whom hath not thy wickedness passed continually?* (Nahum 3:15–19)

Nahum unlocks the mystery of the *locusts* and their *torment* when he refers to the great number of merchants the locusts have created ("*multiplied*"). He is explicit in writing of "*thy crowned are as the locusts,*" which John expresses as, "*on their heads...were as it were crowns of gold, and their faces where as the faces of men.*" In other words, John and Nahum are describing the powers that lead the people upon the earth that back the corporations, businesses, and industries (or whatever name they might have gone by in former times). To keep anyone else in check who might rise up against their way of *multiplying the merchants,* or doing business as usual, these locusts are "*prepared unto battle*"—ready and willing to go to war to protect the secret combinations of moguls, corporations, businesses, and government, all which give them their true power.

9:8 And they had **long** hair as the hair of women, and their teeth were as the teeth of **young** lions.

In the commentary for Revelation 6:12, *hair* is given as a symbolic part of the body that receives revelation and inspiration from God. "*Long hair*" was given in the allegoric story of Samson as that which gave him his great strength and power. Hair is used to cover the head, and unlike the men, the Jewish women were commanded to cover theirs:

> *Every man praying or prophesying, having his head cov-*
> *ered, dishonoureth his head. But every woman that*
> *prayeth or prophesieth with her head uncovered dishon-*
> *oureth her head: for that is even all one as if she were*
> *shaven.* (I Corinthians 11:4–5)

According to Jewish custom and belief, women were not permitted to receive revelation and inspiration from God. Thus, they were to keep their heads covered during meetings and other religious settings where revelation and inspiration was (supposedly) coming from God.

John uses this Jewish belief and custom to describe the *"locusts"* (leaders of humankind) as those who receive no revelation or inspiration from God (*"as the hair of women"*) though their countenance (*length of their hair*) shows power and authority.

The male lion has a long mane indicative of his power within the pride. Male lions protect their own, run off any competition, and kill as they wish—sometimes even members of their own pride, and especially the young cubs. When a hunger needs to be satisfied, the *king of beasts* eats first before all others. True prophets, in lieu of describing how the leaders of the people acquire what they need to sustain their lives, have often used the term *"teeth of young lions."* Lions use their teeth to hunt and kill what they need to eat. Likewise, the leaders of the world use their *"teeth"* to sustain their kingly lifestyles, which upon doing so, corrupt every other aspect of balance and equality in the societal structures of humankind.

The prophets saw the day when the Lord would *"break the teeth of the lions,"* bringing equality and abundance to *all* the inhabitants of the earth; thus debasing the rich and causing the poor to rejoice:

> *By the blast of God they perish, and by the breath of his*
> *nostrils are they consumed. The roaring of the lion, and*
> *the voice of the fierce lion, and the **teeth of the young***
> ***lions, are broken**.* (Job 4:9–10)

*My soul is among lions: and I lie even among them that
are set on fire, even the sons of men, whose teeth are spears
and arrows, and their tongue a sharp sword.* **Break their
teeth, O God, in their mouth: break out the great teeth
of the young lions,** *O Lord.* (Psalms 57:4; 58:6)

9:9 And they had breastplates, as it were breastplates of iron; and the
sound of their wings was as the sound of chariots of many horses running
to battle.

Prophets have used the term *"breastplates"* as a part of certain
clothing worn to illustrate the *intent* of the wearer.

*For **he put on righteousness as a breastplate**, and an
helmet of salvation upon his head; and he put on the garments of vengeance for clothing, and was clad with zeal as
a cloak.* (Isaiah 59:17)

During battle, *breastplates* were worn to protect the vital organs
of the bearer from an enemy's attack. According to the Law of Moses, a
breastplate was made of *cloth* and worn by the High Priest who was given
the authority and supposed power of God to lead and judge the people.
Its dimensions and construction were given in exact specifications
according to the symbolism of the law. It is important to keep in mind
that the Israelites were not living the *Higher Law* of God, which is to do
unto others what you would want done unto you, but were given a *lower
law* of strict ordinances and sacrifices to keep their minds focused on
something rather than their desires to worship the *"golden calf."*

Instead of a breastplate of cloth (representative of a warm and
peaceful covering devoid of the symbols of physical strength or aggression),
John presents the *"locusts"* as having *"breastplates of iron."* This symbolizes the heaviness and hardness of the judgments, burdens, and mistruths of
the leaders that weigh heavily on the people of the earth. This is given in
contrast to the breastplate of Christ which provides the opposite:

*Come unto me, all ye that labour and are **heavy laden**, and I will give you rest. Take my yoke upon you, and learn of me; for I am meek and lowly in heart: and ye shall find rest unto your souls. For my yoke is easy, and my **burden is light**.* (Matthew 11:28–30)

The "*locusts*" use their power ("*wings*") and *ironclad* imposition of will to bring the people into wars and uprisings ("*the sound of chariots of many horses running to battle*"), further causing the "*torment*" and "*hurt*" that John again describes in the next verse.

9:10 And they had tails like unto scorpions, and there were stings in their tails **which hurt the men upon the earth**; and their power was to hurt men five months.

John again reiterates that the cause of humanity's problems come from compliant people ("*tails*") following their leaders and doing their bidding, *hurting* and bringing pain one upon another. Though few in number, the leaders of the earth would have no power or means to hurt others, if it were not for the power given them by their followers ("*in their tails*"). Giving this power to their leaders, the people have brought the torment they feel upon themselves—which is as "*the sting of a scorpion.*" And this *torment* will last as long as mortals continue the process of learning from their experience and mistakes (the cleansing through the "*five months*" as explained in verse 5 above.)

9:11 And they had a king **who ruled** over them, which is the angel of the bottomless pit, whose name in the Hebrew tongue is Abaddon, but in the Greek tongue hath his name Apollyon.

It has already been established that John used the term "*name*" as a figurative expression of the works of the person who is given the "*name.*" In this instance, the "*name*" (works) of the "*king*" who rules over the people of the earth (the *king* is the flesh, or *Lucifer*, or human nature, which controls the works of all people) is **destruction** and **hell**. A proper translation of the words "*Abaddon*" and "*Apollyon*," which words John chose to use to *name* the *king*, literally mean **death** and **destruction**. In other words, the *king* of man is his flesh, or his human nature, which motivates and controls all of his works.

In following our human natures, we create emotional stress and torment (*hell*), and bring inequality and destruction upon each other by the strength of our own arms. Humankind engages in all manner of war and contention in order to protect our property, families, borders, and rights. Those who do not believe as we do, and who might live their lives according to foreign ways that we do not understand, but which we fear might change our own beliefs, are looked upon as enemies of our truths, justifying the hatred and destruction we bring upon them.

Our *flesh* is the "*king who rules over*" us. Human nature indeed creates **destruction** and **hell** for us all.

> *Know ye not, that to whom* [the king] *ye yield yourselves servants to obey, his servants ye are to whom ye obey; whether of sin unto death, or of obedience unto righteousness? But God be thanked, that ye were the servants of sin, but ye have obeyed from the heart that form of doctrine which was delivered you. Being then made free from sin, ye became the servants of righteousness. I speak after the manner of men because of the **infirmity of your flesh**: for as ye have yielded your members servants to uncleanness and to iniquity unto iniquity; even so now yield your members servants to righteousness unto holiness.* (Romans 6:16–19)

> *Love not the world, neither the things that are in the world. If any man love the world, the love of the Father is not in him. For all that is in the world, the **lust of the flesh**, and the lust of the eyes, and the pride of life, is not of the Father, but is of the world.* (I John 2:15–16)

9:12 One woe is past; and, behold, there come two woes more hereafter.

The three *woes* mentioned in *Revelation* 8:13 give us an idea of the spiritual or emotional torment that affects the peace and happiness of our existence. With the blowing of the *fifth trumpet* (warning), John has presented the idea that when human beings are driven by the lusts and desires of their natural state, they create this torment for themselves. This is done by giving power to those who create an atmosphere conducive to the pursuit of human nature (*Lucifer*), which in and of itself has always been an enemy of peace and happiness (*God*).

Since the figurative "*fall of Adam,*" (which is the same figurative expression that John uses as the "*star which fell from heaven upon the earth*" in Revelation 9:1), human beings in their natural state have become enemies to God. They will be forever and ever unless they yield to the enticements of their spiritual natures, and put off their natural states and become *Saints* through the teachings of the One anointed to make sure we become as a little child. This entails becoming submissive, meek, humble, patient, full of love, and willing to submit to all things which are inflicted upon us, even as a child submits to his father.

The *sixth trumpet,* or *woe,* warns us of the greatest culprit in the downfall of our spiritual natures throughout the many years of our learning and development upon the earth. This culprit *slays* us spiritually in the flesh (*a third part*) more than any other *woe* yet described. After we learn of this culprit (the enemy of our peace and happiness) the next and final *woe* is the spiritual shock and feeling of embarrassment most will experience—which will be compounded exceedingly because of all *the warnings* we have received—once the One assigned to our solar system comes again to earth to reveal the truth.

9:13 And **before** the sixth angel sounded, I heard a voice **come** from **between** the four horns of the golden altar which is before God,

The "*golden altar*" is the world, which is figuratively presented as always "*before God.*" The "*four horns*" are at the four corners of the altar, symbolic of the four corners of the earth. The earth was laid out precisely as intended by the Creators according to the laws of nature given for this type of creation. Thus, in symbolic representation of this, the altar was meticulously and precisely constructed for the rebellious Jews:

> *Thou son of man, shew the house to the house of Israel, that they may be ashamed of their iniquities: and let them measure the pattern. And if they be ashamed of all that they have done, shew them the form of the house, and the fashion thereof, and the goings out thereof, and the comings in thereof, and all the forms thereof, and all the ordinances thereof, and all the forms thereof, and all the laws thereof: and write it in their sight, that they may keep the whole form thereof, and all the ordinances thereof, and do them. This is the law of the house; Upon the top of the mountain the whole limit thereof round about shall be most holy. Behold, this is the law of the house. And these are the measures of the altar after the cubits: The cubit is a cubit and an hand breadth; even the bottom shall be a cubit, and the breadth a cubit, and the border thereof by the edge thereof round about shall be a span: and this shall be the higher place of the altar. And from the bottom upon the ground even to the lower settle shall be two cubits, and the breadth one cubit; and from the lesser settle even to the greater settle shall be four cubits, and the breadth one cubit. So the altar shall be four cubits; and from **the altar and upward shall be four horns**.* (Ezekiel 43:10–15)

Before the announcement of the *sixth angel*, there was no indication of the "*four horns*" being mentioned, because many of the things presented figuratively by John were isolated to specific regions of the world known to humankind, and were not worldwide events. Before the *sixth trumpet* sounds, or before the time of the opening of the *sixth seal*, there is no mention of human works being represented in all four corners of the earth.

Though the angels were aware of the exact dimensions of all of the lands of the earth, mortals did not realize that the world was literally divided into two parts, or hemispheres, until the latter times just before the opening of the *seventh seal*, which figuratively occurs in *Revelation*, chapter 10.

What the angel is announcing is a worldwide event that affects the four corners (*"four horns"*) of the world.

9:14 Saying to the sixth angel which had the trumpet, *Sound the warning that* the four angels which are *still* bound in *the bottomless pit which is near unto* the great river Euphrates *shall be* loose.

John has already shown us that the term *"angel"* does not always represent righteousness (see verse 11). However, it is always representative of power and knowledge. Whenever *"four angels"* are mentioned, it is given to mean that whatever the angels are doing, they perform it on a worldwide scale. The *four angels* mentioned here are not righteous angels sent from God, but are from *"the bottomless pit,"* or the effects of human nature.

The city of Babylon, situated next to the Euphrates River, has been used by prophets to describe the great worldliness and wickedness of humankind. Babylon was the first city to become renown worldwide as a center of advanced human expression and desire. It is known for the rise of the world's first urban centers and monarchies, together with the first attempts to write (in cuneiform script), build temples, create monumental works of art, organize a government administration, and build empires.

The Babylonians are known as the "inventors of civilization" and left their influence on many neighboring states. Their progress in literature, philosophy, and astronomy by their ancient scientists was unmatched before or after them, until later when the Roman Empire came about. They were the inventors of one of the world's most accurate calendars, and their science and technology became the foundation of knowledge of most other civilizations of that time.

But in spite of all of these technological, scientific, artistic and literary advancements, the Babylonian culture was one of the most selfish and corrupt societies ever created (until modern times), which led people further and further away from the principles of equality and doing unto others what one would want done unto them.

Throughout the remainder of his *Revelation*, John uses the term "*Babylon*" to express the worldliness and wickedness of the world. Here John is telling us that there will be widespread wickedness coming out of the "*bottomless pit*" and covering the whole earth as did Babylon, which sat "*near unto the great river Euphrates.*"

9:15 And the **key was given to the sixth angel to loose the** four angels **bound in the bottomless pit**, which were prepared for an hour, and a day, and a month, and a year, for to slay the third part of men.

Up until the early part of the 1800's, very little technological and scientific advancements were made beyond what the world had experienced for thousands of years. Then, within just a few decades, humans came up with advancements that would make the ancient Babylonians appear uncivilized and underdeveloped.

Until this time, the angels kept humankind from discovering and understanding certain aspects of natural law that would permit them to make these miraculous advancements upon the earth. In essence, this knowledge and power was kept under *lock* and *key* until "*an hour, and a day, and a month, and a year*" that was "*prepared*" to allow humankind the opportunity to experience what happens when this knowledge is given to the world and misused by those who are ruled by their "*king*" (lusts and fleshly desires).

The angels knew that once humans were allowed to have an understanding of the power of the laws of nature, science, and technology, because of their flesh (human nature), they would harness their use. This would lead to promoting greater destruction and misery upon themselves and on the natural earth upon which they live ("*slay the third part of men*").

John saw the effects of this technology on the earth, and understood the reasons why the Creator would not allow free-willed beings to have this incredible power until the latter days. He knew that it would have been calamitous to the people if they had been given these technologies too soon, having never experienced what would happen as a result of their use and misuse. Humans did not understand right from wrong because they had not yet experienced all of the consequences of making the *wrong* choices.

John understood that humankind would be allowed to experience this technology at the end of times, so they could not advance far enough to completely destroy each other and the earth before the Lord came in his glory to save them from themselves.

9:16 And the number of the army of the horsemen were two hundred thousand thousand and ***their end I could not see, but*** I heard the number of them.

John is telling us here that most of the people of the world will be given the power and ability to use these great technological and scientific advancements. In earlier times, only the rich and powerful (*"locusts"*) partook of the things coming from *"the bottomless pit,"* causing those who followed them to suffer because of their selfishness. But in the latter times, *everyone* gets to partake, some more than others.

John reflects that the number of people is so great that he cannot determine it from viewing how many there actually are. But he *"heard the number of them,"* symbolizing that there are a finite number of people upon the earth participating in the latter days, and experiencing the miracles of modern advancements in technology, science, art, and literature.

These people, however, are the *"horsemen"* of the angels of the bottomless pit. Given what John figuratively expresses as a *horse* and its *rider*, we see that he is presenting that the people of the earth are all participating in the wickedness perpetuated by the advancements of the latter days.

One cannot argue the fact that in modern times there are few, very few, who do unto others what they would want others to do unto them. Their actions and intents are descriptively given in John's continuing presentation of this time period.

9:17 And thus I saw the horses in the vision, and them that sat on them ***rode thereupon***, having breastplates of fire, and of jacinth, and brimstone: and the heads of the horses were as the heads of lions; and out of their mouths issued fire and smoke and brimstone.

Instead of a breastplate of cloth (peace), or one of iron (heavy burdens), these *horsemen* have *"breastplates of fire,"* symbolizing their *burning* intent to use their power and knowledge (*"fire"*) to consume the things of the world upon their lusts. Their intent of having the fine things of the world is given by the presentation of *"jacinth."* The smelly, gross repugnancy of these lusts and desires of their hearts is represented here as the effects of *"brimstone,"* which is another word for sulfur.

To further understand what John is trying to present here, a review of what John means by the presentation of a *horse* and *rider* is needed. (See commentary on Revelation 6:1.)

In this figurative presentation given by John, the *"horsemen"* have the *"horses"* do the killing. Using the expression *"heads of lions"* to describe the horses' heads, John tells us that this power is used without regard to any just purpose, and only because they possess the power and can use it as they will, and as expressed above in the prophets' negative use of the term *"lion"* (see commentary on Revelation 9:8).

9:18 By these three was the third part of men killed, by the fire, and by the smoke, and by the brimstone, which issued out of their mouths.

The burning desire (*"fire"*) humans have for the things of the world creates a *"smoke,"* which blinds their minds to the reality of what their desires and lusts really do to them and those around them (*"the third part of men killed"*), thus creating the tribulations of the world (the putrid smell given as *"brimstone"*). These things are the result of the flatteries and perceptions of modern media invented by those who gain when others accept the words which come *"out of their mouths"* according to the appetites, lusts, and covetousness for material things which the people have cultivated. (This is further explained in the next verse.)

9:19 For their power is in their mouth, and in their tails; for their tails were like unto serpents, and **each of their tails** had heads, and with them they do hurt.

In other words, the laws of nature (such as electronics in the use of phones and computers, nuclear energy, avionics and fuel powered trans-portation, and all manner of technology which is used at the command of the *rider*) are tamed, bridled, and used to *"kill"* the people of the earth. Not just spiritually this time, which was previously represented by John using the term "*hurt*" instead of "*kill*," but literally killing millions of human beings as well as the natural earth upon which they live by the technology and advancements they are allowed to experience.

With modern technology, the powers that be upon the earth do not need other humans to perform much, or most, of the work that is required to create their personal wealth and maintain their power. Therefore, unlike the "*locusts*," which only need the "*sting*" of their "*tails*" to give them power, these "*horsemen*" have their "*horses*" "*kill*" anyone who might stand in their way. John soon reveals that the "*horses*" have power both in "*their mouths*" and in "*their tails*," which "*tails*" also have "*mouths*" that spew out "*fire, smoke, and brimstone*."

The wealthy give power from behind the scenes to politicians and others who belong to a circle of individuals chosen for their public skills. These so chosen, use patriotism and rhetorical words of promise to follow the agendas of the wealthy elite. The words and actions delivered to the people are meant to pacify and to gain the respect of those who are expected to follow them ("*their power is in their mouth*"). The "*tails*," therefore, are given power virtually equal to the main "*heads*" to destroy the peace and happiness that would exist if the people were treated as equals and given equal opportunity to pursue happiness. There is as much power in their "*tails*" as in the "*heads of the tails*," wherein these are also used to ruin peace and happiness being just as successful at destroying as the main "*head*."

Bureaucracy is the "*tails like unto serpents with heads*" expressed by John. Serpents have always symbolized knowledge and wisdom; yet the use of this knowledge is to "*hurt*" instead of promote peace.

Jesus advised his disciples: "*Behold, I send you forth as sheep in the midst of wolves: be ye therefore wise as serpents, and harmless as doves.*" (Matthew 10:16)

Adolf Hitler was one of many modern examples of a *wise serpent*. (When the truth is known, the Founding Fathers of the United States will also be revealed as very *wise serpents*.) Hitler was a small-framed man, yet from his mouth came power and words that elicited allegiance and obedience. He did not do the killing himself. It was done by the bureaucracy who followed ("*tails*") him and used the power of their commands ("*their heads*") to destroy peace and happiness. These "*tails*" also belong to business, law, academia, and the entertainment "*horses*" that destroy the peace and happiness of our world. All the while, they are promoting, through flattery ("*power is in their mouth*"), their own agendas of acquiring more wealth and power.

9:20 And the rest of the men which were not killed by these plagues ***still did*** not ***repent*** of the works of their hands, that they should not worship devils, and idols of gold, and silver, and brass, and stone, and of wood: which neither can see, nor hear, nor walk:

As explained above, the knowledge of technology has given great power to the people of the earth. The advancements in all areas of life have attained unimaginable levels. But even though humans seem to have advanced and have the power to create the perfect society, there is less love, less respect, less forgiveness, and less tolerance in the modern world than at any other time in history.

With the technology that exits today, there is absolutely no reason why there should not be enough free food, clothing, shelter, and health care for every human being upon the earth. Instead of serving the lusts and desires of human nature, which are "*idols of gold, and silver, and brass, and stone, and wood,*" we should be serving a God who can "*see, hear, and walk.*" If we knew God, we would know what He has commanded us to do: Do unto others, what you would have them do unto you. If we lived by this *Law*, there would be neither inequality or poverty on the earth today.

9:21 Neither ***did*** they ***repent*** of their murders, nor of their sorceries, nor of their fornication, nor of their thefts.

Even when we can clearly see that the "*horsemen*" and the "*horses*" (of whom we were warned by the "*sixth angel's trumpet*") are continually causing the problems that "*plague*" our peace and happiness, we stand by and do nothing ("*neither did they repent*") to stop the inequality and poverty that is spreading unabated throughout the entire world. These "*plagues*" are threatening the eminent destruction of the whole human race, and the world created for them.

The human race is being lulled into carnal security where none realizes the wickedness that is taking place. People believe that because they, their families, and their country prosper, that all is well. In the blanket of our imagined security, we continue to abuse each other for the sake of our own gain, which is what John figuratively expresses as *"murders, sorceries, fornication, and thefts."*

Truly this *"woe"* and warning is greater than all others. Mortal humans have no hope of surviving this *"woe"* unless someone more powerful and wiser than any other rescues them. This Annointed One will do this by *"having...the key of the bottomless pit and a great chain in his hand"* to take the perpetrator of all these woes and *"cast him into the bottomless pit, and shut him up, and set a seal upon him"* (see Revelation 20:1–3).

Chapter

REVELATION
UNFOLDED

10:1 And I saw another mighty angel come down from heaven, clothed *as it were* with a cloud *in the day of rain; and he appeared as if he were covered that all upon the earth could not see his face*; and a rainbow *shown from the crown which* was upon his head, and his face was as it were the sun, and his feet as pillars of fire; *and from his countenance came forth a great light upon the earth.*

The *seventh trumpet* to sound, or the *seventh woe,* is an even greater threat to humankind than any of the preceding warnings. This warning gives no portend of demise to a person's physical being, because once a person is dead, the pain, tribulation, and torment of life is over. This final "*woe*" becomes the most dreaded of all, because of the figurative "*never-ending torment*" that will be experienced. It is the time when all people must face the truth of reality, and judge themselves. This will be done according to what they have allowed themselves to believe and understand in connection with the way they have lived their lives, and how they have done unto others. During this time (*the voice of the seventh angel*), the "*mystery of God*" that has been known by all prophets, and understood by "the elect," will be revealed in its fullness.

The Christ, who is the Messiah—the one appointed to teach us how to live at peace with each other upon the planets of this solar system—is the One who will be the "*voice of the seventh angel*." He is the one about whom the "*seventh trumpet*" would have warned the world of his coming had it been sounded. However, John makes no indication that this final *seventh angel's trumpet* has sounded, as he did specifically with the previous *six angels*. This final woe will come without warning, when the world is least expecting it.

Thus spoke Jesus in parable to his disciples:

> *Watch therefore: for ye know not what hour your Lord doth come. But know this, that if the goodman of the house had known in what watch the thief would come, he would have watched, and would not have suffered his house to be broken up. Therefore be ye also ready: for in such an hour as ye think not the Son of man cometh.* (Matthew 24:42–44)

John continues his descirption of the earth's cleansing by referencing the allegorical story of the Great Flood, which ends with a rainbow symbolizing the covenant between God and man that the earth will **never** be physically destroyed again.

John shows this "*mighty angel*" (John *only* refers to *this* angel as "*mighty*") coming "*down from heaven*," which the inhabitants of the earth do not recognize. Even though it has rained upon the earth (revelation and understanding given to the world by true prophets), the "*clouds*" of darkness have shaded it from the "*light*" of the sun, and the people do not know, nor do they understand, Christ as he truly is. Thus, John presents him as being "*clothed as it were with a cloud in the day of rain; and he appeared as if he were covered that all those upon the earth* **could not see his face**."

John borrows this metaphor from Ezekiel:

*As the appearance of the bow that is in the **cloud in the day of rain**, so was the appearance of the brightness round about. This was **the appearance of the likeness of the glory of the Lord**. And when I saw it, I fell upon my face, and I heard a voice of one that spake.* (Ezekiel 1:28)

When the Christ appears in glory, his power will be over all the kingdoms of the earth, represented by the "*crown*" upon his head made of the same gems as the "Breastplate of Judgment," in which are woven the 12 gems (representing the different tribes of Israel) as explained fully in the commentary on Revelation 4:3.

John figuratively expresses that when Christ's "*face*" comes from behind the "*cloud*," and is revealed to the world, it is "*as it were the sun*" because of the light and truth which he shall give to the people of the earth, or the light shining through the *twelve gems* that creates "*a rainbow*" illumination.

Wherever his "*feet*" take him upon the earth, he will bring a light to a world lying in darkness, and which will cause the people to burn ("*fire*") from within ("*feet as pillars of fire*"). Throughout the *Old Testament*, the prophets used a "*pillar of fire*" to describe the Lord leading the people through the night:

*Yet thou in thy manifold mercies forsookest them not in the wilderness: the pillar of the cloud departed not from them by day, to lead them in the way; neither **the pillar of fire** by night, to show them light, and the way wherein they should go.* (Nehemiah 9:19)

10:2 And he had in his hand a little book open **which contained that which was sealed from the foundation of the earth**; and he set his right foot upon the sea, and his left foot on the earth, **even that his whole countenance did fill the earth, even that there was not a part thereof that was not filled with his light**.

John presents figuratively that in Christ's return to the earth ("*mighty angel come down from heaven*"), he will assure that the instructions of what is to be done next with the earth and its people (as contained in the "*Book of Life*"), are being followed and completed as written therein. The expression that "*he set his right foot upon the sea, and his left foot on the earth*" tells us that the whole earth will have knowledge of his arrival, and *all* will know that the world has been placed in his power. He will universally and recognizably establish his stance (*feet*) as a "*pillar of fire.*"

Modern communication technology makes it very easy to understand how one extraterrestrial being might arrive on this planet in one particular location, and at the same time, enable the whole world to tune in to what he says and does.

10:3 And ***he opened the seventh seal and*** cried with a loud voice, as when a lion roareth ***and maketh all afraid***; and when he had cried, ***it was as if*** seven thunders uttered their voices.

Here John presents, figuratively, the ushering in of the Millennial Reign of Christ upon the earth. Once Christ has established his presence, he will spread the truth to the whole earth, and tell the people what needs to be done to establish the proper society so that all can experience peace, happiness, and joy. What he will reveal to the people will be given with power and authority, causing all to submit to his rule:

> *I have sworn by myself, the word is gone out of my mouth in righteousness, and shall not return, That unto me every knee shall bow, every tongue shall swear. Surely, shall one say, in the LORD have I righteousness and strength: even to him shall men come; and all that are incensed against him shall be ashamed.* (Isaiah 45:23–24)

The "*seven thunders*" represent the "*loud voice*" of Christ resonating like a "*lion's roar*" throughout the seven continents of the world. Every inhabitant on planet earth will hear what he has to say.

10:4 And when the seven thunders had uttered their voices, I was about to write *that which they spoke*; and I heard a voice from heaven saying unto me, seal up those things which the seven thunders uttered, and write them not, *for these things shall not come forth unto the children of men until the end of times*.

All true prophets of God know what is going to occur during the Millennial Reign of Christ upon the earth. They know the time frame, the procedure, and all the processes and changes that must take place in order to change a world of chaos and inequality—characterized by humans who do not do unto others as they would have others do unto them—into one of peace and order. John is relating that he was shown what was going to occur (*"those things which the seven thunders uttered"*), but was not allowed to explain to the people in his day, in plainness.

One of the main reasons why he was not allowed to write what specifically takes place during the Millennium is because mortals were not to be given this information at that time. Denying them the truth of these things would allow them the opportunity to experience the full effects of *not* living the way they should, so that *when* they are shown the proper way to live by Christ, they will awaken and realize the truth and effectiveness of his teachings and instructions.

All prophets are likewise commanded to withhold the knowledge they receive of the mysteries of God until the time appointed to reveal them to the people:

> *And at that time shall Michael stand up, the great prince which standeth for the children of thy people: and there shall be a time of trouble, such as never was since there was a nation even to that same time: and at that time thy people shall be delivered, every one that shall be found written in the book. And many of them that sleep in the dust of the earth shall awake, some to everlasting life, and some to shame and everlasting contempt. And they that be wise shall shine as the brightness of the firmament; and they that turn many to righteousness as the stars for*

*ever and ever. But thou, O Daniel, **shut up the words, and seal the book, even to the time of the end**: many shall run to and fro, and knowledge shall be increased. And I heard, but I understood not: then said I, O my Lord, what shall be the end of these things? And he said, Go thy way, Daniel: **for the words are closed up and sealed till the time of the end**. Many shall be purified, and made white, and tried; but the wicked shall do wickedly: and **none of the wicked shall understand; but the wise shall understand**.* (Daniel 12:1–4, 8–9)

10:5 And the **mighty** angel which I saw stand upon the sea and upon the earth lifted up his hand to heaven,

10:6 And sware by **Him** that liveth for ever and ever, who created heaven, and the things that therein are, and the earth, and the things that therein are, and the sea, and the things which are therein, that there should be time no longer, *for the time, times, and half of time have passed. And thus I heard the voice of the seventh thunder speak*.

In this explanation, John sees Christ in the attitude of swearing an oath to the Father that His work will now be done on earth as it is in heaven. His symbolism is borrowed from Daniel:

*Then I Daniel looked, and, behold, there stood other two, the one on this side of the bank of the river, and the other on that side of the bank of the river. And one said to the man clothed in linen, which was upon the waters of the river, How long shall it be to the end of these wonders? And I heard the man clothed in linen, which was upon the waters of the river, when **he held up his right hand and his left hand unto heaven, and sware by him that liveth for ever** that it shall be for a **time, times, and an half**; and when he shall have accomplished to scatter the power of the holy people, all these things shall be finished.* (Daniel 12:5–7)

The Father's work is to fulfill the covenant that He has made with all of us who were created by Him; who were guaranteed that we will *all* eventually experience joy and happiness forever as we exercise our free agency according to our individual desires.

God does not create beings just to leave them in circumstances that would force them to experience suffering and torment without an end, as humans now do upon this earth—only a sadistic Creator would do this. We were created to experience the ultimate balance of nature—happiness. Since this happiness comes from our relationships with each other, and also our ability to interact with our surrounding environs, the covenant Christ is swearing to uphold (*"lifted up his hand"*) is that he will create the proper environment, both socially and physically, so that in the end, we can fulfill the measure of our creation and live in peace and happiness eternally.

The earth has gone on long enough experiencing the effects of the *"locusts"* and the *"horsemen and their horses."* These times of turmoil have been presented figuratively, in their proper timetable as understood by the prophet Daniel, and thereafter borrowed by John, as the *"time, times, and a dividing of time."* A thorough explanation of *"time, times, and half of time"* will be given in the commentary of chapter 11.

> *And he shall speak great words against the most High,*
> *and shall wear out the saints of the most High, and think*
> *to change times and laws: and they shall be given into his*
> *hand until* **a time and times and the dividing of time**.
> *But the judgment shall sit, and they shall take away his*
> *dominion, to consume and to destroy it unto the end. And*
> *the kingdom and dominion, and the greatness of the king-*
> *dom under the whole heaven, shall be given to the people*
> *of the saints of the most High, whose kingdom is an ever-*
> *lasting kingdom, and all dominions shall serve and obey*
> *him. Hitherto is the end of the matter.* (Daniel 7:25–28)

Christ will end these times of turmoil by revealing the truth to the inhabitants of the world according to the established timetable, unless that timetable is shortened in righteousness because the inhabitants of earth have become righteous on their own accord. The truths he will teach will finally set humankind free from all the falsehoods and deceptions that have continually beset them. They will also be relieved from the "*stings*" and "*torments*" delivered by unrighteous leaders who know nothing of the reality of God's covenant of everlasting peace and happiness—which *is* the mystery of God.

10:7 But in the days of the voice of the seventh **trumpet**, when **it** shall begin to sound, **then shall** the mystery of God be **revealed**, as he hath declared to his servants the prophets.

During the "*days*" of Christ, the people of the earth will finally receive the truth concerning the heavens, the earth, and all there is to know about who they are, why they are, and how they came to exist. Unfortunately for the world—and its mighty leaders with their great advancements in science and technology, their pretended knowledge, their religions, their spiritual divinations and imaginations—all these "*locusts*" will be revealed for what they truly are: foolish and selfish mortals who imagined these things up in their hearts to satisfy the lusts of their flesh.

There are no mysteries to those who know truth and reality. Mysteries, theories, speculations, vain imaginations, perceptions, opinions, and beliefs are invented by those who do not know how, why, and when life came into existence. Science's never-ending determination to try to understand and explain reality, leads its followers in a constant race that will continue until One who actually knows what reality is, appears to teach those who seek truth.

Religion is worse than science in its speculative efforts to satisfy the human ego. Religion has created the impetus for people to search how, why, and who they are without having the proper tools to help the people discover the truth for themselves. Religious leaders have convinced their followers that they ("*the locusts*") are chosen by God to teach people truth and lead them on the right path. Yet, neither the religions of the world nor any of their leaders have been able to fulfill the *covenant of the Father* in providing the earth's inhabitants with the happiness and peace He has promised them. Religion and science destroy peace and happiness because of the action and precepts of their "*locusts and horsemen*" who torment the people.

There is no precept of religion or science that comprehends or properly explains *reality*—which is things as they were, as they are, and as they are to come. Science is a type of religion, just as religion is a type of science, wherein the mystery of life *remains* a mystery to those who don't understand it, but pretend to. The aim of both science and religion is one in the same in trying to come to a logical conclusion about why, how, and when humans came into existence.

The only ones who have known true reality and can teach it properly, are those whom others have so named *"prophets of God"*:

> *Surely the Lord God will do nothing, but revealeth his secret unto his servants the prophets.* (Amos 3:7)

These prophets were not received or appreciated by the religions of the world, and science would have nothing to do with their simple message of what the human race needs to do to find the peace and happiness it desires.

Whether their message of truth was given in the Orient by the Buddha, the Middle East by Mohammed, to the ancient Greeks by Socrates, or to the arrogant Jews by a young man, it was the same. This Jewish man, who owned nothing, and was killed because he spoke against the religion to which he and his family belonged, taught the very same message: in order to realize peace and happiness, we must do unto others what we would want them to do unto us—nothing more, nothing less.

The prophet to whom the entire world will listen when the *"voice of his trumpet sounds"* is not like the religious and secular leaders of the world. This prophet does not want to be worshipped or set above another, but considers himself a servant to all:

> *And, behold, one came and said unto him, Good Master, what good thing shall I do, that I may have eternal life? And he said unto him, Why callest thou me good? there is none good but one, that is, God: but if thou wilt enter into life, keep the commandments.* (Matthew 19:16–17)

And I fell at his feet to worship him. And he said unto me, See thou do it not: I am thy fellowservant, and of thy brethren that have the testimony which I gave unto you in the flesh as the man Jesus; worship God for that which He hath given you through me; for he who hath a testimony of that which I did as Jesus hath the spirit of prophecy. (Revelation 19:10)

And he said unto me, These sayings are faithful and true and have been hidden from the foundation of the world because of the wickedness of men; but the Lord God, who called the holy prophets, and who sent His angels to shew unto his servants all things which must shortly come to pass; hath commanded His prophets to write these things and seal them up until the last days before I come again into the world. Behold, I am Jesus Christ, the Son of God, and I come quickly. Therefore, blessed is he that keepeth the sayings of the prophets who have sealed up the prophecy of this book. And I John saw these things, and heard them. And when I had heard and seen, I fell down to worship before the feet of him who shewed me these things. Then saith he unto me, See thou do it not, but worship God who hath sent me; for I am thy fellowservant, and of thy brethren the prophets, and of them which keep the sayings of this book; and this book doth not teach a man to fall down and worship another, but it teacheth a man to worship God and keep His commandments in all things; and these are those things which have been sealed up to come forth unto the children of men. (Revelation 22:6–9)

The mystery of God will no longer be a mystery ("*the mystery of God shall be revealed*"), when the truth is finally brought to the world. And by this truth, we shall all be set free from the chains of hell with which the whole world is bound.

10:8 And the voice which I heard from heaven spake unto me again, and said, Go and take the little book which *was sealed with the seven seals and* is *now* open in the hand of the angel which standeth upon the sea and upon the earth.

John mentions a *"voice from heaven"* (see verse 4) commanding him to first, *"seal up"* the things which he knows, and then to *"take the little book"* from the hand of the angel, who is Christ. This refers to the way in which true prophets of God are called by those who are in charge of this solar system. The "Gods" have not only created Christ to fulfill a specific mission for the earth, but also have called other prophets to do particular works designed specifically for their times. John continues to describe this heavenly *calling*:

10:9 And I went unto the angel, and said unto him, Give me the little book. And he said unto me, Take it, and eat it up; and it shall make thy belly bitter, but it shall be in thy mouth sweet as honey.

10:10 And I took the little book out of the angel's hand, and ate it up; and it was in my mouth sweet as honey, *for that which I read brought much joy to my soul*; *but* as soon as I had eaten it, my belly was bitter.

The prophet Ezekiel put it this way:

And he said unto me, Son of man, I send thee to the children of Israel, to a rebellious nation that hath rebelled against me: they and their fathers have transgressed against me, even unto this very day. For they are impudent children and stiffhearted. I do send thee unto them; and thou shalt say unto them, Thus saith the Lord GOD. And they, whether they will hear, or whether they will forbear, (for they are a rebellious house), yet shall know that there hath been a prophet among them. And thou, son of man, be not afraid of them, neither be afraid of their words, though briers and thorns be with thee, and thou dost dwell among scorpions: be not afraid of their words, nor be dismayed at their looks, though they be a rebellious house. And thou shalt speak my words unto them, whether they will hear, or whether they will forbear: for they are most rebellious. But thou, son of man, hear what I say unto thee; Be not thou rebellious like that rebellious house: **open thy mouth, and eat that I give thee.** *And when I looked, behold, an* **hand was sent unto me; and, lo, a roll of a book was therein;** *And he spread it before me; and it was written within and without: and there was written therein lamentations, and mourning, and woe. Moreover he said unto me, Son of man,* **eat that thou findest; eat this roll, and go speak unto the house of Israel.** *So I opened my mouth, and he caused me to eat that roll. And he said unto me, Son of man, cause thy belly to eat, and fill thy bowels with this roll that I give thee. Then did I eat it; and it was in my mouth as honey for* **sweetness.** (Ezekiel 2:3–10; 3:1–3)

Prophets are "*fed*" the knowledge and understanding of the eternal plan of God. Though it has always been the same, this plan is unknown to the mortal world because of the inability of the human brain to recollect the recorded experiences in the molecules that make up their spirits. This fleshly brain is the veil through which most mortals cannot see (*remember*) while in mortality. The reason for this veil is so that we will have the opportunity to experience the opposite of God's eternal plan of happiness. If we could consciously recall everything our spirits have recorded throughout the eons of millenniums we have existed, we would not be prone to experience the bad, because we would know better.

Every prophet called of God to perform a specific work, must be called in the exact same manner as those before him, as will those after him. Prophets are usually male in gender, giving life to the world through their words, while the more refined and righteous females give life to the world through the birth of a child. All prophets pass through tribulation and rebellion against God before they are called. There has been only one prophet, who from his birth into mortality, did not rebel against God—Jesus Christ; he who could not sin because of the preprogrammed nature of his soul.

In order to keep the other prophets humbled and focused on the work of the Father, instead of on their own fleshly agendas, they are purposely weakened in the flesh in many ways. The story goes that Moses couldn't speak well, and many others were small of stature and uncomely to look upon. This kept them always aware that no matter how much they were given to know, they were *still nothing* and equal to all other people.

Before Jesus came to the people in his role as a prophet, he was preceded by John the Baptist. The Jews could accept John because he was plainly dressed in camel skins, "ate *locusts*" (ironic symbolism here) and lived in the desert. The Jews had a harder time accepting Jesus because he was seen as a beautiful man who dressed normally, had women following after him, and ate and drank with the sinners.

Except for Jesus Christ, all other prophets have passed through years of refinement and preparation until each has arrived, through the use of his own free will, at an emotional state of a broken heart and a contrite spirit. This is further brought upon each by the recognition of the wicked state in which the people of his particular culture live. Each humbles himself before God, and asks for a better understanding of truth. After a period of refinement, and if the supplicant has been chosen to perform a specific work, a Celestial Being will appear and take the veil away from his eyes through certain physical changes.

The prophet Daniel explains it well:

> And whiles I was speaking, and praying, and confessing
> my sin and the sin of my people Israel, and presenting my
> supplication before the LORD my God for the holy moun-
> tain of my God; Yea, whiles I was speaking in prayer,
> even the man Gabriel, whom I had seen in the vision at
> the beginning, being caused to fly swiftly, **touched me**
> about the time of the evening oblation. And he informed
> me, and talked with me, and said, O Daniel, I am now
> come forth **to give thee skill and understanding**. At

the beginning of thy supplications the commandment came forth, and I am come to shew thee; for thou art greatly beloved: therefore understand the matter, and consider the vision. (Daniel 9:20–23)

In order for this understanding to take place, or for the veil to be removed, a physical change must take place on a cellular level in the mortal brain of the prophet. An angel of God who has the knowledge, power, and technology to do so properly, does this "unveiling." John figuratively expresses this by showing that a "*voice from heaven*" did not actually teach him anything, but commanded him to do a *physical* act involving an angel (*take the book and eat it*).

A person might lose substantial memory after being struck violently in the head, thereby changing the physical structure of their brain. Prophets on the other hand, through actual physical contact with an exalted being, receive the ability to remember things *written in the book*. There is no other way to be called as a prophet of God.

Upon having the veil removed so that the eyes of their understanding are more fully opened, prophets rejoice in the great and wondrous plan of the Father in fulfilling His covenant *of happiness* with His creations. This is what is meant by "*it was in my mouth sweet as honey*." But as they go to preach the wonderful good news (*the gospel*), their knowledge becomes "*bitter*" because of the rejection due to the ignorance of the people.

Though it would seem fair of a God who is no respecter of persons to allow Celestial Beings to reveal themselves to *all* those who humble themselves properly with a broken heart and contrite spirit, doing so would negate the purpose of *the veil* and our mortal existence.

The veil allows us to live without a sure knowledge of God, so that we may become who and what we really are according to our individual desires of happiness, and not what we *think* God expects us to become. In other words, most people are good when the spotlight is on them, and when they are told everything they *should* do; but the truer nature of individual souls will shine when they are left to themselves with nobody else around who might influence them to be someone they really are not. Furthermore, if everyone had a sure knowledge of an afterlife of peace, tranquility, and happiness, and we realized that suicide was a choice, not a sin, how many of us would really hang around in the *hell* we have created for ourselves here?

This sure knowledge and instruction is only given to some (prophets) who are to perform specific missions. There are many other prophets and righteous men who become knowledgeable by listening to others who have been given the physical ability to know the mysteries of God:

> *But blessed are your eyes, for they see: and your ears, for they hear. For verily I say unto you, That many prophets and righteous men have desired to see those things which ye see, and have not seen them; and to hear those things which ye hear, and have not heard them.* (Matthew 13:16–17)

Jesus commended those who believe without a physical manifestation:

> *Jesus saith unto him, Thomas, because thou hast seen me, thou hast believed: blessed are they that have not seen, and yet have believed.* (John 20:29)

Speaking to "the elect," Peter said:

> *That the trial of your faith, being much more precious than of gold that perisheth, though it be tried with fire, might be found unto praise and honour and glory at the appearing of Jesus Christ: Whom having not seen, ye love; in whom, though now ye see him not, yet believing, ye rejoice with joy unspeakable and full of glory: Receiving the end of your faith, even the salvation of your souls. Of which salvation the prophets have inquired and searched diligently, who prophesied of the grace that should come unto you: Searching what, or what manner of time the Spirit of Christ which was in them did signify, when it testified beforehand the sufferings of Christ, and the glory that should follow. Unto whom it was revealed, that not unto themselves, but unto us they did minister the things, which are now reported unto you by*

them that have preached the gospel unto you with the Holy Ghost sent down from heaven; which things the angels desire to look into. (I Peter 1:7–12)

John was chosen to prepare a *Revelation* that would reveal to the people of the world what has happened on this earth, and what would take place in the latter days. He received this knowledge from the mouth of Christ, and prepared it in such a way that the mystery would remain hidden until the right time. Today is that time. This book is that venue.

10:11 *And he said unto me, Thou must prophesy again before many peoples, and nations, and tongues, and kings.*

John was commanded to "*seal up*" the things which he heard. He did so in the figurative expressions, metaphors, and allegories he presents in the book of *Revelation*. He knew that no one, without the proper authority and physical changes required in the memory and thinking capabilities of the brain, would be able to unlock the mystery of his words unless that person was given the same *book to eat* (the same mission to perform) that was given to him. Furthermore, John's message was set to come forth in plainness in the latter days by his own mouth. In other words, John himself would guide the unveiling of his written *Revelation*. He would do this by directing the one who would be given the authority to do so, under his supervision. This *Book* fulfills the commandment given to John that he "*must prophesy again*" to the entire world.

Chapter

REVELATION
UNFOLDED

11:1 And the angel *gave* me a reed like unto a rod *and said unto me*, Rise, and measure the temple of God, and the altar, and them that worship therein.

John's calling to prophesy segues into what he is figuratively expressing here. Once a prophet understands his mission, he is commanded to build the kingdom of God upon the earth by teaching exactly what he receives ("*gave me a reed*") from God.

Ancient builders used reeds to measure the materials needed to construct their buildings. The precision of the construction came from the exactness of the measurements taken with the available tools. Later in *Revelation*, Christ is presented as one who "*had a golden reed to measure the city, and the gates thereof, and the wall thereof*" (see Revelation 21:15), signifying that he will set up the kingdom of God upon the earth precisely as the blueprints demand as found in the *Book of Life*. John is simply expressing the idea that his prophetic duty is to help those who "*worship God*" in the figurative "*temple*," upon the figurative "*altar*," to establish and *build* the kingdom of God in their lives. He will do this according to the *precise* mandates of the revealed word of God—the gospel of Jesus Christ, often referred to as *"like unto a rod."*

The *"temple of God"* is the *house* Jesus commanded the people to build upon *a rock* (his words of counsel) with the measuring tool (*"reed"*) he gave them:

> *Therefore whosoever* **heareth these sayings of mine, and doeth them***, I will liken him unto a wise man, which* **built his house** *upon a rock: And the rain descended, and the floods came, and the winds blew, and beat upon that house; and it fell not: for it was founded upon* **a rock***. And every one that heareth these sayings of mine, and doeth them not, shall be likened unto a foolish man, which built his house upon the sand: And the rain descended, and the floods came, and the winds blew, and beat upon that house; and it fell: and great was the fall of it.*
> (Matthew 7:24–27)

John borrowed his symbolism from Ezekiel who presents symbolically the precision of the workmanship needed to build the kingdom of God (*"the temple and the altar"*):

> *In the visions of God brought he me into the land of Israel, and set me upon a very high mountain, by which was as the frame of a city on the south. And he brought me thither, and, behold, there was a man, whose appearance was like the appearance of brass, with a line of flax in his hand, and a* **measuring reed***; and he stood in the gate. And the man said unto me, Son of man, behold with thine eyes, and hear with thine ears, and set thine heart upon all that I shall shew thee; for to the intent that I might show them unto thee art thou brought hither:* **declare all that thou seest to the house of Israel***. And behold a wall on the outside of the house round about, and in the man's hand a* **measuring reed** *of six cubits long by the cubit and*

an hand breadth: so he measured the breadth of the build-
ing, one reed; and the height, one reed. (Ezekiel 40:2–5)

The prophet Zechariah saw the same thing:

I lifted up mine eyes again, and looked, and behold a man
*with a **measuring line** in his hand. Then said I, Whither*
goest thou? And he said unto me, To measure Jerusalem,
to see what is the breadth thereof, and what is the length
thereof. (Zechariah 2:1–2)

John refers to the "*reed like unto a rod*," signifying that his measurement will be the word of God (see commentary on Revelation 2:27). John was given the power to help set up and build "*the temple*" (*kingdom of God*) among those who abide by the commandments ("*them that worship therein*").

11:2 But the court which is without the temple leave out, and measure it not; for it is given unto the Gentiles **to measure**. **And when they measure it**, they shall tread the holy city under foot forty and two months.

John is to teach "the elect" (those who *worship* in the *temple of God* and offer righteous works upon *the altar*) what it takes to set up and establish the kingdom of God upon the earth. But to those who *do not* keep the commandments (always figuratively expressed as *Gentiles*), John is to teach them nothing and establish nothing among them, allowing them to do what they want according to their desires. The Gentiles will *build* and establish their houses, cities, nations, and kingdoms upon the earth using their own *measuring stick* and their own set of blueprints created by "*Lucifer*" (the king who rules over them).

John indicates that *the Gentiles* will do as Isaiah implied in his writings, also giving us the source from where he borrowed his symbolism:

Hear the word of the LORD, ye rulers of Sodom; give ear unto
the law of our God, ye people of Gomorrah. To what purpose
is the multitude of your sacrifices unto me? saith the LORD:

*I am full of the burnt offerings of rams, and the fat of fed beasts; and I delight not in the blood of bullocks, or of lambs, or of he goats. When ye come to appear before me, who hath required this at your hand, to **tread my courts**? Bring no more vain oblations; incense is an abomination unto me; the new moons and sabbaths, the calling of assemblies, I cannot away with; it is iniquity, even the solemn meeting. Your new moons and your appointed feasts my soul hateth: they are a trouble unto me; I am weary to bear them. And when ye spread forth your hands, I will hide mine eyes from you: yea, when ye make many prayers, I will not hear: your hands are full of blood. Wash you, make you clean; put away the evil of your doings from before mine eyes; cease to do evil; Learn to do well; seek judgment, relieve the oppressed, judge the fatherless, plead for the widow.* (Isaiah 1:10–17)

Instead of obeying the words of Christ and building the kingdom of God by doing unto others as they would want done unto them (*seek judgment, relieve the oppressed, judge the fatherless, plead for the widow*), the Gentiles have their own measurement of righteousness. This measurement is their useless beliefs, ordinances, traditions, oblations, and all other *incense* repugnant (*an abomination unto me*) to God as John presented in Revelation 8:3.

Old Testament prose uses "*tread*" to mean the destruction or subduing of something undesirable.

*That I will break the Assyrian in my land, and upon my mountains **tread him under foot**: then shall his yoke depart from off them, and his burden depart from off their shoulders.* (Isaiah 14:25)

*For he bringeth down them that dwell on high; the lofty city, he layeth it low; he layeth it low, even to the ground; he bringeth it even to the dust. The **foot shall tread** it down, even the feet of the poor, and the steps of the needy.* (Isaiah 26:5–6)

"*Holy city*" (or the "*New Jerusalem*," see commentary on Revelation 3:12) is used by John to represent those who keep the commandments of God; and in contrast, the city of *Babylon* is used throughout *Revelation* as those who do not.

To the Gentiles, the gospel of Jesus Christ, which John was called as a prophet to give to the world, is undesirable; therefore they "*tread it under foot forty and two months.*" Here John introduces the first indication of an exact timetable of God's dealings with mortals.

With mathematical precision, John gives the necessary clues to this timetable throughout *Revelation*. Of all the *Old Testament* prophets, only Daniel used a timetable to express exact dates when certain prophecies would be fulfilled. John borrows from Daniel's timetable:

> *And he shall speak great words against the most High, and shall wear out the saints of the most High, and think to change times and laws: and they shall be given into his hand until* **a time and times and the dividing of time.** *...And I heard the man clothed in linen, which was upon the waters of the river, when he held up his right hand and his left hand unto heaven, and sware by him that liveth for ever that it shall be for a* **time, times, and an half***; and when he shall have accomplished to scatter the power of the holy people, all these things shall be finished.* (Daniel 7:25; 12:7)

Notice that Daniel writes "*that it shall be for a* **time, times, and an half***; and when he shall have accomplished to scatter the power of* **the holy people***, all these things shall be finished.*"

John wrote the same thing this way, "*and* **the holy city** *shall they tread under foot forty and two months.*"

The Jewish calendar has twelve months of exactly 30 days each (there is no leap year in the Jewish calendar). Therefore, "*forty-two months*" is "*a thousand two hundred and threescore days.*" "*Forty-two months*" is also "*three and a half*" years. "*Three and a half*" is equal to one (*time*) plus two (*times*) plus one-half (*half a time*). Therefore, when John uses any of these terms, it is given to denote the same amount of time. When he intended to present a specific time period in Revelation, John reverts back to using Daniel's timetable and the *beginning reference point* Daniel established as the fulfillment of certain prophecies.

In chapter 2 of *Revelation*, John establishes his own reference point, which is the year he finishes *"measuring the temple of God,"* or in other words, when he stops preaching the word of God, allowing the Gentiles to corrupt the word of God by coming up with their own measurements. John was he of whom it was written:

> *Peter seeing him saith to Jesus, Lord, and what shall this man do? Jesus saith unto him, If I will that he tarry till I come, what is that to thee? follow thou me. Then went this saying abroad among the brethren, that that disciple should not die: yet Jesus said not unto him, He shall not die; but, If I will that he tarry till I come, what is that to thee? This is the disciple which testifieth of these things, and wrote these things: and we know that his testimony is true.* (John 21:21–24)

As previously explained, the *New Testament* was not edited or collated until hundreds of years after the death of Jesus. John was still alive then, and in disguise visited those responsible for the canonization of the scripture. His writings were profound, and gave the editors a different view of Jesus' ministry than what had been passed down from one generation to the next. John also delivered the manuscript for his *Revelation*, which he knew the editors would never understand because of the symbolic and metaphorical way in which it was written, thus maintaining its integrity for hundreds of years. It is this same John who edited and instructed the compilation of this book, revealing for the first time his exact words and their meanings.

John's reference point for this part of his *Revelation* is the year 570 A.D. It was at this time that he was instructed to stop preaching the gospel of Jesus Christ to the people, especially to his own people, the Jews. There was destined to be one final prophet sent to another people, *the Gentiles*, who would teach them the true gospel of the Father.

This last prophet, of the generation in which John ended his mission, would have nothing to do with Christianity, which at that time, had been corrupted and divided into various sects and beliefs. This last prophet for that generation was the prophet Mohammed, who was born in the year 570 A.D. Without giving reference to the name of Jesus Christ, Mohammed would establish the truth and teach God's will to the people residing in the surrounding lands inhabited by other descendants of Abraham. However, he would establish the same *rock* with the same premise as Jesus' gospel— do unto others as you would have them do unto you.

The world would corrupt (*"tread under foot"*) the gospel of Jesus Christ, change its meaning, and follow after every whim and doctrine that blew into the ears of humankind for the next *"one thousand two hundred and threescore years,"* until once again a *reed* would be given to a prophet to properly *"measure"* and establish the kingdom of God upon the earth.

11:3 And I **have given** power unto my two witnesses **that they may prophesy; but during the** thousand two hundred and threescore days **they shall prophesy** clothed in sackcloth.

11:4 These **witnesses** are the two olive trees, and the two candlesticks standing before the **altar of** God **upon** the earth.

Since the *"altar of God"* figuratively expresses one offering his or her works before God (see commentary of Revelation 6:9), John presents **two witnesses** that give the fruit (*"the olive trees"*) of the gospel and provide the light (*"the candlesticks"*) by which the proper works are determined. In other words, they are witnesses of each other and the words of Christ. These are the Holy Scriptures, or the written words of chosen prophets of God given to witness what God would have the people do. The prophecies contained therein also give portend of what will take place upon the earth according to God's plan.

Although unbeknownst to the rest of the people in his time, John knew that the physical earth consisted of *two separate* landmasses, modernly referred to as the Western and Eastern Hemispheres.

The Jews were not the only people chosen to bring the words of

Christ to the world. From Jewish culture came *the Bible*, which is a historical religious record that culminates in the formation of Christianity as presented in the *New Testament*. There were other religious writings found among different peoples of the earth, given by the specific prophet sent to teach each culture according to its traditions and understanding. The Orient had the writings of Confucius and Lao Tse. The Persians had their prophets, the Greeks had theirs, and there were many others who expounded upon the wisdom they received as chosen prophets of God.

Eastern cultures and their written scriptures were isolated to the Eastern Hemisphere. What the world did not discover at the time, is that after his resurrection, Christ visited the Western Hemisphere and established his gospel among the people of that part of the world too. These also received the testimony and prophesying of ancient prophets, who were sent to them according to God's timetable for the earth.

> *And other sheep I have, which are not of this fold: them also I must bring, and they shall hear my voice; and there shall be one fold, and one shepherd.* (John 10:16)

The evidence of Christ's visit to those in the Western Hemisphere is recorded in the second *"olive tree"* and *"candlestick"* presented as a *"witness"* by John. Upon proper research, those so inclined will find the witness given of Christ and his gospel to the people of the Western Hemisphere.

Daniel prophesies of two different prophets who recorded the same vision that he received. (The **bold** indicates the difference from the *King James Bible*):

> *And the Lord God spake unto me, saying, But thou, O Daniel, shut up the words of the vision which I have given unto thee, for these things shall be as a book that is sealed, even to the time of the end. And in that day, many shall run to and fro seeking for understanding, and knowledge shall be increased, but understanding shall not come to*

*those that have knowledge because of that which is sealed
up in the book. Then I Daniel looked, and, behold, there
stood **two others like unto me, who had received this
same vision and sealed up their words, the one on
this side of the bank of the river, and the other on
that side of the bank of the river**. And the name of him
on this side of the bank was made known unto me, but the
name of the other, I cannot give, for it is also sealed. **And
the one on this side of the bank** said to the man who I
saw in the vision who was clothed in linen, who was upon
the waters of the river, **How long** shall it be to the end of
these wonders?* (Daniel 12:4–6)

In Revelation 6:10, John is revealed as he who has written and
sealed up his words and asks, "*How long, O Lord, holy and true…?*"

Daniel lived in the Eastern Hemisphere ("this side of the bank of the
river"—the water that divides the landmasses). John lived there too, and was
he of whom Daniel refers as the "*one on this side of the bank*" who had the
same vision and sealed up what he saw. However, "*the **other** on that side of
the bank of the river*" who had the same vision and sealed it up is not identified
because "*the name of the other, I cannot give, for it is also sealed.*"
In this verse of *Revelation*, John is not speaking of just any particular
prophet who has been given a vision of the beginning of time to the end of
time. John saw that after the Gentiles had tread the temple court for the
figurative *forty-two months* (*three years and an half*), both "***witnesses***"
would be made known to the world, or the gospel would be taught in its
fullness in all parts of the world. This is further explained in the following
verses as these *witnesses* are killed and figuratively come back to life and
stand upon their feet (see verse 12).
These "*two witnesses*" ("*two olive trees/two candlesticks*") are
received as the Holy Word of God as contained in the scriptures, both those
written in the Eastern Hemisphere (which include, but are not limited to *the
Bible*), and those in the Western Hemisphere. The scriptures which have
been written by the prophets in the Western Hemisphere include some that

will be mentioned but not referenced by name in this book; as there should be no credence given to the few emergent faiths that endorse and hold these witnesses and testimonies as their own.

Because these modern organized religions have corrupted the words of Christ, and therefore do not understand the true meaning of his gospel, John has forbidden their official names to be mentioned. However, a sincere seeker of truth will find these scriptures. When you do, you will discover that there exists a contemporary religion (the *last*) which prophetically mirrors the Jews of John's day (who were the *first*) almost exactly, in its establishment, precepts, and history. Observing the works of this modern-day religion, the humble researcher will know of a surety that this particular organized faith is inspired, owned, and operated by *Lucifer, the prince of the world,* and has little to do with emanating the true gospel of Jesus Christ as taught by John and the others who knew him personally.

As John would say: *"If any man have an ear, let him hear. As the first has done to the holy word, so has the last."*

According to John's personal time frame, all scripture was written and completed before 570 A.D. Because of the wickedness of the world (*"the treading of the Gentiles"*), the prophecies and witness of the scriptures will be hidden from the world (*"clothed in sackcloth"*); meaning that in great mourning, they shall not be revealed to the world. In other words, they will not be understood because of the figurative and metaphorical way in which they are written. An ancient prophet wrote:

> Behold, my brethren, he that prophesieth, let him prophesy to the understanding of men; for the Spirit speaketh the truth and lieth not. Wherefore, it speaketh of things as they really are, and of things as they really will be; wherefore, these things are manifested unto us plainly, for the salvation of our souls. But behold, we are not witnesses alone in these things; for God also spake them unto prophets of old. But behold, the Jews were a stiffnecked people; and **they** despised **the words of plainness, and killed the prophets, and sought for things that they could not understand.** Wherefore, because of their blind-

ness, which blindness came by looking beyond the mark,
*they must needs fall; for **God hath taken away his***
plainness from them, and delivered unto them many
things which they cannot understand, because they
desired it. And because they desired it God hath
done it, that they may stumble. (Source withheld)

John uses this metaphor (*"clothed in sackcloth"*) the same way he used *"sackcloth,"* in *Revelation* 6:12 to represent that which blocks out the light of the sun (*"the sun became black, **clothed in a** sackcloth"*).

11:5 And if any man will hurt them, fire proceedeth out of their mouth, and devoureth their enemies: and if any man will hurt them, he must in this manner be killed.

John is referring to those who misinterpret (*"hurt them"*) the Holy Scriptures either by mistranslating them or presenting them in a way that they were not intended to be presented. The editors of the *New Testament*, for example, transformed the canon of scripture into what they felt best served their interests and agendas at the time. They edited, transposed, added to, and deleted any part that did not fit their perception of the doctrine of Christ, which at the time they began to organize the *New Testament*, was far from what Christ intended. John knew this, and wrote *Revelation* in such a way that they would not understand his words. He includes these religious leaders in his figurative expression of the *"locusts"* (see commentary on Revelation 9:3–10). These, as well as all modern-day religious leaders, never had a clue that he was referring to them.

At the end of *Revelation*, John gives the same warning as he does in verse 5 above:

For I testify unto every man that heareth the words of the
*prophecy of this book, **If any man shall add unto these***
things, God shall add unto him the plagues that are
written in this book: And if any man shall take away

from the words of the book of this prophecy, God shall take away his part out of the Book of Life, and out of the holy city, and from the things which are written in this book. (Revelation 22:18–19)

When Christ comes, the people will be judged according to how they treated each other. When the world's religious leaders teach their followers to do **anything** other than "*do unto another as you would want done unto you,*" they "*hurt*" the word of God by "*trampling it under foot.*" When the scriptures are revealed in their purity, especially the words Christ spoke, these leaders and those who have changed and corrupted the word of God, will be figuratively "*killed*" by the sharp sword coming out of the mouth of Christ.

An ancient prophet who lived in the Western Hemisphere wrote:

O ye wicked and perverse and stiffnecked people, why have ye built up churches unto yourselves to get gain? **Why have ye transfigured the holy word of God, that ye might bring damnation upon your souls***? Behold, look ye unto the revelations of God; for behold, the time cometh at that day when all these things must be fulfilled. Behold, the Lord hath shown unto me great and marvelous things concerning that which must shortly come, at that day when these things shall come forth among you. Behold, I speak unto you as if ye were present, and yet ye are not. But behold, Jesus Christ hath shown you unto me, and I know your doing. And I know that ye do walk in the pride of your hearts; and there are none save a few only who do not lift themselves up in the pride of their hearts, unto the wearing of very fine apparel, unto envying, and strifes, and malice, and persecutions, and all manner of iniquities; and your churches,* **yea, even every one***, have become polluted because of the pride of your hearts. For behold, ye do love money, and your substance, and your* *fine apparel, and the adorning of your churches, more than ye love the poor and the needy, the sick and the afflicted. O ye pollutions, ye hypocrites, ye teachers, who sell yourselves for that which will canker, why have ye polluted the holy church of God? Why are ye ashamed to take upon you the name of Christ? Why do ye not think that greater is the value of an endless happiness than that misery which never dies — because of the praise of the world? Why do ye adorn yourselves with that which hath no life, and yet suffer the hungry, and the needy, and the naked, and the sick and the afflicted to pass by you, and notice them not? Yea, why do ye build up your secret abominations to get gain, and cause that widows should mourn before the Lord, and also orphans to mourn before the Lord, and also the blood of their fathers and their husbands to cry unto the Lord from the ground, for vengeance upon your heads? Behold, the sword of vengeance hangeth over you; and the time soon cometh that he avengeth the blood of the saints upon you, for he will not suffer their cries any longer.* (Source withheld)

The "*fire*" that comes from the truth will "*devour*" the doctrines and precepts of men ("*the enemies*" of the Holy Scriptures). This means that when the true and correct translations and words of the prophets are given, those who have misunderstood or changed the truth of the prophets' words shall be *burned* with the *fire* of embarrassment.

11:6 These ***witnesses*** have power to shut heaven, that it rain not in the days of their prophecy; and ***they*** have power over ***the*** waters to turn them to blood, and to smite the earth with all plagues, as often as they will.

It has already been mentioned that the words of Christ given in the Holy Scriptures ("*their prophecy*") have great "*power*" which can bring "*plagues*" upon those who do not give heed to their warnings and abide by their counsels (see Revelation 22:17–19). When we do not do unto each other what we would want done unto us, we wreak havoc upon a world in which we are collectively connected in many ways, and in this way experience the "*plagues*" together. Disregarding these simple words of Christ hinders us from receiving further light and revelation from God ("*shut heaven, that it rain not in the days of their prophecy*").

The pure and living "*waters*" of truth that would refresh and quench our thirst are turned to "*blood*," which means they no longer refresh us as water does because they are corrupted by the lifestyle we choose to live. Blood gives life to the body, or in other words, it is figuratively given as the intents and desires of our hearts. Instead of our intents and desires refreshing us, as does pure water, when we do not abide by the words of Christ, the "*living water*" is turned into the "*blood*" of the natural man, which we cannot drink to quench our thirst.

The "*power*" of the word of God can either bring peace and happiness, if we abide by it, or cause the torments ("*plagues*") John described in the preceding chapters of *Revelation*, when we do not.

11:7 And when they shall *give* their testimony, the beast that ascendeth out of the bottomless pit shall make war against them, and shall overcome them, and kill them.

John specifically mentions that these "*witnesses*" (the scriptures) bear "*testimony*" of the truth. But as these literary prophets (the written word) unwaveringly testify and prophesy, their words and warnings are ignored because of the frailties of human nature, which fight ("*make war*") against the law and the prophets.

This law is simply:

Therefore all things whatsoever ye would that men should do to you, do ye even so to them: for this is the law and the prophets. (Matthew 7:12)

As mentioned previously, John uses the term "*angel*" and "*beast*" interchangeably. Neither term is used to represent righteousness or wickedness specifically. Chapter 4 uses the term *"beast"* for those angels who do the will of God, and chapter 13 will introduce a *"beast"* opposed to the will of God. Likewise, John uses *"beast"* in this verse to describe the *"angel of the bottomless pit"* (see Revelation 9:11), revealed as our flesh, or human nature, which is *"the king that rules over them."*

Our human natures are opposed to the idea that we are all created equal. This natural tendency comes from our instinct to protect our own life in spite of how our selfish and self-serving interests and actions might affect others.

Jesus taught his disciples that there is a constant war raging between our spiritual natures and our flesh. When we allow ourselves to be overcome and become servants of the *"king"* (our flesh), we are spiritually dead (*"shall make war against them, and shall overcome them, and kill them"*).

Watch and pray, that ye enter not into temptation: **the spirit indeed is willing, but the flesh is weak**. (Matthew 26:41)

From whence come wars and fightings among you? come they not hence, **even of your lusts that war in your members**? *Ye lust, and have not: ye kill, and desire to have, and cannot obtain: ye fight and war, yet ye have not, because ye ask not.* (James 4:1)

Dearly beloved, I beseech you as strangers and pilgrims, abstain from **fleshly lusts, which war against the soul**; (I Peter 2:11)

Let not sin therefore reign in your mortal body, that ye should obey it in the lusts thereof. Neither yield ye your members as instruments of unrighteousness unto sin: but yield yourselves unto God, as those that are alive from the dead, and your members as instruments of righteousness unto God. For sin shall not have domin-

*ion over you: for ye are not under the law, but under grace. What then? shall we sin, because we are not under the law, but under grace? God forbid. Know ye not, **that to whom ye yield yourselves servants to obey, his servants ye are to whom ye obey**; whether of sin unto death, or of obedience unto righteousness? But God be thanked, that ye were the servants of sin, but ye have obeyed from the heart that form of doctrine which was delivered you. Being then made free from sin, ye became the servants of righteousness. I speak after the manner of men because of **the infirmity of your flesh**: for as ye have yielded your members servants to uncleanness and to iniquity unto iniquity; even so now yield your members servants to righteousness unto holiness. For when ye were the servants of sin, ye were free from righteousness. What fruit had ye then in those things whereof ye are now ashamed? **for the end of those things is death**.* (Romans 6:12–21)

The prophets' message contained in the Holy Scriptures is changed, ridiculed, ignored, and "*overcome*" by the power that feeds the lusts and needs of the flesh. John is expressing that as the gospel is given to the world ("*when they give their testimony*"), it is rejected because of human nature.

11:8 And their dead bodies shall lie in the street of the great city, which spiritually is called Sodom and Egypt, where also our Lord was crucified.

The word of God will lie dormant ("*dead bodies shall lie*") in a world ("*street of the great city*") where there are so many other enticements that keep people from treating each other with equality. "*Sodom*" has been used by many prophets to represent a society of people who are led by their lusts; and "*Egypt*" is used to represent the pride and authority that one group of people exercises over another. Isaiah referred to the leaders of the Jews as "*rulers of Sodom*":

*Hear the word of the LORD, ye **rulers of Sodom**; give ear unto the law of our God, ye people of Gomorrah.* (Isaiah 1:10)

*For Jerusalem is ruined, and Judah is fallen: because their tongue and their doings are against the LORD, to provoke the eyes of his glory. The shew of their countenance doth witness against them; and they declare **their sin as Sodom**, they hide it not. Woe unto their soul! for they have rewarded evil unto themselves.* (Isaiah 3:8–9)

*And the **spirit of Egypt** shall fail in the midst thereof; and I will destroy the counsel thereof: and they shall seek to the idols, and to the charmers, and to them that have familiar spirits, and to the wizards. ...Woe to the rebellious children, saith the LORD, that take counsel, but not of me; and that cover with a covering, **but not of my spirit**, that they may add sin to sin: That walk to go down into Egypt, and have not asked at my mouth; to strengthen themselves in the strength of Pharaoh, and to trust in the **shadow of Egypt!** Therefore shall the strength of Pharaoh be your shame, and **the trust in the shadow of Egypt your confusion**.* (Isaiah 19:3; 30:1–3)

John does not use the word "*crucify*" in any other part of *Revelation* except in this verse where he intended to demonstrate that the words spoken by Jesus Christ were unheeded ("*killed*" as explained in verse 7), and the reason Jesus was put to death. He was killed by a world that chose the lusts of the flesh ("*Sodom*") and the pride and authority of its leaders ("*Egypt*") over the simple counsels of which Christ testified and witnessed to the world.

11:9 And they of the people and kindreds and tongues and nations **of the earth** shall see their dead bodies three days and an half, and shall not suffer their dead bodies to be put in graves.

Dead bodies are put into graves so their stench does not torment those who remain. Here John is expressing that the inhabitants of the earth will be well aware of the prophets and Holy Scriptures (*"see their dead bodies"*) that will be available in all parts of the world during a certain time frame (*three days and an half*, see commentary on Revelation 11:2). Though to the world their words seem impotent and insignificant (*"dead bodies"*), they are present to prick the world's conscience. John uses *"see"* here as it refers to *understanding* or *being aware* that the scriptures are available.

In this verse and verses 10 through 12, John borrows the words of Jeremiah and transposes them to illustrate the actions of the masses. While John depicts what the people are doing, Jeremiah illustrates the consequences of their actions:

> *Then will I cause to cease from the cities of Judah, and from the streets of Jerusalem,* **the voice of mirth, and the voice of gladness, the voice of the bridegroom, and the voice of the bride***: for the land shall be desolate. At that time, saith the LORD, they shall bring out the bones of the kings of Judah, and the bones of his princes, and the bones of the priests, and the bones of the prophets, and the bones of the inhabitants of Jerusalem,* **out of their graves***: And they shall spread them before the sun, and the moon, and all the host of heaven, whom they have loved, and whom they have served, and after whom they have walked, and whom they have sought, and whom they have worshipped:* **they shall not be gathered, nor be buried***; they shall be for dung upon the face of the earth. And death shall be chosen rather than life by all the residue of them that remain of this evil family, which remain in all the places whither I have driven them, saith the LORD of hosts.* (Jeremiah 7:34; 8:1–3)

11:10 And they that dwell upon the earth shall rejoice over them, and make merry, and shall send gifts one to another; because these two prophets *are dead which* tormented them that dwelt on the earth.

Jeremiah is indicating what will happen because of their *rejoicing*, by writing, "*Then will I cause to cease from the cities of Judah, and from the streets of Jerusalem, **the voice of mirth, and the voice of gladness**.*"

Humankind is oblivious to the message of the prophets contained in the scriptures. As they eat, drink, and are merry, they pay no attention to those who are hungry, naked, homeless, afflicted, or in prison. As long as one's life is personally satisfying, humans find no need to concern themselves with the plight of those who are not eating, drinking, and making merry. The people believe they are righteous if they are happy. None take notice of the "*dead bodies of the witnesses lying in the street.*" Every once in a while, the odor of the "*prophets' dead bodies*" will "*torment*" their nostrils, but as long as they have a fine warm house, plenty of food, and entertainment to keep their minds occupied, the stench is tolerable.

> *How do ye say, We are wise, and the law of the LORD is with us? Lo, certainly in vain made he it; **the pen of the scribes is in vain.** The wise men are ashamed, they are dismayed and taken: lo, **they have rejected the word of the LORD; and what wisdom is in them?*** (Jeremiah 8:8–9)

In other words, people might acknowledge the scriptures and claim with fervor they are the "word of God," but the words are "*dead*" to them because they do not understand or heed them. Once in a while they might say, "Oh yes, we should do unto others what we would want done unto us," just before they leave their comfortable houses with their exclusionary families, after reading passages of scripture, right after family prayer, and before they get into their automobiles and curse those who disagree with them all the way to their place of employment where they can shield their eyes from those in need.

11:11 And after three days and an half the Spirit of life from God entered into them, and they stood upon their feet; and great fear fell upon them which saw them.

Here it is appropriate to explain John's timetable, and why he chose to use "*three days and an half, forty and two months, a thousand two hundred and threescore days,*" and later, "*a time, and times, and a half a time*" (see Revelation 12:14).

John borrows this timetable from the prophet Daniel. As mentioned previously, John uses days and years interchangeably. Therefore, in each instance where John and Daniel use "*days,*" the exactness of their timetables will be revealed if the reader understands these "*days*" to mean mortal years. What John expresses in Revelation 11:9–19, Daniel demonstrates this way:

> *And he shall speak great words against the most High, and shall wear out the saints of the most High, and think to change times and laws: and they shall be given into his hand until **a time and times and the dividing of time**. But the judgment shall sit, and they shall take away his dominion, to consume and to destroy it unto the end. And the kingdom and dominion, and the greatness of the kingdom under the whole heaven, shall be given to the people of the saints of the most High, whose kingdom is an everlasting kingdom, and all dominions shall serve and obey him. Hitherto is the end of the matter. As for me Daniel, my cogitations much troubled me, and my countenance changed in me: but I kept the matter in my heart.* (Daniel 7:25–28)

Daniel continues presenting his vision by expressing what John illustrates in Revelation 10:6:

> *And I heard the man clothed in linen, which was upon the waters of the river, when he held up his right hand and his left hand unto heaven, and sware by him that liveth for ever that it shall be for **a time, times, and an half; and when he shall have accomplished to scatter the power of the holy people, all these things shall be finished**. And I heard, but I understood not: then said I, O my Lord, what shall be the end of these things? And he*

said, Go thy way, Daniel: for the words are closed up and sealed till the time of the end. Many shall be purified, and made white, and tried; but the wicked shall do wickedly: and none of the wicked shall understand; but the wise shall understand. (Daniel 12:7–10)

After Daniel has prophesied that *the wise shall understand,* he gives an exact clue to the **beginning reference point** of his timetable:

*And from **the time that the daily sacrifice shall be taken away**, and the abomination that maketh desolate set up, there shall be **a** thousand **two hundred and nine-ty days**. Blessed is he that waiteth, and cometh to the **thousand three hundred and five and thirty days**.* (Daniel 12:11–12)

Daniel's beginning point of reference is the year when the Israelites lost the Ark of the Covenant ("*the time that the daily sacrifice shall be taken away,*" circa 1320 B.C.E.). The Jews offered all of their daily sacrifices and oblations upon the altar in relation to the Ark of the Covenant. When the Ark was destroyed and carried off by marauders, the daily rituals ceased.

Though modern calendars have a plus or minus margin of error of about 4 to 8 years, they are sufficiently capable of measuring the timetable Daniel sets forth. "*Time, times, and half of time*" are exact time periods when prophets ("*the two witnesses,*" "*olive trees,*" and "*candlesticks*") were sent into the world to preach the word of God, and also the exact time periods their "*bodies lay dead in the streets,*" or when their words are generally ignored.

According to his timetable, Daniel reveals to the world the exact year when Christ was to be born into the world, whereas John reveals the exact year when Christ will return. Here's how they reveal these important times and dates by using these time frames:

Here is the timetable revealing the date the voice of God is once again heard in the temple, according to Daniel 12:11–12:

1320 B.C.E.

The temple is destroyed and the Ark of the Covenant is lost.

Add 1290 years

"...*a thousand two hundred and ninety days...*"

30 B.C.E.

The time the temple will once again be established.

Add 45 years

."..*cometh to the thousand three hundred and five and thirty days.*"
(The difference between 1290 and 1335 = 45)

15 A.D.

The time the voice of God is once again heard in the temple.

The word of God was once again heard in the temple when Jesus Christ, as a young boy, preached therein, circa 15 A.D. (the slight difference in the age of Christ is not important in light of the margin of error in modern time calculations):

> And **when he was twelve years old**, *they went up to Jerusalem after the custom of the feast. ...And it came to pass, that after three days found him in the temple, sitting in the midst of the doctors, both hearing them, and asking them questions. And all that heard him were astonished at his understanding and answers.* (Luke 2:42, 46–47)

Surely, "Blessed is he that waiteth, and cometh to the" time the Lord's voice was once again heard in the temple.

The following is both Daniel's and John's **beginning reference point** when they mention "*time, times, and half of time.*" Following this timetable, the exact year of the beginning of the Millennial Reign of Christ is revealed:

1950 B.C.E.

This is the beginning of the reference period known as the *time*. This beginning point of reference is the year Abraham, the assumed father and founder of the Jewish faith, received the covenant from God that through his lineage, Christ would come and bless all the nations of the earth:

And in thy seed shall all the nations of the earth be blessed;
because thou hast obeyed my voice (Genesis 22:18)

630 years is the exact period of the *"time."*

For *"time,"* or 630 years, starting at the time Abraham received the covenant, prophets were sent throughout the world to preach the gospel of doing unto others what you would have them do unto you.

1320 B.C.E.

The reference time the prophets end their preaching.

For *"time"* (630 years) their *"dead bodies lay in the streets."* In other words, no prophets are authorized to preach the gospel to the world.

690 B.C.E.

Prophets were once again sent to the earth to bring the gospel to the people for a period of 1260 years, which is the period known as the *"times"* (doubling of time)

570 A.D.

The prophets were once again stopped from preaching throughout the earth.

For *"times,"* or 1260 years, no prophets were sent to the earth to establish the kingdom of God and teach the gospel to the people. This was during John's tenure upon the earth when he writes of the *two witnesses* who prophesied for 1260 years until they were killed and their bodies lie in the street for three and a half days, or until the *"time, times, and half of time"* were finished.

1830 A.D.

This is the beginning of the *"half of time"* when once again prophets would be sent throughout the earth to make one last attempt to turn the hearts of the people toward the covenants, or to the gospel that was given to their fathers. At the end of the *"half of time,"* Christ will come again to the earth.

This explanation might help understand this timetable better:

> *Since the day that God made a covenant with Abraham, he being the first prophet of the span of time known as the "time," there passed 630 years. After that 630 years had passed, God took His prophets and His gospel off of the earth and let Lucifer have the exact same time (630 years) without God's interference. After Satan had his 630 years, God once again began to call and send forth prophets to teach the people of the earth His will, but this time, the time span was twice as long as the first, or "times," which is 1260 years. Then after 1260 years of having the prophets and the gospel of the Father upon the earth, God's influence was taken off the earth for 1260 years, so that Lucifer would not complain that he wasn't given a fair shot at implementing his plan without the interference of the Father. Then after Satan had control for 1260 years, then the Father called His prophets and gave his gospel for the last time, which is the "half of time," or 315 years, before He comes Himself, casts Satan out, and binds him for a long period of time, and basically says, 'Lucifer, you had your chance to implement your plan without MY intervention, now I get the chance to implement MY plan without your intervention.* (Source withheld)

Those readers with eyes that see and ears that hear can deduce the rest of the prophetic equation.

John expresses that after *"three days and an half"*—time (1), *times*

(2), and *half of time* (1/2) = (3 1/2)—the gospel as revealed through the words of all the prophets (who sacrificed their lives in teaching the truth), will be understood when the scriptures are opened and the truths contained therein are unfolded (*"the Spirit of life from God entered into them"*). Those who ridiculed the prophets, (*"them which saw them"*), or ignored their warnings and words, will be confounded when the truthfulness of the gospel is revealed in its purity (*"and they stood up upon their feet"*).

11:12 And they *which saw them* heard a great voice from heaven saying unto *the two witnesses*, Come up hither. And they ascended up to heaven in a cloud; and their enemies beheld them.

This *"voice from heaven"* (spiritual/emotional witness) testifies of the truthfulness of the prophets' words contained in the Holy Scriptures. When one is told to *"come up to heaven,"* the impression is given that favor and acceptance of God has been received. Even though they will not understand all the figurative, metaphoric, and allegoric expressions used by the prophets in the scriptures (*"in a cloud"*), all the people will know that their overall message was God's message and instruction to the earth. That message and instruction has always been: do unto others as you would want them to do unto you, which would ultimately create equality and peace throughout the world.

11:13 And the same hour was there a great earthquake, and the tenth part of the city fell in the earthquake; *and there* were *saved* of men seven thousand; and *this* remnant *was* affrighted, and gave glory to the God of heaven.

Because the translators and editors of the *New Testament* changed and corrupted the text with their personal and varied interpretations, this verse reads differently when given in its true form. Instead of being *"slain,"* the *"remnant"* of *"seven thousand"* was *"saved"* from the effects of the earthquake when *"the tenth part of the city fell."*

John is saying here that when the truth is known, the very foundations upon which people have established their own precepts will be shaken (*"earthquake"*) from under them, and the things in which they once believed and trusted will *fall*. *"The city"* he is referring to is the same *great city* mentioned previously in verse 8, which represents the whole world, especially those who are led by the lusts of the flesh (*Sodom*) and have set themselves up above others (*Egypt*).

John is again borrowing from the stories of the *Old Testament* using the tribes of Israel as his example. The Jewish world was anciently divided into twelve areas known as the twelve tribes of Israel. During a later period, a monarchy was established; but with the death of King Solomon, the state was divided in two. The tribes split along territorial and political lines, with Judah and Benjamin in the south loyal to the house of David, and the rest of the tribes in the north ruled by a succession of monarchies. The southern tribes of Judah and Benjamin constitute the historical forbearers of most of the Jewish people known today. These tribes of the Northern Kingdom are referred to as the "Lost Ten Tribes of Israel."

The reason why ten out of the twelve tribes were lost, is because of the Jews' inability to obey the commandments of God. The prophets have used this historical fact to represent those who are *"lost"* in a world of darkness, or those who do not follow the voice of the prophets. When it refers to the tribes once again being found and unified, this simply means, that one day, they will know the truth and no longer be *"lost."* John uses this inference to point to those who have rejected the words of the prophets (the *"two witnesses"*) and whose false foundations have been shaken.

John borrows *Old Testament* writings in order to imply that a *"remnant"* (*"of men seven thousand"*), that has not given in to falsehoods, has been saved from the *"earthquake"* because their foundation was built upon truth:

> Yet I have **left me seven thousand in Israel,** *all the knees which have not bowed unto Baal, and every mouth which hath not kissed him.* (I Kings 19:18)

John is insinuating here that there will be many, who upon hearing the truth, will say, "Oh, so that's the truth! Good. I can accept that because it makes perfect sense to me." These are those who are not part of any organized religion, or who are humble enough to admit that they know very little about reality. These are not firm in their convictions and beliefs, and doubt the many religious and philosophical rationalizations given by those who present themselves as knowing the truth. These types of individuals will be able to accept the truth once they hear it, *"giving glory to the God of heaven,"* which finally makes more sense than anything else they have heard from the religious and political leaders of their day.

11:14 The second woe is past; and, behold, the third woe cometh quickly.

In Revelation 9:12, John writes, *"One woe is past; and, behold, there come **two woes more** hereafter."* The commentary of 9:12 explains:

> *The sixth trumpet, or woe, warns us of the greatest culprit in the downfall of our spiritual natures throughout the many years of our learning and development upon the earth. This culprit slays us spiritually in the flesh (a third part) more than any other woe yet described. After we learn of this culprit (the enemy of our peace and happiness) the next and final woe is the spiritual shock and feeling of embarrassment most will experience—which will be compounded exceedingly because of all the warnings we have received—once the One assigned to our solar system comes again to earth to reveal the truth.* (Revelation 9:12 commentary.)

John is ready to give further understanding of this *third* and *final woe,* supporting the words of the Lord given to many of the latter-day prophets:

> *Behold, **I come quickly**: hold that fast which thou hast been given of me, that no man take thy crown. ...Behold, I am Jesus Christ, the Son of God, and **I come quickly**. Therefore, blessed is he that keepeth the sayings of the prophets who have sealed up the prophecy of this book. ...And, behold, **I come quickly**; and my reward is with me, to give every man according as his work shall be.* (Revelation 3:11; 22:7,12)

11:15 And **when** the seventh angel sounded, there were great voices in heaven, saying, The kingdoms of this world are become the kingdoms of our **God**, and of his Christ; and he shall reign for ever and ever.

These same "*great voices in heaven*" are the same "*great voice from heaven*" that testified of the truthfulness of the prophets' words in verse 12 (see verse 12 commentary). This "*voice*" is considered a sure spiritual or emotional confirmation of the truth. In other words, the people are left without any doubt as to who this Anointed One ("*his Christ*") is; and by a unanimous voice, they sustain him as their God.

11:16 And the four and twenty elders, which sat before God on their seats, fell upon their faces, and worshipped God,

These are the prophets of God as explained in the preceding chapters, and whose written words John has represented in this part of his *Revelation* as the "*two olive trees, and the two candlesticks standing before the altar of God upon the earth*" (see verse 4). Therefore, it makes sense that the culmination of this part (chapter 11) of John's figurative presentation would end with these prophets ("*four and twenty elders*") *worshipping* before the throne of God.

11:17 Saying, We give thee thanks, O Lord God Almighty, which art, and wast, and art to come; because thou hast taken to thee thy great power, and hast **sent thy Christ to reign upon the earth**.

The prophets are elated that the power of humankind has been taken from men and given to someone who can control the power and use it for the good of all people. For thousands of years, humans have been allowed to exercise their free will upon the earth and do with the earth what they pleased. But in the end, this power will be given to him for whom it was meant—One who does not lead, but serves all equally.

11:18 And the nations were angry **because thou hast** come; and the time of the dead **hast come**, that they should be judged **as the living**, and that thou shouldest give reward unto thy servants the prophets, and to the saints, and them that *reverence* thy name, **both** small and great; and shouldest destroy **the power of** them **who** destroy the earth.

The inhabitants of the earth will not be very happy when their illusory world has been turned upside down. Those who have been judged by the precepts and doctrines of men will now be judged in righteousness according to how they have treated their fellowmen. The reward the prophets, saints, and those that revere the name of Christ will receive, is peace and happiness. Those who wielded unrighteous dominion and power over others will lose their power.

11:19 And the temple of God was opened in heaven, and there was seen in his temple the ark of his testament: and there were lightnings, and voices, and thunderings, and an earthquake, and great hail.

Throughout the preceding chapters, the *"lightnings, and voices, and thunderings, and an earthquake, and great hail"* have all been explained. However, it is important to note that chapter 11 begins with John being given the assignment to measure the temple of God on earth, and ends this part of his *Revelation* with him revealing that the *"temple of God"* is already in heaven, but is now *"opened"* because of what Christ has done on earth. When it is *opened,* or when the people understand what the kingdom (*"temple"*) of God actually is, they will *see* with new eyes of understanding the Ark of the Covenant (*"ark of his testament"*), which anciently contained the written words of the prophets (*"two candlesticks/witnesses"*)—the main theme of this part of John's *Revelation.*

Chapter

Revelation Unfolded

12:1 And there appeared a great *sign* in heaven *showing those things as they are upon the earth. And I saw* a woman clothed *in a robe as if it were* the sun, and the moon under her feet, and upon her head *there was* a crown of twelve stars.

It has already been established that the term *"woman"* is used to represent the human race. Here John is presenting the *"woman"* as the church of God, or in other words, the group of people in mortality who wear *"robes"* (their works) filled with the light of *"the sun"* (the illumination of truth and righteousness). To guide the *"footsteps of the woman"* throughout mortality, the people have been given the prophets of God (*"the moon under her feet"*).

Because John was called as a Jewish prophet, and subsequently used Jewish symbolism and time frames in his expressions throughout *Revelation*, he presents here that the power and authority (*"the crown"*) of truth and righteousness was established through Abraham, whose lineage is the twelve tribes of Israel (*"twelve stars"*). However, this reference is purely figurative, as it has already been explained that the term "*twelve tribes*" represents all those in every culture and in every time period who keep the commandments of God.

12:2 And *the woman was* with child *and was crying and* travailing in birth, *being* pained to be delivered.

The righteous people of the earth who are led by true prophets of God have always been saddened (*"crying and travailing"*) living in a world that wants nothing to do with equality and love, which is the purpose of keeping the commandments of God. The prophets have prophesied of the coming of a Christ (*"the child"*) to the earth to wipe away their tears and relieve them of the pains of trying to live righteously in a corrupt world.

John presents *"the woman with child,"* expressing the hope of the righteous that one day a Messiah would be sent to the earth. But until the *"child is delivered"* (the kingdom of God set up), the woman will still be *"crying and travailing."*

> And he will destroy in this mountain the face of the cover-
> ing cast over all people, and the vail [SIC] that is spread
> over all nations. He will swallow up death in victory; and
> **the Lord GOD will wipe away tears from off all faces**;
> and the rebuke of his people shall he take away from off all
> the earth: for the Lord hath spoken it. And it shall be said
> in that day, Lo, this is our God; we have waited for him, and
> he will save us: this is the LORD; we have waited for him,
> we will be glad and rejoice in his salvation. (Isaiah 25:7–9)

John borrows his symbolism from Jeremiah's description of the earth before it is *"spoiled"* (ruined) by the coming of Christ, figuratively asking the world what good is all its splendor and glory when it finally finds out the truth:

> And when thou art spoiled, what wilt thou do? Though
> thou clothest thyself with crimson, though thou deckest

*thee with ornaments of gold, though thou rentest thy face with painting, in vain shalt thou make thyself fair; thy lovers will despise thee, they will seek thy life. For I have heard a voice as of **a woman in travail**, and the anguish as of **her that bringeth forth her first child**, the voice of the daughter of Zion, that bewaileth herself, that spreadeth her hands, saying, Woe is me now! for my soul is wearied because of murderers.* (Jeremiah 4:30–31)

12:3 And there appeared **before my eyes** another **sign given** in heaven **in likeness of things upon the earth**; and **I beheld** a great red dragon, **which was the serpent which I saw that had power over the bottomless pit. And the serpent had** seven heads and ten horns, and seven crowns upon his heads.

After the righteous who choose to live the gospel of Jesus Christ were presented in his vision as a "*clothed woman*," John saw the cause of all the world's problems: the enticements and influences of the flesh, or human nature. *Dragons* have been presented throughout the scriptures as those who exercise power and control over people. Throughout the presentation of *Revelation*, John uses the terms "*dragon*" and "*serpent*" interchangeably.

Prophets have used the term "*dragon*" and "*owl*" in expressing those who unrighteously control the people with their power or supposed wisdom.

*But the cormorant and the bittern shall possess it; the owl also and the raven shall dwell in it: and he shall stretch out upon it the line of confusion, and the stones of emptiness. They shall call the nobles thereof to the kingdom, but none shall be there, and all her princes shall be nothing. And thorns shall come up in her palaces, nettles and brambles in the fortresses thereof: and it shall be an **habitation of dragons, and a court for owls**. The wild beasts of the desert shall also meet with the wild beasts of the island, and the satyr shall cry to his fellow; the screech* *owl also shall rest there, and find for herself a place of rest. There shall the great owl make her nest, and lay, and hatch, and gather under her shadow: there shall the vultures also be gathered, every one with her mate. ...The beast of the field shall honour me, **the dragons and the owls**: because I give waters in the wilderness, and rivers in the desert, to give drink to my people, my chosen.* (Isaiah 34:11–15; 43:20)

*And all the graven images thereof shall be beaten to pieces, and all the hires thereof shall be burned with the fire, and all the idols thereof will I lay desolate: for she gathered it of the hire of an harlot, and they shall return to the hire of an harlot. Therefore I will wail and howl, I will go stripped and naked: I will make a **wailing like the dragons, and mourning as the owls**.* (Micah 1:7–8)

*I am a **brother to dragons**, and a **companion to owls**. My skin is black upon me, and my bones are burned with heat. My harp also is turned to mourning, and my organ into the voice of them that weep.* (Job 30:29–31)

The "*dragon/serpent*" that "*had power over the bottomless pit*" is figuratively given as our human natures. These are presented as a "*red dragon*" because human nature has led to the bloodshed of billions of people throughout the history of this earth. Because our natures cause us to place a greater value on our own lives than those of others, we have established nations and governments throughout the earth to protect (*horns* are used by an animal for protection) our own lives in spite of what we might have to do to others.

John presents this "*dragon*" has having power and control ("*seven crowns*") over all the seven continents ("*seven heads*"), specifically noting ten kingdoms or governments ("*ten horns*") that had not yet been given power upon the earth at the time John received this vision (see Revelation 17:12).

12:4 And *with* his tail *he* drew *after him* the third part of the stars *which were upon the crown worn by the woman. And the dragon took the crown from the woman* and cast *it* to the earth. And the dragon stood before the woman, *who* was ready to be delivered, to devour her child *after* it was born.

An explanation of "*the third part*" was given in the commentary on Revelation 8:7. John is explaining that because people follow ("*the tail*") after the flesh, they lose their spiritual power ("*crown*"), which causes them to concentrate more on the things belonging to the earth ("*cast it to the earth*"), than on those things which keep them in balance with the righteousness they once knew.

According to *Old Testament* writings, when Moses descended down from the mount with the written "word of God," he encountered the Israelites singing, dancing, and worshipping an idol they had constructed from the things of the earth; this because Moses "delayed to come down out of the mount." Their fleshly desires led them to worship something they could see, feel, and touch, rather than comply with the simple commands they had received in the Ten Commandments Moses had given them.

Upon seeing the corruption their flesh had desired, Moses cast the stones to the earth, giving segue to John's figurative representation of the righteous desires of the children of God ("*the crown worn by the woman*") being cast to the earth.

Before coming down from the mount, Joshua reports that instead of hearing the voices of people with broken hearts and contrite spirits, who are ready to receive the word of God, they heard another sound:

> *It is not the voice of them that shout for* **mastery**, *neither is it the voice of them that cry for being* **overcome**: *but the noise of them that sing do I hear.* (Exodus 32:18)

It is certainly much easier to follow the enticing desires of the flesh to revelry and merrymaking, than it is to treat others as we would want to be treated. Why attempt personal *mastery* in order to *overcome* human nature, when it's so much easier just to give in and have fun?

Another figurative story involving Moses implies the imminent corruption of the people in their ability to follow the word of God when they are "*cast to the earth*" into fleshly mortality. (From this story John took the figurative expressions he uses in *Revelation* 12:4):

When Moses first received his calling as a prophet of God, he had with him a "*rod*," which term was later used by succeeding prophets to signify the "word of God." When he was commanded to cast the rod to the earth, it became a "*serpent*." Moses fled when he saw the serpent, but "*the Lord said unto Moses, Put forth thine hand, and take it by the **tail**. And he put forth his hand, and caught it, and it became a rod in his hand:*" (See Exodus 4:2–4.)

John used Moses' experience to figuratively demonstrate the concept that when a spiritual being who knows the "*word of God/the truth*" (*the rod*) is cast to the earth, it becomes a "*serpent/dragon*." In John's figurative representation, it is the "*tail*" of the dragon that drew away the "*stars of heaven and cast them to the earth*"; therefore, it is this "*tail*" that we must catch and control.

Because the natural man is an enemy of God, and has been ever since he entered mortality, we have no hope of peace and happiness unless we put off the natural man and regain our "*crown*" of righteousness. We do this by keeping the commandments of God in catching ourselves by the "*tail*," and turning it back into the "*rod*" which leads us properly.

To parallel his teachings (the word of God) to those which Moses received upon a *mount*, Jesus went up onto a *mountain* to teach the gospel to the people. Before Christ was born into the world to teach us by word and example what the true commandments of God were, and to reveal to us the hidden mysteries that were withheld since the beginning of time, "*the dragon*" was there waiting to dissuade us. Our flesh overcomes us ("*devour her child*") and entices us to follow our human natures instead of doing unto others what we would want them to do to us.

During the ministry of Jesus Christ, few could give up the things of the world to follow the simple message he taight. As soon as he was born into the world to bring truth, the desires and temptations of the flesh ("*the dragon*") kept the people from receiving his message of righteousness and peace.

12:5 And she brought forth a man child, who was to rule all nations with a rod of iron; and ***before the dragon could devour the*** child ***it*** was caught up ***and taken*** unto God, and to his throne.

Before those who rejected his message killed him, Christ accomplished his mission and left his testimony. In spite of the majority of the people, who choose a different god than the one of whom Christ spoke, Jesus left his example and gave the commandments of God he was instructed to give to the world. His gospel (*"the rod of iron"*) was revealed to the world. Though rejected by the majority, it was established upon the earth in both the Eastern and the Western Hemispheres. Thus his words are verified:

> *And other sheep I have, which are not of this fold: them*
> *also I must bring, and they shall hear my voice; and there*
> *shall be one fold, and one shepherd.* (John 10:16)

The mysteries Jesus could have taught the people were never revealed to the world, and were kept with him, in essence, *"caught up, and taken unto God,"* waiting for the day when the mystery of God *will* finally be revealed (see Revelation 10:7).

12:6 And the woman fled into the wilderness, where ***there was*** a place prepared ***by*** God ***for her. And I saw the four and twenty elders and the four beasts standing before the woman, and it was given them*** that they should feed her there a thousand two hundred and threescore days.

After Jesus Christ was rejected, because the people chose to follow their fleshly natures instead of his *way of life*, the gospel of truth was taken from the people. John uses the same verbiage other prophets have used in describing the pattern that people follow in rejecting the truth.

The following passage from Ezekiel presents in his words exactly what John has presented in his own *Revelation*. Instead of using the term *"woman with child,"* Ezekiel uses *"mother."* Instead of *"crown," "scepters"* are used. Ezekiel leaves out the term *"dragon"*; however, when his writings are read in context, little doubt is left that he refers to the desires of the flesh as the contributing factor to the corruption of the people. Both mention that the righteous are "*cast to the earth*."

Ezekiel mentions that "*her strong rods were broken*," just as John writes of "*a man child who was to rule all nations with a rod of iron*." Both end their presentations by having the "*woman/mother fled/planted*" in the wilderness:

> *Thy **mother** is like a vine in thy blood, planted by the waters: she was fruitful and full of branches by reason of many waters. And she had strong rods for the **scepters** of them that bare rule, and her stature was exalted among the thick branches, and she appeared in her height with the multitude of her branches. But she was plucked up in fury, **she was cast down to the ground**, and the east wind dried up her fruit: her strong rods were broken and withered; the fire consumed them. And now she is plant-ed in the wilderness, in a dry and thirsty ground.* (Ezekiel 19:10–13)

Throughout the *Old Testament*, the prophets have referred to a "*wilderness*" as the place where people are led who do not have access to the fullness of truth. This mortal state is a "*wilderness*," as none have access to the fullness of truth because of the veil over our minds. This *veil*, or inability to know all the mysteries of God, is represented by prophets when they mention the ancient people being led by a "*pillar of fire*" by night (in which a fire obscures the lights in the night sky), and a "*pillar of a cloud*" by day (in which clouds obscure the light of the sun), both insinuating that the people are being led to a place prepared for them (the promised land) without God revealing His mysteries (His light is obscured).

This preset course was established as a wise way for us to experience a "*wilderness*" in comparison to a *promised land*. In other words, so we can experience what it is like to live *without* knowing and understanding truth, in order to appreciate what it is like when we do.

*Yet thou in thy manifold mercies forsookest them not in the **wilderness**: the **pillar of the cloud** departed not from them by day, to lead them in the way; neither the **pillar of fire** by night, to shew them light, and the way wherein they should go. Thou gavest also thy good spirit to instruct them, and withheldest not thy manna from their mouth, and gavest them water for their thirst. Yea, forty years didst thou sustain them in the wilderness, so that they lacked nothing; their clothes waxed not old, and their feet swelled not.* (Nehemiah 9:19–21)

*Thy holy cities are a **wilderness**, Zion is a **wilderness**, Jerusalem a desolation. Our holy and our beautiful house, where our fathers praised thee, is burned up with fire: and all our pleasant things are laid waste.* (Isaiah 64:10–11)

*Oh that I had in the **wilderness** a lodging place of wayfaring men; that I might leave my people, and go from them! for they be all adulterers, an assembly of treacherous men. ...Many pastors have destroyed my vineyard, they have trodden my portion under foot, they have made my pleasant portion a desolate **wilderness**.* (Jeremiah 9:2; 12:10)

When the ancient Israelites (including their leader, Moses) rebelled against God, none of them were permitted to enter into the land of promise. Joshua was the one who finally led the people into the land filled with "milk and honey." *Milk* because the truths when unfolded in plainness are as an infant's food, and *honey* because these truths will be sweet to whomever receives them. This story gave a parallel of those things which occurred when Jesus (Yeshua, whose true name should properly be translated as *Joshua*) arrived to lead the people in truth and righteousness by giving them a manna, which if they partook, would fill them up, never to feel the pains of hunger again:

Then Jesus said unto them, Verily, verily, I say unto you,
Moses gave you not that bread from heaven; but my Father
giveth you the true bread from heaven. For the bread of
God is he which cometh down from heaven, and giveth life
unto the world. Then said they unto him, Lord, evermore
give us this bread. And Jesus said unto them, I am the
bread of life: he that cometh to me shall never hunger; and
he that believeth on me shall never thirst. (John 6:32–35)

In order to parallel the message given throughout scripture of "the first shall be last and the last shall be first," those who oversee the work of God upon this earth waited until the author of this book, who was called to present the "milk and honey" of John's *Revelation*, reached the exact same age as the number of years Joshua had to wait until he was allowed to lead the Israelites into the land of promise (If of any interest, this author's *firstborn* son's name is *Joshua* as well):

And now, behold, the LORD hath kept me alive, as he said,
*these **forty and five years**, even since the LORD spake*
this word unto Moses, while the children of Israel wan-
dered in the wilderness: (Joshua 14:10)

In Revelation 12:6, John gives an exact time of "*a thousand two hundred and threescore days*" instead of the more general time period of "*time, times, and half of time.*" John uses "*three days and an half,*" or "*time, times, and half of time*" to represent *general time periods* when, according to Jewish tradition and history, prophets would be teaching the fullness of the gospel to the people of the earth.

When he intended to give a *specific time period* of a certain event, he distinguishes this time frame from the general one by using "*a thousand two hundred and threescore days.*" This has substantial relevance because by so doing, John gives the reader a clue about the amount of time the fullness of the gospel would be withheld after he was commanded to stop preaching to the world. (This was discussed in the commentary on Revelation 11:2–4.)

The "*place prepared by God*" is not a physical location, but a state of mind, in which those who live the gospel are *placed* as they do unto others what they would have done unto them. It is a *place* of peace, happiness, and an understanding of the fullness of the gospel. It is the *place* that is promised to those who keep the commandments of God and have a true testimony of Jesus Christ and his gospel.

> *But if ye turn unto me, and keep my commandments, and do them; though there were of you cast out unto the uttermost part of the heaven, yet will I gather them from thence, and will bring them **unto the place that I have chosen to set my name there**. Now these are thy servants and thy people, whom thou hast redeemed by thy great power, and by thy strong hand.* (Nehemiah 1:9–10)

12:7 And there ***appeared another sign*** in heaven ***in the likeness of a war being waged both*** in heaven ***and upon the earth***. ***And*** Michael and his angels fought against the dragon; and the dragon and his angels fought ***against Michael***;

As explained in the commentary of Revelation 8:1, "*Michael*" is the figurative expression of the Holy Ghost. The "*war*" that is presented is the constant battle between our flesh ("*Lucifer/the dragon*") and our spirits (*Holy Ghost/"Michael"*). This war was explained in the commentary section on Revelation 11:7.

12:8 And ***at the end of the battle, the dragon and his angels*** prevailed not ***against Michael or the child or the woman***; ***and the*** place ***which had been given to the dragon and his angels was not*** found any more in heaven ***or on earth***.

We were created to experience joy and happiness in our associations with each other. In order to do this, we must overcome and win the battle between our selfish natures and the law of the gospel, which is to do unto others what we would want them to do to us. Until we can live this law, none of us will be ready to live in a world where this is required in order to maintain the peace and happiness we were promised upon creation. God did not create us to experience misery living with each other, or to fear one another, or to put ourselves above each other; we were created to overcome our *flesh*, which fights against our *true* natures while in mortality.

In the end, we must overcome the flesh and learn to respect each other and live the law of the everlasting gospel of His Christ. Luckily, there is more than one planet that will be prepared in the future, upon which we will live forever, and experience those things that bring each of us the different degree of individual happiness we each desire. Before we are entrusted with an eternal body that will never die, we must be able to use it the way it was meant to be used—to experience happiness for ourselves and maintain happiness for others.

12:9 And the great dragon was cast out, that old serpent, called ***Lucifer***, the Devil, ***who is also called*** Satan, which deceiveth the whole world: he was cast out ***of heaven and also out of*** the earth, and his angels were cast out with him.

Isaiah puts it beautifully this way:

How art thou fallen from heaven, O Lucifer, son of the morning! how art thou cut down to the ground, which didst weaken the nations! For thou hast said in thine heart, I will ascend into heaven, I will exalt my throne above the stars of God: I will sit also upon the mount of the congregation, in the sides of the north: I will ascend above the heights of the clouds; I will be like the most High. Yet thou shalt be brought down to hell, to the sides of the pit. They that see thee shall narrowly look upon thee, and consider thee, saying, Is this the man that made the earth to tremble, that did shake kingdoms; That made the world as a wilderness, and destroyed the cities thereof; that opened not the house of his prisoners? All the kings of the nations, even all of them, lie in glory, every one in his own house. But thou art cast out of thy grave like an abominable branch, and as the raiment of those that are slain, thrust through with a sword, that go down to the stones of the pit; as a carcase trodden under feet. Thou shalt not be joined with them in burial, because thou hast destroyed thy land, and slain thy people: the seed of evil-doers shall never be renowned. Prepare slaughter for his children for the iniquity of their fathers; that they do not rise, nor possess the land, nor fill the face of the world with cities. (Isaiah 14:12–21)

The study of the human psyche has long been an interest to those who have taken it upon themselves to analyze, scrutinize, and come up with a solution to the problems human beings experience in life. Their study and search is exhaustive and never-ending, and usually culminates in one observation: the happiness of the creature depends on its ability to reconcile itself with its own existence.

This reconciliation can only be realized when the adaptation to its environment creates a balance, which is defined and recognized by human beings as happiness. If happiness is not experienced, the being cannot justify the purpose for its existence; therefore, it continually seeks the balance of physical and emotional satisfaction by using any *means* at its disposal. This *means* is the flesh. Our innate desire for happiness (the flesh) dictates how this balance is maintained.

Because our human experience appears to have a beginning (birth) and an end (death), which are the only things we know of a surety, we justify any action that will satisfy the pleasures we crave. The satisfaction of these fleshly desires is the essence of who we are, and in our minds, takes precedence over the pursuit of happiness of others with whom we share our existence. We become reconciled to eat, drink, and be merry, for tomorrow we die; and if our eating, drinking, and merriment causes unhappiness to others, it is their problem, not ours, for we have found *our* balance.

This is the course of the flesh, which are the truths, the doctrines and the enticements of "*that old serpent, called Lucifer, the Devil, who is also called Satan, which deceiveth the whole world.*" (Source withheld.)

There is only one way to conquer the flesh and cast Satan out: make sure those with whom you associate have the same ability and means to find happiness as you do. If all beings live to make sure everyone else around them is happy, we would all be happy. In other words, do unto others what you would have them do unto you—the commandment upon which *all* the laws of God, His Christ, and His prophets are predicated; and which, of course, is diametrically opposed to *Lucifer's* plan.

If we were created for our existence to end in misery, then eternal death seems justifiable. But if happiness is to be our end, and for this reason we were created, then eternal life is preferred.

12:10 And I heard a loud voice saying in heaven, Now is come salvation, and strength, and the kingdom of our God, and the power of his Christ *to the earth*; for the accuser of *men* is cast *out*, which *caused them to accuse him* before our God day and night.

John writes of the glorious time when the whole world will finally be aware of what they can do to create an environment of peace and happiness ("*salvation*"). This can only occur when a proper leader directs according to the rule of a righteous law ("*the kingdom of our God*").

Logic should cry that unless this Anointed One comes to the earth in a supernatural, spectacular way, demonstrating a power ("*strength*") and knowledge never known before, the people will doubt his authority. When this alien visits the earth, then will the truth be known that we are not alone in this Universe, and there are others who have progressed in knowledge and understanding far beyond anything we mere mortals can comprehend. Instead of speculation, hypothesis, belief, opinion, or imagination, reality will finally become the norm.

Using logic and reality, how can *Lucifer* be "*the accuser of men?*" Accusing them of what? Of obeying the commandments of God and disrupting his earthly kingdom and glory? Does *Lucifer* go before God and make accusations "*day and night*" about those who do not follow him? It is quite obvious that the original translators of John's words had no clue what he was trying to say when they came up with their own interpretation of this passage.

Part of the great turmoil and embarrassment that the people of the earth will experience when Christ sets up the proper government and society, and reveals reality in all the glory and splendor of logic, is the fact that each of them was, is, and will always be, completely responsible for his or her own actions. No longer can they "*accuse*" a being outside of themselves for the actions that caused their misery. The foolish notion of demonic possession and "*the devil made me do it*" will be "*cast out*" under the truth that we are all individually and independently responsible for what our spirit tells our body to do.

However, this does not discount physical aberrations that cause mental illnesses and how they affect our decisions to think rationally. But true to the intended meaning given of the prophets for "*Lucifer*," in these cases, it *is* the flesh that contributes to our aberrant behavior.

The invention of a "*Lucifer*," "Satan," "the devil," demons or evil spirits, and the likes, has been used by men to make *accusations before God* as to why they have acted contrary to His commandments. With a belief that an outside influence can direct our thoughts and actions, it is very easy for human nature to run its course uninhibited, because the being inside the body is not responsible for what it does. Conversely, in order to establish peace and happiness, one must understand that this "*kingdom of God*" can only be established from within as fast as each of us (being individually responsible) influences the acts that lead to this end.

When the human race finally realizes there is no hell, except for the one which it creates for itself, and that there is no force that can take away an individual's free agency, and that we are solely responsible for how we use the bodies we have been given, we will finally have the ability to do what is necessary to create the peace and happiness associated with the term, "*the kingdom of our God*."

"*The power of his Christ*" is not in forcing us against our will, which not even God can do (so how can we believe the devil can?), but *is* teaching us the things we need to know and understand, in order to be able to create heaven on earth ourselves. When this is accomplished, no longer will men be able "to *accuse*" someone other than themselves—so much for "*man's accuser*."

12:11 *For* they *have gained victory and overcome* him by the blood of the Lamb, and by the word of their testimony *which they have borne; for* they loved not their *own* lives *but kept the testimony of the word even* unto death.

John is explaining how those, who once accused "*Lucifer*" of their wickedness, were able to overcome the temptations of the flesh.

Jesus counseled his disciples:

> *And he that taketh not his cross* [bear the testimony of Christ], *and followeth after me, is not worthy of me. He that findeth **his life shall lose it**: and he that **loseth his life for my sake shall find it**.* (Matthew 10:38–39)

Before he said these words—which were directed at those of us who look to satisfy the natural urges that compel us to save our *own* lives (in spite of what we must do to protect ourselves from others)—Christ explained that he was *not* on earth to provide an excuse for us in treating others badly to protect our own selfish interests. Christ taught that filial bonds (the family) create the most powerful urges of self-protection, and can cause us to act contrary to the way we must live in order to experience true peace and happiness:

> *Think not that I am come to send peace on earth: I came not to send peace, but a sword. For I am come to set a man at variance against his father, and the daughter against her mother, and the daughter in law against her mother in law. And a man's foes shall be they of his own household. He that loveth father or mother more than me is not worthy of me: and he that loveth son or daughter more than me is not worthy of me.* (Matthew 10:34–37)

Once we understand "it's all up to us," and that there is no one else to blame for our misery and unhappiness ("*the accuser cast out*"), our desire to promote this happiness becomes extrinsic, and we begin to look for ways to increase the happiness of others, which will indirectly affect our own. This is the attitude and purpose of the life of Christ. This is the essence and purpose that gave him life, and caused gladness to surge through his veins as he shared his message with the world—this was the "*blood of the Lamb.*" (Refer also to the commentary on Revelation 1:6, 5:1, and especially 5:9.)

12:12 Rejoice, ye that dwell in *the* heavens *and upon the earth! And after I had beheld these things I heard another voice saying, The time of rejoicing is not yet because the devil still reigneth upon the earth*. Therefore, woe to the inhabiters of the earth and *they who dwell upon the islands* of the sea! for the devil is come down unto you, having great wrath, because he knoweth *he shall be conquered and* that he hath but a short time.

John gets excited relating the wonderful promise of peace and happiness we will experience in the kingdom of God once we have overcome the desires of our flesh. However, he knows the time for this salvation is yet to come, and warns us to watch ourselves, much the same way Jesus warned his disciples:

> Watch and pray, that ye enter not into temptation: the spirit indeed is willing, but the flesh is weak. (Matthew 26:41)

Most see death as the end of their existence. With this mentality, we believe we have such a "*short time*" to live and experience the desires of our flesh; therefore, it would seem logical to take advantage of the time we have left, and enjoy life during this "*short time.*" Believing death is the end, the only purpose left for our lives is the satisfaction of our fleshy desires that leads us to immediate satiation of our lusts.

Our human nature fights against anything that stands in the way of fulfilling the needs and desires of our flesh. We are filled with "*great wrath*" when someone or something stands in the way of the immediate gratification of these desires. We fight when either we, or someone we love, is threatened. We are easily annoyed with those who appear happy, but live contrary to our belief system and way of life.

There are many other ways our flesh fights for its own benefit, regardless of what we do to others. This happens because our beliefs are threatened, usually because we are not as happy following our way of life as those who live another way appear to be, i.e., "the grass is always greener on your neighbor's side of the fence." Our egos take precedence over our happiness, and anything that threatens our self-validation fights with this "*wrath*."

John is warning us that our flesh ("*the devil*") will continue to tempt us to remain selfish and self-centered, prohibiting us from doing unto another what we would want done unto us. This is because our flesh has convinced us we have "*but a short time*" before death overwhelms us and "*conquers*" us.

12:13 And when the dragon saw that he was ***to be overcome and*** cast ***out of*** the earth, he ***pursued*** the woman which brought forth the man child, ***to torment her***.

When we believe there is such a "*short time*" between birth and death, we see things with a limited perspective, which encloses our world inside a box made of our earthly experiences, limiting our reality to this box. Inside our box, we see nothing beyond what we have learned since our birth.

Everything we are taught from the time we enter the world encourages us to protect our own interests, which include our immediate loved ones, who are only our "*loved* ones" because they are part of our interests. When someone we might have once loved takes his or her interests somewhere else, our selfish natures are no longer fulfilled by their existence; therefore, we *lose* our love, and could care less what happens to them. Likewise, we are concerned for our loved ones with much more interest than we are for our neighbors, and others whom we do not love, or with whom we have not shared an interest in our mortal experience. This is the natural course of the flesh, and is diametrically opposed to the gospel of Jesus Christ.

The "*woman*" represents the group of people who are resolved to keep the commandments of Jesus Christ ("*the man child*") as he delivered them during his own mortal experience. But as these principles are taught to us, or come knocking on the enclosed reality inside our boxes, we become uncomfortable, and attempt to find a way to justify our cramped reality by discounting the gospel of Jesus. We begin to *"pursue"* ways to fight (*"torment her"*) against the words of Christ.

Christ taught us not to become angry or call another a fool for what he or she might do that does not agree with us. Yet when another threatens the security of our box, they are the "fool" because we are "right." We are angered that our box was even approached, and we satisfy our flesh by fighting against any who might disagree with the living arrangements inside our box. When we are sued in a court of law by someone seeking our money or material goods, how many of us do as Christ commanded? He commanded:

> *And if any man will sue thee at the law, and take away*
> *thy coat, let him have thy cloke [sic] also.* (Matthew 5:40)

If someone strikes us on the left cheek, our flesh will not allow us to take another strike, but encourages us to strike back. We judge others. We measure others. We speak ill of others. We hate and kill our enemies. We lay up for ourselves treasures upon earth, treasuring the clothes we wear ("what moths corrupt"), and our cars and material goods ("what rust corrupts and thieves break in and steal"). We do these things because our flesh has justified our actions in defense of our egos, which are securely housed in the box of our limited reality. We do nothing commanded by Jesus Christ. (See Matthew 6:19–21.)

John sees this battle and presents it here as *"the dragon"* (our flesh), which realizes it has only a *"short time"* to live, so in protection of its desires, it finds any way it can (*"pursues the woman and the man child"*) to ridicule and avoid (*persecute/"torment"*) the truths revealed to us by the mouth of Christ, which will not only bring us peace and happiness while in mortality, but will also allow us salvation in the world to come. The problem is, *"the dragon"* doesn't want us to know of the world to come, and deceives us into believing it all ends when we are dead.

12:14 *Therefore, the elders and the beasts which stood before* the woman *gave her* two wings of a great eagle, that she might fly into the wilderness, into *a* place *prepared for* her, where she is nourished for a time, and times, and half a time, *safe* from the face of the serpent.

This verse parallels Revelation 12:6 in its presentation, but uses the general time frame description of *"time, and times, and half a time"* instead of the more specific time frame used by John in the former verse. Verse six speaks of the *"woman"* fleeing into the wilderness after the *"child was caught up and taken unto God"* representing the state of emptiness and lack of nourishment (*"wilderness"*) the people of the earth would experience for a *specific* time period after the apostasy of the early people who once followed the commandments of Christ. Taken in context, both verses represent the constant war going on between our human natures (the flesh) and our desires for happiness (the spirit).

Here, John expresses the effect that the prophets of God (*"the elders"*) and the unseen angels (*"the beasts"*) have on those who keep the commandments, and have the testimony of Jesus Christ. They have the ability to give power (*"wings"*) to those who listen and obey, to escape the vicissitudes and torments of the flesh. This has always been the case, and is thus presented by John as the time periods: *"time, times, and half a time,"* in which prophets have been called and sent into the world to preach the gospel to the people. (See commentary on Revelation 11:11.)

John borrows the expression of fleeing into the wilderness and to the land of promise (*"the place prepared"*) upon *"eagles' wings"* (with the help of unseen angels) from the Old Testament:

> Ye have seen what I did unto the Egyptians, and how I bare you on **eagles' wings**, and brought you unto myself. Now therefore, if ye will obey my voice indeed, and keep my covenant, then ye shall be a peculiar treasure unto me above all people: for all the earth is mine: (Exodus 19:4–5)

Masterfully, John takes most of his expressions of this part of *Revelation* from the story of Moses, and the exodus of the children of Israel into the wilderness. The part referring to the *"man child"* being born to the *"woman"* with the *"dragon"* waiting to devour him, was inspired by the biblical relation of Pharaoh's edict commanding the Hebrew midwives to kill all males born to the children of Israel. (See verse 4 and 5 above.)

12:15 And the serpent cast out of his mouth water as a ***great river*** after the woman, that he might cause her to be carried away ***because*** of the flood.

The *"great river"* John is referring to is the same one mentioned in Revelation 9:14, the river Euphrates, which carried the excrement of the people who lived in ancient Babylon. This city is always used by John as a figurative expression of materialism, excess, and the things of the earth that satisfy our human lusts. As explained above, all of the desires of our hearts lead us away from treating others as our equal, and doing unto them what we would want them to do to us.

As we pursue the satiation of the lusts of the flesh, our houses get bigger, our closets expand, our bank accounts increase, our storage spaces increase and fill, and the waste of our materialism floods our lives with obstacles that cause us to forget about anything else other than rearranging and reorganizing the contents of our *boxes* in which we are drowning.

Furthermore, there is a deluge of *poison rain* coming from the *clouds of darkness* that blocks the light of the sun, and increases the raging currents of false doctrine and precepts coming out of the mouths of the religious and political leaders; causing the *"great river"* of worldly knowledge to overflow and *"flood"* our minds with the polluted water of our own excrements. The people of the earth live in the pollutions of their own doings, and are drowning in their own waste—filling up the great and abominable pit they have dug for themselves with those who have dug it.

> *But the house of Israel rebelled against me in the wilderness: they walked not in my statutes, and they despised my judgments, which if a man do, he shall even live in them; and my sabbaths they greatly polluted: then I said, I would pour out my fury upon them in the wilderness, to consume them.* (Ezekiel 20:13)

Because they are drowning in the *"flood"* of their own concerns, they forget the poor and the needy, and instead concentrate more on making a car payment and sending their children to college, than worrying about the homeless and deprived who are the least among them, and the least thought about by them. In all these things, they fulfill the words of the prophets:

> Hear this, O ye that swallow up the needy, even to make the poor of the land to fail, Saying, When will the new moon be gone, that we may sell corn? and the sabbath, that we may set forth wheat, making the ephah small, and the shekel great, and falsifying the balances by deceit? That we may buy the poor for silver, and the needy for a pair of shoes; yea, and sell the refuse of the wheat? The LORD hath sworn by the excellency of Jacob, Surely I will never forget any of their works. Shall not the land tremble for this, and every one mourn that dwelleth therein? **and it shall rise up wholly as a flood; and it shall be cast out and drowned, as by the flood of Egypt.** And it shall come to pass in that day, saith the Lord GOD, that I will cause the sun to go down at noon, and I will darken the earth in the clear day: And I will turn your feasts into mourning, and all your songs into lamentation; and I will bring up sackcloth upon all loins, and baldness upon every head; and I will make it as the mourning of an only son, and the end thereof as a bitter day. Behold, the days come, saith the Lord GOD, that I will send a famine in the land, **not a famine of bread, nor a thirst for water, but of hearing the words of the LORD:** And they shall wander from sea to sea, and from the north even to the east, they shall run to and fro to seek the word of the LORD, and shall not find it. (Amos 8:4–12)

12:16 And the earth helped the woman, and the earth opened her mouth, and swallowed up the flood which the dragon cast out of his mouth.

As the *"flood"* of selfishness and lusts are continually rising on the sea of humanity, the effects of their works are being felt by those who do these works, and not by those who have learned to treat others equally. The latter take no interest in material goods, and live their lives in accordance with the simple words of Christ. The natural course of things ("*the earth*") makes trouble for the inhabitants of this planet, while those who are not involved, sit back with the "*seal of God in their foreheads*," and float safely in "the ark" they have prepared according to the commands of God—to wait out the "*five months*" of torrential rains and floods.

Here, John is expressing the fact that the natural course of things always comes backs and bites the hand that goes against nature. This is a natural Karma, if you will, that establishes a natural law of, "What goes around comes around." As the people of the earth go about their lives in lasciviousness, greed, and selfishness, "*the earth*" creates an unavoidable situation in which they must pay for their actions. This natural cause-and-effect creates a protective shield ("*the earth helped the woman*") for those who know better, and do not participate in the lusts of the world. The righteous are sheltered, while those responsible for the earth's demise are "*swallowed up*" in their self-induced flood.

12:17 And ***because the earth helped*** the woman, the dragon was wroth with ***her***, and went to make war with the remnant of her seed ***who were not drowned in the flood and who*** keep the commandments of God, and have the testimony of Jesus Christ.

People feel the effects of their own doings, and cannot find a solution to their problems, because their flesh ("*the dragon*") keeps them from realizing that the answers to *all* their problems are in the words of Christ and his simple mandate of "doing unto others."

Their inability to realize this frustrates them, and they blame anyone but themselves for their predicament. Therefore, it is natural for them to place the blame on those who are not involved in worldly pursuits. These worldly pursuits have become *their* motivation, and are the essence of *their* existence, and the true cause of all their problems.

The "*war*" between "*the dragon*" and those who are saved ("*the remnant of her seed*") from the "*great flood*," is continual, and will one day culminate in a final battle John will later present as "*Armageddon*."

Chapter

R**EVELATION**
UNFOLDED

13:1 And I *saw another sign in heaven in likeness of the kingdoms of the earth*. And *I* saw a beast rise up out of the sea and stand upon the sand of the sea, having seven heads and ten horns, and upon his horns ten crowns, and upon his heads the name of blasphemy.

The "*beast*" referred to here is the same beast John later describes in Revelation 17:3. This "*beast*" is a "*beast of the earth*," unlike the "*four beasts of heaven*" mentioned previously by John. To properly understand what this "*beast*" represents, it is necessary to review what John later reveals in *Revelation*.

The "*woman*" who is described previously as being in the "*wilderness*," is presented later as "*sitting upon a scarlet coloured beast, full of names of blasphemy, having seven heads and ten horns*" (17:3). The "*woman in the wilderness*" represents those saints who escaped the "*dragon.*" However, in Revelation 13:6–7, the "*beast*" is finally allowed to "*overcome the saints*," and gain "*power over all kindreds, and tongues, and nations.*" This prepares the reader appropriately to see the "*woman sitting upon the beast.*"

The description of the "*woman*" and the "*beast*" gives the reader all the information needed to understand what this "*beast*" represents:

> *And I was carried away in the spirit into the wilderness where I saw a woman sit upon a scarlet coloured beast,* **full of names of blasphemy, having seven heads wtih seven crowns and ten horns**. *And the woman was arrayed in purple and scarlet colour, and decked with gold and precious stones and pearls, having a golden cup in her hand full of abominations and the filthiness of her fornication: And upon her forehead was a name written, MYSTERY, BABY-LON THE GREAT, THE MOTHER OF HARLOTS AND ABOMINATIONS OF THE EARTH.* (Revelation 17:3–5)

The "*beast*" represents a political and social design established ("*rise up*") by the societies of humankind ("*out of the sea*") to satisfy the desires of human nature. This design "*stands upon the sand of the sea,*" meaning it covers the entire earth, as the "*sand of the sea*" represents the people of the earth:

> *That in blessing I will bless thee, and in multiplying I will multiply thy seed as the stars of the heaven, and as* **the sand which is upon the sea shore**; *and thy seed shall possess the gate of his enemies*; (Genesis 22:17)

The unquenchable desire for money, materialism, and worldly comforts to satiate human lust, is what the "*beast*" offers the "*woman*." The governments and democracies ("*ten horns*") of the world ("*seven heads*"/continents) are set up to please those whom they govern. When a democracy reigns with power, its sole purpose is to satisfy the wants of the constituents who support it. It cares nothing for the mandates of God ("*the name of blasphemy*"), which would create equality by providing for the needs of all people of the earth. The purpose of the "*beast*" is to allow for and provide the material wants and lusts of the heart ("*a woman sit upon a scarlet colored beast*").

In modern terms, the best way to describe what the *"beast"* promises is: "The American Dream." Later in *Revelation,* John presents how this hope and dream has *"overcome the saints"* of God, and is the desire of the whole world.

13:2 And the beast which I saw was like unto a leopard, and his feet were as the feet of a bear, and his mouth as the mouth of a lion: and the dragon gave him his power, and his seat, and great authority.

In the first part of this verse, John has borrowed heavily from Daniel in the presentation of the governments and powers that represent *"the beast."* Whereas Daniel writes of separate and *"diverse"* governments, John makes no such distinction, and figuratively expresses all as *"one beast"*:

*Daniel spake and said, I saw in my vision by night, and, behold, the four winds of the heaven strove **upon the great sea**. And four **great beasts came up from the sea**, diverse one from another. The first was **like a lion**, and had eagle's wings: I beheld till the wings thereof were plucked, and it was lifted up from the earth, and made stand upon the feet as a man, and a man's heart was given to it. And behold another beast, a second, **like to a bear**, and it raised up itself on one side, and it had three ribs in the mouth of it between the teeth of it: and they said thus unto it, Arise, devour much flesh. After this I beheld, and lo another, **like a leopard**, which had upon the back of it four wings of a fowl; the beast had also four heads; and dominion was given to it. After this I saw in the night visions, and behold a fourth beast, dreadful and terrible, and strong exceedingly; and it had great iron teeth: it devoured and brake in pieces, and stamped the residue with the feet of it: and it was diverse from all the beasts that were before it; and it had ten horns. I considered **the horns**, and, behold, there came up among them another little horn, before whom* *there were three of the first horns plucked up by the roots: and, behold, in this horn were eyes like the eyes of man, and a mouth speaking great things.* (Daniel 7:2–8)

The *"beast"* has great power over the people of the earth. Its strength is powerful and exercised in darkness (*"leopards"* are dark and hunt at night). It moves with force, crushing under its *"feet"* anything that rises against it (there is no animal as strong in its feet/paws as the *"bear"*). The sound of its voice is both intimidating and fierce (*"the mouth of a lion"*) to all who dare challenge it.

"His power, and his seat, and great authority" as mentioned in the latter part of this verse, comes only one way: by the voice and election of the people who are driven by the *"power"* of the flesh (*"the dragon gave him his power"*) to hope and desire for what the *"beast"* can offer them. Though it *"sits upon many waters,"* *"the seat"* (throne) of this *"beast"* is established firmly in the midst of the people who devour more of the earth's resources in pursuit of their fleshly lusts than anyone else in the world. From its most powerful *"seat,"* the *"beast"* rules the world with its economic policies, laws, and mandates. In former times, it was Rome that maintained this *"seat and great authority"*; in modern times, **THE UNITED STATES OF AMERICA** *is* **THE SEAT OF THE BEAST**.

13:3 And I saw one of his heads as *if* it were wounded *even unto* death; *but* his deadly wound was healed: and all the world wondered after the beast *and bowed down before him*.

In order to properly understand what John is establishing here as *"one of his heads"* being *"wounded,"* and also to fully understand the rest of the figurative expressions presented in Chapter 13, it is imperative to introduce a brief and concise history of Roman Law.

Laws are the basis of any human society, and govern those subjected to them. A society of people that lives to fulfill its selfish desires, no matter what the cost might be to others, will establish laws which codify and support these desires—this premise is the *"beast"* John presents throughout this part of *Revelation*. One of the *ten horns* upon one of the *"seven heads"* of this "*beast*" was the Great Roman Empire that extended into all parts of the continent (Europe, one of the "*seven heads*") on which it was established.

Though there were other governments established throughout the world at the time of the Romans, (and all were set up under the premise of the "*beast,*") none compared to the Roman Empire, which has been called by historians as one of the greatest civilization in the history of the world.

From the 6th Century B.C.E., the principles, procedures, and institutions of Roman law dominated both Western and parts of Eastern civilization. Most of the current legal systems of Western Europe are based on Roman law, and are called *civil law* systems. The United States claims *common law* as its precedent, but there is little doubt of the influence Roman law had on its establishment.

Roman law began as an attempt to codify a single set of legal principles for all citizens, but selectively (with purpose) protected the rights and supported the agendas of the educated and elite, who could read, write, and establish such laws and convince the people to follow them. The Roman republic developed the *jus civile*, or civil law, the beginnings of which were based on both custom and local legislation that applied only to Roman citizens. Later, the Romans developed the *jus gentium*, or the law of nations, which were rules of international law that applied to interactions between Romans and foreigners. Eventually, these laws became a massive compendium produced and manipulated by the magistrates and governors from the elitist class.

Roman law was divided into two parts: the written law, and the unwritten law. The unwritten law was based on custom and tradition, while the written law came primarily from legislation by those who held the power over the people. These included their edicts, proclamations, and any resolutions that supported their power. Their laws covered every type of legal issue including contracts, inheritance of property, family law, business organizations and criminal acts, *all* of *which* centered on the desires to earn, sustain, and keep individual and family wealth secured and controlled.

With time, Roman law steadily expanded as new ideas and laws were introduced when necessary in order to protect a Roman citizen's right to accumulate and maintain wealth. Because of the corruption and greed of government officials, the legal books became contradictory and confusing.

This is how the Romans dug a *"pit"* for themselves out of which they could not climb, eventually filling it with those who dug it. The *"smoke"* that rose out of the *"pit"* produced *"locusts"* (see comentary on Revelation 9) that tormented and struck fear in the hearts and the minds of the people under the influence of Roman law. The *"beast"* prevailed over the people and would eventually lead to their demise. The Great Roman Empire was *"wounded"* and fell; and great was the fall thereof.

Though Roman government policies and laws were *"wounded"* when the Great Empire fell, they did not *"die"*; but *"his deadly wound was healed"* when later empires incorporated Roman customs and laws into their societies. These later empires had just as strong a desire to accumulate individual and family wealth as did the Romans, and thus the people *"wondered after the beast."*

A number of years later, the Byzantine emperor Justinian I appointed a commission to examine the body of Roman law and determine what should be kept and what should be discarded. From this effort came the *Corpus Juris Civilis*, or Body of Civil Law, which is a codification of Roman law that became the chief book of law that remained of the *"wounded"* Roman Empire. Of course, the Byzantine leaders chose those laws which supported their incessant lust for material wealth, as did the Romans before them.

Throughout Medieval Times, Roman law influenced the legal system of the Catholic (worldwide) Church, as well as almost every country in Europe. Consequently, church leaders (*"the locusts"*) became the wealthiest and most powerful people in the world, *"blaspheming"* in word and deed the gospel of Jesus Christ, which demands equality for all individuals.

13:4 And they worshipped the dragon which gave power unto the beast: and they **praised** the beast, saying, Who is like unto the beast? who is able to make war with him?

Today, people are pursuing the lusts and desires of the flesh (*"worshipped the dragon"*) which give life and *"power"* to the systems of government (*"beast"*), both politically and spiritually. These systems allow the people the ability to realize their dreams of worldliness, or they at least provide their citizens with the glimmer of hope that they *might*. People strive their whole lives to become popular, accepted, and obtain as much money as they can, not only for their immediate fleshly needs, but also for the future when they hope they will not have to work.

Because this type of focus is self-centered or family-centered, it is *"praised"* and supported through political patriotism and religious affiliation. This attitude leads to a more isolated human being, which leads to a more tightly knit family unit, which then forms communities, cities, states, and nations that set up borders to protect those rights that are *"praised"* as virtuous and righteous. They protect their borders against all others who do not believe as they do, many times forcing their beliefs upon others by extending the borders of their system of human desire supported by the force of law. The only way their beliefs can be protected and promulgated, is through **war**. When this value system is accepted and protected by the strongest governments, and praised by the people, *"who is able to make war with"* it?

13:5 And there was given unto him a mouth speaking great things and blasphemies; and power was given unto him to continue forty and two months.

Some historians have marked the official end of the Roman Empire as circa 478 A.D.; however, John was alive during the course of its downfall, and personally determined from his own prophetic perspective that it continued for a longer period of time. Eventually, remnant governments were assimilated into the Byzantine Empire around the year 570 A.D. This is John's reference point used in Revelation 11:2, when he was commanded to not preach the fullness of the gospel any longer amongst the people to whom he had been sent.

This date was also used by John to mark the period known as the *"times"* (see commentary on Revelation 11), in which there would be no more effort made by the prophets of God to preach to the Jewish people, who by this time, were scattered throughout the world into every nation and kingdom, both on the Eastern and the Western Hemispheres.

The influence of this quest for personal wealth and easy living spread throughout the world (*"a mouth speaking great things"*), promising the kings, priests, and warriors great wealth as they conquered other peoples and nations, and brought them under their subjection. For these *"forty and two months"* (1260 years according to John's timetable), this *"beast"* would continue to devour the inhabitants of the earth. It did this through the strength of the secular kings and the religious priests who ruled over the people, completely disregarding (*"speaking...blasphemies"*) the tenets of the gospel of Jesus Christ, which command us:

> But I say unto you, Love your enemies, bless them that curse you, do good to them that hate you, and pray for them which despitefully use you, and persecute you; That ye may be the children of your Father which is in heaven: for he maketh his sun to rise on the evil and on the good, and sendeth rain on the just and on the unjust. (Matthew 5:45)

The people were convinced by the *"beast"* (*"a mouth speaking great things"*) that there was no other way to protect their self-interests, their families, their communities, their cities, and their nations unless they did so by killing their enemies.

13:6 And he opened his mouth in blasphemy against God, to blaspheme his name, and his tabernacle, and them that dwell in heaven.

The people were no longer doing the works (*"his name"*) commanded by God. No one was attempting to establish the kingdom of God (*"his tabernacle"*) anywhere on earth; nor were the people being led by spiritual beings, angels, or prophets sent from heaven, and which the *sun* and the *moon* (*"that dwell in heaven"*) represent.

13:7 And it was given unto him to make war with the saints, and to overcome them: and power was given him over all kindreds, and tongues, and nations.

The people give the *"beast"* (*"and it was given unto him"*) his power by supporting the kings, queens, presidents, magistrates, and religious leaders who speak (*"mouth speaking great things"*) to them. The leaders decieve their followers into believing that one's religious and patriotic duty is to support their nation and their church leaders. Even the righteous humble peasants (*"the saints"*) who live in harmony with each other and with nature, striving to do unto each other what they would want done unto them when allowed to do so, are overcome by the deceiving words of the "*beast*," and the power of "*the dragon*" that rages in their flesh. Eventually, the whole world is overcome.

13:8 And all that dwell upon the earth shall worship him, whose names are not written in the Book of Life of the Lamb slain from the foundation of the world.

The only ones who do not worship the "*beast*" (and there were few during this 1260 years or "*forty and two months*") are those who have subdued "*the dragon*" (desires of the flesh) within, and live (*"whose names"*/works) according to the example and the teachings of the gospel of Jesus Christ. This is the same teaching that has always been taught from the foundation of the world, and is the only way to eternal life (the instructions and directions in "*the Lamb's Book of Life*" received from the Father).

During Medieval Times (appropriately called The Dark Ages), no religious leader could teach or lead the people in truth and righteousness. This was because they, more than the people who followed them, were led by "*the dragon*," their master, which gave much power to "*the beast*." Catholic and orthodox religious leaders were the richest and most revered men on earth. They called and anointed the kings and political leaders, and influenced or directly controlled almost all political decisions.

13:9 If any man have an ear, let him hear.

Review the commentary on Revelation 2:7, keeping in mind that by unfolding the mystery of *Revelation* in this book, what was only known to very few, is now available for all the world to hear and understand:

What ye hear in the ear, that preach ye upon the housetops.
(Matthew 10:27)

13:10 He that leadeth into captivity shall go into captivity: he that killeth with the sword must be killed with the sword. Here is the patience and the faith of the saints.

The course of action taken by the religious and political leaders during these tumultuous and unsettled times led to the invasion and occupation of other lands which were filled with the material goods and slaves these leaders needed to support their lifestyles. Explorers and conquerors were sent by the leaders of their nations to find new lands and subdue them, bringing back to their financiers the plunder of their many wars and *"captivity."*

There was no other way to support their governments' greed and material lust without going into other countries, *"killing"* any who defended themselves with *"the sword,"* and *"leading into captivity"* the conquered people, so that their homeland would gain from the exploits. The leaders had already exploited their own nation's resources, and promised their citizens prosperity. To fulfill these promises, the governments went beyond their borders, usually doing so without the consent and knowledge of the citizens that supported them.

The *"saints"* of God, or those who *"elect"* to keep His commandments and have received the *"seal of God in their foreheads,"* know that war only leads to war, and captivity only leads to captivity, because a nation is not doing unto another nation what they would want done to them in the same situation. With *faith* and *patience, the saints* await the coming of the One anointed to bring peace to this planet without war, and without captivity, but with the overwhelming strength of love and truth.

Whereas the prophets use *"beasts"* to symbolize a menagerie of strong and vicious animals (*leopards, bears, lions*), this new system of laws and government is always presented as a *"lamb."* But before this *"Lamb"* establishes a kingdom of peace, *"another beast,"* different from the first, pretending to be *"like a lamb,"* must rise *"up out of the earth"* and replace the first *"beast, which was wounded and healed."* This "*psuedo-lamb*" promises to fulfill the desires of the mortal flesh without "*the sword*" or "*captivity,*" (so it shall deceive the people of the earth into believing).

13:11 And I beheld another beast coming up out of the earth; and he had two horns like a lamb, and he spake as a dragon.

Christianity became the religion of choice for the monarchies and aristocracies of the Middle Ages. Christianity was used to introduce false notions and doctrines, which were incorporated into the early Catholic Church. It taught the people that one who sinned against God (a sin being anything that was contrary to the mandates and commandments of the Church and its leaders), could not only be recompensed and forgiven by the leaders of the Church through communion and confession, but most importantly, by the payment of tithes and offerings. This blind obeisance sustained the lifestyles of the leaders who benefited the most, not only with material goods, but by maintaining strict control over the minds of the people.

The corrupted doctrine that Jesus died on the cross for our sins (instead of Christ's simple message of love your neighbor as yourself) benefited these leaders greatly because of the people's desire to feel emotionally balanced and right with God. To the people, the Church was God, and the leaders were His appointed spokesmen.

No longer were there vagabond prophets of God, coming forth out of the wilderness dressed in sackcloth and ashes, eating honeycomb and locusts and living without material wealth—not allowing themselves to be put above another in any type of leadership position. These types were not "blessed" with the riches and luxuries that were indicative of the leaders of the Church; therefore, not being blessed with these things by the god who rules the earth ("*the dragon*"), why would the people accept them as being divinely appointed?

Having the power of the "*beast*" and being supported by "*the dragon,*" the Church and its people spread throughout the earth, fighting wars and conquering other nations in the name of their god—material wealth and political gain. This was the "*first beast,*" which was figuratively presented by John to represent the Roman Empire and its system of government and laws, as explained previously.

"*Another beast*" came forth, not from "*out of the sea*" as did the first, but "*out of the earth*," which had *soaked up the blood* from the wound received by the *first beast*. This represents the fact that the Roman Empire was established over time, as the inhabitants of the earth pursued their fleshly desires. The peoples of the world ("*the sea*") established this form of society, in which the rich minority reigned over and exploited the poor majority in order to maintain itself. Having been thus established "*in the earth*," this final "*beast*" came "*up out of the earth*," or in other words, was established by the rich and powerful who had already gained (received the *blood soaked into the earth*) from the "*healed wound of the first beast*" before it.

After the European powers had discovered new lands filled with gold, silver, precious herbs, spices, and fertile uncharted territory, they sent people there, and guarded these new colonies with armies and navies. These nations colonized these new lands with one purpose in mind: to exploit the natural resources and tax the people living there.

The Americas became a prize to the Europeans. The native peoples of this new land were seen as corrupt and *evil demons* who had no belief in the "*lamb*" of God; therefore, they were expendable for the promotion of orthodox Christianity. In just a short time, those who had gained riches and power among the new colonies in America formed this "*other beast*."

Rich American landowners began to see the distance between them and the government they were supporting as an opportunity to gain even more personal wealth and power. Why should they remain subjected to other powers and pay part of their wealth to a government many miles across the vast ocean, when they could just as easily set up their *own* government, collect taxes from their *own* citizens, and eliminate the tax forced upon them? As a result, they presented themselves as Christian believers full of peace with love for all men, and spoke great words of equality that all are endowed with certain inalienable rights from God ("*like a lamb*").

In time, this new "*beast*" would rise up, and though it was "*like a lamb*," it had what no lamb is endowed with—"*horns*." Horns are for protection, and are grown upon the head as a warning sign to others that, "We might look like a *lamb*, but we will defend ourselves (*two horns like a lamb*) against any who mess with us."

When other nations struggled to survive their own revolutionary wars and pled with the United States for help, America was not willing to risk going to war for nations they did not believe could survive. However, the true reason why the United States did not go to war for these nations, was that American leaders understood that these rebellious nations did not intend to submit themselves to the laws and government of the United States, and wanted to form their own governments. If the rich landowners and politicians would not personally gain from another nation's desire to be free, why should they involve themselves? From their point of view, as long as the other European powers did not intervene, the government of the United States could let other rebellious colonies fight it out amongst themselves.

The American motherland, Great Britain, was torn between monarchical principle and a desire for new markets. South America as a whole, constituted at the time, a much larger market for English goods than the United States, which had rebelled against them. Instead of war, the United States negotiated the purchase of lands from other European countries, who could see their power slipping away in these foreign parcels of America. With adroit political wrangling, the wealth of the United States increased unlike any other nation ever before it, all the while whispering sweet fragrant empty words of freedom and democracy to the people, who were exploited to perpetuate the "*beast*" that was supported by "*the dragon*."

While the European nations were fighting among themselves for dominance in the Eastern Hemisphere, the "*other beast*" was establishing its "*seat*" securely in the Western.

After the American Founding Fathers had successfully seduced the people into fighting a revolutionary war and establishing *them* as patriotic leaders, these wealthy and powerful land and business owners made sure that "law and order" served them well. A subsequent president, James Monroe, summed up the purpose of American power, and the new society of "*freedom*" they had created in what became known as The Monroe Doctrine.

The Monroe Doctrine essentially proclaimed that the United States was informing the powers of the Old World that the American continents were no longer open to European colonization, and that any effort to extend European political influence into the New World would be considered by the United States as "dangerous to our peace and safety" (protected by the "*two horns like a lamb*"). The United States would not interfere in European wars or internal affairs, and expected Europe to stay out of American affairs. Over time, this new "*beast*" coalesced this Doctrine into an identifiable policy, raising a standard of an independent American foreign policy so strong that future administrations could not ignore it.

Well did Daniel prophesy concerning the United States of America:

> *Then I would know the truth of the fourth beast, which was diverse from all the others, exceeding dreadful, whose teeth were of iron, and his nails of brass; which devoured, brake in pieces, and stamped the residue with his feet; And of the ten horns that were in his head, and of the other which came up, and before whom three fell;* **even of that horn that had eyes, and a mouth that spake very great things, whose look was more stout than his fellows. I beheld, and the same horn made war with the saints, and prevailed against them**; (Daniel 7:19–21)

13:12 And he exerciseth all the power of the first beast before him, and causeth the earth and them which dwell therein to worship the first beast, whose deadly wound was healed.

English law became the basis of American law, and drew its power and establishment from Roman law. English ecclesiastical courts applied canon law, which was based on Roman law, and the universities of Oxford and Cambridge taught both. Scholars have long noted the similarities between Roman and English laws. Most important to the success of the "*beast*" was that much of western European *commercial law* (which contained Roman law), became part of English law without much change. (NOTE: This paragraph was included as a pseudo tongue twister, demonstrating the use of the same laws with the same purpose, a vicious circle, which is to enrich those in power.)

The legal systems of most continental European nations owe their basic structures and categories to Roman law; however, what was most important to the "*beast*" was ensuring the reception of Roman law and the political principles it contained. Roman law that had been produced in a centralized state under a sovereign emperor, could now be used to buttress the arguments of the rich and powerful as they struggled to assert their sovereignty and influence over the ignorant majority.

At the same time the rich were benefiting from the establishment of laws that would protect their lusts for power and material goods, they were also consolidating their power and expanding the role of government administration. Only those who were trained in the law—lawyers—could fill these new positions in government. The majority of the people had no clue from whence their government and courts obtained their laws, and knew little of their true purpose and meaning. And as long as the fleshly needs of the masses were met, or as long as they *believed* their government could provide them with the ability to meet these needs, the people loved their pretended democracy.

European customary law had developed in an agrarian (relating to the farmers and other laborers who produced the bulk of the nation's resources) economy. Roman law, on the other hand, supported the rich by enforcing written and verbal contracts that supported their agenda to gain wealth, and which were needed for an economy where commerce played an increasingly larger role.

John pulled no punches when he figuratively expressed that this new "*beast*" "*exercised all the power of the first beast before him.*" This "*beast*" would subsequently "*cause the whole earth*"—its environs and resources, as well as all "*them which dwell therein*"—to fall down and "*worship*" a set of societal laws and precepts set up solely on one premise: whatever needs to be done to the earth or to another in order to fulfill the desires of the flesh ("*the dragon*"), and support and promote self-worth, is good.

Why should the people do unto others what they would have others do unto them, when doing so would not give them more material wealth, more worldly acceptance, and more power over those who are not seen as their equals? The "*beast*" has indeed "made war with the saints, and prevailed against them." (See Daniel 7:21.)

13:13 And he doeth great wonders, so that he maketh fire come down from heaven on the earth in the sight of *the beast*,

It was an obscure and relatively unknown American prophet who made the following prophecy:

> *For I the Lord cannot look upon sin with the least degree of allowance; Nevertheless, he that repents and does the commandments of the Lord shall be forgiven; And he that repents not, from him shall be taken even the light which he has received; for my Spirit shall not always strive with man, saith the Lord of Hosts. And again, verily I say unto you, O inhabitants of the earth: I the Lord am willing to make these things known unto all flesh; For I am no respecter of persons, and will that all men shall know that the day speedily cometh;* **the hour is not yet, but is nigh at hand,** *when my Spirit shall be taken from the earth,* **and the devil shall have power over his own dominion**. (Source withheld)

This prophecy was given in November of 1831. Shortly after this time ("*the hour is not yet, but is night at hand*"), mortals began to discover the knowledge and understanding ("*fire come down from heaven*"—see commentary on Revelation 4:5) of some of the mysteries of God.

The American lifestyle (the "*other beast*" and the "*he*" referred to in this verse) influenced the scientific and technological advancements needed to satisfy the appetites of its belly. For thousands of years, the greatest minds on earth could not decipher the mysteries and riddles of scientific observations, which were necessary to control the powers of nature for the benefit of mortal man. The secrets of kinetic energy, theorized and speculated on by the great minds of science, were kept hidden away. Unable to utilize what they understood, the world advanced very little from the time of the Ancient Egyptians until the time of the isolated colonies of the American pilgrims.

The extraordinary power of electricity was kept hidden from the very foundations of the world so that humankind would not discover its potential and use it inappropriately. The ancient prophets knew of this great power, yet none of them mentioned it to his contemporaries, guarding this incredible mystery that is a small, but important portion of the power of a God. They knew that when the earth was approaching its last days of exercising universal free agency and democracy, it would be safe to allow *the devil to have power over his own dominion*; thus permitting the use of this knowledge (*"fire"*) so "he" could experience the effects of this power when used improperly.

Not one ancient prophet who received knowledge of the latter days prophesied anything but great wickedness upon the earth. They saw the computers, the medical advancements, and the technological cornucopia of ease and wealth, given to those who would experience the effects of this *"fire from heaven,"* but they prophesied of nothing but wickedness.

As the world began to lust more and more after the ease and comforts that this *"fire"* provided them, the *"great furnace of the bottomless pit"* was stoked and fueled (see Revelation 9:1–2). Nature's power was bridled, and the *"beast"* was given the ability by *"the dragon"* to hold the reigns in his hands, taking the *"horse"* and its *"rider"* anywhere he so desired.

13:14 And them that dwell on the earth *are deceived* by the means of those miracles which he had power to do in the sight of the beast; *by* saying to them that dwell on the earth, that they should make an image to the beast, which had the wound by a sword, and did live.

As technology began to provide immediate pleasures and satisfaction to humankind, faith in an unseen God, and any hope of an afterlife, became less and less important to *"them that dwell on the earth."* New advancements and apparent *"miracles"* were introduced with each new generation. In a brief amount of time (compared to the thousands of years that humans existed without the *miracles* of science and technology), mortals have gained power to travel hundreds of miles per hour through the sky, and to entertain themselves with these wonderful *"miracles."*

These *"miracles"* provide large amounts of leisure time, and instead of working as expected by their Creator (*"in the sweat of **thy face** shalt thou eat bread, till thou return unto the ground; for out of it wast thou taken: for dust thou art, and unto dust shalt thou return"*—Genesis 3:19), the people of the earth search for ways to be free from all labor. *"Them,"* so *"deceived,"* live by the "sweat of the **faces**" of the poor, causing them to grind at the wheel of an economy that feeds the wants and needs of the *"deceived."*

"Grinding the faces of the poor" as prophesied, is the result of those who believe that their individual and family goals of financial wealth and independence are more important than another's. The *"other beast that came out of the earth like a lamb,"* opened up and developed a land where these miracles could be seen (*"sight of the beast"*) and believed. Millions of people around the world were deceived into believing that the "American Dream" was equally attainable for all.

Prophetically, the Statue of Liberty, a figurative representation of the *"image"* of the *"beast"* (a graven image), was constructed and erected in order to entice the *"deceived"* to sit upon the *"beast"*; while the *"woman"* stands upon the *"sea,"* welcoming the world to come into her bed and enjoy *"her fornication"* (Revelation 17:1–5).

The giant *"image—a woman clothed in a robe"* holds a torch in her right hand (giving the appearance of righteousness) offering "enlightenment" (*"fire come down from heaven"*) to the world, and is profoundly represented by the *"seven heads,"* or *seven rays* (seven continents of the world) jutting from *"her crown."*

The chains on her feet, by which she was bound, have been unlocked (see Revelation 3:10), giving her power to do the *"miracles in the sight of the beast."* In her left hand she holds a book, symbolizing a diary of her unrighteous works (*left hand*), which she has accomplished and recorded therein.

What is written upon the book she holds?

Chiseled in **Roman** *numerals* in honor of the *"first beast, which had the wound by a sword, and did live,"* is the celebrated and *"worshipped"* (holy day) holiday: July 4, 1776. This is the celebrated day this *"other beast rose out of the earth with two horns like a lamb,"* deceiving them that dwell upon the earth by saying, "Bring us your tired, your poor, your huddled masses" and we will *"face"* them toward the grinding wheel that feeds *"the dragon,"* and has given us this great *"power."*

The *"image of the beast"* is the illusory belief that all peoples of the earth have the ability to achieve a life of freedom from work, oppression, and sadness under the current economic policies and laws of the United States' form of democracy. To support the lifestyle of one rich person, at least **ninety-nine** poor people are needed to fulfill their selfish "Dream." Food needs to be picked, garbage needs to be removed, hotels need to be staffed, and raw materials need to be produced and turned into the products that the rich use to live their desired "standard of living."

The *"deceived of the earth"* are convinced that if they are not *"worshipping the image"* (living this standard of living), then they have not arrived, and they are not successful; therefore, they are not happy. Thus, these are they who are *"deceived."*

13:15 And he had power to give life unto the image of the beast, that the image of the beast should both speak, and cause that as many as would not worship the image of the beast should be killed.

The US government and its laws have the power to guarantee a person a high standard of living (*"power to give life unto the image"*). Corporate and business law, as well as diverse litigation in US courts, has created personal and family wealth for the few who have heard the great and marvelous words and promises of financial independence spoken by the *"beast"* that is *"that horn that had eyes, and a mouth that spake very great things, whose look was more stout than his fellows."* (Daniel 7:20)

The lure of financial independence can be figuratively expressed as the mythical 'Siren's Song' (the very great things that *"the beast's mouth speaks"*) that metaphorically caused many ships to steer off course and wreck. Profound are the words of a contemporary song that reflect its title:

Beware the siren song
A song of delirious beauty
Though you want to sing along
A song full of promised delight
Lash yourself onto the mast
A song that will lead you to madness
Till the siren song has passed
A song that ends only in pain

Through the wind and through the rain
Through the long night of tempting
Of torment and of doubt
He cried out in his pain
But this captain stayed the course
Guiding the ship through danger
Past the siren's melody
On to the promise of home.

Beware the siren song
Try not to listen
Make sure the ropes are strong
Focus your vision
Beware the siren song
A song of beauty
Guide your ship on the right course.

And the ocean is so deep
Blackening water is raging
As the ship is tossed about
A speck in the infinite void
And the map is old and worn
Stained with the tears of captains
Who have sailed this way before
To follow the song of the heart.

(*Brave Combo, <u>Siren Song</u>, Hernandez, Carter/Don Cenobio Music, BMI*)

The Roman Empire, and those who claimed citizenship under its realm, set the precedent for the standard of living currently perpetuated by the United States (*"that they should make an image to the beast, which had the wound by a sword, and did live"*). Like the Romans, Americans believe they are the greatest of all peoples of the earth, and that they deserve the finest standard of living possible, regardless of what supporting this *"image"* does to other nations and people.

Any nation that makes an attempt of independence and sovereignty by severing its *economical ties* with the United States will be invaded, conquered, and occupied (*"as many as would not worship the image of the beast should be killed"*). Oil-rich countries that refuse to bow down to the pressure of American interests, are threatened and subdued. If a country has no economical relevance in sustaining the American lifestyle, it is left alone until it does.

All nations of the earth hearken to the speech of the beast and have bowed in worship, genuflecting with their arms splayed and overflowing with the natural resources their nation can offer this *"image"*; if not, they *"should be killed."* If a nation's resources can support the American standard of living, it has no choice but to bow down before the *"image of the beast."*

13:16 And he causeth all, both ***righteous and wicked***, small and great, rich and poor, free and bond, to receive a mark in their right hand, or in their foreheads:

A *"mark"* is left after something has been accomplished or experienced. The works of Shakespeare left a *"mark"* on the literary world. After a well-attended parade, a *"mark"* is left by the amount of litter left in the street. Jesus left his *"mark"* upon the world, and kept the *"mark"* in his hands and feet, which will one day prove him to be he who was anointed to become the Christ of this solar system. By no choice of their own, the Jews were *"marked"* for annihilation by Hitler's regime, and those who John describes as *"the saints"* of God, receive a *"mark"* in their forehead as has been explained previously.

There is not a person in this world that has not received the *"mark of the beast"* in his or her *"right hand"*—**not one**! It is impossible to live in this world without being affected in some way by commercialism, money, or the economic structures set up by the societies of the earth. Jewish custom taught that what one does with one's *"right hand"* is a reflection of the actions one makes in his daily life. What one thinks and focuses upon, is represented by a *"mark"* in the *"forehead."*

The greatest portion of our waking hours are spent in pursuit (*"mark in right hand"*) of the lifestyle (*"the image of the beast"*) we have imagined in our minds (*"mark in their foreheads"*) for our families and ourselves. Those who have the mark, or *"seal of the Father in their forehead" think* of others and how their actions affect the least among us, trying in every way possible to do unto others what they would want done unto them. Nevertheless, because *"the beast has overcome the saints,"* they too, have the *"mark of the beast in their right hand."* They too are unable to live without it in a world which steadily revolves around the idea of doing whatever is necessary in order to assure a secure life for the individual and the family.

13:17 And that no man might buy or sell, save he that had the mark, or the name of the beast, or the number of his name.

We cannot buy or sell in this world unless we involve ourselves in its economies. We have idolized the almighty dollar, prostrating ourselves before it, and worshipping all it can do for us.

It has become our God.

The more we have, the more secure we feel, and the more we worship it. Our bank accounts, our retirement accounts, our investments, our promised pensions, and our life insurance policies give us the false sense of security that our future is provided for and secure. The *"number of his name"* is the accounting and value system we have established to perpetuate the *"beast."* It is money. Without it, *"no man might buy or sell."*

13:18 Here is wisdom. Let him that hath understanding count the number of the beast: for it is the number of a man; and his number is Six hundred threescore and six.

Here John capitalizes on the metaphors, symbolism, and figurative expressions borrowed from the *Old Testament.* He knew that only those who are wise and have a proper understanding of truth, would be able to make the connection between the riddle he gives here, and the reality of what the *"number of the beast"* is.

How foolish the world has become. How arrogant and deceived are those who unknowingly carry the mark of the beast prominently displayed in their right hand and in their forehead, yet ignorantly believe they would never allow anyone to mark their right hand with 666, which they have erroneously named the "mark of the beast."

Look carefully at the actual text, and you will note that John did not write "666 (*"six hundred threescore and six"*) **is** the *mark of the beast,* nor did he say "666" is the **_number_** of the beast. He specifically and purposefully wrote that the number "666 corresponded to" the **"number** *of the beast, which is the **number** of a man, and his number is six hundred threescore and six."* Neither did John say: *"is the number of **man** (as in 'mankind'),"* but he specifically wrote: *"is the number of **a** man,"* meaning **a** particular man.

That particular *man* to whom John was pointing those who *"hath understanding,"* is Solomon. *"His number"* corresponds to "money," as in the amount of *"gold"* he received in a one-year period:

> *Now the weight of gold that came to **Solomon** in one year was **six hundred threescore and six talents of gold**.* (I Kings 10:14)

> *Now the weight of gold that came to Solomon in one year was **six hundred and threescore and six talents of gold**;* (II Chronicles 9:13)

You will notice that this chapter of *Revelation* suffered less than most canonized scripture at the hands of those who took it upon themselves to decide what portions needed to be altered or deleted. These powerful prophetic passages retained their basic meaning in spite of translation difficulties. With the possible exception of verse 1, these verses appear almost exactly as John intended, when they were first given in such plainness and simplicity that even a child could have figured it out; but few have, because the people and their leaders do not have "*understanding.*" They are the blind being led by the blind, stumbling forward toward the pit they have dug for themselves. A pit into which they will fall headlong and become consumed in the fire that burns fervently with the fuel from the bodies of those who have dug it and fallen therein.

"*Here is wisdom,*" wrote John;

The "*name of the beast*" is **The God of This World** (our natural selves).

The "*image of the beast*" is the *dream* or vision of material prosperity that is "*imaged*" or imagined (the "American Dream").

The "*mark of the beast*" is displayed in how we worship him (our works).

The "*number of the beast*" is money.

...And upon "*his number, his name*" is inscribed:

In GOD We Trust

The god that has the "*great power and authority*" in this world is the necessity and pursuit of money. It is in *this* graven "*image*" we do trust!

For those with "*eyes that see and ears that hear,*" John's *Revelation* cannot make the point more clear.

Chapter

R̄EVELATION
UNFOLDED

14:1 And I looked, and, lo, *in the midst of this beast I saw as it were* a Lamb *that* stood on the mount *Zion*, and with him *were those of the* hundred forty and four thousand, having his Father's name written in their foreheads.

New Testament editors used the name "*Sion*" instead of the actual name "*Zion*," which was used throughout the *Old Testament*, and which John intended for this part of his *Revelation*. To early Christians, who didn't understand what John was trying to express here, "*mount Sion*" was the place they established by tradition where Jesus ascended up into heaven in sight of the apostles. Though modern religious scholars, who know even less than their earlier counterparts, argue amongst themselves as to the exact significance of "*mount Sion*," there is no mistake in how John intended its use.

According to Jewish history, King David overthrew a great fortress of the Jebusites called *Zion*, which was situated in the land of Jerusalem, and later renamed the City of David. This fortress was built to protect the people and promote peace with their enemies. The Jews referred to the

City of David as the birthplace of peace, thus renaming it *Jerusalem*. To symbolize the birth of the *"prince of peace,"* Jesus was born in Bethlehem, another city referred to as the *"City of David"* by the Jews. When the Jews renamed the City of David, *"Jerusalem,"* they believed they were literally establishing a foundation of peace. Little did they realize that their prophesied *Messiah* would one day roam the streets of their great city, preaching the gospel of peace that they would reject. Furthermore, the term *"New Jerusalem"* is used by John to represent the peace that Christ will establish upon the earth during his Millennial Reign.

"Mount Zion" and *"Jerusalem"* were used interchangeably by many of the *Old Testament* prophets, whose purpose in using the term was to illustrate a place of peace and righteousness:

> *A Song and Psalms for the sons of Korah. Great is the LORD, and greatly to be praised in the city of our God, in the mountain of his holiness. Beautiful for situation, the joy of the whole earth, is* **mount Zion**, *on the sides of the north, the city of the great King.* (Psalms 48:1–2)

> *How beautiful upon the mountains are the feet of him that bringeth good tidings, that publisheth peace; that bringeth good* **tidings of good**, *that publisheth salvation; that saith unto* **Zion**, *Thy God reigneth!* (Isaiah 52:7)

> *But upon* **mount Zion** *shall be deliverance, and there shall be holiness; and the house of Jacob shall possess their possessions.* (Obadiah 1:17)

In this verse, John is presenting the establishment and foundation of peace (*"mount Zion"*) experienced by those in the world (*"in the midst of this beast"*) who choose to live the gospel of peace, which is nothing more or less than doing unto others what they would want done unto them. These are those whose cognitive paradigm (thinking patterns/*"Father's name written in their foreheads"*) is structured around the gospel of the *Lamb*—creating peace and harmony by doing to others what one would want done to them in all situations.

He numbers these as those who have heard the voice of the prophets and followed their counsel. As previously mentioned, the "*hundred forty and four thousand*" represents the figurative expression of the number of people during the 6000 years leading up to the Millennium, who have heeded the words of the prophets ("*the twenty and four elders*"). (See commentary on Revelation 7:4.)

In the next few verses John describes this peace:

14:2 And I heard a voice *as if it came* from heaven, *even* as the voice of many waters, and *also* the voice of a great thunder; and *the sounds* I heard *were like unto* the voice of harpers harping with their harps:

One of the greatest mysteries of human emotion is *why* we think, *why* we seek beauty, and *why* we seek peace and happiness. Other animals in the natural world seek only to fulfill the demands of the instincts that motivate them. Our 'spirit' is the name we ascribe to the unseen gaseous entity that enters into a body of flesh created by mortal parents. This entity enters our body upon our first breath.

Our spirit has recorded all of our past experiences; and outside of mortality, our spirit exists with the ability to recall every experience that we have ever had. Before this life (figuratively, "*as if it came from heaven*"), we knew the plan the Creator had outlined for us. It was a plan of balance and harmony, and something that felt comfortable and right. This emotional knowledge is embedded in the molecules that make up our spirits.

This should not be hard to understand, with the ability of modern science to program and create databases on a molecular level. Can one imagine what science will be able to do in 500 more years? 1000? 10,000? Stored information on DNA molecules unseen to the mortal eye gives enough proof that it is possible to store information on molecules of elements that are still unknown to mortals, which are these unseen elements that make up the spirit.

Once a conscious being has experienced something long enough, a comfort level is reached. If this comfort level is breached by change, it creates feelings of confusion, depression, frustration, and a longing to undo the change and return to the pre-experienced, or previous state of balance and comfort. If a creature exists for thousands of years recording continual experiences of peace, equality, harmony, and joy, it would likely have some serious moments of imbalance and discontent if it were forced to live for a few years (72 or so) in a completely different environment.

Those on the earth who pay attention to their innermost feelings will hear the "beat of a different drummer" than those who only pay attention to what the world offers them. These do not hear a drum, but the gentle strum of a "*harp*," which since its inception, has always been one of the most soothing musical instruments to the mortal soul. John uses the expression "*harpers harping with their harps*" to show how the "spirit of God," or remembering the true nature of our spirits, will take away the evil (frustrations, depressions, miseries, etc.) from our minds. He again borrows from *Old Testament* writings:

> *But the spirit of the LORD departed from Saul, and an evil spirit from the LORD troubled him. And Saul's servants said unto him, Behold now, an evil spirit from God troubleth thee. Let our lord now command thy servants, which are before thee, to seek out a man, who is a cunning **player on an harp**: and it shall come to pass, when the evil spirit from God is upon thee, that he shall play with his hand, and thou shalt be well. And Saul said unto his servants, Provide me now a man that can play well, and bring him to me.* (I Samuel 16:14–17)

The man found by Saul's servants was none other than David:

> *And it came to pass, when the evil spirit from God was upon Saul, that **David took an harp, and played with his hand: so Saul was refreshed, and was well, and the evil spirit departed from him**.* (I Samuel 16:23)

John used this symbolism to point us toward the "*son of David*," a *harp player*, who has the ability to *"refresh us"* and cause the *"evil spirit"* to depart:

> The book of the generation of **Jesus Christ, the son of David**. (Matthew 1:1)

Those people (*"voice of many waters"*) who listen to what they feel and remember outside of this world (*"voice from heaven"*), will hear a *"voice"* speak as forceful as *"great thunder"* (the truth), but which will soothe their soul, as does the music from a *"harp."*

14:3 And they sung as it were a new song **to them, but** before the throne, and before the four beasts, and the ***four and twenty*** elders **the song was not new**; and no man could learn that song but **those of** the hundred and forty and four thousand, which were redeemed from the earth.

Only those who listen to the voice of the prophets (*"four and twenty elders"*) will understand what the servants (angels/*"four beasts"*) are doing for our benefit upon this earth in mortality. These servants of the plan of God already know the *"song,"* and sing it in tune with the rhythm and beat arranged by the *"song's"* Great Composer. However, to those in mortality who choose to listen to its melody, it is *"as it were a **new** song to them,"* because of their inability to recall their former experiences stored within their spirit. It is a *"song"* they are familiar with, and which they will sing while listening to the *"harpers harp."*

Isaiah said it beautifully:

> And the ransomed of the LORD shall return, and come to Zion with **songs and everlasting joy upon their heads: they shall obtain joy and gladness, and sorrow and sighing shall flee away**. (Isaiah 35:10)

14:4 These are they which were not defiled with **the woman who sits upon the beast**; for they **remain as** virgins, **committing no fornication**

with her. These are they which follow the Lamb whithersoever he goeth. These **are the** redeemed from among men, **and are** the firstfruits unto God and to the Lamb.

In chapter 2, John first introduced the woman Jezebel as a representation of the wicked works of the world. It is with this woman that the people of the world "*commit fornication*," or "*sleep in the bed with her*" (see commentary on Revelation 2:20–23). John again uses being "*defiled*," or "*committing fornication with the woman*," as a representation of those who are seeking after the glory, honor, and material things of the world.

Once a person has heard the truth, and begins to do what is heard instead of just listening and doing nothing, that person figuratively begins to bring forth fruit. The "*firstfruits*" mentioned by all prophets are those things which are the first we do once we have come to a knowledge of the truth. When the truth is known, the pursuit of worldly education, pleasure, and worldly lusts are the *first* things overcome. Thus, those who have given these things up ("*virgins*," who have not committed "*fornication with the woman*") **are** like "*the firstfruits unto God and to the Lamb.*"

James put it this way using the same metaphor of our *lusts conceiving sin* in fornication:

> *Blessed is the man that endureth temptation: for when he is tried, he shall receive the crown of life, which the Lord hath promised to them that love him. Let no man say when he is tempted, I am tempted of God: for God cannot be tempted with evil, neither tempteth he any man: But every man is tempted, when he is **drawn away of his own lust, and enticed**. Then **when lust hath conceived, it bringeth forth sin**: and sin, when it is finished, bringeth forth death. Do not err, my beloved brethren. Every good gift and every perfect gift is from above, and cometh down from the Father of lights, with whom is no variableness, neither shadow of turning. Of his own will begat he us with the word of truth, **that we***

*should be a kind of firstfruits of his creatures. Wherefore, my beloved brethren, let every man be swift to hear, slow to speak, slow to wrath: For the wrath of man worketh not the righteousness of God. Wherefore lay apart all filthiness and superfluity of naughtiness, and receive with meekness the engrafted word, which is able to save your souls. But **be ye doers of the word, and not hearers only**, **deceiving your own selves**.* (James 1:12–22)

14:5 And in their mouth was found no guile: for they are without fault before the throne of God.

One of the worst and most common human propensities is *guile*. Few pass through a day without using guile in some form. Guile is cunning behavior used to deceive people into thinking something that the beguiler does not really feel; usually in order to get something from another, or to elicit a manipulated response desired by the beguiler. It is a clever skill used by most humans to get what they want. For example, guile is used to compliment a person in a way that is not really true, such as, "Yea, that skirt looks good on you. Don't worry about it!" when to you, the skirt doesn't compliment the wearer. Another example is when a salesman presents a product without disclosing how much profit is being made; this is *"guile."* These and many other forms of guile exist to perpetuate the *"beast."*

Guile opposes the *Royal Law*—Do unto others as you would have them do unto you. All of those who use *"guile"* for whatever reason (99.9% of humans do), are at fault of adding to, or creating, unhappiness and misery for others.

One of the reasons why others despised Jesus, is because he did not use guile. He spoke the truth no matter whom or what it offended. John specifically included *"guile"* here to demonstrate what we all know to be an eternal truth that will always lead to peace and happiness: Honesty is the best policy.

For even hereunto were ye called: because Christ also suffered for us, leaving us an example, that ye should follow his

steps: Who did no sin, neither was guile found in his mouth:
(I Peter 2:21–22)

14:6 And I saw ***an*** angel fly in the midst of heaven, having the everlasting gospel to preach unto them that dwell on the earth, to every nation, and kindred, and tongue, and people,

The *"everlasting gospel"* is simply a guideline of how we should treat each other so that we all have the same opportunity to experience joy and happiness, which is the reason why we exist. As he has all throughout his *Revelation*, John uses the term *"angel"* here to represent those who have been given power and authority over what goes on here upon the earth. As previously mentioned, these angels are exalted beings far more advanced than any mortal. They come from other solar systems, some from other galaxies, to oversee the planets of this solar system, assuring that all things follow their outlined course of providing happiness for those who are assigned here.

In these latter times, they have allowed the knowledge (*"fire"*) to come down from heaven, figuratively, to make it possible that *"every nation, and kindred, and tongue, and people"* has the opportunity to learn of each other, and to learn the things that are necessary to promote *peace* and *equality*—the forerunners of *joy* and *happiness*.

As these latter times progress, the world will become more closely connected unlike any other time in its short human history. Through the means of communication being introduced, the day will come when every living soul will have access to knowledge; not necessarily the truth, but vast amounts of information. As we begin to experience the effects of this knowledge, we are able to discern the difference between what brings lasting happiness, and what causes our stresses and unhappiness.

All of our experience, understanding, wisdom, and knowledge that we gain in mortality, will lead us to one ubiquitous conclusion: Doing unto others what we would have them do unto us in all situations is the only way to lasting happiness—this is the *"everlasting gospel"* of which John speaks.

14:7 Saying with a loud voice, **Behold those who** fear God and give glory to him; for the hour of **your** judgment is come; **for ye** worship **not** him that made heaven, and earth, and the sea, and the fountains of waters.

As the knowledge of this gospel spreads throughout the world, it becomes very apparent that the people of the world who *claim* religious affiliations actually worship God with their mouths, (pretending to be of one sect or another), but do not treat each other with kindness according to the tenets of Christ's gospel. The universal teaching of love, to which all religions make claim, is preached, but hardly ever practiced.

Well did Isaiah prophesy:

> *Wherefore the Lord said, Forasmuch as this people draw near me with their mouth, and with their lips do honour me, but have removed their heart far from me, and **their fear toward me is taught by the precept of men**:* (Isaiah 29:13)

The religions of the world teach their congregations to *"fear God and give glory to him,"* but forget that God is not "One" to be feared; and that the only *"glory"* He ever expects, comes as a result of one doing good works to another:

> *Let your light so shine before men, that they may see your good works, and **glorify your Father** which is in heaven.* (Matthew 5:16)

The mission and purpose of Jesus Christ is to teach people how to love each other and treat each other correctly, so that one day we all might reside in eternal bodies in a place where we can fulfill the measure of our creation—happiness. In this, he glorified God:

> *Father, glorify thy name. Then came there a voice from heaven, saying, I have both glorified it, and will glorify it again.* (John 12:28)

*I have glorified thee on the earth: **I have finished the work which thou gavest me to do**.* (John 17:4)

Though they have been convinced otherwise, modern-day Christians perpetuate hate against the homosexuals, non-Christians, and those who choose to abort the flesh of their own bodies before the spirit enters therein. They generate many other biases and prejudices contrary to loving thy neighbor as thyself. The persecution of their neighbor, their *"fear of God,"* and the erroneous way in which they *"worship,"* illuminates what they fear the most—damnation (ignorance) instead of salvation (knowledge of truth).

As does every other religion upon earth, Christian sects exalt themselves above others who do not fit their description of "righteousness." The Muslims believe the prophet Mohammed was the last prophet to live upon earth, and worship him as they do Allah, which is the name for the Islamic God. The Hindus believe they are correct. The Buddhist disagrees.

The whole world is filled with *"the gospel"* of what we should do, but few *"worship"* the **true** God who *"made heaven, and earth, and the sea, and the fountains of waters."* Why? Because we are so involved in the grandeur and glory of the *"beast,"* and that *"great city Babylon"* which provides for our every desire and pleasure, that we pay no attention to the *"mark in our right hands and foreheads."*

As John reveals in the next verse, the angels have something to say about this *abomination* that makes our souls *desolate*:

14:8 And there followed another angel, saying, Babylon is *falling*, is *falling*, *even* that great city, because she *makes* all nations *that partake* of her fornication drink of the wine of the wrath *of God*.

Our actions are being observed by those who oversee the progression of this solar system. Each angel's mission is to assure that the plan written in the *"Book of Life"* is followed according to the eternal laws which have always and forever governed the Universe. With their vast knowledge and experience, they understand the structured steps that we mortals will take upon this earth as we use our free agency—gaining the much-needed experience to help us find our happiness. This is why it is easy for them to show John the course that will be followed in the future.

Because the people have become selfish and family-centered, they are being devoured by the *"beast"* that has *"deceived them by the means of the miracles"* (see Revelation 13:14). They have ignored forgiveness, loving your enemies, doing good to others who hurt you, not judging or measuring another, and caring for the least among them. They have alienated themselves from each other, and are in a self-protective mode of existence. When each person seeks only his or her own welfare, an emotional war ensues, which often leads to a physical war, where the combatants fight until each *"fall"* by the other's sword.

John presents the *"falling of Babylon"* after *"the seat of the beast"* is set up in the latter days, and the world has begun to feel its effects. There is no denying that the United States' influence is felt worldwide. Its citizens consume more of the earth's resources, by far, than any other nation in the world (*"she makes all nations...partake of her fornication"*). Its consumption formulates and controls the world markets. It gives no forgiveness or mercy to its enemies, makes no excuses for itself, and is constantly engaged in expanding its economical presence throughout the world.

From the commentary of Revelation 6:17, we understand what John refers to as *"the wrath of God"*:

"John has shown us the stages and effects of human development when we are left to our own devices with complete control over our environment and actions. Our Father and Creator does not get angry as we prefer to think, or have been taught by false leaders and teachers. John has led us to quite a different understanding of what is meant when we speak of the "the wrath of God," which refers to His non-intervention in the affairs of humankind. When we are undeserving, we are left to suffer the full effects of our self-imposed situations. He has taught us that when we do not live by the Royal Law, we do not receive the intervention or divine instruction from above through righteous and true prophets— the sun is darkened (no light or revelation is given) because of our wickedness. As a result of rejecting the prophets and killing them, the moon is turned into blood. This is the 'wrath of God'."

God's message of love and "doing good unto others" has no affect on our lives when we selfishly pursue what's best only for ourselves and our families. The further we stray from compliance to His *Royal Law*, the more we become comfortable with the "*beast*" and its ways, and subsequently, the less we learn of God and His ways. We are left to ourselves to "*drink and become drunken from the wine*" we have poured in our own glasses, staggering as we "*fall.*"

14:9 And the third angel followed them, saying with a loud voice, If any man worship the beast and his image, and receive his mark in his forehead, or in his hand,

14:10 The same shall drink *from a* cup of wine *which is a* mixture of the wrath of God *and His* indignation, which is poured out *upon the earth*; and he *who shall drink thereof* shall be tormented with fire and brimstone in the presence of the holy angels, and in the presence of the Lamb:

14:11 And the smoke of their torment *shall ascend* up *before God* for ever and ever; and they *shall* have no rest day nor night, who worship the beast and his image, and whosoever receiveth the mark of his name.

These verses relate the emotional turmoil that will be felt by those who worship the "*beast*" when they are confronted with the truth. The people of the earth do not understand the mysteries of God or merit His intervention ("*the wrath of God*"), because of "*His indignation.*" Indignation is not anger in this instance, but annoyance because somebody or something seems unfair or unreasonable, which is how God views those who mistreat others. "*A cup from which*" the wicked "*drink their wine*" will not be clean, as they are reminded of their works and beliefs ("*wine*") when "*the Lamb and the holy angels*" make their "*presence*" known.

When the truth is known, those who have (directly or indirectly, knowingly or unknowingly) caused unhappiness to another person will feel an embarrassment and torment ("*fire*"), and will be repulsed by the repugnant smell ("*brimstone*") of what they have done with their free agency.

These are those of whom Jesus Christ spoke when he said:

*Then shall he say also unto them on the left hand, Depart from me, ye cursed, into everlasting fire, prepared for the devil and his angels: For I was an hungered, and ye gave me no meat: I was thirsty, and ye gave me no drink: I was a stranger, and ye took me not in: naked, and ye clothed me not: sick, and in prison, and ye visited me not. Then shall they also answer him, saying, Lord, when saw we thee an hungered, or athirst, or a stranger, or naked, or sick, or in prison, and did not minister unto thee? Then shall he answer them, saying, **Verily I say unto you, Inasmuch as ye did it not to one of the least of these, ye did it not to me**. And these shall go away into everlasting punishment: but the righteous into life eternal.* (Matthew 25:41–46)

*Not every one that saith unto me, Lord, Lord, shall enter into the kingdom of heaven; but he that doeth **the will of my Father which is in heaven**. Many will say to me in that day, Lord, Lord, have we not prophesied in thy name? and in thy name have cast out devils? and in thy name done many wonderful works? And then will I profess unto them, I never knew you: depart from me, ye that work iniquity. Therefore whosoever **heareth these sayings of mine, and doeth them**, I will liken him unto a wise man, which built his house upon a rock:* (Matthew 7:21–24)

"*These sayings of mine*" have nothing to do with going to church, praying to God, paying a tithe or offering, proclaiming the name of Christ or Mohammed, protesting abortion or homosexuality, or volunteering a miniscule amount of your overall life to obtain the "feel-good" sensation of "I have done good." "These sayings" are the gospel of Jesus Christ, and the guidelines he gave to teach us how to live in equality and peace. The entire "rock" upon which we should build our "house" is found in the gentle words of the Beatitudes, which are given exclusively in Matthew, chapters 5, 6, and 7.

Anything other than these commandments are the commandments, precepts, and doctrines of men. These are the doctrines and precepts of those who want you to go to their church, pay them your money, proclaim a name they do not know, and protest and support efforts of hate and persecution. They do many things to justify the time you spend listening to these "*locusts*," and the money that you pay them.

How great shall be the embarrassment of those who find out their Lord did not attend church or support any *ordained* minister. The "*tormented*" and embarrassed will be in the presence of a man who once lived on their earth, who is their Lord, and also in the presence of other exalted beings who have progressed far beyond modern humans ("*the holy angels*"). Christ loved his enemies, sinners, and friends equally; and will say to those spoken of above, "*I gave you the simple commandments, which were **the will of my Father which is in heaven**, who is also your Father, and you did none of them.*"

The Lamb will not have to say, "Depart from me, ye that work iniquity," because those who worship *the* beast,

> *the kings of the earth, and the great men, and the rich men, and the chief captains, and the mighty men, yea even every man who bringeth bondage upon another who is not free,* [shall hide] *themselves in the dens and in the rocks of the mountains; And these* [shall say] *to the mountains and rocks, Fall on us, and hide us from the face of him that sitteth on the throne, and from the wrath of the Lamb, whose countenance we cannot bear.* (Revelation 6:15–16)

14:12 And I heard a voice from heaven saying unto me, Write, Here is the patience of the saints: here are they that keep the commandments of God, and the faith of Jesus.

14:13 Blessed are the dead which die in the Lord from henceforth: Yea, saith the Spirit, **because** they **shall** rest from their labours **because** their works follow them.

Those who listen to "these sayings of mine and doeth them" are those "whose house is built upon the rock." No matter what the "*beast*" throws at them to deceive them and disrupt their peace, in "*patience*," they remain steadfast and immovable in keeping the commandments and counsels of Christ.

These "*saints*" understand the will of the Father, as it is forefront in all their thoughts ("*the seal of God in their foreheads*"). They ridicule and judge none, worship none, fear none, and are unaffected by the vicissitudes created by the "*beast*" and those who have received his "*mark*." They experience the affects of Christ's promise:

> *All things are delivered unto me of my Father: and no man knoweth the Son, but the Father; neither knoweth any man the Father* [or receives the seal of the Father in their forehead], *save the Son, and he to whomsoever the Son will reveal him. Come unto me, all ye that labour and are heavy laden, and **I will give you rest**. Take my yoke upon you, and learn of me; for I am meek and lowly in heart: and ye shall find rest unto your souls. **For my yoke is easy, and my burden is light**.* (Matthew 11:27–30)

14:14 And I looked, and behold a white cloud, and upon the cloud one sat like unto the Son of man, having on his head a golden crown, and in his hand a sharp sickle.

To understand who this "*one...like unto the Son of man*" is, we must refer to the scriptures already presented, and see from where John borrowed his metaphors. This "*one*" is a prophet of God. He has "*on his head a golden crown*":

> *And in the midst of the throne were four and twenty seats: and upon the seats I saw four and twenty elders sitting, clothed in white raiment; and they **had on their heads crowns of gold**.* (Revelation 4:4)

Prophets were often referred to in *Old Testament* scripture as *"Son of man,"* when being spoken to by a heavenly Being:

> *So thou, **O son of man**, I have set thee a watchman unto the house of Israel; therefore thou shalt hear the word at my mouth, and warn them from me.* (Ezekiel 33:7)

This prophet is unknown by the people of the world (*"sits upon a cloud,"* which signifies his presence is kept obscure), but in his hand is a *"sharp sickle."* Sickles were used in historic times to cut down the wheat. Then the kernels, which are nutritious, could be separated from the chaff—which has no nutritional value.

John the Baptist prophesied of Christ:

> *John answered, saying unto them all, I indeed baptize you with water; but one mightier than I cometh, the latchet of whose shoes I am not worthy to unloose: he shall baptize you with the Holy Ghost and with fire: Whose fan is in his hand, and he will thoroughly purge his floor, and will gather the **wheat** into his garner; but **the chaff he will burn with fire unquenchable**.* (Luke 3:16–17)

"Like unto" Christ, this prophet of whom John speaks, bears *"his name"* (does the same works Christ did), and has the necessary tools in his hand to *gather the wheat and burn the chaff.*

However, this prophet does what all prophets of God usually do after they are called: he sits with the tools in hand, sometimes in rebellion, humbly admitting that he is not worthy of such great responsibility and authority (the *"golden crown"*):

> *The four and twenty elders fall down before him that sat on the throne, and worship him that liveth for ever and ever, and **cast their** crowns **before the throne**, saying, Thou art worthy, O Lord, to receive glory and honour and*

power: for thou hast created all things, and for thy pleasure they are and were created. (Revelation 4:10–11)

It takes an *"angel with a loud voice"* to convince the prophet to get busy doing what he was called to do:

14:15 And another angel came out of the temple, crying with a loud voice to him that sat on the cloud, Thrust in thy sickle, and reap: for the time is come for thee to reap; for the harvest of the earth is ripe.

The *"angel with a loud voice"* tells this modern-day prophet, *"the time is come for thee to reap."* He is commanded to begin the process that will allow the separation of the wheat from the chaff. His *"sharp sickle"* is his knowledge of the mysteries of God that cuts down the doctrines and precepts of men which encase (*the chaff*) the hearts and souls (*the wheat*) of humankind.

As he presents truth (*"thrust in thy sickle"*), he destroys the strong stems (religions and doctrines of men), which have grown out of the earth and shield the wheat from the *"rain"* (revelation) and the *"light of the sun."* Once the wheat stalks are cut down, they are threshed; which means they are crushed and tossed into the air where the *"wind"* blows the chaff away, allowing the wheat to fall to the ground. This is the *"wind"* mentioned in Revelation 7:1 (see commentary) that the angels were commanded to not allow to *"blow upon the earth."* Once the people have heard the truth, those who heed it are as the separated wheat that will be placed in a secure granary—safe from the fire that will consume the harvested field.

14:16 And he that sat on the cloud thrust in his sickle on the earth; and **began to reap** the earth.

14:17 And **when he stopped reaping for a season**, another angel came out of the temple which is in heaven, he also having a sharp sickle **like unto the first**.

This modern prophet begins to do his job, but is sluggish in his efforts. In the beginning, he shrinks from his duties (*"stopped reaping"*) after he is rejected and persecuted by the *"beast."* In order to help him, *"another angel"* is sent with the same tool (*"sharp sickle"*).

14:18 And another angel came out from the altar, which had power over fire; and cried with a loud cry to ***the first*** that had the sharp sickle, saying, Thrust in thy sharp sickle, and gather the clusters of the vine of the earth; for her grapes are fully ripe.

This time, an *"angel, which had power over fire"* (the ability to give knowledge and truth to whomever the angel so chooses) comes *"out from the altar"* (the place upon which the people present their offerings to God). In other words, this *"angel"* does not come from heaven, but is already involved in his own mission upon the earth. He also cries with *"a loud cry"* telling this prophet to, *"Thrust in thy sharp sickle."*

These servants of God (*angels*) are among the people of the earth; and only manifest themselves when they are needed to carry out the work planned for this earth and its inhabitants. Prophets have special access to their help, if and when it is appropriate to assure the prophet's mission is completed. The mission of this *"one like unto the Son of Man"* is to *"bear the name of Christ,"* and reveal the truths and mysteries of God. His mission will *"seal"* those upon the earth (who *"elect"* to serve God and keep His commandments) *"in their foreheads,"* so that when the *"angels"* who hold the *"vials"* pour out the *"seven plagues"* upon the earth (which John presents in the next chapters), these *"elect"* will not be affected.

14:19 And the ***one like unto the son of Man*** thrust in his sickle into the earth, and gathered the vine of the earth, and cast it into the great winepress of the wrath of God.

This final prophet completes his job by presenting the truth to the world much the same way it was told to Joel's contemporaries:

Proclaim ye this among the Gentiles; Prepare war, wake up the mighty men, let all the men of war draw near; let them come up: Beat your plowshares into swords, and your pruninghooks into spears: let the weak say, I am strong. Assemble yourselves, and come, all ye heathen, and gather yourselves together round about: thither cause thy mighty ones to come down, O LORD. Let the heathen be wakened, and come up to the valley of Jehoshaphat: for there will I sit to judge all the heathen round about. **Put ye in the sickle, for the harvest is ripe: come, get you down; for the press is full, the fats overflow; for their wickedness is great.** *Multitudes, multitudes in the valley of decision: for the day of the LORD is near in the valley of decision. The sun and the moon shall be darkened, and the stars shall withdraw their shining. The LORD also shall roar out of Zion, and utter his voice from Jerusalem; and the heavens and the earth shall shake: but the LORD will be the hope of his people, and the strength of the children of Israel. So shall ye know that I am the LORD your God dwelling in Zion, my holy mountain: then shall Jerusalem be holy, and there shall no strangers pass through her any more. And it shall come to pass in that day, that the mountains shall drop down new wine, and the hills shall flow with milk, and all the rivers of Judah shall flow with waters, and a fountain shall come forth of the house of the LORD, and shall water the valley of Shittim. Egypt shall be a desolation, and Edom shall be a desolate wilderness, for the violence against the children of Judah, because they have shed innocent blood in their land. But Judah shall dwell for ever, and Jerusalem from generation to generation. For I will cleanse their blood that I have not cleansed: for the LORD dwelleth in Zion.* (Joel 3:9–21)

The *"vine of the earth"* is the works of the people upon it. The *"fruit"* (what the works of the people produce) of this vine will be *"cast into the great winepress of the wrath of God,"* in that the truth will be withheld from them because they give no heed to this final prophet. Neither God nor His servants will intervene in saving humankind from its own demise. Its *"fruit"* is crushed and trodden upon, creating a wine that inebriates the whole earth, causing all that drink from the same cup to stagger and *"fall."*

14:20 And the winepress was trodden without the **holy** city, and blood came out of the winepress, even unto the horse bridles, by the space of a thousand and six hundred furlongs.

John borrows from the allegoric description he later uses of the *"holy city"* in Revelation 21. The city has four walls of the same height, length, and breadth. The measurement he uses for the entire city is 12,000 furlongs, which means when divided into four walls, gives the product of 3,000 furlongs each for the length, height, and breadth of each wall.

John describes the effects of the wicked works of the people (*"blood coming out of the winepress"*) as reaching over half-way up the walls *"without the holy the city"* (*"a thousand and six hundred furlongs"* is over half of 3000), signifying a *constant majority* of human works are corrupt and wicked.

The *"bridle"* is what steers and directs the horse. In other words, because the people reject the truth, God does nothing (*"great winepress of the wrath of God"*) to help save them from the results of their works (*"blood"*), which lead them (*"the horse bridles"*) as they go.

John has set the stage for the angels to withdraw their intervention, and allow the world to reap the punishments it has brought upon itself.

Chapter

R EVELATION
UNFOLDED

15:1 And *after these things* I saw another sign in heaven *in the likeness of those things upon the earth*; *and* great and marvelous *were these things*. *And I beheld as it were*, seven *servants* having *power over* the seven last plagues; for in them is filled up the wrath of God.

In Revelation 1:20, John introduces the "*seven servants*" as a figurative expression of those throughout the world ("*seven continents*") who are righteous.

After the introduction of technological and scientific advancements ("*great wonders*") used by mortals to aid in their pursuit of financial independence and material substance, those who have separated themselves from the world ("*seven servants*") by choosing to follow the tenets of the gospel of Christ, will not be affected ("*having power over*") by the worldwide ("*seven*" continents) consequences ("*plagues*") of the unquenchable thirst for money and materialism.

The example of a "*servant*" intended by John can be given as one who "*has power over*" the cravings, to name a few for example: to eat too much, shop too much, and worry too much. Those who understand and practice the "*easy burden and yoke*" of Christ's gospel will be at peace, and understand the purpose for the trials and tribulation in the world. Those who do not, will experience the result of "*the wrath of God*," which has previously been described as the non-intervention of heavenly guidance. (See commentary on Revelation 6:17.)

15:2 And I saw as it were a sea of glass mingled with fire, and ***upon it stood those seven servants who*** had gotten the victory over the beast, and over his image, and over his mark, and over the number of his name; ***and as they played their*** harps ***they sang the song*** of God.

John uses the figurative expression "*sea of glass*" to describe the ability of having an eternal perspective of all things (see the commentary of Revelation 4:6). Having an eternal perspective "*mingled*" with knowledge of real truth ("*fire*") gives a person "*victory over*" the cares and worries of the world.

Those thus victorious, have no desire to live the "American Dream" and isolate themselves from others by surrounding themselves with a white picket fence that encloses their self-contained family. These have won the battle with their human nature by slaying the "*dragon/beast*" inside, and have no desire to earn more than another ("*number*"), own more than another ("*mark*"), or be more than another ("*image*"). They live ("*sing*") the gospel of doing unto others, forgiveness, and loving their enemies ("*the song of God*"), which creates the peaceful and soothing music as does a "*harp*."

15:3 And they sing the song of Moses the servant of God, ***which is*** the song of the Lamb, saying, Great and ***marvelous*** are thy works, Lord God Almighty; just and true are thy ways, thou King of saints.

The following verses are from one of the last books included in the *Old Testament*. The text has been translated properly. (The **bold** indicates the difference from the *King James Bible*):

*But unto you that fear my name shall the Sun of righteous-
ness arise with healing in his wings;* **and the windows of
heaven shall be opened up so that this light can shine
upon you and warm you and give you comfort.** *And ye
shall go forth, and grow up as calves of the stall,* **which are
fed by the hand of the Lord.** *And* **he shall lead you
forth from the stalls among the** *wicked,* **and** *ye shall
tread* **upon them, even as grown cattle walk upon the
remnants of a burnt field;** *for they shall be ashes under the
soles of your feet in the day that I shall do this, saith the
LORD of hosts.* **And now, I would that** *ye* **should** *remember the law of Moses my servant, which I commanded unto
him in Horeb for all Israel, with the statutes and judgments*
**that I gave unto your fathers that they might look for-
ward to the day of the Lord. And ye are their children,
therefore, the law that I have given them, even so shall
ye do.** *But in the last days the heart of the children
shall be turned away from the law and the statutes
and judgments of their fathers; and their fathers shall
mourn for them. For I have promised their fathers and
have made my covenant with them. But their children
do not know them.* Behold, I will send you Elijah the
prophet before the coming of the great and dreadful day of
the LORD: And he shall **plant in the hearts of the children
the promises made to their** fathers, lest I come and smite
the earth with a curse **and the whole earth be utterly
wasted at his coming.** (Malachi 4:2–6)

The true Law of Moses had nothing to do with what the *Old
Testament* presents in the esoteric and ritualistic ordinances described
therein. These priestly ministrations were the *lower law* given to the
Israelites after they had rejected the *higher.* The symbolism and metaphoric statutes and judgments of the Law of Moses (as given in the *Old
Testament*) point to the gospel of Jesus Christ. When Christ lived upon
earth in mortality, he fulfilled this law, and gave a new law:

*And he said unto them, These are the words which I
spake unto you, while I was yet with you, that all things
must be fulfilled, which were written in the law of Moses,
and in the prophets, and in the Psalms, concerning me.*
(Luke 24:44)

*Therefore all things whatsoever ye would that men should
do to you, do ye even so to them: **for this is the law and
the prophets**.* (Matthew 7:12)

Just before he taught the people not to get angry with each other,
not to lust after each other, not to sue each other, and not to judge each
other, but instead, to forgive each other and love their enemies, Christ said:

*Think not that I am come to destroy the law, or the
prophets: I am not come to destroy, but to fulfil. For verily I say unto you, Till heaven and earth pass, one jot or
one tittle shall in no wise pass from the law, till all be fulfilled. Whosoever therefore shall break one of these least
commandments, and shall teach men so, he shall be called
the least in the kingdom of heaven: but **whosoever shall
do and teach them**, the same shall be called great in the
kingdom of heaven. For I say unto you, That except your
righteousness shall exceed the righteousness of the scribes
and Pharisees, ye shall in no case enter into the kingdom
of heaven.* (Matthew 5:17–20)

When one "*sings the song of Moses*," and does the things that Christ
taught ("*song of the Lamb*"), it is easy to exclaim, "*Great and marvelous are
thy works, Lord God Almighty; just and true are thy ways, thou King of
saints.*" This is because treating others as one wants to be treated really
works by creating peace and happiness! With this understanding, one has
"*power*" over the consequences of depression, confusion, and fear (the
things that "*plague*" us with unhappiness).

15:4 ***For we*** shall not fear thee, O Lord, and ***shall*** glorify thy name ***with our song***; for thou art holy ***and*** all nations shall come and worship before thee; for thy judgments are made manifest ***unto us***.

How is God to be feared?

The translators of *New Testament* writings, who had been taught to fear God, misinterpreted John's original writings to read the way they believed. Those who sing the *"song of God"* will do the works commanded of Him (*"glorify thy name with our song"*) and let their light shine before men, that they may see good works by which God is glorified (refer to Matthew 5:14–16).

Those who *"fear"* God preach "hell, fire, and damnation" upon those who do not. They send out missionaries without the love of the true God, but are convinced they demonstrate their love toward their neighbor by warning them. Yet in all the scriptures, which they claim to be the "word of God," where can one verse be found wherein Christ condemns the sinner and preaches "hell, fire, and damnation," except to those who piously "fear God"?

Preachers, ministers, evangelists, and modern-day "Holy Ones" preach of a God they neither know nor understand. They cannot carry the tune of *"the song"* that those who are redeemed of the world, and who have an eternal perspective of all things, sing in perfect harmony. The *"sea of glass mingled with fire"* upon which these "elect" stand, allows them to spread love, tolerance, forgiveness, and hope instead of vain imaginations of "hell, fire, and damnation."

When the truth is finally revealed, and the world is taught this eternal perspective, *"all nations"* of the earth will come to understand the judgment and wisdom of the eternal plan of the Creator. These are the *"judgments made manifest"* to those who so choose to accept them.

Well did the Psalmist sing his song:

The law of the LORD is perfect, converting the soul: the testimony of the LORD is sure, making wise the simple. The statutes of the LORD are right, rejoicing the heart: the commandment of the LORD is pure, enlightening the eyes. The fear of the LORD is clean, enduring for ever: the judgments of the LORD are true and righteous altogether. More to be desired are they than gold, yea, than much fine gold: sweeter also than honey and the honeycomb. Moreover by them is thy servant warned: and in keeping of them there is great reward. (Psalms 19:7–11)

15:5 And after ***I had beheld these things***, I looked, and, behold, ***inside*** the temple in heaven the tabernacle of the testimony was opened:

By writing "*the tabernacle of the testimony was opened,*" John is figuratively presenting the same thing that he did in Revelation 14:6–7: the everlasting gospel being preached and available to the world.

John was taught by Jesus that the stories and traditions of the Jews had no relevance to a person's righteousness. The ordinances and rituals were allowed to be practied by the Jews as symbolic pointers to teach them how to get along with each other, and to give them "busy work" to keep their minds centered on spiritual matters instead of worldly pursuits (*worshipping the golden calf*).

According to Jewish legend and tradition, the Israelites refused to go up to the mount to speak with God, but sent Moses to do it for them. This was the first indication that mortals did not want to receive the simple truths of the mysteries of God, but would rather listen to another mortal tell them what they needed to know and do. Because they refused the plainness and simplicity of the *higher law*—which is the law Jesus taught—Moses went up on the mount and received a law of ordinances and rituals that were so embedded with esoteric meaning and filler that the Jews had no idea of their intent.

This truth is contrary to the precepts of orthodox *Bible* believers, who want to accept that the Ten Commandments was the *only* thing written upon the stone tablets Moses brought down from the mount. This foolishness couldn't be further from the truth. Here are some biblical excerpts to illustrate what really happened:

And Moses brought forth the people out of the camp to meet with God; and they stood at the nether part of the mount. (Exodus 19:17)

The Israelites were frightened and would not approach God. In comparison, because of the *"fear"* of God taught by the religious leaders of the world today, why would anyone believe God is approachable? But the opportunity to know Him and hear His voice has always been an option for those who have *"eyes that can see"* Him for who He really is, and *"ears that can hear"* His true voice.

And the LORD said unto Moses, Come up to me into the mount, and be there: and I will give thee tables of stone, and a law, and commandments which I have written; that thou mayest teach them. (Exodus 24:12)

Various instructions and precise details, which are also a part of the Law of Moses, are detailed in Exodus 24:13 to 31:17 (a large amount). These "busy laws" of building a tabernacle, an altar, and an ark, and adorning them, along with all the works to be done with each, were given after the people had rejected the simple laws Moses had taught them. If they had not been written down on the "tablets," how did Moses remember them in such detail?

And he gave unto Moses, when he had made an end of communing with him upon mount Sinai, two tables of testimony, tables of stone, written with the finger of God. (Exodus 31:18)

And Moses turned, and went down from the mount, and the two tables of the testimony were in his hand: the tables were written on both their sides; on the one side and on the other were they written. And the tables were the work of God, and the writing was the writing of God, graven upon the tables. (Exodus 32:15–16)

The people still demonstrated their natural behavior and desire to worship someone or something they could see with their mortal eyes, by building a golden idol and worshipping it. Moses threw down the stones and broke them, but was later commanded to "hew" two more stones so that this "busy work" would always be carried wherever the Israelites went.

> *And the LORD said unto Moses, Hew thee two tables of stone like unto the first: and I will write upon these tables the words that were in the first tables, which thou brakest.* (Exodus 34:1)

The Israelites made a *"tabernacle"* (a portable temple) that had the "Ark of the *Testimony"* ("Covenant" is used interchangeably) within it, which contained the "busy work" parts of the Law of Moses. The ark was always veiled and enclosed so that the people could not see it. Only those ordained with proper authority could touch it or look upon it and read those things Moses heard with his own ears. In other words, as John says throughout his *Revelation*, "*If any man have an ear, let him hear*." The Israelites had ears, but they did not want to meet God and hear Him.

In this verse of *Revelation*, John is figuratively saying that the "*temple*" is now open for *all* to see (understand) the "*tabernacle of testimony*." In other words, those who *do not fear* God and want to approach Him and hear the "*testimony*" from His own mouth, can do so without having it shielded from their view by a veil, or by having it revealed to them through another mortal (prophet).

15:6 And the seven *servants* came out of the temple, having *power over* the seven plagues, clothed in pure and white linen, and having their breasts girded with golden girdles.

According to the Law of Moses, in order for the priests to officiate in their office within the tabernacle, behind the veil, and around the Ark of the Covenant, they were instructed to dress in special clothing specifically sewn for the sacred purpose:

*And thou shalt embroider the **coat of fine linen**, and thou shalt make the mitre of fine linen, and thou shalt make **the girdle** of needlework. And for Aaron's sons thou shalt make coats, and thou shalt **make for them girdles**, and bonnets shalt thou make for them, for glory and for beauty. ...And they shall be upon Aaron, and upon his sons, when they come in unto the tabernacle of the congregation, or when they come near unto the altar to minister in the holy place; that they bear not iniquity, and die: it shall be a statute for ever unto him and his seed after him.* (Exodus 28:39–40, 43)

In this verse, John presents those who are *"coming out of the temple,"* and can now look upon the *"tabernacle of the testimony"* and recognize it for what it really is. These have a whole new perspective on life, which gives them *"power over the seven plagues."* They are clothed with righteousness (*"pure and white linen"*) *"having their breasts girded"* with a proper understanding of truth, which encases the adulations of joy and peace emanating from their breasts. (See also the reference to the *"golden girdle"* of Christ described in Revelation 1:13.)

15:7 And one of the four beasts gave unto the seven *servants* seven golden vials full of the wrath of God, who liveth for ever and ever.

To properly understand what these *"golden vials"* contain, John makes a metaphoric parallel between the *"seven servants"* presented here having the *"vials,"* and the *"seven angels"* he presented in chapter 8 having the *"trumpets"* (as mentioned in the commentary on chapter 8):

"John expresses this period of silence in his Revelation as the time in which warnings are given of what will happen to the human race if it continues to disregard the commandments of God. Trumpets are symbolically given as announcements or warnings, and each of the "seven angels" has one "trumpet" that sounds a warning pertaining to a specific effect caused by wickedness. These warnings pertain to

things that are spiritual, or those things which turn our hearts away from peace, harmony, and the love we should have one for another. Later, in chapter 16, the servants have vials in their hands, which they are commanded to pour out upon the earth. Each vial represents the actual spiritual and physical effects of humankind's wickedness, and corresponds to the spiritual warnings given by each of the angels with the trumpets that sound when humans act contrary to the Royal Law of God. The pouring out of the vials spoken of later in John's Revelation, cause much tribulation to come upon the earth after humankind has been warned by the trumpeting angels and has ignored the warnings."

When John first mentioned *"vials,"* he set up another metaphoric parallel in which he compares *"the four and twenty elders"* (prophets of God) to all those who have heeded their warnings and followed their counsel (*"seven servants"*/righteous of the world):

> *And when he had taken the book, the four beasts rejoiced, and the four and twenty elders fell down before the Lamb, having every one of them harps, and **golden vials** full of the smoke of incense, which are the prayers of saints.* (Revelation 5:8)

The *"seven angels"* whose trumpets sounded *"in heaven"* and warned us of the impending *"plagues,"* were presented as doing so *"in heaven,"* whereas the *"seven servants"* will be commanded to *"Go your ways, and pour out the vials of the wrath of God **upon the earth**."* Since the *"wrath of God"* is non-intervention in the actions of humankind, given so that we can experience consequences and learn from them; it makes sense that those with an eternal perspective (*"seven servants"*), would *"go their way upon the earth and pour out"* what they have been given upon the rest of the people. They give the world *nothing*, and do *nothing* to aid it, as it suffers the consequences of disregarding the *"trumpets of warning heard in heaven."*

This parallels Jesus Christ's thoughts in the parable of the ten virgins:

And the foolish said unto the wise, Give us of your oil; for our lamps are gone out. But the wise answered, saying, Not so; lest there be not enough for us and you: but go ye rather to them that sell, and buy for yourselves. And while they went to buy, the bridegroom came; and they that were ready went in with him to the marriage: and the door was shut. Afterward came also the other virgins, saying, Lord, Lord, open to us. But he answered and said, Verily I say unto you, I know you not. Watch therefore, for ye know neither the day nor the hour wherein the Son of man cometh. (Matthew 25:8–13)

John gives a clue to his meaning when, as the "*seven servants*" are pouring out their vials upon the earth, he mentions in Revelation 16:15:

Behold, I come as a thief. Blessed is he that watcheth, and keepeth his garments upon him, lest he walk naked, and they see his own shame.

No matter how much knowledge those who have overcome the world gain from the truth and the eternal perspective they possess, all of their explanations, understandings, wisdom, and pure knowledge of truth will be disregarded, or unaccepted by those who haven't gotten "*victory over the beast*" and do not stand on a "*sea of glass mingled with fire.*"

This clear understanding will be as a "*vial filled with the wrath of God poured out upon*" the others who have no such understanding. The mere fact that these seven servants understand the mysteries of God and the rest of the world does not (though all have been given the same opportunity), justifies the consequences of the plagues from which they suffer.

It is important to keep in mind that John presents these servants as having the *exact same vial filled with the exact same thing*—"*the wrath of God.*" He does not say that each of them has a different "*plague*" in his vial.

15:8 And the temple was filled with smoke *and all were blinded* from the glory of God, and from his power; and no man was able to enter into the temple *because of the smoke* till the seven plagues of the seven *servants* were fulfilled.

This verse parallels the period of *"silence for the space of about a half an hour"* presented in Revelation 8:1. A pure knowledge of God, His power, and His mysteries will not be known (*"no man was able to enter into the temple"*) until the inhabitants of the earth suffer the consequences (*"seven plagues"*) of *not* following His plan and mandates. When *"smoke"* is present, none can see what it hides. But one day the *"smoke"* will clear, and all will have a perfect knowledge of those alien Beings who live on another planet in another solar system, or galaxy, and with whose advanced technology and understanding we have been given the opportunity of life and the ability to experience happiness.

Chapter

Revelation Unfolded

16:1 And I heard a great voice out of the temple saying to the seven **servants**, Go your ways, and pour out the vials of the wrath of God upon the earth.

Because the people will not seek wisdom and follow the simple gospel of "do unto others what you would have them do unto you," *the plagues* will begin to torment and annoy them as thus it is sung in "*the song of Moses the servant of God*":

> *If thou wilt not observe to do all the words of this law that are written in this book, that thou mayest fear this glorious and fearful name, THE LORD THY GOD;* **Then the LORD will make thy plagues wonderful, and the plagues of thy seed, even great plagues, and of long continuance, and sore sicknesses, and of long continuance.** (Deuteronomy 28:58–59)

16:2 And the first went *his way*, and poured out his vial upon the earth; and there fell noisome and grievous *sores* upon the men which had the mark of the beast, and upon them which worshipped his image.

No prophet could more eloquently describe what John is alluding to in this verse than Isaiah:

> *Ah sinful nation, a people laden with iniquity, a seed of evildoers, children that are corrupters: they have forsaken the LORD, they have provoked the Holy One of Israel unto anger, they are gone away backward. Why should ye be stricken any more? ye will revolt more and more: the whole head is sick, and the whole heart faint.* **From the sole of the foot even unto the head there is no soundness in it**; **but wounds, and bruises, and putrifying sores**: *they have not been closed, neither bound up, neither mollified with ointment.* (Isaiah 1:4–6)

Throughout the *Old Testament*, "*sore*" is used as an adjective or an adverb to describe a condition such as being "*sore afraid*":

> *And when Pharaoh drew nigh, the children of Israel lifted up their eyes, and, behold, the Egyptians marched after them; and they were* **sore afraid**: *and the children of Israel cried out unto the LORD.* (Exodus 14:10)

...or being "*sore distressed*":

> *Moreover the children of Ammon passed over Jordan to fight also against Judah, and against Benjamin, and against the house of Ephraim; so that Israel was* **sore distressed**. (Judges 10:9)

...or being "*sore athirst*":

*And he **was sore athirst**, and called on the LORD, and
said, Thou hast given this great deliverance into the hand
of thy servant: and now shall I die for thirst, and fall into
the hand of the uncircumcised?* (Judges 15:18)

The *"sores"* mentioned in this verse have nothing to do with actual
abrasions or lesions on the skin, but all to do with the things that annoy, irri-
tate, offend, and distress those who are constantly worrying about how to
make money today, how they are going to make more money tomorrow, and
pine over the money they spent yesterday on the things that *moth corrupts*
(clothes) and all the other things which *thieves break through and steal*:

*Lay not up for yourselves treasures upon earth, where moth
and rust doth corrupt, and where thieves break through and
steal: But lay up for yourselves treasures in heaven, where
neither moth nor rust doth corrupt, and where thieves do
not break through nor steal: For where your treasure is,
there will your heart be also.* (Matthew 6:19–21)

Though not intended by John as physical ailments, those *"who have
the mark of the beast and worship his image"* will also experience other
"sores" (which annoy and disrupt their happiness) such as cancer, diabetes,
and many other diseases caused by poor diet and lack of exercise exacer-
bated by *"worshipping the beast."* He who has *"gotten the victory over the
beast"* will not feel the affects of *the noisome pestilence* as he *establishes
upon his hands the mark* (work) of the Lord by doing unto others.

The *"servant"* in this verse has *"poured out his vial,"* and sings in
harmony with the Psalmist:

*Let thy work appear unto thy servants, and thy glory unto
their children. And let the beauty of the LORD our God be
upon us: **and establish thou the work of our hands
upon us; yea, the work of our hands establish thou
it**. He that dwelleth in the secret place of the most High*

shall abide under the shadow of the Almighty. I will say of the LORD, He is my refuge and my fortress: my God; in him will I trust. Surely he shall deliver thee from the snare of the fowler, and from the noisome pestilence. He shall cover thee with his feathers, and under his wings shalt thou trust: his truth shall be thy shield and buckler. Thou shalt not be afraid for the terror by night; nor for the arrow that flieth by day; Nor for the pestilence that walketh in darkness; nor for the destruction that wasteth at noonday. (Psalms 90:16 through 91:6)

16:3 And the second *servant* poured out his vial upon the sea; and it became as the blood of a dead man; and every living soul died in the sea.

Those who do not understand the gospel of Christ and do not possess an eternal perspective, will not understand the intent for which the gospel is given. Their works become dark (*"as the blood of a dead man"*), and give no life to them; whereas the gospel of Christ and its intent (his pure *"blood"* which is red and life-giving) gives eternal life to the body, in that it can assure us peace and happiness forever.

> *How much more shall the blood of Christ, who through the eternal Spirit offered himself without spot to God, purge your conscience* **from dead works** *to serve the living God?* (Hebrews 9:14)

> *Forasmuch as ye know that ye were not redeemed with corruptible things, as silver and gold, from your vain conversation received by tradition from your fathers; But with the* **precious blood of Christ**, *as of a lamb without blemish and without spot:...Seeing ye have purified your souls in obeying the truth through the Spirit unto unfeigned love of the brethren, see that ye love one another with a pure heart fervently:* (I Peter 1:18–19, 22)

John presents this *"servant pouring out his vial upon the sea,"* wherein *"every living soul dies."* This represents everyone upon the earth (see previous commentary on the significance of *"the sea"*) being *"dead,"* because their works do not bring a life of peace and happiness as promised by obeying the gospel of Christ (the red and pure blood), but are dark like *"the blood of a dead man."*

16:4 And the third **servant** poured out his vial upon the rivers and fountains of waters; and they **also** became **as the** blood **of a dead man**.

The *"rivers and fountains of waters"* are the source of quenching human thirst for knowledge and understanding. These represent secular leaders, popes, priests, bishops, prophets, pastors, evangelists, spiritual gurus, therapists, motivational speakers, or anyone who presents him or herself as one from whom others may obtain knowledge and inspiration. Usually for a price, these *"rivers and fountain of waters"* appease the thirst of their followers by virtue of their worldly degrees and honors, or by subtle manipulation, which makes one *think* their thirst is quenched, only to awaken the next day still parched and thirsty.

Seldom is counsel drawn from these deep wells full of *"the blood of a dead man"* that leads an individual to understand that the "kingdom of God" is **within**, and *no other* can lead a person to this kingdom of peace and tranquility. If the people were led to the simple and light burden of the gospel of Jesus Christ, these *"rivers and fountain of waters"* would no longer be necessary. The only well from which one needs draw for understanding and inspiration is the one mentioned by Christ:

> But whosoever drinketh of the water that I shall give him
> shall never thirst; but the water that I shall give him
> shall **be in him a well of water springing up into**
> **everlasting life**. (John 4:14)

16:5 And I heard the **servant who poured out his vial upon these** waters say, Thou art righteous, O Lord, which art, and wast, and shalt be, because thou hast judged **them by their works**.

In this verse, John further expounds upon the corrupted *"waters"* by proclaiming that the counsel and commandments of the Eternal God (*"O Lord, which art, and wast, and shalt be"*) are proper and righteous.

Withholding His intervention from the people (*"pouring out of his wrath"*) is directly linked to their works. The greater the heed given to the commandments of God, the more His mysteries are revealed. Those who give no heed to His commandments are given a lesser portion of understanding until they know *nothing* concerning the mysteries of God. When they know nothing concerning His mysteries, they (the *"frogs"*—see verse 13) must seek to quench their thirst for knowledge and understanding from the sources available to them: *"rivers and fountains"* overflowing with the *"blood of a dead man."*

The concept of gaining more understanding by complying with the gospel of Jesus Christ is comparable to freeing the mind, and allowing thoughts to process without the restrictions of worry and stress. In essence, Christ's counsels can be summed up as: don't worry, be happy.

Little children are happy because they have no worry of what they will eat or drink or where they will lie down come nightfall. They do not worry about whether they are better than or as good as everyone else. They have no worries about accomplishing vain goals, and are completely satisfied playing alone or with other little children, who share their uncluttered minds. The older they become, the more experiences they gain from a world filled with "grown children," who worry about everything except what truly makes them happy—being who they were in the beginning—little children.

Therefore, the more worries and stresses we have in our lives, the less we understand about reality and happiness—the mysteries of God. Because we lack happiness, we are convinced that we must seek it from others we assume have the authority and ability to help us find it. These are the *"rivers and fountains of waters"* described by John.

16:6 For they have shed the blood of saints and prophets, and thou hast given them blood to drink; for they are worthy.

The *people* were not the ones that killed Christ and the prophets. The masses do not have a problem seeking *within* for peace, without having to perform certain ordinances or pay money to others to get it. The *"rivers and fountains of waters"* (the *"they"* to which John refers in this verse) lose their honor and glory when confronted by true *"saints and prophets"* of God. They have every reason to rid themselves of their competition—either by physically murdering them, or spiritually "shedding their blood" by causing the people to reject their message.

Because the people would rather *"drink blood"* from the corrupted *"waters,"* they do not deserve to "understand the mysteries of God" or receive His intervention in their lives. Thus, *"they are worthy"* to have the *"vial full of the wrath of God"* poured out upon them.

16:7 And I heard another *voice* out of the altar say, Even so, Lord God Almighty, true and righteous are thy judgments.

This voice came from *"out of the altar,"* which represents the place where people present their works upon the earth in mortality. The prophet who is upon the earth during the times these plagues are tormenting and annoying the world, testifies by his works (*"voice"*) that the people are not listening to truth, but instead are appeasing their thirst for knowledge by drinking corrupted *"water."* This prophet was given the power to provide the "cup" from which people could drink the pure water mentioned by Christ:

> *For whosoever shall give you a cup of water to drink in my name, because ye belong to Christ, verily I say unto you, he shall not lose his reward.* (Mark 9:41)

16:8 And the fourth *servant* poured out his vial upon the sun; and power was given unto him to scorch men with fire.

Two questions have *"plagued"* (annoyed and confounded) the so-called "Great Minds" of the human race: First, "Which came first, the chicken or the egg?" Secondly, "Why did the human race exist for thousands of years without discovering how to use electricity and other forms of energy to serve the needs of humankind? Why in only a few hundred years of harnessing and using this *"power,"* does our world now change so drastically every few years? Was Democritus, the Greek Philosopher who postulated the existence of the atom circa 500 B.C.E., much less intelligent than Albert Einstein? Or perhaps both were fools compared with a true understanding of the mysteries of God?"

The first question was figuratively answered by John in verse 5 of this chapter:

Thou are righteous, O Lord, which art, and wast, and shalt be... .

There have always been chickens, there have always been eggs, there have always been Gods—question answered.

The second question was answered in the commentary of Revelation 13:14, but is further expounded on in this verse. The "*sun*" represents knowledge or an understanding ("*fire*"/light) of the power of God. This "*power*" is given to the world without the guidance and intervention of God (the wrath "*poured from the vial upon the sun*"). The children of God have been allowed in these final times to play with "*fire*" without adult supervision. This is so they will learn by their own experience that it burns, and when it does, it hurts!

16:9 And men were scorched with great heat, and blasphemed the name of God **who** hath power over these plagues; **but** they repented not to give him glory.

The environments of the world are being destroyed because of the great advancements in technology and science ("*great heat*") the human race is using to gratify their lusts. But far more devastating is the fact that these technologies cause people to become more and more selfish; because now a person can sit home, earn their money, be entertained, and not worry about what is happening to a neighbor living ten feet away divided by a white picket fence.

"*Giving glory to God*," as previously mentioned, is nothing more or less than loving your neighbor as yourself. For the most part, even when we love one another, we isolate ourselves behind our "picket fences," and *"blaspheme His name"* by not doing His works (loving *all* of His children as we love the few that we claim to "love").

Though these wonderful technological advancements could save our lives and bring equality and more happiness to the world, we use them in ways that go against the gospel of Jesus Christ; therefore, even though we are being *"scorched"* by this *"great heat"* (having this great knowledge) *"we repent not to give God glory."* Furthermore, by doing it *God's way*, we would have *"power over these plagues."*

Isaiah uses the same figurative expressions to depict the comfort given to those who follow the Lord:

> *They shall not hunger nor thirst; neither shall **the heat nor sun smite them**: for he that hath mercy on them shall lead them, even **by the springs of water shall he guide them**.* (Isaiah 49:10)

16:10 And the fifth **servant** poured out his vial upon the seat of the beast; and his kingdom was full of darkness; and they gnawed their tongues for pain,

Those who pursue the selfish course of the "American Dream" disregard all tenets of the gospel of equality. This "Dream" is exactly what it is: a dream. In order to dream this way, the world has been pacified and lulled (to sleep) into carnal security. Once the *"vial of the wrath of God"* is poured out upon the earth, those who keep us awake are silenced.

> *For the LORD hath poured out upon you the spirit of deep sleep, and hath closed your eyes: the prophets and your rulers, the seers hath he covered.* (Isaiah 29:10)

After the establishment of the United States and its capitalistic economical principles, the entire world followed suit—either by the sheer necessity to survive, or by force.

In the next chapter (17), John gives an even greater explanation of the things he is presenting here. He is shown the other nations of the earth ("*ten horns*") who are of "*one mind, and shall give their power and strength and their kingdom unto the beast*" (see Revelation 17:13, 17). This "*beast sits upon the sea*" (sea of humanity), and has thus established its "*seat*" upon the earth. The effects of "*the seat of the beast*" have caused "*his kingdom*" to be "*full of darkness*":

> And in that day they shall roar against them like the roaring of the sea: and if one look unto the land, **behold darkness and sorrow, and the light is darkened in the heavens** thereof. (Isaiah 5:30)

The correct English definition for the word "*gnawed*" used here by John is the intransitive verb: "to cause somebody constant anxiety or distress." Being in pursuit of the "Dream," and in all aspects of a capitalistic economy, the ability to outsmart, outthink, and outspeak ("*tongue*") one's neighbor is essential to success. However, in doing so, an atmosphere of anxiety and stress ("*pain*") is created as we try to out-succeed each other. Well did Jeremiah prophesy:

> **And they bend their tongues like their bow for lies***: but they are not valiant for the truth upon the earth; for they proceed from evil to evil, and they know not me, saith the LORD. Take ye heed every one of his neighbour, and trust ye not in any brother: for every brother will utterly supplant, and every neighbour will walk with slanders. **And they will deceive every one his neighbour, and will not speak the truth: they have taught their tongue to speak lies, and weary themselves to commit iniquity. Thine habitation is in the midst of deceit***; through deceit they refuse to know me, saith the LORD. (Jeremiah 9:3–6)

16:11 And blasphemed the God of heaven because of their pains and their sores, **but still they** repented not of their deeds.

Isaiah presents what John is describing in this verse, like this:

*And when they shall say unto you, Seek unto them that have familiar spirits, and unto wizards that peep, and that mutter: should not a people seek unto their God? for the living to the dead? To the law and to the testimony: if they speak not according to this word, it is because there is no light in them. And they shall pass through it, hardly bestead and hungry: and it shall come to pass, that when they shall be hungry, they shall fret themselves, and curse their king and their God, and look upward. And they shall look unto the earth; and behold trouble and darkness, dimness of anguish; and **they shall be driven to darkness**.* (Isaiah 8:19–22)

In these latter times, humans have little need for a God they cannot see, hear, touch, or experience. They use their "*belief*" in God to assuage their inner longings to make sense out of a world gone amuck. The sale of self-help books (*familiar spirits*), which teach a person about "self-help" instead of how to help others less fortunate, dominates the book markets.

These are some of the "*false prophets*" of whom John writes. They set themselves up as one "trained" in the ministration of effective catharsis that relieves one of "*their pains and their sores*." Their emotional fix lasts about the week their fee covers, after which, one must return and pay more money for an additional week of a temporary "feel good about myself" sensation. If one does not have a therapist (*wizards that peep*), he or she is considered in denial, and all the more in need of one—therapists see other therapists! Pure and lasting happiness is nowhere to be found in most of these attempts to "help-the-self," as is evident every day, as *hate* increases and *love waxes cold*:

And then shall many be offended, and shall betray one another, and shall hate one another. And many false prophets shall rise, and shall deceive many. And because iniquity shall abound, the love of many shall wax cold. (Matthew 24:10–12)

People cannot see that the only solution to their problems is found in forgiveness, love for neighbor and enemy, and treating each other as they would want to be treated. When they do these things, they find happiness. However, the happiness is short-lived when convinced by the "*beast*" that happiness is not in how your neighbor is doing, but in how YOU are doing; therefore, in spite of the obvious, "*still they repented not of their deeds.*"

16:12 And the sixth ***servant*** poured out his vial upon the great river Euphrates; and the water thereof was dried up, that the way of the kings of the east might be prepared.

When God makes no intervention into our lives ("*wrath of God poured out of the vial*") there is no "revelation from heaven" ("*rain*"). When there is no rain, rivers "*dry up.*"

The "*great river Euphrates*" was mentioned and explained in the commentary on Revelation 9:14: "*The city of Babylon, situated next to the Euphrates River has been used by prophets to describe the great worldliness and wickedness of humankind.*"

After many years of following the course of the "*beast*" (the course of the *river Euphrates*, and also the King's Highway that leads to the *river Euphrates* mentioned below) without divine intervention ("*wrath from the vial*"), which would have us treat each other appropriately, the economic stability of the world and its ability to obtain the "American Dream" will literally "*dry up.*" It will become more challenging for a person to achieve the illusory "Dream," and acquire the material possessions for which the heart longs. Means of income will become harder and harder to come by as technology replaces the laborer with machines and robots.

No longer will human life be valued as it once was. Human beings who die in wars on one side will be considered heroes—and the enemy, merely expendable casualties of war. The way of life and the standard of living the human race is accustomed to, and the source of its leisure and abundance, will literally "*dry up.*"

John uses a simple expression to represent *why* the "*water thereof was dried up.*" In order that a "*way might be prepared*" to help those who are seeking the "*Christ child*" (*the one the dragon was ready to devour upon birth*), material possessions and the ability to acquire them must be inhibited sufficiently to help cause a change of heart. One is either seeking for the things of the earth, or seeking to serve God—"Ye cannot serve God and mammon":

> *For where your treasure is, there will your heart be also.*
> *The light of the body is the eye: if therefore thine eye be sin-*
> *gle, thy whole body shall be full of light. But if thine eye be*
> *evil, thy whole body shall be full of darkness. If therefore the*
> *light that is in thee be darkness, how great is that darkness!*
> *No man can serve two masters: for either he will hate the*
> *one, and love the other; or else he will hold to the one, and*
> *despise the other. Ye cannot serve God and mammon.*
> (Matthew 6:21–24)

John contrasts the "*the kings of the east*" in this verse with "*the kings of the earth and of the whole world*" in verse 14. One represents those who allow righteousness to "rule over them" (or be their king), and the other represents those who allow "mammon" to rule over them.

Anciently, there existed trade routes of vital importance to the commerce of the Middle East. They began in Egypt, and led to the Euphrates River. One was called Via Maris (meaning the "*Way of the Sea,*" and according to John's figurative expressions: "*the way*" of the "*people of the earth*"), and the other was called The King's Highway.

Merchants would carry their merchandise along these routes to the Euphrates, where they would float their wares down to Babylon. The ancient merchants' version of the "American Dream" was dependent upon the river. If it were to ever "*dry up,*" that would be the end of their income, or at least it would make it much harder for them to make their exchanges.

John uses the reference of "*the kings of the east*" (*wise men* who came from the east in search of the prophesied "*Christ child*" destined to save the world) as his figurative expression of those who are seeking to comply with the gospel of Christ:

> *Now when Jesus was born in Bethlehem of Judaea in the*
> *days of Herod the king, behold, there came **wise men***

from the east to Jerusalem, Saying, Where is he that is born King of the Jews? for we have seen his star in the east, and are come to worship him. (Matthew 2:1–2)

"*The way*" to live the gospel of Jesus Christ is cleared and "*prepared*" before us as the things of the world and its desires are "*dried up.*" As a person begins to see the futility in finding happiness in the things of the world, one's heart is "*prepared*" that it "*might*" begin to seek for the things that truly bring happiness—loving others as one does oneself.

16:13 And *because the water was dried up* I saw three unclean spirits like *unto* frogs come out of the mouth of the dragon, and out of the mouth of the beast, and out of the mouth of the false prophet.

Frogs live in or near bodies of water that give them life. When the water is "*dried up,*" "*frogs*" seek out other bodies of water to sustain them. In verse 4, John has presented the "*rivers and fountains of water*" as corrupted with "*blood.*" These polluted "*waters*" come forth from the mouths of religious, secular, and other spiritual leaders of the earth. When these desperate and distressed "*frogs*" seek for "*water*" and life in the mouths of these, and enter therein, they find "*blood*" instead, and "*come out of the mouth*" of those who do not possess the "*living waters*" of the gospel of Christ.

As the means of the economies of the world "*dry up,*" as has been explained, those people of the earth who are full of <u>selfishness</u>, <u>lust</u>, and <u>hate</u> ("*three unclean spirits like unto frogs*") seek life from those (f*amiliar spirits*) who they believe can give them life. These leaders and spiritual guides, in turn, play on the desires of human nature ("*the dragon*") and the image of worldly success ("*the beast*"), all the while pretending to administer good and sound doctrine (whether spiritual or secular) to the people.

The gospel of Jesus Christ, which includes unconditional forgiveness and loving our enemies as our friends, presents the only message anyone needs to know and understand in order to be happy. In contrast, anyone who does not teach this simple message is who John has referred to as a "*false prophet.*" Therefore, the term John uses ("*false prophet*") always represents any person who *claims* to be good and teach truth, but who pollutes the *pure and living water* by teaching anything more or less than the simple message of Jesus Christ.

Even more than the spiritual gurus (*"false prophets"*) who invent breathing patterns, chakras, regions of the solar plexus, and other such nonsense (causing a person to concentrate and focus more on themselves than on how their chants and esoteric ways affect others), ministers of organized religion give an even clearer model of a *"false prophet."* These dress in fancy clothes, drive fancy cars, live in expensive houses, and receive incomes and stipends from their church, all the while preaching of Christ and his gospel. The message these ministers give causes their congregations to desire (lust after) the things of the world by the examples they inadvertently set for them. The followers are erroneously convinced that their leaders are "blessed" with riches from God because of their righteousness; therefore, they erroneously conclude that *all* who seek after the same riches that a "man of God" possesses, must surely be justified. They then believe these riches are condoned as righteous blessings of God.

What these leaders fail to point out from their adorned pulpits is that Jesus Christ and his apostles had very, very little in way of earthly possessions. These *"false prophets"* preach "family values" to their congregations, which is really only someone's clever guise to subtly persuade any who will listen, to further divide themselves into families, nations, churches, or groups (*selfishness*). They do this by drawing on their own precepts and doctrines, and causing great inequalities and separation among God's children, which in turn, evolves further into condemning others who are not of the same family, nation, church or group (*hate*).

Well did Christ speak of them:

The scribes and the Pharisees sit in Moses' seat: All therefore whatsoever they bid you observe, that observe and do; but do not ye after their works: for they say, and do not. For they bind heavy burdens and grievous to be borne, and lay them on men's shoulders; but they themselves will not move them with one of their fingers. But all their works they do for to be seen of men:

they make broad their phylacteries, and enlarge the bor-
ders of their garments, And love the uppermost rooms at
feasts, and the chief seats in the synagogues, And greet-
ings in the markets, and to be called of men, Rabbi, Rabbi.
(Matthew 23:2–7)

16:14 For they are the spirits of devils *which work* miracles *and* go forth
unto the kings of the earth and of the whole world, *gathering them for*
the battle of that great day of God Almighty.

The people of the earth have gained hope and strength from listening
to religious leaders, spiritual gurus, self-help consultants, and therapists. The
market for books, trinkets, and everything sold with the purpose of giving
a person hope in a world filled with despair and darkness has become substantial and extensive. Those involved in this market do not "sell" their
wares *only* for money. Glory, prestige, honor, and worldly praise are some
of the other rewards these "*false prophets*" receive from those who listen to
them and seek out their wisdom.

The "*miracles*" they "*work*" are the gentle persuasions of the therapist's voice as the depressed and miserable seek relief, which they receive
temporarily through a "*miracle.*" The "*miracles*" also come in the trinkets
provided by spiritual gurus, and in the hypnotic state in which their adher-
ents are placated through breathings, chants, chakras, yoga poses, and
everything else done to relieve the "*sores*" and "*plagues*" of the masses. All
these things lead a person away from the simple solution to the world's
problems by the effects of the "*miracles*" provided as a substitute for: forgiveness, loving your neighbor as yourself, and treating your enemy with
respect and love.

Not to be ignored, are the businesses catering to the need for entertainment by those who are miserable and stressed—by providing them with
their wares. These include, but are not limited to: video games, computer
games, entertainment websites, sports heroes, and the appropriately called
"*stars*" of music, cinema, and stage. These all add to the "*flood that comes*
forth from the mouth of the dragon" to destroy "*the woman who brought*
forth the man child." (See commentary on chapter 12.)

The entertainment world is a *"miracle"* in and of itself. Nothing is more effective in helping a person forget about the reality of the miseries experienced in the *"real"* world than going to a movie, playing a video game, attending a sporting event, or closing our ears with earphones that block out everything but the soothing music to which we listen and direct our attention. A person becomes lost in the emotional *"flood"* of their team winning or losing a game, in a movie presenting a fantasy world that is not real, or in a video game in which the players become *"God"* and control the virtual world that has replaced their reality—in these worlds they create their own realities.

All these things are the *"miracles"* that assuage the hurting and afflicted soul that has been taught to *lust* after the "American Dream," *hate* others because of their differences, and *selfishly* isolate themselves in a world that has no concern for anyone but the *"self."* These are the *"miracles"* by which all upon the earth have been deceived:

> *And deceiveth them that dwell on the earth by the means*
> *of those miracles which he had power to do in the sight of*
> *the beast; saying to them that dwell on the earth, that they*
> *should make an image to the beast, which had the wound*
> *by a sword, and did live.* (Revelation 13:14)

These *"spirits of devils"* have taken power over all those (*"the kings of the earth and of the whole world"*) who should have retained this power within, and allowed no one to "rule over them." There is a *"gathering"* taking place, in which the words of Christ (*"sword"* from his mouth) come up against the ways of the world. This *"battle"* wages within each of us every day, as we wage a war with the desires of our flesh (*"the dragon"*). We pursue this battle by chasing the dream that we should be special and esteemed above others and have all our heart's desire (*"the image of the beast"*).

The swords we use to fight this *"battle"* are provided by the *"false prophets."* We, the distressed *"frogs"* who are feeling *"gnawed,"* cannot help but *hop* into *"the mouths"* of those to whom we look for *"water"* to bring us life—when *"the river"* that has sustained us has *"dried up."* The swords with which to fight the Lamb continue to come out of their *"mouths,"* because we continue to listen to their words and pattern our lives after theirs.

We distressed *"frogs"* do not consciously recognize the One against whom we are fighting. Our leaders and others in whom we put our trust, will continue to depict this unseen "threat" as our worst enemy, until we are convinced by *"the dragon, the beast, and the false prophet"* that he, this **One** who some say is the Anti-Christ, is nothing but a *"thief"* who comes to take away our worldly possessions, knock down our picket fences, and destroy our families and our happy homes.

Therefore, because we are distressed *"frogs"* out of water, we seek out and listen to *"the dragon, the beast, and the false prophet."* We have busied ourselves in many ways, attempting to secure our worldly possessions and protect our beloved families from this enemy that we consciously do not recognize. **Who is this** enemy, this threat, this happiness-robbing Anti-Christ, against whom we are fighting?

Here is a clue from Matthew 10:34: **One** came saying:

Think not that I am come to send peace on earth: I came not to send peace, but a sword. (Matthew 10:34)

Yes, our worst enemy *"sits upon a white horse"* with a *"sharp two-edged sword coming out of his mouth"* to slay us and take away all the glory of the world we created for our own pleasure. He slays those we love and worship: our sports, movie and music stars, our secular leaders, our religious leaders and all *"false prophets."* He comes to destroy the "American Dream." For this reason, he was referred to by Isaiah as "the Prince of Peace."

Is there any wonder why we must *"gather for battle?"* Have not *"the dragon, the beast, and the false prophet"* blown their trumpets and prepared us for this war?

Even so, those whose happiness lies in worldly pleasures, selfish endeavors, or material possessions are justified to war against him, because the enemy with whom they will fight in this *"great battle"* admits he is a *"thief,"* and that he is coming *"to steal"*:

16:15 *If any man have an ear, let him hear what the spirit sayeth*: Behold, I come as a thief. Blessed is he that watcheth, and keepeth his garments *upon him*, lest he walk naked and see his *own* shame.

Though John mentions Christ as a *"thief"* in Revelation 3:3, he has led us into a proper understanding of what Christ meant when he said:

> But know this, that if the goodman of the house had known in what watch **the thief would come**, he would have watched, and would not have suffered his house to be broken up. Therefore be ye also ready: for in such an hour as ye think not **the Son of man cometh**. (Matthew 24:43–44)

Christ's gospel robs us of our pride, our materialism, and our disrespect for others and their beliefs. He robs us of our family units, communities, nations and borders, and makes us equal to others in all things. He robs us of our heroes, our leaders, even all those to whom we look as the quintessential example of a successful human being. He robs us of our ignorance, our degrees, our doctorates, and our worldly intelligence that creates our classes, our castes, and our divisions. He robs us of our businesses, corporations, and all other means by which the *"miracles"* of this life have divided us and caused us misery.

He is truly a *thief*.

John again refers to our *"garments"* as our works and understanding. These *"garments"* are the *"white robes"* given to all those who have the *"seal of God in their forehead,"* and who *"should rest yet for a little season"* as has been previously explained in the commentary of Revelation 6:11. He warns those who have been enlightened by the truth to keep on their *"garments,"* or they will be *"sore"* ashamed when *"the battle"* is finally over.

16:16 And *they were* gathered together into a place called in the Hebrew tongue Armageddon.

In order to understand what John is presenting as "*a place*" where this "*great battle*" between Christ and the world ensues, it is imperative to understand what the word "*Armageddon*" means "*in the Hebrew tongue.*"

The word *Armageddon* is derived from "Mount Megiddo," *Har Megido* in Hebrew. This was the ancient site of the Great Battle of Megiddo. This battle occurred circa 609 BC, between the armies of Egypt and the armies of the kingdom of Judah.

The Egyptians and the Assyrians were allied together to fight the powerful Babylonians who were threatening to take over that part of the world. On this particular occasion, as the Egyptians went forth to aid the Assyrians, they were *blocked* by the armies of Judah at a place called Via Maris (the "*Way of the Sea*") near Mount Megiddo ("*Armageddon*"). The armies of the kingdom of Judah confronted the Egyptians at this particular spot (Via Maris), not because Judah was allied with Babylon, but because the two found themselves face to face.

John was very close to Christ while he lived upon the earth. Jesus knew of the biblical prophecies concerning his own mission and how they played out during his lifetime. Of course, with Jesus present, John was able to gain an insight into things that others did not understand. John borrows from a prophecy of Isaiah to illustrate this "*place*" where the "*battle*" between good (doing unto others as you would have them do unto you) and evil (not doing unto others) takes place.

The armies of Egypt, of course, represent our worldliness and the lusts and desires of the world. The armies of Judah represent the commandment to love your neighbor as yourself. Remember: **ALL** the law and the prophets are predicated upon this law:

> *Therefore all things whatsoever ye would that men should do to you, do ye even so to them: for this is the law and the prophets.* (Matthew 7:12)

The allegiance formed between Egypt and Assyria represents the allegiance of all those who teach anything other than the *Royal Law*. As Egypt went to the aid of Assyria, the armies of Judah "*blocked*" their way at Via Maris, creating a very important allegoric representation that

John used in presenting his message.

This encounter between these two armies holds eternal significance for each of us. Isaiah prophecies of the significance of *this place*:

*Nevertheless the dimness shall not be such as was in her vex-
ation, when at the first he lightly afflicted the land of Zebulun
and the land of Naphtali, and afterward did more grievous-
ly afflict her by the way of the sea* [Via Maris as written in the
Latin Bible], *beyond Jordan, in Galilee of the nations. The
people that walked in darkness have seen a great light: they
that dwell in the land of the shadow of death, upon them hath
the light shined. Thou hast multiplied the nation, and not
increased the joy: they joy before thee according to the joy in
harvest, and as men rejoice when they divide the spoil. "For
thou hast broken the yoke of his burden, and the staff of his
shoulder, the rod of his oppressor, as in the day of Midian.*
**For every battle of the warrior is with confused noise,
and garments rolled in blood; but this shall be with
burning and fuel of fire***. For unto us a child is born, unto
us a son is given: and the government shall be upon his
shoulder: and his name shall be called Wonderful, Counsellor,
The mighty God, The everlasting Father, The Prince of Peace.
Of the increase of his government and peace there shall be no
end, upon the throne of David, and upon his kingdom, to
order it, and to establish it with judgment and with justice
from henceforth even for ever. The zeal of the LORD of hosts
will perform this.* (Isaiah 9:1–7)

Compare this to the *New Testament*:

*That it might be fulfilled which was spoken by Esaias the
prophet, saying, The land of Zabulon, and the land of
Nephthalim,* **by the way of the sea** [Via Maris], *beyond
Jordan, Galilee of the Gentiles; The people which sat in
darkness saw great light; and to them which sat in the*

*region and shadow of death light is sprung up. From that
time Jesus began to preach, and to say, Repent: for the
kingdom of heaven is at hand.* (Matthew 4:14–17)

Though mentioned in Isaiah and spelled out in Matthew, it is not
understood by Biblical scholars that Via Maris is *the actual place* where
the world heard the word of God for the first time from the mouth of a
mortal Jesus who was sent to the world with the *"sword of truth"* coming
out of his mouth.

As the ways of the *"dragon, the beast, and the false prophet"*
become more evident and widespread in the lives of the people, they are
confronted by the words of Christ. Each of us has *"the light of Christ"*
within us, or better, the ability to understand that forgiveness, love, com-
passion, and caring for one another brings more peace and happiness than
our own selfish pursuits and desires. When these two values meet, our conscience, which is the *"light of Christ,"* weighs the decision to love others,
or love ourselves—and a *"battle"* ensues. It is *"the place"* where the words
of Christ (the army of Judah) that teach us to love one another *"block"* the
selfish desires of our human heart (the army of Egypt).

It is no accident as to why Christ instructed John to use this particular historic battle near Mount Meggido as a reference to the end times—for
those with *"eyes that see."* How the Army of Judah fared in the battle against
the Army of Egypt is a historic fact, whose results should ***put every reader
on alert*** regarding the *"Battle of Armageddon"* prophesied to take place in
the latter days, and which is taking place right now.

The *"place"* where our choices are *"gathered together"* (our own Via
Maris) is in our own conscience. In this quiet place, the word of truth meets
up with the word of the world—this is the battlefield—yes, our own
"Armageddon."

John uses the outcome of the *battle* fought at Mount Megiddo
(*"Armageddon"*) to explain what occurs when the *"battle"* in our conscience takes place. The armies of Egypt (lusts and worldly desires) eventually overcome the kingdom of Judah (those things not of the world which
bring us happiness, i.e., forgiveness, love of enemies, etc). Later, the great
nation of Babylon (*"the seat of the beast"*) rises up and destroys Egypt and

her allies (the same ones we surrender to and allow to consume our lives), and sits alone upon the great *"sea of humanity,"* and rules and reigns as *"the mother of harlots and the abominations of the earth."*

As this world wars amongst itself for riches, glory, materialism, etc., the "still small voice," or the "light of Christ," *blocks* our actions, usually for just a few moments, before we disregard it and forget about the peace it could bring.

Therefore, if our conscience "be" our guide, one need only look quietly within and around oneself to notice which side is winning the *"Battle of Armageddon."* One will soon recognize that those who are the most at *"peace"* and do not fight on the battlefield, are the few who love *all* others unconditionally according to the commandments of Christ.

16:17 And the seventh *servant* poured out his vial into the air;

The editors, compilers, and subsequent translators of the *New Testament* made some major errors in the placement of John's words in the next few verses. When John originally wrote the work, there were no chapters or verses. When the task was set to divide the text, it was done according to what made sense to those who took the task upon them. With a correct translation and positioning of John's words, this part of *Revelation* makes logical sense as he intended.

16:18 And there fell upon men a great hail out of heaven, every stone about the weight of a talent: and men blasphemed God because of the plague of the hail; for the plague thereof was exceeding great.

John's intent here becomes self-evident with a proper understanding of what *"hail"* is, but more importantly, with *how* it is formed:

(As the definition is read, keep in mind all that has been unfolded thus far in John's expressive symbolism.)

Hail is formed in huge cumulonimbus clouds, commonly known as *thunder*heads. When the *sun* shines brightly during the day, the air close to the ground is heated. Hot air is less dense, and therefore lighter than cold air, thus causing it to rise and cool. As it cools, its capacity for holding moisture decreases. When the rising, warm air has cooled so much that it cannot retain all of its moisture, water vapor condenses, forming clouds. The condensing moisture *releases heat of its own* into the surrounding air, causing the air to rise faster and give up even more moisture.

These thunderheads contain vast amounts of energy in the form of *updrafts* and *downdrafts*. These vertical winds reach very high speeds. "*Hail*" grows in the storm cloud's main *updraft*. Snow and rain coexist in this central *updraft*.

As the snowflakes fall, liquid water freezes onto them, forming ice pellets that will continue to grow as more and more droplets are accumulated. Upon reaching the bottom of the cloud, some of the ice pellets are carried by the *updraft* back up to the top of the storm. As the ice pellets once again fall through the cloud, another layer of ice is added, and the *hailstone grows even larger*. Typically, *the stronger the updraft, the more times a hailstone repeats this cycle,* and *consequently, the larger it grows.* Once the hailstone becomes too heavy to be supported by *the updraft,* it falls out of the cloud toward the surface of the earth. The hailstone reaches the ground as ice since it is not in the warm air below the thunderstorm long enough to melt before reaching the ground.

To understand what John is trying to present, one needs to see the "*downdrafts*" as what comes from heaven, and the "*updrafts*" as what comes from the earth. The "*downdrafts*" are the mysteries of God and the eternal truths given to the world in the latter days, as has been explained as the increased technology and advancements that were kept from the knowledge of the world for thousands of years until the end of times. The "*updrafts*" are the way humankind uses this knowledge.

The world is *not* using this great knowledge to love one another and do good, but rather to elevate one above another (like unto "*mountains*" rising above the earth), and isolate one from another (like the "*islands*" of the sea). (See verse 21.)

As our use of this knowledge becomes self-evident through our scientific and technological evolution, we create the *"great hail out of heaven."* *"Every stone"* becomes a *portion of knowledge* we have obtained. (A specific *portion* is the definition of *talent* used in the parable by Jesus in Matthew 25:14-30, and *pound* used in the same context in Luke 19:11–27.)

Nothing humans have done to themselves will ever outweigh (*"weight of a talent"*) the consequences (*"plagues"*) of the portion of intelligence they used to create money (*"the number of the beast"*). Money is the great and magical **un**equalizer! It turns a piece of paper into any material possession desired, large or small. It turns a poor man into a rich one. It turns a meek person into one full of pride. It turns a heart from peace to lofty goals and aspirations. It turns an innocent child into a stressed and unhappy adult.

Because of God's non-intervention (*"vial of His wrath poured out into the air"*) in telling us how to properly use this knowledge of the eternal laws of nature, we use it as we please—contrary to His *Royal Law*; thus *"blaspheming"* God, and causing a great burden (*"weight"*) upon ourselves. All of the world's problems (*"the great plague of the hail"*) are directly linked to our inability to create equality among ourselves.

16:19 And ***after the seven plagues of the seven servants were fulfilled I heard*** great voices, and thunders, and lightnings ***coming*** out of the temple of heaven from the throne, saying, It is done.

In Revelation 15:8, John tells us:

*And the temple was filled with smoke and all were blinded from the glory of God, and from his power; and no man was able to enter into the temple because of the smoke **till the seven plagues of the seven servants were fulfilled**.*

But after the *"smoke"* has cleared, we hear *"the voices, the thunder and lightning coming out of the temple,"* revealing the truth and the wondrous mysteries of God. The time and season of our ignorance and the misuse of our world and each other is over—*"It is done!"*

16:20 And there was a great earthquake, such as was not since men were upon the earth, so mighty an earthquake, and so great. And the great city was divided into three parts, and the cities of the nations fell: and great Babylon came in remembrance before God, to give unto her the cup of the wine of the fierceness of his wrath.

Because of the truths that are being revealed (which start with these truths being unfolded at this time throughout the pages of this book), every house built upon a sandy foundation shall fall. This is because the very foundations upon which the people of the world have built, are shaken by the truth so powerful, that it creates "*so mighty an earthquake, and so great.*"

The truth shall shake the earth violently, and there shall be no more borders or nations, no religions, no values placed on one human life above another, nor on material possessions; no more families inside picket fences who do not know their neighbors across the street, no more money, no more race, no more inequality. A human will never again be considered a foreigner, an illegal alien, but all will simply be a *human*—each equally a child of God.

The world shall surely suffer in its drunken state of ignorance from drinking from "*the cup of the wine of the fierceness of his wrath,*" or in other words, because we did not have God's intervention in our lives.

John has used the expression "*three parts*" or "*third*" to again lead us into the concept of equality (see commentary on Revelation 8:7).

The world will then be divided into "*three parts*" according to the desires of happiness of its inhabitants, and each will be able to choose in which part they desire to live; and it will not matter in which, for **ALL** will belong to the kingdom of our God and His Christ—worlds without end.

16:21 And every ***mountain*** fled away, and the ***islands*** were not found.

There shall never again be one person or group isolated away from another in inequality, nor shall there ever again be one placed above another in a world where the *Royal Law* becomes the **ONLY** law—worlds without end.

Chapter

REVELATION
UNFOLDED

17:1 And there came one of *the four beasts* which had the seven vials *which were given to* the seven *servants*, and talked with me, saying unto me, Come hither; I will show unto thee the judgment of the great whore that sitteth upon many waters:

Here John alludes to his own presence upon the earth during the fulfillment of these latter-day prophecies. For the first time, he writes of an angel who "*came...and talked with me, saying unto me, Come hither.*" Previously, John relates his involvement in the prophecies of the future (in comparison to the time he wrote *Revelation*) in a way that shows the effect of a vision:

> *And there appeared a great sign **in heaven** showing those*
> *things as they are upon the earth.* (Revelation 12:1)

John figuratively expresses his physical involvement upon the earth during the fulfillment of his prophecies—as the angel (*"one of the four beasts*") in charge of overseeing what is taking place upon the earth comes to him, and tells him to come and see for himself what is happening.

John is setting up the introduction of the actual proof of what is taking place in the latter days, and who "*the woman*" is, and what the "*beast*" is upon which she sits. Chapter 17, exclusively, describes "*the woman*" and "*beast*" with verifiable historical detail that cannot be denied. Then, Chapter 18 goes on to describe the "*the judgment of the great whore that sitteth upon many waters,*" or better, what is going to happen when Christ comes to the earth and reveals the truth.

17:2 With whom the kings of the earth have committed fornication, ***who are*** the inhabitants of the earth ***who*** have been made drunk with the wine of ***the cup of*** her fornication.

Again, a "*king*" receives power as we give it to him. He rules over us and tells us what to do because of this power. "*The kings of the earth*" are those who have allowed their fleshly lusts and desires to rule over them.

John uses the word "*fornication,*" because it alludes to our sexual desires which are the strongest lusts of human nature. People become "*drunk with the wine of the cup of her fornication*" when they pursue ("*drink*") the lusts of the flesh: money, success, inequality, prestige, honor, glory, etc., and enjoy the effects of what they drink ("*the wine of the cup*"). In comparison, those who "*drink of the wine of the wrath of God*" as mentioned in Revelation 14:10, are *feeling* the effects of His non-intervention in their lives.

17:3 So he carried me away in the spirit into the wilderness ***where*** I saw a woman sit upon a scarlet coloured beast, full of names of blasphemy, having seven heads ***with seven crowns*** and ten horns.

Being "*carried away in the spirit*" means a person begins to understand the truth with an enlightened perspective. It is the same as having the "*eyes of your understanding*" opened up (see commentary on Revelation 11:19). Many who read this book are "*carried away in the spirit,*" as it opens their eyes to truths never known before. These words did not come from God or any spirit, but were written by the author, who knows the truth, and has given it to readers the way they can understand. Likewise, John is figuratively presenting that the angel is showing him how to understand all things he previously saw in vision.

The woman who *"fled into the wilderness"* in Chapter 12, is now seen sitting *"upon a scarlet coloured beast."* The color *"scarlet"* is used by the prophets to signify wickedness, and is usually always referring to worldliness. Traditionally, *"scarlet"* is the color of flame, and may also refer to the color of *"blood"* (see commentary on Revelation 5:9).

> *Come now, and let us reason together, saith the LORD: though your sins be **as scarlet**, they shall be as white as snow; though they be red like crimson, they shall be as wool.* (Isaiah 1:18)

> *They that did feed delicately are desolate in the streets: they that were **brought up in scarlet** embrace dunghills. For the punishment of the iniquity of the daughter of my people is greater than the punishment of the sin of Sodom, that was overthrown as in a moment, and no hands stayed on her.* (Lamentations 4:5–6)

> *The shield of his mighty men is made red, the valiant men are **in scarlet**: the chariots shall be with flaming torches in the day of his preparation, and the fir trees shall be terribly shaken.* (Nahum 2:3)

Wickedness and worldliness keep people from figuratively being *"carried away in the spirit"*, or *"seeing through the veil"*, in order to receive an enlightened perspective. With symbolic purpose, Moses was commanded to construct the veil that covered the entrance to the Ark of the Covenant with *"purple and scarlet"* (the exact colors with which *"the woman is arrayed"*), demonstrating that worldliness and wickedness keep people from seeing and knowing the mysteries of God. If the veil of wickedness is removed, the people can see the truth with their own eyes.

*And thou shalt make a vail [sic] of blue, and **purple**, and*
***scarlet**, and fine twined linen of cunning work: with*
cherubims shall it be made: (Exodus 26:31)

"*The woman sits upon the beast,*" which carries her where *it* wants
to go because it is not "*bridled.*" Its unique features will be explained in
detail in the following verses. The "*woman*" (the children of God—see
commentary on Revelation 12:1), who was once righteous, and was helped
in the wilderness against "*the dragon,*" has now tamed and rides the "*beast*"
in glory. "*She*" has become the whore of all the earth.

The gospel of Jesus Christ ("*the man child delivered of the woman*")
can help people against their fleshly lusts and desires ("*the dragon*"). But
once the beast came along, "*the woman*" decided it was better to ride in
glory rather than wander around in the "*wilderness*" alone. Humans have
bent their hearts and souls to the gratification of their selfish desires, which
perpetuate societies based on materialism, consumption, and selfishness.
The people ride around on these desires without "*bridle*" or spur, which
would direct the "*beast*" upon which they ride.

Because thy rage against me, and thy tumult, is come up
into mine ears, therefore will I put my hook in thy nose,
*and my **bridle in thy lips**, and I will turn thee back by*
the way by which thou camest. (Isaiah 37:29)

17:4 And the woman was arrayed in purple and scarlet colour, and decked
with gold and precious stones and pearls, having a golden cup in her hand
full of abominations and ***the*** filthiness of her fornication:

"*The woman's*" wardrobe is symbolic of the works she performs.
John does a good job of describing the intent and purpose of the world, i.e.,
gaining material things we perceive as "*precious.*" The "*golden cup in her
hand*" is full of rampant materialism and worldly desire. The people of the
earth are the "*golden cup*" held in "*her hand*" as described previously in the
commentary of Revelation 5:8.

17:5 And upon her forehead was a name written, MYSTERY, BABYLON THE GREAT, THE MOTHER OF HARLOTS AND ABOMINATIONS OF THE EARTH.

John leaves no doubt what the woman represents. The *"name"* is presented *"upon her forehead"* to illustrate a constant yearning and desire—the fact that humans waste every moment of *concentration and thought* in their continual pursuit of the *"beast,"* its *"image,"* and the *"number of his name."*

17:6 And I saw the woman drunken with the blood of the saints, *who are* the martyrs of Jesus: and when I saw her, I wondered with great admiration *because of her glory and her beauty*.

John sees all people as wicked and corrupt. He borrows from Ezekiel's figurative expression of *"being drunken with blood"* to illustrate that the people of the earth (*"the woman"*) have overcome all righteousness (*"saints"*), and live no part of loving your neighbor as yourself (*"martyrs of Jesus"*). The people are *"drunk"* with the waters of *"the rivers and fountains"* which were turned to *"blood"* (see commentary on Revelation 16:4).

Ezekiel uses the expression to illustrate the Lord eventually overcoming all wickedness:

> And, thou son of man, thus saith the Lord GOD; Speak unto every feathered fowl, and to every beast of the field, Assemble yourselves, and come; gather yourselves on every side to my sacrifice that I do sacrifice for you, even a great sacrifice upon the mountains of Israel, *that ye may eat flesh, and drink blood*. Ye shall eat the flesh of the mighty, and drink the blood of the princes of the earth, of rams, of lambs, and of goats, of bullocks, all of them fatlings of Bashan. And ye shall eat fat till ye be full, and *drink blood till ye be drunken*, of my sacrifice which I have sacrificed for you. Thus ye shall be filled at my table

with horses and chariots, with mighty men, and with all men of war, saith the Lord GOD. And I will set my glory among the heathen, and all the heathen shall see my judgment that I have executed, and my hand that I have laid upon them. (Ezekiel 39:17–21)

John "*wonders*" how the world can be filled with so much wickedness but have so much opportunity. Stores in America are full of food, clothing, and anything the heart desires. Just the waste in discarded, uneaten food alone, could feed all the hungry of the world. But instead of eating what is needed to live, people live to eat.

The prosperity brought to the world through modern technology could feed, clothe, house, and take care of the basic necessities of every human being. Yet, poverty and inequality continue to increase as the rich become richer and the poor become poorer. Is it any wonder why John "*wonders with great admiration because of her glory and her beauty*"?

17:7 And the angel said unto me, Wherefore didst thou marvel? ***Thou knowest not*** the mystery of the woman, and of the beast that carrieth her, which hath the seven heads ***with crowns*** and ten horns. ***Behold***, I will tell thee:

John prepares to receive a more concise explanation of the "*beast*" he saw and described in Chapter 13. It will be explained why the world, though it exists in all its "*glory*" and progression, is so full of wickedness.

17:8 The beast that thou sawest was, and is not; and shall ascend out of the bottomless pit, and go into perdition: and they that dwell on the earth shall wonder ***after the beast***, whose names were not written in the Book of Life from the foundation of the world, when they behold the beast that was, and is not, and yet is.

The "American Dream," money, and being successful and accepted by others ("*the image, number, and mark of the beast*")—all these are abstract illusions created in the minds of human beings as they seek happiness and fulfillment in mortality. John sets up a conundrum to illustrate something that doesn't really exist (*"was, and is not, and yet is"*). All of these things have led (*"shall ascend out"*) to the corruption and unhappiness of the human race as we attempt to gratify the yearnings of our desires (*"bottomless pit"*).

Truly as the Preacher wrote, all is vanity:

*Vanity of vanities, saith the Preacher, vanity of vanities; all is vanity. ...And I gave my heart to seek and search out by wisdom concerning all things that are done under heaven: this sore travail hath God given to the sons of man to be exercised therewith. I have seen all the works that are done under the sun; and, behold, **all is vanity and vexation** of spirit. That which is crooked cannot be made straight: and that which is wanting cannot be numbered. ...Then I looked on all the works that my hands had wrought, and on the labour that I had laboured to do: and, behold, all was vanity and vexation of spirit, and there was no profit under the sun.* (Ecclesiastes 1:2, 13–15; 2:11)

Though required for our experience and understanding, none of our worldly works and desires will follow us out of mortality, as they are not part of the eternal plan of God. In other words, *"their names"* (works) *"are not written in the Book of Life,"* which is the eternal instruction book of law and creation followed by those who create all things "by the book" so their creations can experience happiness. *"They that dwell on the earth"* cannot imagine a world without pursuing goals of success and the "American Dream."

The *"wonder"* comes from their inability to find happiness in what appears to be a world loaded with opportunity. They *"wonder"* what has caused the hell (*"perdition"*) and misery upon earth while they are pursuing (their works/*"names"*/goals) what everyone has been convinced and deceived into believing is a worthy cause (basically everything *"not written in the Book of Life"*).

Ezekiel expresses it figuratively, but eloquently:

Thine heart was lifted up because of thy beauty, thou hast corrupted thy wisdom by reason of thy brightness: I will cast thee to the ground, I will lay thee before kings, that they may behold thee. Thou hast defiled thy sanctuaries by the multitude of thine iniquities, by the iniquity of thy traffick [sic]; therefore will I bring forth a fire from the midst of thee, it shall devour thee, and I will bring thee to ashes upon the earth in the sight of all them that behold thee. All they that know thee among the people shall be astonished at thee (and they that dwell on the earth shall wonder after the beast): thou shalt be a terror, and never shalt thou be any more. (Ezekiel 28:17–19)

17:9 And here is the mind which hath wisdom *and understanding*: The seven heads are seven mountains, on which the woman sitteth.

Simply put: The whole world is affected and influenced by worldliness and materialism.

17:10 And *the seven crowns* are seven kings: five are fallen, and one is, and the other is not yet come; and when he cometh, he must continue a short space.

These "*seven kings*" are ones which John considered major worldwide powers: The Egyptian (1), Assyrian (2), Babylonian (3), Persian (4), Greek (5), Roman (6), and British (7) empires.

John wrote *Revelation* during the reign of the Roman Empire ("*one is*") which rose to power after the first "*five had fallen.*" The British Empire had "*not yet come,*" and when it reached the full height of its vast power, it would only "*continue a short space*" in comparison with the reign of the other "*seven kings,*" until an eighth comes out from it.

"The eighth is of the seventh" and, of course, is the United States of America.

17:11 And the eighth is of the **seventh and receives its power from** the beast that was, and is not, **and yet is** and **which** goeth into perdition.

The USA survives on the illusion of success, money, and the vain imagination of those everywhere who center their lives on self-development and family values. Their promotion of these values leads people further and further away from the *Royal Law* of love your neighbor as yourself.

By following American values, it is easy to forget that all indigenous groups and minorities, Native Americans, African slaves, Mexican laborers, or any slave laborer who works for mere pennies, are our *neighbors*, and the "little ones" to whom Jesus Christ made reference. Self-fulfillment, self-development, and its fleshly lusts (*"the dragon"*/worldly illusions), are the focus of our human desires and gratification.

This *"dragon"* gives power to a *"beast"* the USA created through world domination by virtue of its military strength derived from this technological supremacy (*"receives its power from the beast"*). Nevertheless, because of all these abstract illusions the USA supports and perpetuates, it has created a literal hell upon earth for many, many people (*"which goeth into perdition"*).

17:12 And the ten horns which thou sawest are ten kings, which have received no kingdom as yet; but receive power *from* the beast as kings *for the last* hour with **the eighth.**

These latter-day *"ten kings"* can be better understood and delineated as John intended by the areas of power in which the ten most prominent languages and their dialects are spoken: Arabic countries (1), Chinese (2), English (3), scattered European dialects such as Dutch, Serbo-Croatian, etc. (4), French (5), German (6), Italian (7), Japanese (8), Russian (9), and the Spanish speaking countries (10).

None of these countries would survive in the contemporary world without *"receiving power from the beast."* If they do not do as the *"beast"* does, their countries would be overrun or occupied by one that does:

*And he had power to give life unto the image of the beast, that the image of the beast should both speak, **and cause that as many as would not worship the image of the beast should be killed**.* (Revelation 13:15)

The world financial markets are directly linked to each other in many ways, and find their sustenance from the pursuit of the *"image of the beast,"* its *"number,"* and its *"mark"* (*"receive power from the beast"*).

Every one of them at some time or another has been dependent on US aid, either financially or for protection in times of war. For example, without the US intervention in the First and Second World Wars, Europe would have been conquered by a few, if not one, of the *"ten kings."* The intervention and involvement of the United States of America is paramount to the successful proliferation of the *"beast"* and its policies and values.

17:13 These **all** have one mind, and shall give their power and strength unto the beast.

The United Nations, the World Bank, and many other unified world organizations (*"these all have one mind"*) are set up under the ruse that they exist to protect and promote peace (thus John presents the *"ten kings"* as *"horns"* upon the *"beast"*—see commentary on Revelation 13:11). Their true purpose is to maintain stability in the financial and economic markets of the world. When there is stability, there is peace. They promote the "American Dream," and finance projects that provide the material goods and services of the world—causing more division between classes—but do little to teach people how to love, forgive, and live in peace with others as equals.

17:14 These shall make war with **those who follow** the Lamb, and **those who follow** the Lamb shall overcome them; for **they know the Lamb** is Lord of lords, and King of kings: and they that **follow** him are called, and chosen, and faithful.

Those who follow the *Royal Law* and base their lives on the gospel of Jesus Christ as outlined specifically in chapters 5, 6, and 7 of Matthew (the Beatitudes), will not be "*overcome*" by the temptations of the world or the "*plagues*" that consequently follow. Their stress levels are nonexistent because they understand the abstractness of human desires and worldly goals, and focus more on finding happiness and pursuing intrinsic emotional peace than on worldly success.

17:15 And he saith unto me, The waters which thou sawest, where the whore sitteth, are peoples, and multitudes, and nations, and tongues.

The whole earth and all its inhabitants are affected by the desire to get gain and rise above others. The world is filled with darkness, and great is that darkness, because the "*whore*" who "*sits*" upon it shields the sunlight.

17:16 And the ten horns which thou sawest upon the beast, these shall *cause the peoples, and multitudes, and nations, and tongues to* hate the whore, and *they* shall make her desolate and naked, and shall eat her flesh, and *they shall* burn her with fire.

Isaiah eloquently puts it this way:

Through the wrath of the LORD of hosts is the land darkened, *and the people shall be as the fuel of the fire: no man shall spare his brother. And he shall snatch on the right hand, and be hungry; and he shall eat on the left hand, and they shall not be satisfied: they shall eat every man the flesh of his own arm*: (Isaiah 9:19–20)

And I will feed them that oppress thee with their own flesh; and they shall be drunken with their own blood, as with sweet wine: and all flesh shall know that I the LORD am thy Saviour and thy Redeemer, the mighty One of Jacob. (Isaiah 49:26)

*But **your iniquities have separated between you and
your God**, and **your sins have hid his face from you**,
that he will not hear. For your hands are defiled with
blood, and your fingers with iniquity; your lips have spoken lies, your tongue hath muttered perverseness. None
calleth for justice, nor any pleadeth for truth: **they trust
in vanity**, and speak lies; they conceive mischief, and
bring forth iniquity. They hatch cockatrice' eggs, and
weave the spider's web: he that eateth of their eggs dieth,
and that which is crushed breaketh out into a viper. Their
webs shall not become garments, neither shall they cover
themselves with their works: their works are works of
iniquity, and the act of violence is in their hands. Their
feet run to evil, and they make haste to shed innocent
blood: **their thoughts are thoughts of iniquity**; wasting
and destruction are in their paths. **The way of peace
they know not**; and there is no judgment in their goings:
they have made them crooked paths: whosoever goeth
therein shall not know peace. Therefore is judgment far
from us, neither doth justice overtake us: we wait for
light, but behold obscurity; for brightness, but we walk in
darkness. We grope for the wall like the blind, and we
grope as if we had no eyes: we stumble at noonday as in
the night; **we are in desolate places as dead men**.*
(Isaiah 59:2–10)

The nations of the world set up economic policies that do not provide for the necessities of the masses. The wealthy use these policies to
take advantage of the poor by paying low wages. Because of these policies, a corporation or business can release an employee from work at will.
When they are treated as an expendable resource, the masses begin to hate
the "system," their governments, and the premise for which these exist—
greed and profit.

Immigrant workers who come to a country to work in order to survive, then establish residency and help build the country's infrastructure,

which of course, is always controlled and maintained by the wealthy. When it becomes more profitable to replace the laborers with machines or out-source their jobs to another country with cheaper labor, the people rise up in rebellion and protest. Poverty increases, crime increases, and in time, the once prosperous and peaceful country is filled with civil uprisings and unrest.

The economic policies and the illusory standard of living (*"the flesh of the whore"*) once promised to the people, no longer becomes a reality, and the hope and promise of the "American Dream" becomes a *"desolate and naked"* promise that is *"eaten up"* in their anger and frustration.

> *Pour out thy fury upon the heathen that know thee not, and upon the families that call not on thy name: for* ***they have eaten up*** *Jacob, and devoured him, and consumed him, and have* ***made his habitation desolate***. (Jeremiah 10:25)

The very essence of the illusion (a decent standard of living) unat-tainable for the masses is limited to those (*"the ten horns/kings"*) who control and have power over their lives. The people are no longer ignorant of what is happening, and with a knowledge of truth (*"fire"*), cause their governments constant problems with protests and uprisings against their leaders, and fight against the deceit behind government agenda and policy (*"burn her with fire"*).

17:17 For ***the beast*** hath put in their hearts to fulfill his will; and ***these*** agree ***with the eighth***, and give their kingdom unto ***him***, until the words of God shall be fulfilled.

There is no doubt that the powers of the earth (*"the ten kings/horns"*) have only one desire: Commit *"fornication with the woman, the whore of all the earth."*

17:18 And the woman which thou sawest is that great city, which reigneth over ***all*** the kings of the earth.

This "*woman*" is the worldly desires and aspirations of all of the inhabitants of the world, which are presented by the prophets as "*BABYLON THE GREAT.*" She truly "*reigneth over all the kings of the earth,*" making them drunk as they drink from "*her cup*" overflowing with "*abominations and filthiness.*"

Chapter

REVELATION
UNFOLDED

18:1 And after these things I saw another angel come down from heaven, having great power *over fire; that by the flame of his fire* the earth *might be* lightened with *the* glory *of God.*

This angel has brought an understanding of truth (*"fire"*) to the earth during the manifestation of the things John has written concerning the latter days. This is the same angel described in Revelation 14:15, who cried to the *"one like unto the Son of man sitting upon a cloud."* This angel brings the knowledge of truth to this *"one with the sickle in his hand"* to be given to the world.

With a pure and true knowledge of the gospel, those who hear this truth and "elect" to follow its precepts will begin to do good works, by which *"the earth might be lightened."* This is the light Christ instructed his disciples to shine before the world to show *"the glory of God."*

18:2 And he cried mightily with a strong voice, saying, Babylon the great is fallen, is fallen, and is become the habitation of devils, and the hold of every foul spirit, and a cage of every unclean and hateful bird.

18:3 For all nations have drunk of the wine of the wrath of her fornication, and the kings of the earth have committed fornication with her, and the merchants of the earth are waxed rich through the abundance of her delicacies.

Here John describes why the *"one who had the sharp sickle in his hand"* had to thrust in his sickle.

John borrows from the prophet Jeremiah:

Your iniquities have turned away these things, and your sins have withholden good things from you. For among my people are found wicked men: they lay wait, as he that setteth snares; they set a trap, they catch men. **As a cage is full of birds, so are their houses full of deceit: therefore they are become great, and waxen rich.** *They are waxen fat, they shine: yea, they overpass the deeds of the wicked: they judge not the cause, the cause of the fatherless, yet they prosper; and the right of the needy do they not judge.* (Jeremiah 5:25–28)

18:4 And I heard another voice *as if it came* from heaven, saying, Come out of her, my people, that ye be not partakers of her sins, and that ye receive not of her plagues.

Notice in this verse that there is no one present, or visually seen, speaking with John. When he writes of a *"voice coming from heaven,"* John is relaying the essence of personal revelation, which is best described as an intrinsic or inner communication, in which a lasting balance and peace is achieved by the individual. Fleeting happiness is experienced by those who make claim to personal revelation but deceive themselves by their own vain and foolish imaginations. A *pure revelation* that is unadulterated by our own minds or the opinions of others is one whose end always brings us a calmness, peace, and balance forever.

When people have no worldly worries, and are not caught up in the race to achieve, obtain, and succeed in this life, a great peace and calmness comes over them. In other words, if we do *"not partake of her"* (BABYLON THE GREAT) *sins,"* we do not *"receive of her plagues"* (stress, frustration, depression, loneliness, self-deprecation).

18:5 For her sins have reached *even* unto *the* God *of* heaven, and *she shall remember* her iniquities *in the Day of Judgment.*

An accounting of what we have done in this life will come to our remembrance when we learn the truth. Only *we* know what *we* have done, why *we* have done it, and to whom we have done it. As we learn the truth, our anguish and punishment will come from within.

Here John describes the sins of the world in the latter days as surpassing the wickedness of any other time period in history. It's like saying a person's actions have reached the pinnacle of wickedness and beyond. For example: Hitler's treatment of the Jews *"reached far beyond"* the normal atrocities of warfare. He goes on to say what our punishment for this will be:

18:6 *For when the Lamb cometh he shall* reward her even as she rewarded you, and *recompense* double unto her according to her works: in the cup which she hath filled, *it shall be filled* to her double.

Feeling *remorse* and deep *embarrassment* is a double punishment. Each of these feelings is unique in its type and intensity. One comes from previous actions, and can be outwardly forgiven by another, but the other cannot be forgiven, except by the one who experiences its intrinsic effects.

Those who do not treat others as they would want to be treated will suffer from this *"double"* punishment. Not only will they feel great *remorse* for treating others badly (*"reward her even as she rewarded you"*), but they will also feel *embarrassed* because of their ignorance when they thought they were doing the *right* thing.

For example, the pursuit of riches to support one's family with material goods, sending one's children to college, and retiring from work to travel to the Bahamas, all *seem* to be noble and just causes; but the consequences that come to others by fulfilling these selfish desires are unknown or ignored by those who pursue them. Not only will the "selfish one" feel bad (**remorse**) for the pain caused to those who f*ace the mill and grind* (see commentary on *"grind the face of the poor"* on Revelation 13:14), but the **embarrassment** for thinking the cause was *just and noble*, when it has caused so much misery, will be much harder to overcome. Human beings would rather appear selfish than stupid.

Furthermore, one who condemns and ridicules women, for example, who are forced to sell their bodies to support their children's necessities (even at times forcing their own children into this prostitution) will also suffer double. When the truth is known that capitalism, corruption, and patriotic, class, and family greed are the direct cause of this necessitated employment, those who so condemned prostitutes, will be mightily *embarrassed* if Christ comes to earth with Mary Magdalene at his side.

John borrows the figurative expression from those prophets before him:

> *For mine eyes are upon all their ways: they are not hid from my face, neither is their iniquity hid from mine eyes. And first I **will recompense their iniquity and their sin double**; because they have defiled my land, they have filled mine inheritance with the carcases of their detestable and abominable things.* (Jeremiah 16:17–18)

> *Speak ye comfortably to Jerusalem, and cry unto her, that her warfare is accomplished, that her iniquity is pardoned: for she hath received of the LORD's hand **double for all her sins**.* (Isaiah 40:2)

18:7 How much she hath glorified herself, and lived deliciously, so much torment and sorrow give her: for she saith in her heart, I sit a queen, and am no widow, and shall see no sorrow.

The people of the earth have no remorse for what they do. They take that which is good and make it evil, and that which is evil they make good. Though the natural environment is being destroyed and consumed at alarming rates; though disparity and inequality run rampant in the course of dividing one class of people from another, those who cause these things sit in comfortable houses, drive expensive cars, adorn themselves with lavishness, and proclaim their happiness and deserved success.

Well does Ezekiel prophesy of "*her*":

Thou art the land that is not cleansed, nor rained upon in the day of indignation. There is a conspiracy of her prophets in the midst thereof, like a roaring lion ravening the prey; they have devoured souls; they have taken the treasure and precious things; they have made her many widows in the midst thereof. Her priests have violated my law, and have profaned mine holy things: **they have put no difference between the holy and profane, neither have they showed difference between the unclean and the clean,** *and have hid their eyes from my sabbaths, and I am profaned among them. Her princes in the midst thereof are like wolves ravening the prey, to shed blood, and to destroy souls, to get dishonest gain.* **And her prophets have daubed them with untempered morter** [SIC]**, seeing vanity, and divining lies unto them,** *saying, Thus saith the Lord GOD, when the LORD hath not spoken.* **The people of the land have used oppression, and exercised robbery, and have vexed the poor and needy: yea, they have oppressed the stranger wrongfully.** *And I sought for a man among them, that should make up the hedge, and stand in the gap before me for the land, that I should not destroy it:* **but I found none.** *Therefore have I poured out mine indignation upon them; I have consumed them with the fire of my wrath: their own way have I recompensed upon their heads, saith the Lord GOD.* (Ezekiel 22:24–31)

18:8 Therefore shall her plagues *be manifested* in *the* day *of the Lord*, death, and mourning, and famine; and she shall be utterly burned with fire: for strong is the Lord God who judgeth her.

When the truth is revealed how actions, desires, and lifestyles have affected the poor, the needy, and the downtrodden, and the One who is expressing this truth is recognized as a "God" (*"strong is the Lord who judgeth her"*) that none can deny, then these actions, desires, and lifestyles shall be as *"dead."* Those who lived contrary to the truth will *"mourn,"* not only because of what they have done, but also from the affects of their *"double"* punishment. The things which they lusted after and sought all the days of their lives, even those things which nourished their lives and brought them their perceived temporary "happiness," will never be "eaten" again; thus, they will experience a *"famine."* Truly they will be *"burned with"* knowledge of the truth (*"fire"*).

John proceeds to describe this *"death," "mourning,"* and *"famine"* in the next few verses.

Verses 9 through 20 are easy to follow and comprehend, in light of what has been explained so far. These verses should leave little doubt in the reader's mind what the consequences of extravagance and avarice are. They should help one understand the true meaning behind *"burning"* and *"weeping, wailing, and gnashing of teeth."* The resultant *"mourning"* is how the people will feel when the truth is finally revealed.

These next few chapters will yield more insight into *"the plagues, the locusts, the bottomless pit, the dragon, the beast, the whore"* and other figurative expressions John used in his writings to describe our human interactions in relation to the *Royal Law* of Christ. All of his metaphors and symbolic writing lead the reader to these last few chapters (chapters 18 through 22).

In chapter 18, the true *"suffering"* and *"burning"* that will take place when Christ returns to the earth to reign is described in detail as it really is. No longer will the "hell, fire, and damnation" preaching of the *"false prophets"* make sense. No longer will the esoteric and fantasized explanations of the *Apocalypse* hold water, when given the explanations in this book received from the mouth of the original author himself.

Apocalypse in Greek means disclosure. It is a term applied to the disclosure of something to certain, privileged persons that is hidden from the masses. John's original title is modernly referred to as the ***Apocalypse of John***. Since Biblical scholars had no clue what was meant in his metaphorical text, they agreed to name it in the English Bible: the *Revelation of St. John the Divine*, or the *Book of Revelation of Jesus Christ, the Messiah*.

Now that the "disclosure" has been unfolded, and presented throughout the pages of this book, the whole world will be held accountable for compliance or rejection of its truths.

Chapters 19 through 22 describe the events during the Millennial Reign of the One who holds the key to peace, happiness, and eternal truth— the One the world does NOT know, but will recognize as the man called in the English language, Jesus, the Christ.

18:9 And the kings of the earth, who have committed fornication and lived deliciously with her, shall bewail her, and lament for her, when they shall see the smoke of her burning,

The "*kings of the earth*" have been explained previously, and have nothing to do with the leaders of the people, but are consistent with John's presentation of those who seek after the things of the world:

> A "*king*" *receives power as we give it to him. He rules over us and tells us what to do because of this power. "The kings of the earth" are those who have allowed their fleshly lusts and desires to rule over them.* (Commentary on Revelation 17:2.)

Since the "*her*" presented in this verse represents the worldly desires and abominations of the world, it is logical that these things cannot be burned with fire from a match, but will be "*burned*" with the "*fire*" (knowledge of the truth) that pursuing these things is contrary to the *Royal Law*.

Of itself, fire does not actually exist, but is a reaction caused by elements being forced from their natural state of stability and balance.

When this state of balance is disrupted, energy is given off in the form of heat until all the elements have been changed. The residue which remains is carbon, the basic element of all living things. Smoke consists of residual particles suspended in the air resulting from the incomplete combustion of element, and is an unwanted by-product of fires.

If all money, material goods, honors, and worldly glories lose their value when the *Royal Law* becomes the *Universal Law*, there will be a residue (*"smoke"*) of hope and concern that everything a person values might have at least *some* eternal value. This is *"the smoke"* that will come from *"the burning"* that will cause people to *"bewail"* and *"lament"* their losses.

When doctors and lawyers are told, for example, that their education, their techniques, their knowledge, their laws and procedures, their medicines, and everything that brought them riches, recognition, and respect are useless, because Beings of a greater understanding can heal with a touch, these *educated ones* will experience a *"burning."* They will realize that nothing they have done in mortality is of any eternal worth. When they think back on all the money they spent, the hours they studied, and the honors they received, they will cling to a hope (residual/*"smoke"*) that at least *some* of what they did was worthy of their money, effort, and the sacrifice of their mortal time.

These residual particles of pride that remain suspended in the air (*"smoke"*) will be the cause of their torment. IF they could allow it to burn, admit they were deceived, and get on with the ways of the Lord, there would be no *residual* emotions or regrets remaining to cause their lamentations.

When the truth is revealed and *"burns"* all falsehoods and vanities, the people will stand in awe, unable to do much about it. When they finally realize (*"when they shall see the smoke of her burning"*) that all their works have been in vain, and have no real eternal value in the eternal plan of God (*"their names"*/works *are not written in the Book of Life"*), some of them will wish they still lived in ignorance and inequality (*"bewail her and lament for her"*).

18:10 ***And these shall stand*** afar off ***fearing*** her torment, saying, Alas, alas that great city Babylon, that mighty city! for in one ***day*** is thy judgment come.

It will be the hope of those willingly and eagerly *"committing for-nication with the whore"* (involving themselves in worldliness) to blend in with the crowd, and not be noticed for what they have done or how they have lived their lives. They will wish to put themselves *"as far away"* from their works as possible. Thus, *"these shall stand afar off fearing."* They will wish to pretend that their works never happened, that the degrees adorning their walls are not theirs, that the expensive cars in their drive-ways are someone else's, and that the white picket fence which has kept their family isolated from others, while *the poor ground at the wheel* to feed and sustain their worldliness, won't be noticed.

Oh, they will be noticed alright! Because their *"names"* will be all over their many good *"deeds,"* titles, and registrations that anyone can match to the *"name"* still written upon the mailbox out front!

18:11 And the merchants of the earth shall weep and mourn over her; for no man buyeth their merchandise any more:

18:12 The merchandise of gold, and silver, and precious stones, and of pearls, and fine linen, and purple, and silk, and scarlet, and all thyine wood, and all manner vessels of ivory, and all manner vessels of most precious wood, and of brass, and iron, and marble,

18:13 And cinnamon, and odours, and ointments, and frankincense, and wine, and oil, and fine flour, and wheat, and beasts, and sheep, and horses, and chariots, and slaves, and souls of men.

In these verses, John mentions items of material worth to the people of *his* day. However, he specifically mentions many of the things that were used in the ancient construction of the temple, the Ark of the Covenant, tabernacle, veil, and other valuables used in the rituals and ordinances. The temple and its contents were the most valuable religious icons to the Jews, both temporally and spiritually. John teaches that none of these things will have value or significance when the truth is revealed.

The *"souls of men"* is a figurative expression of the value placed on a laborer in comparison to a *"merchant"* or ruler; and also refers to the value placed on those who, for example, attend church and believe in God in comparison to those who do not.

Those who pick up and dispose of garbage and the waste of human indulgence, and are currently some of the least valued, in "*one day*" shall be esteemed and exalted as much as any movie star or sports athlete ("he who is abased shall be exalted"). However, the garbage man will not be "*standing afar off weeping and wailing,*" but will rejoice as his tears are wiped away from his cheeks.

Likewise, those who could not accept the gods, values, examples, and models of spirituality presented by the world's organized religions, will not suffer either when they discover that none of the principles taught or presented were the truth.

John has figuratively presented the devaluation of all things, both spiritual (the things of the temple) and material (the things of the world), even all things upon which the inhabitants of the earth have placed a value. When there exists no value, nothing can be bought or sold any longer, as is the business of "*the merchants of the earth.*"

18:14 And the fruits that thy soul lusted after are departed from thee, and all things which were dainty and goodly are departed from thee, and thou shalt find them no more at all.

A person's soul does not lust after food; a body of flesh does. John presents "*the fruit that thy soul lusted after*" as the premise of this verse, in which he explains that honor, prestige, glory, popularity, being *Number One*, and all other vain emotional goals humans set for themselves, will no longer be worthy of time, attention, or pursuit.

John further expresses that these things will no longer have a value in a world where all things are equally available for all people. When Christ himself prefers to pick strawberries in the field instead of sit as a CEO of World Inc, he will solidify the concept of equality for all, the greatest is the least, the first is the last, and our Creator is unequivocally and without question NOT a respecter of persons.

Proverbs puts it this way:

When thou sittest to eat with a ruler, consider diligently what is before thee: And put a knife to thy throat, if thou be a man given to appetite. **Be not desirous of his dainties: for they are deceitful meat. Labour not to be rich: cease from thine own wisdom.** *Wilt thou set thine eyes upon that which is not? for riches certainly make themselves wings; they fly away as an eagle toward heaven. Eat thou not the bread of him that hath an evil eye, neither desire thou his dainty meats: For as he thinketh in his heart, so is he: Eat and drink, saith he to thee; but his heart is not with thee. The morsel which thou hast eaten shalt thou vomit up, and lose thy sweet words.* (Proverbs 23:1–8)

Jesus summed it up saying:

For whosoever exalteth himself shall be abased; and he that humbleth himself shall be exalted. Then said he also to him that bade him, When thou makest a dinner or a supper, call not thy friends, nor thy brethren, neither thy kinsmen, nor thy rich neighbours; lest they also bid thee again, and a recompense be made thee. But when thou makest a feast, call the poor, the maimed, the lame, the blind: And thou shalt be blessed; for they cannot recompense thee: for thou shalt be recompensed at the resurrection of the just. (Luke 14:11–14)

18:15 The merchants of these things, which were made rich by her, shall stand afar off for the fear of her torment, weeping and wailing,

These "*merchants*" are not only those who promoted and gained from buying and selling material goods, but include "*merchants*" who profit off those in need of spiritual or psychological help. Whether these *spiritual merchants* receive their income hourly, weekly, monthly, yearly, by stipend, or through their transportation, health care, or other benefits, provided for free by those deceived into believing their contrived positions of spiritual and emotional value, they will bewail the end of their authority and income, and hope others will not remember (*"stand afar off for the fear"*) how they had once deceived the world.

18:16 And saying, Alas, alas, that **great harlot** that was clothed in fine linen, and purple, and scarlet, and decked with gold, and precious stones, and pearls; *yea, even that great city which reigneth over the kings of the earth*.

18:17 For in one **day** so great riches is come to nought. And every ship-master, and all the company in ships, and sailors, and as many as trade by sea, stood afar off,

In the writings of the prophet Ezekiel, a vivid description is given that depicts what will take place when the Lord reveals himself (truth) to the world.   Ezekiel uses the city of Tyrus, which was destroyed by the Babylonians, as a figurative backdrop for the event.   (See Ezekiel 27:2 through 28:24 for a full and revealing account; and with an understanding of John's symbolism, Ezekiel's words come to life with extraordinary meaning.)

John borrows from Ezekiel's metaphors and illustration to present the same ideas. By reading both texts, one soon realizes that the prophets use real situations as representations of real truths. The metaphors John has chosen to borrow from Ezekiel are easy to understand when they are read in context with what has already been explained.

> *Thy riches, and thy fairs, thy merchandise, thy mariners, and thy pilots, thy calkers, and the occupiers of thy merchandise, and all thy men of war, that are in thee, and in all thy company which is in the midst of thee, **shall fall into the midst of the seas in the day of thy ruin**.* (Ezekiel 27:27)

18:18 And cried when they saw the smoke of her burning, saying, What city is like unto this great city!

*And they shall take up a lamentation for thee, and say to thee, How art thou destroyed, that wast inhabited of sea-faring men, **the renowned city**, which wast strong in the sea, she and her inhabitants, which cause their terror to be on all that haunt it!* (Ezekiel 26:17)

*And in their wailing they shall take up a lamentation for thee, and lament over thee, saying, **What city is like Tyrus**, like the destroyed in the midst of the sea?* (Ezekiel 27:32)

18:19 And they cast dust on their heads, and cried, weeping and wailing, saying, Alas, alas, that great city, wherein were made rich all that had ships in the sea by reason of her costliness! for in one *day* is she made desolate.

*And shall cause their voice to be heard against thee, and shall cry bitterly, and shall **cast up dust upon their heads**, they shall wallow themselves in the ashes:* (Ezekiel 27:30)

(Take note of the change of sequence in the following verses compared to the accepted *King James* translation.)

18:20 And ***I saw in the likeness of things upon earth*** a mighty angel ***in heaven take*** up a stone like a great millstone ***and hang it about her neck***, and cast ***her*** into the sea, saying, ***because of her*** violence shall that great city Babylon be thrown down, and shall be found no more at all.

The "*violence*" to which John refers is revealed in Ezekiel:

By the multitude of thy merchandise they have filled the midst of thee with violence, *and thou hast sinned: therefore **I will cast thee as profane out of the mountain of God**: and I will destroy thee, O covering cherub, from the midst of the stones of fire.* (Ezekiel 28:16)

This "*violence*" is the way the poor are treated as they play their part in bringing riches and profit to the wealthy corporations and businesses ("*merchants*") of the world. These poor who "face the grinding wheel" ("*like a great millstone*") day after day, are "fed from the crumbs that fall from the rich man's table," even a table overflowing with fruits, not from the sweat of the rich man's brow, but of the poor laborers', who are desirous to be "fed the crumbs" from his table. (Note: another English definition of the Hebrew word used to indicate *millstone* is: "heavy burden or load.")

In this verse, John leads the reader into one of the most profound yet most disregarded parabolic masterpieces ever given by Jesus:

> *There was a certain rich man, which was clothed in purple and fine linen, and fared sumptuously every day: And there was a certain beggar named Lazarus, which was laid at his gate, full of sores, And desiring to be fed with the crumbs which fell from the rich man's table: moreover the dogs came and licked his sores.*

> *And it came to pass, that the beggar died, and was carried by the angels into Abraham's bosom: the rich man also died, and was buried; And in hell he lift up his eyes, being in torments, and seeth Abraham afar off, and Lazarus in his bosom. And he cried and said, Father Abraham, have mercy on me, and send Lazarus, that he may dip the tip of his finger in water, and cool my tongue; for I am tormented in this flame. But Abraham said, Son, remember that thou in thy lifetime receivedst thy good things, and likewise Lazarus evil things: but now he is comforted, and thou art tormented.*

> *And beside all this, between us and you there is a great gulf fixed: so that they which would pass from hence to you cannot; neither can they pass to us, that would come from thence. Then he said, I pray thee therefore, father, that thou wouldest send him to my father's house: For I*

have five brethren; that he may testify unto them, lest they also come into this place of torment. Abraham saith unto him, They have Moses and the prophets; let them hear them. And he said, Nay, father Abraham: but if one went unto them from the dead, they will repent. And he said unto him, If they hear not Moses and the prophets, neither will they be persuaded, though one rose from the dead. (Luke 16:19–31)

This parable is one that the rich of the world would rather not understand or have revealed to them. It basically states in profundity the same thing Christ said from the beginning, i.e., the poor and meek shall inherit the kingdom of God and find happiness, and the rich will find it much harder.

And when Jesus saw that he was very sorrowful, he said, How hardly shall they that have riches enter into the kingdom of God! For it is easier for a camel to go through a needle's eye, than for a rich man to enter into the kingdom of God. (Luke 18:24–25)

Of course, as they suppose, the rich work hard for their riches and earn a lifestyle which allows them to "fare sumptuously every day." But who does the "beggar full of sores desiring to be fed from the crumbs of the rich man's table" represent? He represents those standing at "the rich man's gate," in the employment lines to get a job, or on the street corner as an "illegal alien," looking for any type of work—no matter what "crumbs" they are paid to relieve them of their many "sores" and hunger. These are the "little ones," or better, "the least amongst us."

The rich outwardly appear very happy with their worldliness. They feel they are blessed. In what blessed state, does one suppose, are those who receive minimum wage or less, for their labor in the hot sun all day? And to which of these would death be a relief rather than a curse?

After hearing this parable in Jesus' day and realizing the significance of it, those who followed Christ wondered how it was possible that *anyone* could live in the world without committing some *offense* against the *Royal Law* of Do Unto Others.

Jesus answered them appropriately in continuation of his discussion of the rich man and Lazarus, the beggar:

> *Then said he unto the disciples, It is impossible but that offences will come: but woe unto him, through whom they come!* **It were better for him that a millstone were hanged about his neck, and he cast into the sea,** *than that he should offend one of these little ones.* (Luke 17:1–2)

In this verse in *Revelation*, John is figuratively reiterating what Christ taught as the truth. When equality is restored on the earth, no longer will there be any "little ones," who receive the "offenses" of those who could care less about them. Even though they sit at a gate begging to be fed with crumbs, one day all will be invited into the house of the Lord where they will find before them a table spread with the glorious fruits of truth.

Appropriately following John's figurative prose, the "*angel*" did well when he followed the words of Christ and "*hung a millstone about the neck*" of the "*whore of all the earth and cast her into the sea!*"

18:21 And the voice of harpers, and musicians, and of pipers, and trumpeters, shall be heard no more at all in thee; and no craftsman, of whatsoever craft he be, shall be found any more in thee; and the sound of a millstone shall be heard no more at all in thee;

> *And I will cause the noise of thy songs to cease; and the sound of thy harps shall be no more heard.* (Ezekiel 26:13)

18:22 And the light of a candle shall shine no more at all in thee; and the voice of the bridegroom and of the bride shall be heard no more at all in thee: for thy merchants were the great men of the earth; for by thy sorceries were all nations deceived.

John borrows from Jeremiah's prophecies to restate his premise:

Moreover I will take from them the voice of mirth, and the voice of gladness, **the voice of the bridegroom, and the voice of the bride, the sound of the millstones, and the light of the candle.** *And this whole land shall be a desolation, and an astonishment; and these nations shall serve the king of Babylon seventy years.* (Jeremiah 25:10–11)

The books of Job and Proverbs back up the premise:

For there shall be no reward to the evil man; **the candle of the wicked shall be put out.** (Proverbs 24:20)

Yea, the light of the wicked shall be put out, and the spark of his fire shall not shine. The light shall be dark in his tabernacle, **and his candle shall be put out with him.** *The steps of his strength shall be straitened* [SIC], *and his own counsel shall cast him down.* (Job 18:5–7)

Only through Christ (truth) will come the power to unveil the sorceries for what they are, and once and for all confound the ultimate deception of humankind (the ways of the world). In other words, the wisdom of man (*"light of a candle"*) shall be put out by the "snuffer" of Christ—the word of truth.

18:23 And in her was found the blood of prophets, and of saints, and of all that were slain upon the earth.

The words of the prophets (i.e., the *"blood of the prophets and saints"*) have been misinterpreted, denied, ignored, and turned from *red blood,* which can give life to the whole body, to the dark blood of the *"slain"* (dead). Here John does not mean the literal death of the body and the blood that gives it life, but the figurative blood "of the spirit," which is the same blood of which Christ informed his enemies:

Verily, verily, I say unto you, Except ye eat the flesh of the Son of man, and drink his blood, ye have no life in you. Whoso eateth my flesh, and drinketh my blood, hath eternal life; and I will raise him up at the last day. (John 6:53–54)

Worldliness has truly slain the prophets and the saints, and their "*blood*" has stained the hands of "*the woman which thou sawest is that great city, which reigneth over all the kings of the earth*" (see commentary on Revelation 17:18).

With reason should a rejoicing be made over her demise as John proclaims:

18:24 Rejoice over her, *all ye who are in* heaven, and *all* ye *upon the earth who have heeded the words of the* holy apostles and prophets; for God *shall avenge* you on her.

Chapter

Revelation Unfolded

19:1 And after these things I heard *as it were the* voice of *a great multi-tude* in heaven, saying, Alleluia; Salvation, and glory, and honour, and power, unto the Lord our God. *And the Lamb slain from the foundation of the world stood before the throne with the Book of Life in his right hand*;

Continuing his thoughts from the last verse in chapter 18, John writes of all those who are assigned to this solar system (*"a great multitude"*) who have experienced many years of human existence without living the *Royal Law.* After experiencing the opposite, it is easy to praise (*"Alleluia"*) and give *"glory and honor to God"* for His eternal plan, which will be taught and instituted upon this earth by the Christ (*"the Lamb"*) who was prepared to lead us from the beginning. It is only by adherence to this plan that we can experience happiness (*"salvation"*), which is the end of all Christ's teachings.

The Anointed One strictly follows (*"his right hand"*) the instructions given in *"the Book of Life,"* which he received from the Creator of us all.

19:2 *And the Lamb said*, True and righteous are *thy* judgments *O Lord God Almighty*: for *thou hast* judged the great whore, which did corrupt the earth with her fornication, and *now thou must avenge* the blood of *thy* servants at her hand.

Christ is commenting that the instructions he followed in teaching the law of the gospel (*"thy judgments"*/Royal Law/Do Unto Others) is the only way to find peace and happiness, proving (*"thou hast judged"*) that the ways of materialism, selfishness, and personal gain (*"the great whore which did corrupt the earth"*) are the cause of all human dilemma and problems.

The *intent* of the law (*"blood of thy servants"*) is to treat others equally under the *Royal Law*. This will be "*avenged*" as Christ opens the seventh seal and comes again to the earth, this time with power and the glory of God to enforce (*"avenge the blood"*) the *Royal Law* upon the inhabitants of the world by the power of the truths he will speak.

19:3 And again *the voice of a great multitude* said, Alleluia *and Amen!* And *the* smoke *of* her *torment* rose up for ever and ever.

Those who are "*as it were the voice of a great multitude in heaven*" have seen the difference of living in mortality and experiencing both: partaking of worldliness (*"committing fornication with the whore"*) *and* living the law of the gospel (*"saving oneself for marriage"*—in this case, the marriage of the Lamb as John will soon present—one is either fornicating, or saving oneself for marriage).

Because they are satisfied with the lesson, and with the knowledge they have now gained from experience, they praise the ways of God, and finalize their testimony by saying, "Amen!" *Amen* is a Hebrew word that stems from the word "aman," which means "to be faithful, support, or confirm."

As formerly established, "*smoke*" is defined as the leftover particles of a substance which were not torn apart by the heat of fire. We will "*for ever and ever*" remember how we were "*tormented*" living in a world without the *Royal Law* as its foundation. These memories will always keep us singing praises to God and honoring the law He has established for our happiness.

As eternal, resurrected beings, our memory of misery (the opposite of happiness) might become dulled through the passage of time. Luckily for us, we will have advanced technology and the ability to tune our "television sets" to whatever is taking place on a planet in another solar system, where humans like we once were, exist. These humans, who are a living example of our past civilizations, have not yet had enough experience to know for sure that the eternal plan of God is *"for ever and ever" praiseworthy* and *right*. Seeing them in their misery becomes our reminder.

19:4 And the four and twenty elders and the four beasts *and the Lamb* fell down and worshipped God that sat on the throne, saying, Alleluia *and* Amen!

Those who have been called upon this earth (the prophets/*"four and twenty elders"*), those who have come to this solar system unseen to get us through our process of salvation (the angels/*"four beasts"*), and the One "anointed" prepared (Christ/*"the Lamb"*) to oversee that everything is going "by The Book," will acknowledge and praise God for all that is done—by confirming, supporting, and being faithful to the plan forever and ever (*"Amen!"*).

19:5 And *the* voice *of the Lamb* came out of the throne, saying, Praise our God, all ye his servants, and ye that fear him *not*, both small and great.

With the authority of his position, Christ takes charge of the rest of the plan for the earth. He is setting up for his reign upon the earth (*"the opening of the seventh seal"*) by asking all to support the plan of God.

19:6 And I heard the voice of a great multitude, and as the voice of many waters, and *also* as the voice of mighty thunderings, saying, Alleluia *and Amen*: for the Lord God omnipotent reigneth.

Everyone who is "dead," will join together with those behind the scenes in one "voice." These include those "dead" by evil works in mortality (*"voice of a great multitude"*), those exsisting as spirits (*"voice of many waters"*) and awaiting rebirth, or resurrection (being "born-again" from dead works to righteousness), and the "voice of mighty thunderings." (See commentary on Revelation 4:5.) Those angels behind the scenes exercise the power of God to fufill the plan of salvation for all who have not yet received it. With "*one voice,*" all these agree with, support, confirm, and pledge their faithfulness to the plan of God, knowing that He holds power over creation, and will implement His power ("*omnipotence*") through the reign of Christ for the last part of human existence as we know it.

19:7 Let us be glad and rejoice, and give honour to him: for the marriage of the Lamb is come, and his wife hath made herself ready. *Behold, I am the bridegroom prepared for my wife.*

Here it is appropriate to include the correct translation and interpretation of the parable of "The Marriage of the King's Son" as recorded in the book of Matthew, chapter 22, from which John has taken his expressions:

> **1** *And the Pharisees and high priests were wont to show the people their authority. And they questioned Jesus*, *saying, Are we not those who have been chosen by God to receive his kingdom?* And Jesus answered and spake unto them again by parables, and said,

> **2** The kingdom of heaven is like unto a certain king, *who* made a marriage for his son *who would rule over the people in his stead. And he prepared for the day of the wedding, inviting those who were of the same household as his son.*

> **3** And *when the day of the wedding cometh, he* sent forth his servants to call them that were bidden to the wedding *of his son. And because they were of the same household,* they would not come.

> **4** Again, he sent forth other servants, saying, Tell them *who* are bidden, Behold, I have prepared my dinner *for those who are kindred and most familiar to my son*;

and they shall come first before those who shall be bidden last. **Behold,** my oxen and my fatlings are killed, and all things are ready *at the table*; come, *therefore,* unto the marriage.

5 But they made light of it, *because they were familiar with the son and accustomed to his ways. And they made each an excuse* and went their ways, one to his farm, another to his merchandise, *excusing themselves because of their own business.*

6 And the remnant, *who were not familiar with his son, and were the last to be bidden*, took his servants, and entreated them spitefully, and slew them, *because they saw that the kindred who knew the son did not go up to the wedding, thus making a mockery themselves, saying, Behold, there is no wedding, for even those of his own household do not go.*

7 But when the king heard thereof, he was wroth *with those who killed his servants*; and he sent forth his armies, and destroyed those murderers, and burned up their city.

8 Then saith he to his servants, The wedding is ready, but they which were bidden, *both the first and the last*, were not worthy.

9 Go ye therefore into the highways, and as many as ye shall find, *tell them of my son and* bid *them come* to the marriage.

10 So those servants went out into the highways, and gathered together all as many as they found, both bad and good, *even all those who knew not of his son*; and the wedding was furnished with guests.

11 And when the king came in to see the guests, he saw there a man which had not on a wedding garment; *for the servants provided all those bidden with a garment for the wedding, but this man choose not to wear the wedding garment, casting it aside on the highway from whence he came.*

12 And *the king* saith unto him, Friend, how camest thou in hither not having a wedding garment? *Did not my servants provide thee with one?* And *the man* was speechless, *not being able to make excuse, because the servants stood close by to testify that they had given him a robe to wear as the king had commanded them.*

13 Then said the king to the servants, Bind him hand and foot, and take him away, and cast him into *prison, where he* shall weep and gnash *his* teeth.

14 For many are called, but few *have* chosen *to wear the wedding garment which hath been provided for them. And ye leaders of the Jews are those who have been called to the wedding, but come forth naked, having no garment for yourselves or for those who follow you.*"

The "*bride/the Lamb's wife*" in the parable is the kingdom of God set up in truth and righteousness upon the earth, which is in direct contrast to the "*whore of the whole earth with whom the kings commit fornication.*" This is further verified in Revelation 21:9.

19:8 And to *those bidden to the marriage* was granted that *they* should be arrayed in fine linen, clean and white: for the fine linen is the righteousness of saints.

The "*white robes*," "*wedding garment*," and "*fine linen*," all represent the actions of those who have given their lives and attitudes to following the precepts of the king's *Royal Law*. When we live this way, we make ourselves "*ready*" for "*the marriage*," which is the unification of all truth, and is the context used by both Jesus and John.

There is no secret how the world will respond to an *alien*-type Being visiting this earth from another solar system (with many others like him), who looks like us, but has the knowledge and advanced technology that would take us tens of thousands of years to replicate. Christ will bring **truth** to the earth, and by the truth he brings, we will judge ourselves and our own beliefs. Of course, there is no literal physical "*burning*"; our Creator is not sadistic. The "*burning, wailing, and gnashing of teeth*" comes from realizing one's mortal experience, beliefs, understanding, and "truths" are in actuality not real, nor in line with the *Royal Law*.

As mentioned previously, there will be two types of personal suffering: **embarrassment** and **remorse**. Those who listen to the message of Christ given by his proper servants are not "*burned*," i.e., they do not feel embarrassed or remorseful. It is easy to avoid the feeling of remorse. This is done by obeying the *Royal Law*. Each of us is solely responsible for the remorse we will feel for what we have done to another, or allowed to be done to "the least among us" by standing by and doing nothing. As we fulfill the *Law*, our life feels lighter and freer, and our minds awaken to the reception of truth and light, which will enable us to avoid embarrassment.

Truth is how things really are—not how things are theorized to be, or speculated upon based on observation. Science and religion are not truths. These are human cognitive abstractions that help a free-willed thinker find some balance in an existence where they are unsure (live by faith) of themselves. Well can it be said: Religion and Science are fools' attempts to prove to everyone else that they are not foolish.

Once we are confronted by a Being we recognize as our superior, or better, one who knows a lot more than we do, there will be no more faith, and no more living with unsure feelings of why and how we exist. To avoid the embarrassment of the confrontation of real truth against established perceptions, those so clothed and ready for "*the marriage*" will be filled at the "*supper*."

19:9 And he *which spoke* saith unto me, Write *these truths; for* blessed are they which are called unto the marriage supper of the Lamb. And he saith unto me, These *shall know* the true sayings of God *which he has hidden from them from the foundation of the world.*

This *"marriage supper"* is a feast of real truth and those things that can never be discovered when we are constantly engaged in our worldly pursuits. The mysteries of God (*"the true sayings of God"*) are spread out upon the table. Since our existence and purpose is the pursuit of happiness, we are filled by this food and hunger no more as we partake of things that are eternal and real, and not the things of the world that leave us forever hungering for more.

The *meat* provided for the *"supper of the Lamb"* will not be the flesh of the world, but *"the flesh of the Lamb"* slain to provide us with the happiness we desire. John did not intend for his writings to be interpreted any other way than how they were originally written. He did not write "the marriage supper of the king's son," but as intended: *"the marriage supper"* at which is served *"the flesh of the Lamb"* (as opposed to having some other *"meat"* served). John further reveals this in verses 17 and 18, in which people are given *"the flesh of the Lamb"* so they no longer have to *"eat the flesh of the kings and mighty"* men of the earth.

19:10 *And then I knew with whom I spoke* and I fell at his feet to worship him. And he said unto me, See thou do it not: I am thy fellowservant, and of thy brethren that have the testimony *which I gave unto you in the flesh as the man* Jesus; worship God *for that which He hath given you through me*; for *he who hath a* testimony of *that which I did as the man* Jesus *in the flesh, hath* the spirit of prophecy.

John here gives the first indication that Christ does *not* want to be and should *not* be worshipped. Revelation 22:8–9 reiterates this important principle of truth, as does Christ's own words:

> *Why callest thou me good? there is none good but one, that is, God: but if thou wilt enter into life, keep the commandments.* (Matthew 19:17)

I can of mine own self do nothing: as I hear, I judge: and my judgment is just; because I seek not mine own will, but the will of the Father which hath sent me. (John 5:30)

Then there arose a reasoning among them, which of them should be greatest. And Jesus, perceiving the thought of their heart, took a child, and set him by him, And said unto them, Whosoever shall receive this child in my name receiveth me: and whosoever shall receive me receiveth him that sent me: for he that is least among you all, the same shall be great. (Luke 9:46–48)

19:11 And I saw heaven opened, and behold a white horse *and he that rode had a book in his right hand which had the seven seals, six already open and one left*; and he that *spoke with me* sat *there* upon *and* was called Faithful and True, and in righteousness he doth judge and make war.

Christ's mission is to wield the sword of truth and cut asunder all the falsehoods of the world—which create inequality and inhibit the happiness of humankind. The *"war"* he *"makes"* is truth and righteousness (*"Faithful and True"*) against falsehoods and injustice. He rides a "white horse" because the earth is returned to the state it was when humankind began its existence in peace and purity as explained in the commentary of *Revelation*, chapter 6, regarding the *"rider"* upon a *"white horse."*

19:12 His eyes *are* as a flame of fire, and on his head *are* many crowns; and he *has* a name written, that no man *knows*, but he himself.

A *"flame"* is the light produced by fire. Because of his knowledge (*"fire"*), Christ sees things (*"his eyes"*) with an eternal perspective, which always guides his actions, or in other words, is the light by which he sees. The authority and power (*"many crowns"*) is given to Christ to do what needs to be done in this solar system. Our *"name"* is expressed symbolically as our works *"which no man knoweth saving he that receiveth it"* (see Revelation 2:17). Christ has and will accomplish works (*"a name written"*) that no other human being has done, is doing, or will ever do in this solar system.

19:13 And he *is* clothed with a vesture dipped in *his own* blood *and the blood of those who were killed upon the altar*; and his name is called The Word of God.

John describes Christ as he did in his other writings:

In the beginning was the Word, and the Word was with God, and the Word was God. The same was in the beginning with God. All things were made by him; and without him was not any thing made that was made. In him was life; and the life was the light of men. And the light shineth in darkness; and the darkness comprehended it not. ...That was the true Light, which lighteth every man that cometh into the world. He was in the world, and the world was made by him, and the world knew him not. He came unto his own, and his own received him not. But as many as received him, to them gave he power to become the sons of God, even to them that believe on his name: Which were born, not of blood, nor of the will of the flesh, nor of the will of man, but of God. And the Word was made flesh, and dwelt among us, (and we beheld his glory, the glory as of the only begotten of the Father,) full of grace and truth. (John 1:1–5, 9–14)

Christ lost "*his own blood*" upon the cross. In this verse, John ties in "*the blood of those who were killed upon the altar*" (those who performed their works here in mortality) with Christ's blood. Mortality is the "*altar*" upon which these works are offered. These are those of whom Christ spoke when he said:

And he that taketh not his cross, and followeth after me, is not worthy of me. He that findeth his life shall lose it: and he that loseth his life for my sake shall find it. (Matthew 10:38–39)

The symbolism of all *"vesture"* in the scriptures is the results of the actions and works of an individual. Jesus told his disciples that they must follow his example ("take up his cross, and followeth after him") in all things. In essence, the righteous must *"dip"* their own *"vesture"* in the *"blood"* of Christ.

19:14 And the armies which *are* in heaven followed him upon white horses, clothed in fine linen, white and clean.

The prophet Joel describes with eloquence the same thing John describes in this verse:

> *A fire devoureth before them; and behind them a flame bur-*
> *neth: the land is as the garden of Eden before them, and*
> *behind them a desolate wilderness; yea, and nothing shall*
> *escape them. The appearance of them is as the appearance*
> *of horses; and as horsemen, so shall they run. Like the*
> *noise of chariots on the tops of mountains shall they leap,*
> *like the noise of a flame of fire that devoureth the stubble,*
> *as a strong people set in battle array. Before their face the*
> *people shall be much pained: all faces shall gather black-*
> *ness. They shall run like mighty men; they shall climb the*
> *wall like men of war; and they shall march every one on*
> *his ways, and they shall not break their ranks: Neither*
> *shall one thrust another; they shall walk every one in his*
> *path: and when they fall upon the sword, they shall not be*
> *wounded. They shall run to and fro in the city; they shall*
> *run upon the wall, they shall climb up upon the houses;*
> *they shall enter in at the windows like a thief. The earth*
> *shall quake before them; the heavens shall tremble: the sun*
> *and the moon shall be dark, and the stars shall withdraw*
> *their shining: And the LORD shall utter his voice before*
> *his army: for his camp is very great: for he is strong that*
> *executeth his word: for the day of the LORD is great and*
> *very terrible; and who can abide it?* (Joel 2:3–11)

19:15 And out of his mouth goeth a sharp sword, *even The Word of God* that with it he should smite the nations: and he shall rule them with a rod of iron: and he treadeth *the fruit of the vine with* fierceness *which is in* the winepress of wrath of Almighty God.

This "*rod of iron*" was used by John in Revelation 12:5, to express the way in which Christ will correct the falsehoods and corruption upon the earth. Whether it is in the story of Moses or the words of Proverbs, the term "*rod*" has been used throughout written scripture to express a means of correction. It is interchangeable with "*staff*," which is used by a shepherd to direct sheep and ward off the wolves.

"*Iron*" is the significant adjective borrowed from written scripture by John to demonstrate what this particular means of correction ("*rod*") can do:

> *Thou shalt break them with a rod of iron*; *thou shalt dash them in pieces like a potter's vessel.* (Psalms 2:9)

> *And the fourth kingdom shall be strong as iron: forasmuch as iron breaketh in pieces and subdueth all things: and as iron that breaketh all these, shall it break in pieces and bruise.* (Daniel 2:40)

"*Iron*" represents *eternal truths* that cannot be negated or changed by the precepts and doctrines of men. It is interchangeable with the terms "*word of God*" or "*word of truth*," which will correct and change the human value of "Do unto yourself what is needed to be happy" to "Do unto others what you would have them do unto you," thus creating happiness for everyone.

John expresses the products of our misuse of the eternal principles of happiness outlined by our Creator as "*the fruit of the vine*"; whereas the world is "*the vine*" and the actions of the people is its "*fruit*." Because of the non-intervention of God in mortality ("*wrath of God*"), the "*fruit*" is as if it is in the "*winepress of the wrath of God*." Christ will "*tread*" with zeal ("*fierceness*") upon this "*fruit*," crushing it under his feet, which were previously described by John as being "*feet like unto fine brass.*"

19:16 And he hath on his vesture and *under* his thigh a name written, KING OF KINGS, AND LORD OF LORDS.

Our legs hold our bodies upright and carry us through life down the roads of our own choosing. The strongest and most significant muscle of the leg is the *"thigh."* In *Old Testament* tradition, when a covenant or promise was made, it was done by the one making the promise placing a hand under the thigh of the one benefiting from the promise. In other words, it is a way of signifying that a promise and covenant has been made:

> *And Abraham said unto his eldest servant of his house, that ruled over all that he had,* **Put, I pray thee, thy hand under my thigh.** *...And the servant put* **his hand under the thigh of Abraham** *his master,* **and sware to him concerning that matter.** (Genesis 24:2, 9)

> *And the time drew nigh that Israel must die: and he called his son Joseph, and said unto him, If now I have found* **grace** *in thy sight, put,* **I pray thee, thy hand under my thigh, and deal kindly and truly with me;** *bury me not, I pray thee, in Egypt.* (Genesis 47:29)

Christ's *"name"* (his works) is to fulfill the promise and covenant (*"under his thigh"*) he made to us when he took *"the Book of Life from the right hand"* of the Creator to be our leader, our *"King of Kings, Lord of Lords"*—leading us in truth (*"rod of iron"*) and righteousness.

Isaiah gives his own metaphors and figurative expressions of this beautifully:

> *For thou hast broken the yoke of his burden, and the staff of his shoulder, the rod of his oppressor, as in the day of Midian. For every battle of the warrior is with confused noise, and garments rolled in blood; but this shall be with burning and fuel of fire.* **For unto us a child is born,**

unto us a son is given: and the government shall be upon his shoulder: and his name shall be called Wonderful, Counsellor, The mighty God, The everlasting Father, The Prince of Peace. Of the increase of his government and peace there shall be no end, upon the throne of David, and upon his kingdom, to order it, and to establish it with judgment and with justice from henceforth even for ever. *The zeal of the LORD of hosts will perform this.* (Isaiah 9:4–7)

19:17 And I saw an angel standing in the sun; and he cried with a loud voice, saying to all the fowls *of the air,* Come and gather yourselves together unto the supper of the great God *and eat the flesh of the Lamb which was slain for you*;

John presents a servant of God (*"an angel"*) introducing the knowledge of truth (*"standing in the sun"*) to the *"fowls of the air."* John uses *"fowls of the air"* to represent the people of the earth who are searching for truth. Birds are dependant on both land and air to gain their daily sustenance; however, unlike the beasts of the field, *"fowls"* are not specifically bound to either.

This figurative representation is made of those who seek for truth from the inspiration of *heaven* through personal revelation, and from the doctrines of men upon the *earth.* The *angel* is inviting all to come to a *"supper"* in which the truth (*"flesh of the Lamb"*) will be provided for them, so they no longer need to depend on the heavens or the earth for understanding.

And he said, **Whereunto shall we liken the kingdom of God?** *or with what comparison shall we compare it? It is like a grain of mustard seed, which, when it is sown in the earth, is less than all the seeds that be in the earth: But when it is sown, it groweth up, and becometh greater than all herbs, and shooteth out great branches;* **so that the fowls of the air may lodge under the shadow of it.** (Mark 4:30–32)

When the *king's son* returns to the *"kingdom"* from war, having *"conquered"* his enemies (all falsehoods), a celebratory feast is given in his honor. Anciently, it was said of those who conquered others:

And the Philistine said unto David, Am I a dog, that thou comest to me with staves? And the Philistine cursed David by his gods. And the Philistine said to David, ***Come to me, and I will give thy flesh unto the fowls of the air****, and to the beasts of the field. Then said David to the Philistine, Thou comest to me with a sword, and with a spear, and with a shield: but I come to thee in the name of the LORD of hosts, the God of the armies of Israel, whom thou hast defied. This day will the LORD deliver thee into mine hand; and I will smite thee, and take thine head from thee;* ***and I will give the carcases of the host of the Philistines this day unto the fowls of the air****, and to the wild beasts of the earth; that all the earth may know that there is a God in Israel.* (I Samuel 17:43–46)

This same connotation of *"conquering"* is what John intended with the righteous twist given by Jesus in his parables, and in *"gathering yourselves together unto the supper of the great God."* At such a *"supper,"* the *"flesh"* of one's enemy is certainly not to be served. When we attend a *"feast"* put on by God, we will be eating what *He* has prepared and slain (see commentary on verse 9), so that we do not have to eat the flesh of the enemy.

When Christ *"conquers"* his enemies by teaching and revealing truth to the world, the people will *"eat his flesh and drink his blood"* as he so indicated to the Jews:

I am the living bread which came down from heaven: if any man eat of this bread, he shall live for ever: and ***the bread that I will give is my flesh****, which I will give for the life of the world. The Jews therefore strove among themselves, saying, How can this man give us his flesh to eat? Then Jesus said unto them, Verily, verily, I say unto* *you,* **Except ye eat the flesh of the Son of man, and drink his blood, ye have no life in you.** *Whoso eateth my flesh, and drinketh my blood, hath eternal life; and I will raise him up at the last day. For my flesh is meat indeed, and my blood is drink indeed.* **He that eateth my flesh, and drinketh my blood, dwelleth in me, and I in him.** *As the living Father hath sent me,* **and I live by the Father: so he that eateth me, even he shall live by me.** (John 6:51–57)

No longer will the people be living as the world lives, but will *live by the Father,* or better, *"eat the flesh"* (Christ's) that has been provided at *"the supper of the great God."*

19:18 That ye *no longer* eat the flesh of kings, and the flesh of captains, and the flesh of mighty men, and the flesh of horses, and of them that sit on them, *nor* the flesh of *any man,* free *or* bond, small *or* great.

Once the inhabitants of the world are *"fed"* the truth, they are no longer dependent upon (*"eat the flesh"*) those who ruled them (*"kings"*), those who guided and led them (*"captains"*), those who put themselves above them (*"mighty men"*), or those who set up governments, economies, and societies (*"horses"*) and their bureaucracies (*"them that sit on them"*). Neither will *"the flesh of any man"* be consumed any more; in other words, no one will trust in the arm of flesh, not of his neighbor, not of his friend, nor of his own.

Isaiah describes the latter days leading up to the Millennium in this way:

Through the wrath of the LORD of hosts is the land darkened, *and the people shall be as the fuel of the fire: no man shall spare his brother. And he shall snatch on the right hand, and be hungry; and he shall eat on the left hand, and they shall not be satisfied:* **they shall eat every man the flesh of his own arm:** (Isaiah 9:19–20)

Jeremiah reiterates:

Thus saith the LORD; **Cursed be the man that trusteth in man, and maketh flesh his arm,** *and whose heart departeth from the LORD.* (Jeremiah 17:5)

There will be only *one* truth—one *"flesh"* to eat, one *"blood"* to drink. Those who do not do unto others as they would have others do unto them (*"eat the flesh of Christ"*) with true and unselfish intent (*"drink the blood of Christ"*) will have no part in the kingdom of God established upon the earth during his Reign, nor at any other time throughout eternity—worlds without end.

19:19 And I saw the beast, and the kings of the earth, and *their captains and their mighty men and* their armies, gathered together to make war against him that sat on the horse, and against his army.

The societies and economies of this world, and the *"merchants"* of the earth who gain from them, are not going to go away by laying down their arms and giving up—there is too much to lose. How can the "American Dream" possibly be invalidated without those who believe they have achieved it standing up to protect their material possessions, their college degrees, their knowledge, and their status over others?

They will stand to protect their interests in spite of what *their interests* have done to the world and to their neighbors. There will be only one thing brought to their attention as they realize they stand firmly on the *"left hand of the Lord."* When it is brought to their attention, they will *still* resist the fact that their "American Dream" has created an international nightmare:

Then shall he say also unto them on the left hand, **Ye have departed** *from* **those things which ye received of** *me,* **because ye did not understand those things which I had commanded you and did not want that I should reign over you. Therefore, are** *ye cursed* **with an** *everlasting fire, prepared for the devil and his angels,* **who** *are mine enemies, who would not that I should reign over them, and who are those who did not seek me and do that which I commanded of them;* For I was an hungred, and ye gave me no meat *that I might be filled, but ye gave me those scraps which fell from your table, which table was arrayed with all manner of fine food and wine;* I was thirsty, and ye gave me no drink *that I might not thirst again, but ye gave me to drink of a cup, when you of a whole well draw your water;* I was a stranger, and ye took me not in *because ye feared least I take from you that which ye keep in your house; but ye caused me to sleep in the streets away from your house where ye would notice me not;* **I was** naked, and ye clothed me not **with that with which ye clothed yourselves;** **I was** sick, and in prison, and ye visited me not, **nor did ye concern yourselves with me, for ye believed I had received as a punishment a just reward of sickness or imprisonment.** Then shall they also answer him, saying, Lord, when saw we thee an hungred, or athirst, or a stranger, or naked, or sick, or in prison, and did not minister unto thee? Then shall he answer them, saying, Verily I say unto you, Inasmuch as ye did it not to one of the least of these, **who are equal to you in all things in my eyes,** ye did it not to me. And these shall go away into an everlasting punishment **reserved for those who would not have the King rule over them;** but the righteous **shall know of their righteousness and enter** into life eternal. (Matthew 25:41–46. Correct translation given in bold.)

19:20 And **when he had opened the seventh seal** the beast was taken, and with him the false prophet that wrought miracles before him, with which **the beast** deceived them that had received **his** mark, and them that worshipped his image. These both were cast alive into a lake of fire burning with brimstone.

Argue as they may, when the Millennial Reign of Christ begins ("*opening of the seventh seal*"), all those who have lived deliciously off of the labor and work of the poor, and who have exalted themselves above others, will feel an embarrassment and a "*burning*" when they come to a knowledge of the truth ("*lake burning with fire*"). Of course, they will not be destroyed, for they are loved just as much as those who lived miserably upon the earth as a direct result of their actions and inactions. They will remain "*alive*," and come to a realization of what their worldly desires have done to others. The stench of these actions ("*brimstone*") will become apparent to them as the truth is revealed ("*cast into the lake of fire*") by those much more knowledgeable than they, and to whom they now must bow in subjection to the eternal law of Do Unto Others.

19:21 And the remnant *of the beast and the false prophet, even all those from whose* flesh the fowls *of the air* were filled, were slain with the sword of him that sat upon the horse, which sword proceeded out of his mouth.

Any who remain ("*remnant*") still believing they were justified in worldly pursuits, or seeking truth in following the false preaching of religious leaders, spiritual gurus, or self-help promoters, will be sorely confounded by the truth that Christ will reveal to the world. Then those on his "*right hand*" will be told:

> *And in that day when the Son of man shall come in his glory, and all the holy angels with him, then shall he sit upon **his** throne **upon this earth, which the Father hath put in his power. And he shall be made King over all the people.** And before him shall be gathered **the people of** all the nations **of the earth**, and he shall separate them one from another, as a shepherd divideth his sheep from the goats **when he calleth them forth to be put in their pens.** And he shall set the sheep on his right hand, **for these are those who received his word and kept his commandments**, but the goats **are those who**

did not receive his word, nor would they keep his commandments, and they shall be set on the left. *Then shall the King say unto them on his right hand, Come, ye blessed of my Father, inherit the kingdom prepared for you from the foundation of the world, **for ye received me and understood my commandments and kept them**; For I was an hungred, and ye gave me meat **that I might eat and always be filled**; I was thirsty, and ye gave me drink **that I might drink and thirst no more**; I was a stranger, and ye took me in **that I might have always where to lay my head**; I was naked, and ye clothed me **that I might never be naked**; I was sick, and ye visited me **that I might not be afflicted any longer**; I was in prison, and ye came unto me **that I might know of your love for me**. Then shall the righteous answer him, saying, Lord, when saw we thee an hungred, and fed thee? or thirsty, and gave thee drink? When saw we thee a stranger, and took thee in? or naked, and clothed thee? Or when saw we thee sick, or in prison, and came unto thee? **And this they shall say because they kept the commandments of the Lord without being told that which they should do, because they did that which was righteous of their own accord in all things**. And the King shall answer and say unto them, Verily I say unto you, Inasmuch as ye have done it unto one of the least of these my brethren **who are like unto me**, ye have done it unto me. **And if ye had the desire to do it unto the least of these, but ye could not, but would if ye could, ye have also done it unto me**.* (Matthew 25:31–40)

Chapter

REVELATION
UNFOLDED

20:1 And *in the likeness of things upon the earth* I saw an angel come down from heaven having a great chain in his hand, *and he took* the key *to* the bottomless pit *from the star which had fallen unto the earth*, which is the Devil, and Satan.

Revelation 9:1 reads:

And the fifth angel sounded, and I saw as it were a star fall from heaven unto the earth: and to him was given great power and the key to the bottomless pit which was dug by those upon the earth.

It was explained that the world was given the "*key*" (understanding) to new technologies that were not revealed to the world since the beginning of time. This new understanding stoked the "*great furnace*" at the bottom of the "*deep pit*" (which was dug by the inhabitants of the earth) and created "*the smoke*" out of which "*the locusts*" came to torment and cause misery (see commentary on Revelation 9:1–2).

Here, John expresses figuratively that this understanding (*"the key"*) will be taken back. In other words, Christ will not allow the use of any technology that had previously been used to create inequality and destroy the environs of the earth because of our human lusts (*"the Devil, and Satan"*).

20:2 And he laid hold on the dragon, that old serpent, and bound him *with the great chain for* a thousand years,

20:3 And cast him into the bottomless pit and *locked it* up, and set a seal upon *it*, that *the dragon* should deceive the nations no more, till the thousand years should be fulfilled, *but* after that, he must be loosed a little season.

John presents the time periods expressed in his *Revelation* as *"seals"* in which important and crucial events occur in the world. After Christ brings the truth to the world, and people realize his laws and counsels are just and necessary to create peace and happiness, a time period (*"seal"*) will be established. This way, the inhabitants of the world can finally experience mortality living under the law of Christ without the fear of contrasting ideals.

The truth will be revealed of who *"the dragon"* really is, and how it has affected the world negatively. Human nature (*"the dragon"*) will be subdued by the *Royal Law* of Christ. However, people will not lose their free agency to act and live as individually desired, but upon proper introspection, most humans will realize where the *"old serpent"* belongs—*"cast into the bottomless pit and locked up."*

20:4 And I saw *the dead upon the earth and* the souls of them that were beheaded for the witness of Jesus, and for the word of God, and *who* had *chosen* not to *worship* the beast, neither his image, neither *receive* his mark upon their foreheads, or in their hands; and they lived and reigned with Christ a thousand years. And I saw *as it were* thrones *which were given them of Christ*, and they sat upon them, and judgment was given unto *the world because of* them:

All those who *preceded* Christ, and lived upon the earth *"witnessing of him"* by their works, are figuratively expressed here as *"them that were beheaded."* John gives reference and accolade to his namesake John the Baptist, who *preceded* Christ, *testified* of him, and was *beheaded* for his accusation of wickedness against King Herod. Few could preach the true intent of *"the word of God"* like John the Baptist:

> *And now also the axe is laid unto the root of the trees: every tree therefore which bringeth not forth good fruit is hewn down, and cast into the fire. And the people asked him, saying, What shall we do then? He answereth and saith unto them, **He that hath two coats, let him impart to him that hath none; and he that hath meat, let him do likewise**. (Luke 3:9–11)*

Those who live the *Royal Law* (who have two coats and give to them who have none) comply with the rule of do unto others as you would have them do unto you, and prove to the world that it can be done, no matter in what state or condition of wickedness the people exist.

Because these *"beheaded"* ones proved it possible, it leaves no excuse for any other whose works have been *dead* (*"the dead"*). The power and authority (*"throne upon which they sit"*) of their example will be the *"means of judgment"* for the rest of the world. It has been said by some that we will be brought before the *"judgment seat of Christ"* to be judged of our works. This *"judgment seat,"* is that upon which those will sit, who in spite of the world and its ways, followed the laws of Christ, and will be *"judges"* in a sense, of those (*"the dead"*) who will claim it was impossible.

20:5 *And the dead were raised by the power of the Lamb*, but the rest of the dead ***who were the remnant that chose to continue to worship the beast and his image and his mark will*** not ***live*** again until the thousand years ***are*** finished. This is the first ***death***.

Those whose works are not true to the law of Christ (*"the dead"*) are reborn (*"resurrected"*—see verse 6) as they accept Christ and his laws.

This *"resurrection"* or "rebirth" has nothing to do with the physical flesh. John's intended meaning is found in Jesus' answer to Nicodemus:

> *Jesus answered and said unto him, Verily, verily, I say unto thee, Except a man be born again, he cannot see the kingdom of God. Nicodemus saith unto him, How can a man be born when he is old? can he enter the second time into his mother's womb, and be born? Jesus answered, Verily, verily, I say unto thee, Except a man be born of water and of the Spirit, he cannot enter into the kingdom of God. That which is born of the flesh is flesh; and that which is born of the Spirit is spirit.* (John 3:3–6)

Those who accept Christ are *"raised up"* from their bellies upon which they crawled all their mortal days, eating dust of the earth that failed to quench their hunger and thirst. Those who reject the law of Christ, and with their free will choose to continue the ways of the *"beast"* and the worldliness it promotes, shall be removed from the earth, and *"will not live again"* while the *"seal"* remains unbroken upon the bottomless pit. This is considered the *"first death,"* in comparison with the *"second death"* that will be mentioned later.

20:6 Blessed and holy is he that hath part in the first resurrection; *for* on such the second death **shall have** no power, but they shall be priests of God and **his** Christ, and shall reign with him a thousand years.

John refers to those who have *"part in the first resurrection"* (*"raised up"*) as those who accept Christ and his laws as mentioned in the above commentary. *"Priests"* is a figurative expression taken from the Mosaic priesthood, and utilized by John to express those who can now enter beyond the veil of the tabernacle and observe and touch the Ark of the Covenant.

Those who experience the *"first death"* are removed from the earth to observe in a spiritual state of existence how things go for a period of time under the absolute rule of Christ. If after the thousand years, there are those who still believe that the ways of the *"beast"* (worldliness and personal gratification no matter what happens to others) are better for them than the rule of the *Royal Law*, they shall be removed from this solar system forever ("*the second death*"). But for a "*short time*," these will be given the opportunity to make their case and attempt to convince the rest of us that the 6000 years we experienced before the Millennial Reign of Christ were better than the last thousand years with him.

20:7 And when the thousand years are expired, *the dragon* shall be loosed out of his prison *with those who followed him*,

20:8 And *they are as* Gog and Magog *and* shall go out *again* to deceive the nations which are in the four quarters of the earth; *and all the inhabitants of the earth*, the number of *which is* as the sand of the sea, *shall be gathered* together to battle.

John borrows his figurative expression "*Gog and Magog*" exclusively and purposefully from Ezekiel chapters 38 and 39 (a highly recommended read and study). The figurative battle between the Lord and *Gog and Magog* as presented in Ezekiel, is very similar (exact in many words and expressions) as John's description of the destruction of the wicked when the Lord reigns. There is no other reason why John chose the term "*Gog and Magog*."

For the last time, the idea of selfishness, exaltation, riches, power, and worldly glory, will come up against the equality and strict code of *love thy neighbor as thyself*. "*This great battle*" will allow the free agency of all who desire to give their opinions, ideas, and perspectives for their eternal existence. Unlike the "*Battle of Armageddon*," which is one waged within our conscience, this "*battle*" will be one of words—Christ (the One anointed to teach us to treat each other good) pitted against *Lucifer* (our fleshly desires). Everyone who so desires to speak out in favor of or against the plan our Creator has established for this solar system, shall be given the opportunity to speak and attempt to convince the rest of us of their logic.

20:9 And *the armies of Gog shall go* up on the breadth of the earth, and *compass* the camp of the saints about, and the beloved city; and *I saw* fire *come* down from God out of heaven, and *devour* them *who fought against the Lamb*.

No matter what opinions might be held, no matter how much logic might be presented, the experience and knowledge of eternity (*"fire come down from God out of heaven"*) possessed by Him and those who helped create this solar system by following the laws and order of the Universe, shall *"devour"* anything that stands against them. Those who have lived for a thousand years without the illusion of the "American Dream," have fallen in love with the *"bridegroom's wife,"* and now enjoy the standard of living that the laws of Christ have established and provided for them.

The kingdom of God upon earth (*the city"*) has truly become a *"beloved city."*

20:10 And the devil, ***who is the dragon*** that deceived them, was cast into the lake of fire and brimstone, where the beast and the false prophet are, ***who are*** tormented day and night for ever and ever.

The realization that our human natures (*"the dragon"*) must be controlled in order to establish peace and happiness, will be foremost in our minds. The truth (*"fire"*) helps us smell the putrid odors (*"brimstone"*) we leave behind, after we have come to realize the damage to happiness caused by the illusory "American Dream" (*"the image of the beast"*), and the empty counsels of religion and self-help and spiritual gurus (*"false prophets"*).

20:11 And I saw a great white throne, and him that sat on it, from whose face the earth fled away; and the ***veil that covered the host of*** heaven ***dissolved and heaven was rolled together as a scroll***; and there was found no place for ***those who had been cast into the lake of fire and brimstone***.

The righteous (*"white"*) power and authority (*"throne"*) of our Creator will cause all of our previous *earthly* works to *flee* from before His face (*"from whose face the earth fled away"*). Unfortunately for many, they will not be able to justify to the *"One who sits on the throne,"* the *good works* they did that were actually evil.

Jesus prophesied:

> *Not every one that saith unto me, Lord, Lord, shall enter into the kingdom of heaven; but he that doeth **the will of my Father which is in heaven**. Many will say to me in that day, Lord, Lord, have we not prophesied in thy name? and in thy name have cast out devils? and in thy name done many wonderful works? **And then will I profess unto them, I never knew you: depart from me, ye that work iniquity**.* (Matthew 7:21–23)

Our works in mortality are figuratively recorded in heaven ("*rolled together as a scroll*") as a witness against us (see commentary Revelation 6:14). Once "*the veil*" has been dissolved, and we understand the truths of eternal reality, we will find there is no place for those things that take away from our happiness.

> *And **all the host of heaven shall be dissolved, and the heavens shall be rolled together as a scroll**: and all their host shall fall down, as the leaf falleth off from the vine, and as a falling fig from the fig tree.* (Isaiah 34:4)

20:12 And I saw the **quick and the** dead, small and great, stand before **the Lamb of** God; and the books were opened: and another book was opened, which is the Book of Life: and **all** were judged out of those things which were written in the books, according to their works.

> *I charge thee therefore before God, and the Lord Jesus Christ, who shall judge the quick and the dead at his appearing and his kingdom;* (II Timothy 4:1)

The "*books*" that "*were opened*" are what is written in the "*scrolls of heaven*," which are an accounting of our works. Our experiences will be compared with the eternal laws and order of heaven, which are written in "*the Book of Life*." The laws and order of the Universe are eternally established, and will always be as they always have been forever. If our works do not conform to what is written in the *"other book that was opened, which is the Book of Life,"* we will judge ourselves with remorse and embarrassment (*"punish her double"*).

20:13 And the sea gave up the *quick* which were in it; and death and hell delivered up the dead which were in them: and *all* were judged every man according to their works.

Whether alive (*"quick"*) upon the earth physically, or in doing righteous works (those from *"the sea"* of humanity) during the reign of Christ, or *"dead"* in the spirit realm where one exists as a spirit entity, or performing *"dead works"* which have led to the experience of *"hell"* upon earth, we all must confront our inner selves, and compare what we believe, and how we have acted upon these beliefs, with the eternal truths of God. In other words, alive or dead, good or bad, all will be (figuratively) brought before the judgment seat of Christ.

20:14 And whosoever was not found written in the Book of Life was cast into the lake of fire. This is the second death.

Upon comparing who we truly are, with how we know things have to be in order to maintain the balance of the Universe (those things *"written in the Book of Life"*), those of us who cannot conform, will feel the burning of this knowledge (*"cast into the lake of fire"*). Those who refuse to conform their beliefs and actions with the eternal plan of God *"written in the Book of Life,"* will be removed forever from existence (*"this is the second death"*). *"Brimstone"* is not mentioned here, because there will be no continual remembrance of the stench caused by unrighteous works.

20:15 And *then are* death and hell cast into the lake of fire.

With the knowledge and advanced technology of the truth (*"lake of fire"*) there will be no more *"death"* and no more *"hell."*

Chapter

REVELATION
UNFOLDED

21:1 I saw *as it were* a new heaven and a new earth *because* the first heaven and the first earth were passed away; *for the earth had fled and the mountains thereof* and there *were* no more *isles of the* sea.

John's presentation here is not a *physical* transformation of the earth but a *spiritual* one. He writes previously regarding those who isolate themselves from others (*"islands"*) and those who lift themselves above others (*"mountains"*):

> *And every mountain fled away, and the islands were not found.* (Revelation 16:21)

John's figurative expressions are in line with the eloquence of Isaiah:

> *The LORD shall go forth as a mighty man, he shall stir up jealousy like a man of war: he shall cry, yea, roar; he shall prevail against his enemies. I have long time holden my*

peace; I have been still, and refrained myself: now will I cry like a travailing woman; **I will destroy and devour at once.** *I* **will make waste mountains and hills, and dry up all their herbs; and I will make the rivers islands, and I will dry up the pools.** *And I will bring the blind by a way that they knew not; I will lead them in paths that they have not known: I will make darkness light before them, and crooked things straight. These things will I do unto them, and not forsake them.* (Isaiah 42:13–16)

21:2 And I John saw *in the heavens a likeness of* the holy city, *a* new Jerusalem, coming down from God out of heaven, prepared as a bride adorned for her husband.

This is figuratively expressed as the influence of heaven ("*coming down from God*") creating a whole "*new Jerusalem.*" The term "*Jerusalem*" literally means "*foundation of peace*" (see commentary on Revelation 14:1).

Again Isaiah expresses it wonderfully in his writings:

That he who blesseth himself in the earth shall bless himself in the God of truth; and he that sweareth in the earth shall swear by the God of truth; because the former troubles are forgotten, and because they are hid from mine eyes. For, behold, **I create new heavens and a new earth:** *and the former shall not be remembered, nor come into mind. But be ye glad and rejoice for ever in that which I create: for, behold,* **I create Jerusalem a rejoicing, and her people a joy.** (Isaiah 65:16–18)

21:3 And I heard a great voice out of heaven saying, Behold, **the marriage is complete**; the tabernacle of God is **now** with men, and **the Lamb** will dwell with them, and they shall be his people, and **his Word** shall be with them and be their God **instead of wood and stone**.

*And **the Word** was made flesh, and dwelt among us, and*
we beheld his glory, the glory as of the only begotten of the
Father, full of grace and truth. (John 1:14)

This unification (*"marriage"*) between the will of our Creator (*"his*
Word") and our mortal reality will produce peace and happiness upon the
earth. Instead of worshipping gods of *"wood and stone"* (desires and
worldly possessions), *"his Word shall be our God."*

In ancient times, the prophets used *"wood and stone"* to describe the
idols people worshipped instead of the Lord. *"Stone"* represents material
possessions which are not *"burned up"* with the knowledge (*"fire"*) of truth;
whereas *"wood"* represents our worldly aspirations of honor, glory, fame, and
prestige that are easily consumed by this *"fire"*:

*And there ye shall serve gods, the work of men's hands, **wood***
***and stone**, which neither see, nor hear, nor eat, nor smell.*
(Deuteronomy 4:28)

And have cast their gods into the fire: for they were no
*gods, but the work of men's hands, **wood and stone**:*
therefore they have destroyed them. (II Kings 19:18)

Ezekiel brings John's intentional message to light with his own words:

And that which cometh into your mind shall not be at all,
*that ye say, We will be as the heathen, **as the families of***
***the countries, to serve wood and stone**. As I live, saith*
the Lord GOD, surely with a mighty hand, and with a
*stretched out arm, and with fury poured out, **will I rule***
***over you**: And I will bring you out from the people, and*
will gather you out of the countries wherein ye are scat-
tered, with a mighty hand, and with a stretched out arm,
and with fury poured out. And I will bring you into the
*wilderness of the people, and there will **I plead with you***
***face to face**.* (Ezekiel 20:32–35)

21:4 And God shall wipe away all tears from their eyes; and there shall be no more death, neither sorrow, nor crying, neither shall there be any more pain: for the former things are passed away *and all things have become new, even new heavens and a new earth*.

The thoughts of Solomon were wise and profound as he considered how the works of men oppress each other and create *"tears"*:

> *So I returned, and considered all the oppressions that are done under the sun: and **behold the tears of such as were** oppressed, **and they had no comforter**; and on the side of their oppressors there was power; but they had no comforter. Wherefore I praised the dead which are already dead more than the living which are yet alive.* (Ecclesiastes 4:1–2)

John describes their comforter and how he will console them as did the prophet Isaiah:

> *And he will destroy in this mountain the face of the covering cast over all people, and the vail* [sic] *that is spread over all nations. He will swallow up death in victory; **and the Lord GOD will wipe away tears from off all faces**; and the rebuke of his people shall he take away from off all the earth: for the LORD hath spoken it. And it shall be said in that day, Lo, this is our God; we have waited for him, and he will save us: this is the LORD; we have waited for him, we will be glad and rejoice in his salvation...For, behold, I create **new heavens and a new earth: and the former shall not be remembered, nor come into mind**.* (Isaiah 25:7–9; 65:17)

It can be said that when we learn truth, we experience new thoughts and ideas that enlighten our minds to a *whole new world*. As a new understanding of God and His mysteries are revealed to us (truth/"*new heavens*"), we will begin to create a literal heaven on earth ("*new earth*").

21:5 And he that *stood before* the throne said, Behold, I make all things new *by the Word of God*. And he said unto me, Write: *This Word is* true and faithful.

The truth which is heard coming from the mouth of Christ is *"the Word of God."* Everything he does (his works/*"name"*) is called *"The Word of God"* (see Revelation 19:13); therefore, Christ *is* in no uncertain terms *"the Word of God"*:

> In the beginning was the Word, and the Word was with God, and **the Word was God**. The same was in the begin-ning with God. (John 1:1–2)

During his Millennial Reign, he will teach the same *"word"* he taught when he was in the flesh, upon which *"word"* all the law and the prophets are established, and is the same "word given since the beginning of time" and forever: Do unto others what you would have them do unto you.

21:6 And he said unto me, It is done. I am *the Christ*, Alpha and Omega, the beginning and the end. I will give unto him that is athirst of the fountain of the water of life freely.

This *"Word"* (*"the Christ"*) is the ONLY law that will ever be given for the salvation and happiness of the human race. A Christ (Anointed One) was created to give this *"word,"* and make sure it is enforced in this solar system. There is no other being created like him, and this *"word"* is absolute and final (*"Alpha and Omega, the beginning and the end"*).

"The Word" is like a seed. If the seed is planted in good land, it will bring forth fruit in patience:

> Now the parable is this: **The seed is the word of God**. Those by the way side are they that hear; then cometh the devil, and taketh away the word out of their hearts, lest they should believe and be saved. They on the rock are they,

*which, when they hear, receive the word with joy; and these
have no root, which for a while believe, and in time of temptation fall away.   And that which fell among thorns are
they, which, when they have heard, go forth, and are choked
with cares and riches and pleasures of this life, and bring
no fruit to perfection.   But that on the good ground are they,
which in an honest and good heart, having heard the word,
keep it, and bring forth fruit with patience.* (Luke 8:11–15)

In the story of Moses, the Israelites were in constant search for the
"good ground" or promised land. Once they found the "good ground" where
"the seed" could be planted (i.e., where they could live the word of God),
they could not enter, because they were being led by Moses and his laws.
Not even Moses could enter into the "good ground."

The story of Moses is figurative of mortality (*"the wilderness"*),
and the eventual inheritance of a *"new earth"* ("good ground") where *"the
Word"* can be lived (*the seed planted*) and the fruit of happiness harvested.
Joshua eventually led the Israelites into the "good ground," and with
intended figurative precision, the true translation of the name "Jesus" is
the same name used in the *Old Testament* text for "Joshua."

One of the major reasons the Jews would not accept *Jesus/Joshua*
to *lead them into the promised land,* was because he told the Jews the Law
of Moses was no longer necessary, and was replaced by his teachings, and
none of it needed to be observed any longer. He instructed his apostles in
truth, many times referring to Jewish customs and traditions as fables:

*Not giving heed to Jewish fables, and commandments of
men, that turn from the truth.* (Titus 1:14)

*For we have not followed cunningly devised fables, when
we made known unto you the power and coming of our
Lord Jesus Christ, but were eyewitnesses of his majesty.*
(II Peter 1:16)

Neither give heed to fables and endless genealogies, which

*minister questions, rather than godly edifying which is
in faith: so do.* (I Timothy 1:4)

There was no real truth in the Law of Moses because it was set up
to be allegoric, figurative, and metaphoric, and would never lead a person
to the *promised land* ("*salvation*").

The only way to salvation is through the grace and truth of
"*Joshua*" Christ:

*For the law was given by Moses, but grace and truth came
by Jesus Christ.* (John 1:17)

21:7 He that overcometh *this world* shall inherit all things; and I will
make him a son *of* God.

The only purpose for the "*Word of God*" is to bring happiness to a
person alive in a body of flesh and blood who is associating with others of
like nature, in a world created for the purpose of experiencing happiness.
Without the "*Word*" to guide us in our interactions with each other, we are
overcome with inequality, misery, and sorrow.

"*The Father*" is the essence of happiness, and the purpose for
which we were created; thus, He is God, our Creator. "*Becoming a son of
God*" is simply an expression used to demonstrate we have fulfilled the
purpose for which we were created. When left to ourselves to create
inequality, misery, and sorrow, we are not *children of God*, but *children
of the flesh* (the devil, Satan, Lucifer) which are the opposite of God and
happiness. Christ's mission was to teach us how to return to "*the Father*"
(happiness) and become "*sons of God.*"

*He was in the world, and the world was made by him, and
the world knew him not. He came unto his own, and his
own received him not. But as many as received him, to
them* ***gave he power to become the sons of God,*** *even
to them that believe on his name.* (John 1:10–12)

For if ye live after the flesh, ye shall die: but if ye through the Spirit do mortify the deeds of the body, ye shall live. **For as many as are led by the Spirit of God, they are the sons of God.** (Romans 8:13–14)

21:8 But *those who are* the fearful, and unbelieving, and the abominable, and murderers, and whoremongers, and sorcerers, and idolaters, and all liars *who shall not forsake these things*, shall have their part in the lake which burneth with fire and brimstone *and upon whom* the second death *will have power*.

Once the premise of equality has been established by the rule of the *"Word of God,"* those who have lived contrary to this law will suffer great remorse and embarrassment, and will remember their *putrid smelling* (*"brimstone"*) actions. Those who continually refuse to change their ways and subject themselves to this new rule of law, will experience the *"second death"* and be removed from this solar system forever.

There are very, very few mortals who do not fit into one of the categories of *abominations* John has outlined in this verse. In each *sin*, John has presented figurative equivalents as the opposition of Christ's teachings:

Those who are *"fearful"* know better than to treat others as they would not want to be treated:

For if we sin wilfully after that we have received the knowledge of the truth, there remaineth no more sacrifice for sins, But **a certain fearful looking for of judgment** *and fiery indignation, which shall devour the adversaries.* Hebrews 10:26–27)

The *"unbelieving"* who see mortality as their only beginning and end, and want to make the best of it (according to their fleshly lusts and desires) before they die, care little for others or the earth on which they live. However, these *"unbelievers"* also include those who believe in God, but judge others, condemn others' lifestyles and beliefs, and in many other ways violate the *Royal Law*:

Unto the pure all things are pure: but unto them that are defiled and **unbelieving** *is nothing pure; but even their mind and conscience is defiled.* **They profess that they know God; but in works they deny him**, *being abominable, and disobedient, and unto every good work reprobate.* (Titus 1:15–16)

Little do humans realize, that according to the way in which Christ taught, a *thought* is just as condemning as the action associated with the thought. Those who are married and lust after another in their heart are adulterers, just as those who hate others are *"murderers"*:

Whosoever hateth his brother is a murderer: *and ye know that no murderer hath eternal life abiding in him.* (I John 3:15)

The *"whoremongers"* described here are those who perpetuate and support the *"whore of the world,"* or she with whom *"the merchants of the earth commit fornication."* There are no business ventures instituted for profit among the societies of the earth that promote Christ-like values.

The *"sorcerers"* (religious leaders, spiritual gurus, self-help promoters) sustain their glory and lifestyles from their advice and counsel. The true counsel that can lead to everlasting happiness is offered by Christ for free.

I will give unto him that is athirst of the fountain of the water of life freely. (Revelation 21:6)

The *"idolaters"* are those who worship those things made of *"wood and stone"* as has been previously explained.

The world is filled with *"liars"* who spread gossip and unsubstantiated rumor, or outright lies against another to fulfill their desired personal agenda. Those who make and perpetuate lies must *"forsake these things"* in order to live in peace under the rule of *Royal Law*.

21:9 And there came unto me one of *the four beasts* which had the seven vials *which were given to the seven servants who had power over* the seven last plagues, and talked with me, saying, Come hither, I will shew thee the bride, *who is now* the Lamb's wife.

When God does not intervene in our mortal lives, we cause ourselves misery and create hell upon earth. John mentions the angel (*"one of the four beasts"*) who had power over the *"wrath of God"* (non-intervention) contained in the *"seven vials."* Now that God's intervention has come to the earth, and He has interceded to establish *"new heavens and a new earth,"* this angel ends his power and authority by presenting how God's intervention will now take place:

21:10 And he carried me away in the spirit to a great and high mountain, and shewed me that great city, the holy Jerusalem, descending out of heaven from God,

In the next few verses, John borrows heavily from the *Old Testament* to present a beautiful figurative expression of the kingdom of God on the earth during the Millennium:

> *And it shall come to pass in the last days,* **that the mountain of the LORD's house shall be established in the top of the mountains, and shall be exalted above the hills;** **and all nations shall flow unto it.** *And many people shall go and say, Come ye, and let us go up to the mountain of the LORD, to the house of the God of Jacob; and* **he will teach us of his ways, and we will walk in his paths:** *for out of Zion shall go forth the law, and the word of the LORD from Jerusalem.* **And he shall judge among the nations, and shall rebuke many people:** *and they shall beat their swords into plowshares, and their spears into pruninghooks: nation shall not lift up sword against nation, neither shall they learn war any more. O house of Jacob, come ye, and let us walk in the light of the LORD.* (Isaiah 2:2–5)

The *"Word of God"* is what people will learn that will finally end all war, and motivate people to care for each other ("beat their swords into plowshares"). Isaiah presents Christ as "he who shall judge among the nations and rebuke many people." In this sense, John continues his *Revelation* by presenting the kingdom of God on earth metaphorically, in comparison with the "Breastplate of Judgment" worn by the High Priest as described in Exodus, and represented in the following verses:

21:11 Having the glory of God: and her light was like unto a stone most precious, even like a jasper stone, clear as crystal;

In the commentary of Revelation 4:3, it is explained that Christ is presented as *"like a jasper stone,"* which figuratively represents Benjamin, the last son of Israel, whose name literally means "Son of My Right Hand."

The things Christ teaches will be the *"light"* by which all will see, and use to guide their lives and actions. His instruction truly will be *"clear as crystal,"* and give an eternal perspective as explained as the *"sea of glass mingled with fire"* (see commentary on Revelation 15:2).

> *For God, who commanded the light to shine out of darkness, hath shined in our hearts, **to give the light of the knowledge of the glory of God** in the face of Jesus Christ.* (II Corinthians 4:6)

21:12 And had a wall great and high, and had twelve gates, and at the gates twelve **cherubim by which all must pass whose** names **are** written thereon, which are the names of the twelve tribes of the children of Israel:

> *And the stones shall be with the names of the children of Israel, twelve, according to their names, like the engravings of a signet; every one with his name shall they be according to the twelve tribes.* (Exodus 28:21)

The walls of this city are *"great and high,"* so that none can enter therein except they enter through one of the *"gates."* Our works (*"names"*) will determine whether or not we will be allowed to pass by the "*twelve cherubim*" and enter through one of the "*twelve gates.*"

The equality of the judgment of Christ is expressed in "*thirds*" as explained previously in the commentary of Revelation 8:7: *Many of the Old Testament prophets used the term "third" to exemplify three distinct expressions of the whole of humankind from which corruption usually occurs: there are those who serve, those who do not, and those who are served. The symbolic use of "thirds" expresses that all people, no matter in which "third" they are found, will be judged and treated equally according to the Royal Law of Christ.*

Using this allegory of "*thirds,*" John divides the gates appropriately:

21:13 On the east three gates; on the north three gates; on the south three gates; and on the west three gates.

No matter from which direction of the earth the city is approached, one must enter therein through one of "*twelve gates.*" Humans derive their happiness either by serving others, being served by others, or serving oneself, all perfectly acceptable desires of happiness as long as the *Royal Law* is obeyed.

And they shall come from the east, and from the west, and from the north, and from the south, and shall sit down in the kingdom of God. (Luke 13:29)

21:14 And the wall of the city had twelve foundations, and in them the names of the twelve apostles of the Lamb.

Throughout his *Revelation,* John expresses the "*twelve tribes of Israel*" as a symbolic representation of all people "*in every nation.*" Specifically referring to the Jews who constitute the tribes of Israel, the twelve apostles were those who were chosen by Jesus to preach the gospel to them. The "*foundations*" of truth and righteousness were established for *the children of the twelve tribes of Israel* by those so anointed by Christ ("*the twelve apostles of the Lamb*").

Then Peter opened his mouth, and said, Of a truth I per-
ceive that God is no respecter of persons: But in every
nation he that feareth him, and worketh righteousness,
is accepted with him. ***The word which God sent unto***
the children of Israel, preaching peace by Jesus
Christ*: he is Lord of all: That word, I say, ye know,*
which was published throughout all Judaea, and began
from Galilee, after the baptism which John preached.
(Acts 10:34–37)

21:15 And he that talked with me had a golden reed to measure the city,
and the gates thereof, and the wall thereof.

The angel (*"he that talked with me"*) who withheld the intervention
of God (*"vials of the wrath of God"*) from the earth, possesses the knowledge of the proper way in which the kingdom of God should be established
upon the earth (*"golden reed"*). John mentions in Revelation 11:1 that he
was *"given a reed"* to establish the kingdom of God among those who
would listen, thus intervening into the lives of those who seek God and
keep His commandments (see commentary Revelation 11:1–2).
The judgements we make in how we treat each other simply determines whether or not we belong to the kingdom of God. When God intervenes in our lives, we each receive a *"golden reed"* by which to measure our
actions. The measure of these judgments (*"golden reed"*) is expressed
properly in the colloquialism: *Obey the Golden Rule.* These are things we
feel in our hearts which are located in our *breasts.*

John utilizes these sentiments by presenting the true meaning of
the kingdom of God upon earth as the "Breastplate of Judgment," which he
presents in metaphorical prose in the next few verses:

21:16 And the city lieth foursquare, and the length is as large as the
breadth: and he measured the city with the reed, twelve thousand furlongs.
The length and the breadth and the height of it are equal.

*And thou shalt make **the breastplate of judgment** with cunning work; after the work of the ephod thou shalt make it; **of gold,** of blue, and of purple, and of scarlet, and of fine twined linen, shalt thou make it. **Foursquare it shall be being doubled; a span shall be the length thereof, and a span shall be the breadth thereof.*** (Exodus 28:15–16)

21:17 And he measured the wall thereof, an hundred and forty and four **thousand** cubits, according to the measure of a **man's arm** that is, **and not of the golden reed** of the angel.

John again alludes to the 144,000 being the righteous "elect," who over the 6000 years preceding the Millennium, listened to the words of the prophets ("*four and twenty servants*") of God (see commentary on Revelation 7:4). A "*man's*" works are done with his "*arms.*" John writes that the kingdom of God is established ("*measured*") by a man following the counsel of the holy prophets, and performing his works ("*man's arm*") accordingly.

21:18 And the building of the wall of it was **done** of jasper **and emerald**: and the city was **overlaid with** pure gold, **the streets** like unto clear glass.

John uses "*jasper*" because the "*builder of the wall*" is as Benjamin (*Son of My Right Hand*), the twelfth stone, and "*emerald*" because he is from the loins of Judah, the forth stone placed in the "Breastplate of Judgment." Christ set the walls and measured them by his "*word.*" If the people cannot keep his commandments, they will not be able to climb over the "*great and high wall.*"

According to the Law of Moses, the Ark of the Covenant was to be "*overlaid with pure gold.*" This Ark contained the "*word of God,*" which were the instructions given to Moses to guide the children of Israel.

And thou shalt overlay it with pure gold, within and without shalt thou overlay it, and shalt make upon it a crown of gold round about. (Exodus 25:11)

The stones of the "Breastplate of Judgment" are also encased in gold:

"they shall be set in gold in their inclosings.[sic]"
(Exodus 28:20)

Anyone who walks according to the *"Word of God"* will see things clearly (*"like unto clear glass"*), and always maintain an eternal perspective of all things as they walk along *"the streets of the city,"* which all lead to eternal happiness (see also commentary on Revelation 15:1–5).

21:19 And the foundations of the wall of the city were garnished with all manner of precious stones. The first **to garnish the foundations** was jasper; the second, **onyx**; the third, a **beryl**; the fourth, an **amethyst**;

21:20 The fifth, **agate**; the sixth, **ligure**; the seventh, **diamond**; the eighth, **sapphire**; the ninth, **an emerald**; the tenth, a **carbuncle**; the eleventh, a **topaz**; the twelfth, a **sardius**.

The uninspired collaborators and editors of the *New Testament* canon started to describe *"the foundations of the city"* as John intended, with *the last* stone (*"jasper,"* which was placed last on the "Breastplate of Judgment") being *the first one* placed to *"garnish the foundations of the wall of the city."*

To create the impression of equality for all people no matter of what nation, John intended to indicate what he learned from Jesus when it was said:

*But many that are **first shall be last**; and the **last shall be first**.* (Matthew 19:30)

*And they shall come from the east, and from the west, and from the north, and from the south, and shall sit down in the kingdom of God. And, behold, there are **last which shall be first, and there are first which shall be last**.* (Luke 13:29–30)

Though John uses the term *"the children of Israel"* to represent all the peoples of the world, in latter times the Gentiles accepted *"The Word"* before the Jews did. They were *first* to" *garnish the walls"* with their works.

21:21 And the twelve gates were *as* twelve pearls, *each of the gates* was of one pearl: and the street of the city was pure gold, as it were transparent glass.

There is only *"one pearl"* to which John was referencing in his intent of this verse, only *one* **Word**, *one* baptism, *one* religion, *one* way: the gospel of Jesus Christ. Only his teachings lead into (*"gates"*) the city of happiness—the kingdom of heaven.

> *Again, the kingdom of heaven is like unto a merchant man, seeking goodly pearls: Who, when he had found one pearl of great price, went and sold all that he had, and bought it.* (Matthew 13:45–46)

> *For all the law is fulfilled in one word, even in this; Thou shalt love thy neighbour as thyself.* (Galatians 5:14)

21:22 And I saw no temple therein: for the Lord God Almighty and the Lamb are the temple of it.

The Jewish temple was their most sacred sanctuary. Held up above other beliefs as a trophy, the Jews claimed that only therein could one receive the ordinances of salvation. Christ was hated and rejected for his blasphemy against the Jews and their traditions, including the sacredness of their temple:

> *But I say unto you, That in this place is one greater than the temple.* (Matthew 12:6)

No ordinances or rituals are needed to be happy (reach salvation). *"The Word"* is all one needs to experience happiness around others of like natures, who are seeking this emotional balance. (See also commentary on Revelation 11:2.)

21:23 And *there was found no darkness in* the city *and it* had no need of the moon to shine in it *and reflect the light* of the sun; for the glory of God did lighten it, and the Lamb is the light thereof.

The commentary on Revelation 6:12 states:

> *The prophets are those who teach and preach to the people who live in darkness, reflecting the light they receive from God to the people who are in need of harsh reminding to return to the commandments of God. The moon has no light of its own, but reflects the light of the sun that shown yesterday and the sun that will shine tomorrow, giving this light to a darkened world. The prophets of God are metaphorically presented as the moon.*

No longer will prophets be needed, because all will know and see what prophets know.

21:24 And the nations of them which are saved shall walk in the light of it: and *no longer shall* the kings of the earth bring their glory and honour into it.

21:25 *But* they *which are saved* shall bring the glory and honour of *all* nations into it.

Worldly glories, honors, degrees, certificates, awards, winnings, accomplishments, or anything else that puts one above another (*"glory and honor of the kings of the earth"*), will no longer be of any value or importance. *"The glory and honor"* experienced will be in the righteous works and happiness of the inhabitants of the city, who esteem all flesh equally, no matter which gate one has entered in: to serve, be served, or serve oneself. Finally, the world will see that God is no respecter of persons.

21:26 And the gates of it shall not be shut at all by day *and* there shall be no night there.

The eternal truths of God will be available anytime forever for all to know and utilize for their individual happiness.

21:27 And there shall in no wise enter into it any thing that defileth, neither whatsoever worketh abomination, or maketh a lie: but *only* they *whose names* are written in the Lamb's Book of Life.

The formula for happiness is as eternal as the elements. The "*Book of Life*" is symbolic of the ingredients for this formula. The ingredients are the way we treat and associate with each other (our works/"*names*"). Those who serve us (God and His angels) will provide all things we need in order to live and be happy. Our only responsibility is to do unto others what we would have them do unto us. Those who cannot abide this *Royal Law* "*shall in no wise enter into the New Jerusalem,*" the city of happiness.

Thank God!

EPILOGUE:

John's *Revelation* ends with a personal testimony from Christ—witnessing of himself, and the purpose of his work and the work of his servants, the prophets. To disrupt its flow with commentary would take away from its climatic nature, and subject the reader to an intellectual mentality that was not intended by John the Beloved. Correctly translated and written in its original prose, John's epilogue culminates and coalesces his intended message with divine efficacy.

The purpose of mortal existence has been made clear. Though the mysteries of life seem as numberless as the sands upon the seashore, when the fire of knowledge heats our conscious souls, these sands are turned to glass, through which we no longer see ourselves alone in a mirror. Our vision extends beyond our self into the reality of how we react to and with each other.

We thirst incessantly for happiness, only to find that our thirst cannot be quenched in selfishness by following the natural course of mortal lust, but is solely dependent on how we treat others, and how they treat us in our mutual associations. If we fail to recognize this true source of lasting happiness, we become plagued with misery from the sores that seep with hatred, intolerance, anger, and depression. To assuage these unquenchable pains and sorrows, we dig deeper into the earth, seeking isolation and personal fulfillment, only to find the pit which we have dug for ourselves is bottomless and full of darkness and despair.

Our natures become a furnace of selfish pursuits—caused by our fear of others and lack of concern for anyone outside ourselves. From the smoke that rises comes more torments and sorrows. The heat brings more thirst, more longing, more isolation; and when we desire a drink to quench this thirst, a sponge of vinegar is given of others who fear us as much as we fear them.

There is only one cup of water that will ever fulfill our thirst, and which can only be drawn from one river. It is water that flows throughout all the earth—nourishing and providing sustenance for the tree of life whose fruits are delicious to the taste, and whose leaves can heal the curse of humanity. We cannot change this water, nor can we add to it; for anything but the purity of its refreshing coolness will augment our plagues and increase our sores.

For thousands of years, we have tried to cultivate and nourish the tree of life by depending on our own cup of water; but we have failed to find the elusive Holy Grail from which flows a river of happiness. Only *One* holds this cup in his hand; not to be worshipped for his offering, but allowed the ability to drink from it with us. Without partaking of the life-giving refreshment that is in the cup he is holding, we will forever be athirst.

Many earths have come and gone; many solar systems have been created and organized to offer the tree of life and its fruit. Many more will come. But to us, there is only one. In it we can find the gift of life we were promised by the covenant of our Creator. He prepared the way. He has shown us this way, and has illuminated our path all along. His words are embedded in our souls, and have proven time and time again to be the only way to eternal life:

> *I have created you in my image, therefore ye are my children whom I love. And even as I have eternal joy, I have created you that ye might also have this joy. And for no*

other purpose have I created you except that ye might have joy. **Behold, ye shall have joy as ye associate one with another according to the free will that I have given to each of you, even according to my image in which ye were created.** *And this joy ye shall receive when ye have become perfected in me and have received a body of flesh and bone as ye see that I have. For this is my work and my glory: to bring to pass your eternal lives that ye might forever experience this joy as I experience it.*

These are His words. There is no other word. It has always been the same word, and will continue to be written in the Book of Life forever:

To experience everlasting joy we must do unto others what we would have them do unto us in all things. Upon this foundation rests the purpose of creation and the eternal state of happiness.

There is no other way—worlds without end.

Chapter

REVELATION
UNFOLDED

22:1 *And the Son of man appeared before me* and he shewed me a pure river of *the* water of life, clear as crystal, proceeding out of the *kingdom* of God and of the Lamb.

22:2 In the midst of the street of it, and on either side of the river, was there the tree of life, which bare twelve manner of fruits, and yielded her fruit every month *according to its seasons*; and the leaves of the tree were for the healing of the nations.

22:3 And there shall be no more curse *because of that which was hidden*, but the throne of God and of the Lamb shall be in it *where God shall reign in truth and righteous*; and his servants shall serve *Him, who have overcome the world*.

22:4 And they shall see *His* face *and know Him*; and *His* name shall be in their foreheads, *because their works have been His works*.

22:5 And there shall be no night there; and they need no candle, neither **the** light of the *moon*; for the sun, *who is the* Lord God giveth them light *according to their works*; and they shall reign *in His kingdom* for ever and ever.

22:6 And he said unto me, These sayings are faithful and true *and have been hidden from the foundation of the world because of the wickedness of men*; *but* the Lord God *who called* the holy prophets *and who* sent *His angels* to shew unto *His* servants *all* things which must shortly *come to pass, hath commanded His prophets to write these things and seal them up until the last days before I come again into the world*.

22:7 Behold, *I am Jesus Christ, the Son of God, and* I come quickly. *Therefore*, blessed is he that keepeth the sayings of the *prophets who have sealed up the* prophecy of this book.

22:8 And I John saw these things, and heard them. And when I had heard and seen, I fell down to worship before the feet of *him who* shewed me these things.

22:9 Then saith he unto me, See thou do it not, *but worship God who hath sent me*; for I am thy fellowservant, and of thy brethren the prophets, and of them which keep the sayings of this book; *and this book doth not teach a man to fall down and worship another, but it teacheth a man to* worship God *and keep His commandments in all things; and these are those things which have been sealed up to come forth unto the children of men*.

22:10 And he saith unto me, *Therefore*, seal not the sayings of the prophecy of this book *any longer*, for the time is at hand *when it shall come to pass that kings shall shut their mouths; for that which had not been told them shall they see; and that which they had not heard shall they consider. And these things shall be preached upon the housetops to all the people. And there shall be no more excuse for the wickedness of a man*.

22:11 And he that is unjust, let him be unjust still *in that which he believeth*; and he which is filthy, let him be filthy still *in those works which he doeth*; and he that is righteous, let him be righteous still *in the works that he hath chosen for himself to do*; and he that is holy, let him be holy still *and stand in a holy place and wait for me to come*.

22:12 And, behold, I come quickly; and my reward is with me, to give every man according as his work shall be.

22:13 I am Alpha and Omega, the beginning and the end, the first and the last *and have revealed all things unto my servants, the prophets, that they might preach repentance and teach men the commandments of God*.

22:14 Blessed are they that do His commandments, that they may have right to the tree of life, and may enter in through the gates into the *holy* city, *which is the kingdom of God*.

22:15 For without are *those men who are like* dogs *who ceaselessly bark unto others of their own*, and sorcerers *who deceive others and set themselves up as a source of light,* and whoremongers, *who are led by the lusts of their hearts*, and *also the* murderers, and idolaters, and whosoever loveth and maketh a lie.

22:16 I Jesus have *been* sent *by God to send forth* mine *servants to* testify *of* these things in the churches *that have been set up among men. And this have I commanded them to testify unto the people, that* I am the root and the offspring of David, and the bright and morning star.

22:17 *I am he who hath sent forth the word of God by my own mouth and by the power of* the Spirit, and *who hath come to prepare* the bride *for the wedding; and who saith*, Come *unto me*. And *to* him that heareth *I* say, Come *and partake of the living waters, which are the words that I have spoken and given unto the world*. And let him that is athirst come. And whosoever will, let him *come also and* take the water of life freely *so that he shall never thirst*.

22:18 For I testify unto every man that heareth the words of *life given in the words of* prophecy of this book, If any man shall add unto these things, God shall add unto him the plagues that are written in this book, *for in these things which are written ye shall know of that which must surely come to pass upon the earth*.

22:19 And if any man shall take away from the words of *life given in* the book of this prophecy, God shall take away his part out of the Book of Life, and *he shall be kept* out of the holy city, and from the *holy* things which are written in this book.

22:20 He which *hath testified of* these things, saith, Surely I come quickly. Amen. Even so, come, Lord Jesus.

22:21 The grace of our Lord Jesus Christ be with you all. Amen

Tasharrafna Ismi J.

APPENDIX

THE APOCALYPSE OF JOHN THE BELOVED

The Revelation of John, a servant of God, which was given unto him of Jesus Christ; to show unto those who believe on his name things which must shortly come to pass. And God sent and signified it by His Son unto John, who bore record of the word of God, and who bareth testimony of Jesus Christ, who gave unto him the word. And John, a witness in the flesh of Christ, testifeth of all things that he saw.

Blessed are they who read and understand the words of this prophecy, and keep the commandments of God, for these shall understand those things which are written therein. For the time of the coming of the Lord draweth nigh.

Now this is the testimony of John to the servants of the seven churches which are in Asia; or in other words, all the servants of God upon the earth: Grace be unto you, and peace, from him who is, and who was, and who is to come. And who hath been sent forth from before the throne of God to testify unto those who are the servants of the seven churches which are in the world.

Therefore, I John, a faithful witness, bear record of the things which were delivered me of the angel of God, who is Jesus Christ, the first begotten of the Father in the flesh; and he who was risen first from the dead and who shall overcome Lucifer, the prince of the kings of the earth. And unto him who loved us, giving us of the glory of the Father by providing the way whereby we might be washed from our sins, because of his own blood; which was shed as an example to us that we might have his spirit to be with us always. And who hath power to make us kings and priests unto God, his Father; and to the Father be glory and dominion for ever and ever. Amen.

Behold, he cometh in the clouds with tens of thousands of his saints from the kingdom of God, clothed with the glory of his Father. And every eye shall see him, and they also who pierced him and rejected the word that he gave unto them by his own mouth, and by the mouths of his seven servants, which he hath sent unto the seven churches. And all kindreds of the earth who worship the prince of the kings of the earth shall wail because of him. Even so, Amen.

For he saith, "I am Alpha and Omega, the beginning and the ending."

And thus saith the Lord, who is, and who was, and who is to come, the Anointed One of the Almighty, called by Him to save the world.

I John, who also am your brother and companion in tribulation, and who also belongeth to the church of the Lamb of God (which is the kingdom and patience of Jesus Christ), was in the isle that is called Patmos; having been exiled from the world for the word of God which I have given to the world, and also for the testimony which I have given of Jesus Christ, he who gave the word unto me.

I was in the Spirit pondering upon the word of the Lord, and heard behind me a great voice, as of a trumpet, saying, "I am Alpha and Omega, the first and the last, the beginning and the ending, the Lord who is, and who was, and who is to come, the Almighty. Greetings, my friend. Unto thee shall be given that which none other of thy brethren hath known, even those things which shall come to pass before I come again upon the earth to take the throne which my Father hath given me. And what thou seest, write in a book as the Spirit shall command thee; writing that which hath been sealed, so that it shall remain sealed unto all those who are not called by my name.

"Behold, thou shalt send it unto the seven churches which are in Asia: unto Ephesus, and unto Smyrna, and unto Pergamos, and unto

Thyatira, and unto Sardis, and unto Philadelphia, and unto Laodicea. For behold, these are the churches of men who have strayed from my ordinances and broken mine everlasting covenant. Therefore, they shall not have these things given unto them in plainness, that they might be tried in their faith concerning me."

And as I turned again to see the voice that spake with me, I beheld a vision. And in the vision, I saw seven golden candlesticks. And in the midst of the seven candlesticks, was the Son of man, of whom I bore record of to the world, being one of his eyewitnesses in the flesh. And he was clothed with a garment down to the foot, and girt about the paps with a golden girdle. His head and his hairs were white like wool, as white as snow. And his eyes were as a flame of fire, for any who looked upon them in unrighteousness would burn from within. And his arms and his feet like unto fine brass, as if they were burned in a furnace, and his voice as the sound of many waters. And he had in his right hand seven stars, which he kept always before him. And out of his mouth went a sharp two-edged sword that slew all those who came forth, except those who he held in his right hand. And his countenance was as the sun which shineth in its strength.

And when I saw him, I fell at his feet as if I were dead. And I dared not look upon him, knowing the wickedness of my ways. And he laid his right hand upon me, saying unto me, "Fear not. I am the first and the last. I am he that liveth, and was dead; and behold, I am alive for evermore, Amen. And have the keys of hell and of death, which is the sword that thou sawest proceeding forth from my mouth. And thy sins are forgiven thee. Write the things which thou hast seen, and also the things which thou shalt see, which are the things which are, and the things which shall be hereafter, even that which shall befall thy people of the latter days.

Behold, the mystery of the seven stars which thou sawest in my right hand, and the seven golden candlesticks: The seven stars are the servants of God of the seven churches, which are the righteous of the world. And the seven candlesticks which thou sawest are the seven nations of the world wherein the servants shall dwell and shine and give their light unto the world.

"Unto the servant of the church of Ephesus write: These things saith he that holdeth the seven stars in his right hand, who walketh in the midst of the seven golden candlesticks, 'I know thy works, and thy labour, and thy patience, and how thou canst not bear them which are evil; and how thou hatest them who belong to the church of the devil. And thou hast tried them which say they are apostles of the Lamb, and are not, and hast found them liars because of their works, which are evil. And thou hast borne, and hast patience; and for my name's sake hast laboured, and hast not fainted.'

"Nevertheless, I have somewhat against those whom thou servest; because they have left their first love because of the anger they have for their enemies, who are not of thee. Preach repentance unto them, saying: 'Remember therefore from whence thou art fallen. And repent, and do the first works which were given thee by thy first love; or else I will come unto thee quickly, and will remove my servants out of their place. And I will remove the light from upon thy candlestick, except thou repent. But this thou hast in thy favor: the hate that thou hast is for the deeds of the Nicolaitians, which I also hate. For they take that which is good and make it evil; and that which is evil, they make good.'

"He that hath an ear, let him hear what the Spirit saith unto the churches: 'To him that overcometh the works of this world will I give to eat of the tree of life, which is in the midst of the paradise of God. And the paradise of God is the eternal happiness of His kingdom.'

"And unto the servant of the church in Smyrna write: These things saith he who teacheth his will to the first and the last, even he who was dead, and is now alive, "I know thy works and tribulation and poverty. But thou art rich as to the things of God, and I know the blasphemy of them which say they are Jews, and are not, but are of the church of the devil whose desires are the appetites of the flesh.

"'Fear none of those things which thou shalt suffer in the flesh. Behold, the servants of the devil shall cast some of you into prison, that ye may be tried and tested in your faith. And ye shall have tribulation. But be ye steadfast, as they who restrain from eating the food and wine of the king for ten days. And ye shall become strong in the Spirit, as they did who received the crown of life. And if thou art faithful unto death, I will give thee also a crown of life.'

"He that hath an ear, let him hear what the Spirit saith unto the churches: 'He that overcometh the things of this world shall not be hurt of the second death, which shall come upon all those who eat the food of the kings of this world.'

"And to the servant of the church in Pergamos write: These things saith he who hath the sharp sword with two edges that proceedeth forth from his mouth, and cuts asunder those who deny him and do not the works of God, 'I know thy works, and where thy heart dwellest. Even when thou dwellest where Satan's seat is, thou hearest me, and thou holdest fast my name; and hast not denied me in thy faith, even as in those days wherein Antipas was my faithful martyr (who was slain among you), where Satan dwelleth and exerciseth his power. Yea, even then, thou didst not betray me.

"'But I have a few things against thee, because thou hast there, them that hold the doctrine of Balaam, and envy those things he offered unto Balac; to cast a stumblingblock before the children of Israel, commanding them to eat things sacrificed unto idols, and to commit fornication with unbelievers. So hast thou also them that hold the doctrine of the Nicolaitians, which thing I hate. For thou knowest that I esteem all flesh the same; and no man is above another, for I am no respecter of persons. Repent, or else I will come unto thee quickly, and will fight against them that are of the Nicolaitians with the sword of my mouth.'

"He that hath an ear, let him hear what the Spirit saith unto the churches: 'To him that overcometh the flesh of this world, will I give to eat of the hidden manna, which is that which shall save them. Not as it did their fathers in the wilderness, for they are dead; but unto him who receiveth this manna, I shall give eternal life. And I will give him a white stone, which shall be a light unto perfection to those who receive it. And in the stone a new name shall be written, which no man knoweth saving he that receiveth it.'

"And unto the servant of the church in Thyatira write: These things saith the Son of God, who hath eyes like unto a flame of fire, and his feet are like fine brass, 'I know thy works. Yea, I know that they are full of charity and service and faith. And thy patience I have seen, and thy works I have also seen; and the last to be more than the first, and this because thy works are many. Notwithstanding, I have a few things against thee, because thou sufferest that woman dressed in scarlet, even the whore of all the earth, (who is as Jezebel who killed the prophets), who called herself a prophetess so that she could teach and seduce my servants to commit fornication with her, and to eat things sacrificed unto the idols who are her gods.

"'And I shall give her and those who sleep in her bed space to repent of their fornication. And if they do not repent, behold, those who are in her bed, and them who commit adultery with her, I will cast into great tribulation, except they repent of their deeds. And I will kill her children with death; yea, they shall be cut asunder by the sword of my mouth. And all the churches shall know that I am he who searcheth the reins and desires of the heart. And I will give unto every one of you according to your works and the desires of your hearts.

"'But unto those of you who are righteous, I say (and also unto the rest in Thyatira, even as many as have not followed this doctrine and committed fornication with this woman dressed in scarlet; and which have not known the depths of the ways of Satan, even as she speaks as if his ways are good to seduce you, but they are not), Behold, I will put upon you none other burden except that which I have already commanded you. But that which ye have already from me, hold fast till I come.'

"And to him that overcometh, and keepeth my commandments unto the end, to him will I give the power to live in my kingdoms. And I shall rule over them with the word of God; and they shall be in my hands as the vessels of clay in the hands of a potter. And he shall receive this power by faith, given with equity and justice even as I received of my Father and do His will. But those who do not overcome, their vessels shall be broken to shivers. And I will give those who have overcome all that I have, even all that the Father hath given me, the bright and morning star. He that hath an ear let him hear what the Spirit saith unto the churches.

"And unto the servant of the church in Sardis write: These things saith he who hath the seven stars, which are the seven servants of God, 'I know thy works, that thou hast declared a name by which thou livest that can give thee eternal life; but thou art dead. Be watchful therefore, and strengthen those who remain with thee, who are ready to die because they know not the name by which they are called, and whose works I have not found perfect before God. Remember therefore, how thou hast received and heard the name thou hast been given, and hold fast to the rod of truth I have given you; and repent of thy slothful ways. Watch and prepare for my coming. But if therefore thou shalt not watch, I will come on thee as a thief; for thou shalt not know what hour I will come upon thee.'

"'Thou hast a few who remember their names, even in Sardis, who have not defiled their garments. And they shall walk with me in white raiment, for they are worthy and are called by my name. He that overcometh the world, the same shall be clothed in white raiment. And I will not blot out his name out of the Book of Life, but I will confess his name before my Father, and before his angels. He that hath an ear, let him hear what the Spirit saith unto the churches.'

"And to the angel of the church in Philadelphia write: These things saith he that is holy, he that speaketh truth, he that hath the key of the house of David, which openeth, and no man shutteth; and shutteth, and no man openeth, 'I know thy works. Behold, I have set before thee an open door, which I have unlocked with the key; and no man can shut it. I have unlocked it and opened it up for thee; for thou hast a little strength, but hast kept my word, and hast not denied my name. Nevertheless, there are those among you who envy the key which I have given unto thee, and they pretend to be with thee, but they are not.

"'Behold, I will make them of the synagogue of Satan, which say they are of the house of Israel, but are not, but do lie. Behold, I will not give them the key, but I shall give unto thee a crown, and make them to come and worship before thy feet, and to know that I have loved thee. Because thou hast kept my word with patience, I also will keep thee from the hour of temptation (which shall come upon all the world), to try them that dwell upon the earth. For Satan shall be loosed and a key given unto those who follow him, that they may unlock the chains by which he has been bound.

"'Behold, I come quickly. Hold that fast which thou hast been given of me, that no man take thy crown. For him that overcometh, will I make a pillar in the temple of my God; and he shall dwell in this sanctuary and go no more out. And I will write upon him the name of my God, and he shall dwell in the city of my God, which is the new Jerusalem, which cometh down out of heaven from my God. And I will write upon him the new name, which no man shall know saving he that receiveth it. He that hath an ear, let him hear what the Spirit saith unto the churches.'

"And unto the angel of the church of the Laodiceans write: These things saith he who hath the final word, who is the faithful and true witness of this word, which word was in the beginning of the creation of God, 'I know thy works, and from thy cup I cannot drink because thou offerest a drink unto me that is neither cold nor hot. I would that thou would bring forth a drink offering of cold or hot. So then because thou offerest that which is lukewarm, and neither cold nor hot, I will spue it out of my mouth. For thou sayest, because of the blessings of the Lord I am rich with gold and fine raiment, and increased with goods, and have need of nothing; but thou knowest not that thou art wretched, and miserable because thou art poor, and blind, and naked. I counsel thee to buy of me that gold which is tried in the fire, that thou mayest be rich. And purchase of me without price white raiment, that thou mayest be clothed so that the shame of thy nakedness does not appear. And anoint thine eyes with my eyesalve, that thou mayest see.'"

And behold, thus saith the Lord unto all the churches, "As many as I love, I rebuke and chasten. Be zealous therefore, and repent. Behold, I stand at the door, and knock. If any man upon hearing my voice shall open the door, I will come in to him, and will sup with him, and he with me. To him that overcometh the sins of this world, will I grant to sit with me in my kingdom; even so it shall be as I also overcame, and am set down with my Father in His kingdom. He that hath an ear, let him hear what the Spirit saith unto the churches."

After this, I looked; and still in the vision, I beheld. And it appeared as if a door was opened in heaven. And I heard again the first voice (which was as it were of a trumpet talking with me) which said, "Come up hither, and I will show thee things which must be hereafter."

And immediately, I was taken in the spirit and beheld a throne set high in heaven. And one sat on the throne. And I looked and saw near unto the throne, another who sat; and was to look upon like a sardine and jasper stone, and also like unto an emerald. And I saw as it were the appearance of fire, and it shown in brightness as a rainbow round about the throne. And in the midst of the throne were four and twenty seats. And upon the seats, I saw four and twenty elders sitting, clothed in white raiment. And they had on their heads crowns of gold. And out of the throne proceeded four beasts. And lightnings and thunderings and voices came out of seven lamps of fire burning before the throne in the midst of the four beasts, which each gives its light to the seven servants of God.

And before the throne there appeared a sea like unto a looking glass of crystal; and it was in the midst of the throne where the four and twenty elders sat. And round about the throne were the four beasts full of eyes before and behind. And each beast had the likeness of four faces: the first was like a lion and the second like a calf; and the third like a face as a man, and the fourth was like a flying eagle. And the four beasts had each of them four wings about him. And they were full of eyes within; and they rest not day and night, saying, "Holy, holy, holy, Lord God Almighty, which was, and is, and is to come."

And when those beasts give this glory and honour and thanks to Him that sat on the throne, who liveth for ever and ever, the four and twenty elders fall down before Him that sat on the throne, and worship Him that liveth for ever and ever, and cast their crowns before the throne, saying, "Thou art worthy, O Lord, to receive glory and honour and power. For thou hast created all things, and for thy pleasure they are and were created."

And I saw in the right hand of him who sat on the throne the Book of Life. And it was full of words written within and on the backside, and sealed with seven seals. And I saw the four beasts, who are the angels of God in their power, proclaiming with a loud voice as if it were a trumpet, "Who is worthy to open the book, and to loose the seals thereof?"

And no man in heaven above the earth, neither below the earth, was able to open the book, neither to look thereon. And I wept much, because no man was found worthy to open and to read the book, neither to look thereon. And one of the elders saith unto me, "Weep not. Behold, the Lion of the tribe of Juda, the Root of David, hath been prepared to open the book, and to loose the seven seals thereof."

And I beheld, and lo, in the midst of the throne and the four beasts, stood the elders and a Lamb as if it were to be slain; having twelve horns and twelve eyes, which are the twelve servants of God sent forth into all the earth. And he who was prepared, came and took the book out of the right hand of Him that sat upon the throne. And when he had taken the book, the four beasts rejoiced, and the four and twenty elders fell down before the Lamb, having every one of them harps, and golden vials full of the smoke of incense, which are the prayers of saints. And they sung a new song, saying, "Thou art worthy to take the book, and to open the seals thereof. For thou wast prepared as a lamb to be slain; to redeem us to God out of every kindred, and tongue, and people, and nation by thy sweat and blood. And thou hast the power to exalt us and make us kings and priests unto our God. And we shall inherit the kingdom God upon earth."

And I beheld, and I heard the voice of many spirits round about the throne where the beasts were and where the elders stood. And the number of them was ten thousand times ten thousand, and thousands of thousands; saying with a loud voice, "Worthy is the Lamb that is to be slain to receive this power from God, to give unto us the riches of life in wisdom, and strength. And we will for ever give him honour and glory for this blessing."

And every creature which is above the earth, and on the earth, and under the earth, and such as are in the sea, and all that are with them, heard I saying, "Honour and glory be unto Him who hath blessed us, and who in power sitteth upon the throne, and hath given unto us the Lamb, glory to Him for ever and ever."

And the four beasts said, "Amen." And the four and twenty elders with the golden vials fell down and worshipped him that liveth for ever and ever. And when the Lamb opened one of the seals, I saw and heard as it were, the noise of thunder, and one of the four beasts saying, "Come and see."

And I saw, and beheld a white horse upon the earth: and he that sat on him had a crown given unto him, and around and about the crown appeared a rainbow; and he went forth conquering, and to be conquered. And when he had opened the second seal, I heard the second beast say, "Come and see."

And there went out upon the earth another horse that was red. And a crown of power was given to him that sat thereon to take peace from the earth; and there was given unto him a great sword, because it was allowed that they should kill one another. And when he had opened the third seal, I heard the third beast say, "Come and see."

And I beheld, and lo, a black horse went forth upon the earth. And he that sat on him had a pair of balances in his hand. And I heard a voice that came from the throne which was in the midst of the four beasts say, "Let them sell a measure of wheat for a penny, and three measures of barley for a penny; for thou seest that they hurt not the oil and the wine." And when he had opened the fourth seal, I heard the voice of the fourth beast say, "Come and see."

And I looked, and beheld a pale horse upon the earth. And his name that sat on him was Death; and Hell followed with him. And power was given unto them over the fourth part of the earth: to kill with sword, and with hunger, and with death, and with the beasts of the earth. And when he had opened the fifth seal, I saw the souls of them upon the earth who were slain upon the altar for the word of God, and for the testimony which they held.

And the four and twenty elders cried with a loud voice, saying, "How long, O Lord, holy and true, dost thou not judge them that dwell on the earth and avenge their blood, which has been spilt upon the altar?" And white robes were given unto every one of them who were sacrificed upon the altar. And it was said unto them that they should rest yet for a little season, until their fellowservants and their brethren, who would also be killed upon the altar as they were, should fulfill their works.

And I beheld when he had opened the sixth seal, and lo, there was a great earthquake, and the earth reeled to and fro like a drunkard. And the sun became black, clothed in a sackcloth made of hair, because the moon was turned into blood. And the stars of heaven fell unto the earth because of the great earthquake, even as a fig tree casteth her untimely figs, when she is shaken of a mighty wind.

And it came to pass that the heavens opened as a scroll is opened when it is rolled together; and every mountain and island was moved out of its place because of that which was written therein. And the kings of the earth, and the great men, and the rich men, and the chief captains, and the mighty men, yea even every man who bringeth bondage upon another who is not free, hid themselves in the dens and in the rocks of the mountains. And these said to the mountains and rocks, "Fall on us, and hide us from the face of him that sitteth on the throne, and from the wrath of the Lamb, whose countenance we cannot bear. For the great day of his wrath is come, and who among us shall be able to stand?"

And after these things, I saw four angels ascending from the east standing on the four corners of the earth, holding the four winds of the earth; that the wind should not blow on the earth, nor on the sea, nor on any tree. And I saw another angel ascending from the east, having the seal of the living God to give to those who overcome the world. And he cried with a loud voice to the other four angels, to whom it was given to hurt the earth and the sea by the winds which they held, saying, "Hurt not the earth, neither the sea, nor the trees, till we have sealed the servants of our God in their foreheads."

And I heard the number of them which were sealed in their foreheads with the name of the Father. And they were among all the nations of the earth, and there were sealed an hundred and forty and four thousand of all the scattered tribes of the children of Israel. Of the tribe of Juda were sealed twelve thousand. Of the tribe of Reuben were sealed twelve thousand. Of the tribe of Gad were sealed twelve thousand. Of the tribe of Aser were sealed twelve thousand. Of the tribe of Nephthalim were sealed twelve thousand. Of the tribe of Manasses were sealed twelve thousand. Of the tribe of Simeon were sealed twelve thousand. Of the tribe of Levi were sealed twelve thousand. Of the tribe of Issachar were sealed twelve thousand. Of the tribe of Zabulon were sealed twelve thousand. Of the tribe of Joseph were sealed twelve thousand. Of the tribe of Benjamin were sealed twelve thousand.

After this I beheld, and lo, this great multitude, which no man could number, of all nations and kindreds and people and tongues, stood before the throne and before the Lamb, clothed with white robes and palms in their hands, and cried with a loud voice, saying, "Salvation to our God who sitteth upon the throne, and unto the Lamb whom He hath given to us."

And this great multitude stood with the elders and the Lamb round about the throne, and about the four beasts, who were the angels of God. And they fell before the throne on their faces, and worshipped God, saying, "Glory and thanksgiving and honour we give unto our God for ever and ever, for his blessings and wisdom and power and might. Amen."

And one of the elders spake unto me, saying, "Who are these who are arrayed in white robes? And from whence did they come?"

And I said unto him, "Sir, thou knowest."

And he said to me, "These are they who came out of great tribulation, and have washed their own robes, and made them white in the blood of the Lamb. Therefore they are before the throne of God, and serve him day and night in his kingdom. And He that sitteth on the throne shall dwell with them. They shall hunger no more, neither thirst any more; neither shall they need the sun to give them light, nor any heat. And God shall wipe away all tears from their eyes. For the Lamb which is in their midst and before the throne shall feed them, and shall lead them unto living fountains of waters."

And before he had opened the seventh seal, there was silence in heaven about the space of half an hour. And during the silence, I saw seven angels who stood before God; and to them were given seven trumpets to sound. And another angel came from upon the earth and stood at the altar, having a golden censer filled with much incense; that he should offer it with the prayers of all saints upon the golden altar which was before the throne. And the smoke of the incense from the golden censer, which came with the prayers of the saints, ascended up before God out of the angel's hand. And he who sat upon the throne turned away because of the burnt incense before Him. And the angel took the censer, and filled it with fire from the altar, and cast it into the earth. And it was filled with voices, and thunderings, and lightnings, and these caused a great earthquake.

And when the censer was emptied upon the earth, the seven angels which had the seven trumpets prepared themselves to sound. The first angel sounded, and there followed hail, and fire mingled with the hail, which appeared as blood; and they were cast upon the earth. And the third part of trees was burnt up, and all green grass was burnt up.

And the second angel sounded; and as it were, a great mountain burning with fire was cast into the sea. And the third part of the sea became blood. And the third part of the creatures which were in the sea that and had life, died. And the third part of the ships were destroyed.

And the third angel sounded, and there had fallen a great star from heaven, burning as it were a lamp. And it fell upon the third part of the rivers, and upon the fountains of waters. And the name of the star is called Wormwood. And the third part of the waters from the rivers and the fountains became wormwood. And many men died of the waters, because they were made bitter.

And the fourth angel sounded, and the third part of the sun was smitten, and the third part of the moon, and the third part of the stars. And because a third part of them was darkened, the day shone not for a third part of it, and the night likewise received no light. And I beheld, and heard an angel flying through the midst of heaven, saying with a loud voice, "Woe, woe, woe, to the inhabiters of the earth by reason of the other voices of the trumpets of the three angels, which are yet to sound!"

And the fifth angel sounded, and I saw as it were, a star fall from heaven unto the earth. And to him was given great power, and the key to the bottomless pit, which was dug by those upon the earth. And when he had unlocked the bottomless pit and opened it, there arose a smoke out of the pit. And the sun and the air were darkened by reason of the smoke made by a great furnace in the pit. And there came out of the smoke locusts, and they went out upon the earth. And unto them was given power, and their power was in their tails, as the scorpions of the earth have power.

And it was commanded them that they should not hurt the grass of the earth, neither any green thing, neither any tree, but only those men which have not the seal of God in their foreheads. And to the locusts it was given that they should not kill them, but that they should be tormented five months until they are healed from their hurt. And their torment was as the torment from the tail of a scorpion when he striketh a man. And in those days shall men seek relief from their torment, and shall not find it. And because of the torment, they shall desire to die, but they shall find no relief, and death shall flee from them.

And the shapes of the locusts were like unto horses, and their riders were prepared unto battle. And on the heads of the riders were as it were crowns like gold, and their faces were as the faces of men. And they had long hair as the hair of women, and their teeth were as the teeth of young lions. And they had breastplates, as it were breastplates of iron. And the sound of their wings was as the sound of chariots of many horses running to battle. And they had tails like unto scorpions, and there were stings in their tails which hurt the men upon the earth. And their power was to hurt men five months.

And they had a king who ruled over them, which is the angel of the bottomless pit, whose name in the Hebrew tongue is *Abaddon*. But in the Greek tongue hath his name *Apollyon*. One woe is past. And behold, there come two woes more hereafter. And before the sixth angel sounded, I heard a voice come from between the four horns of the golden altar which is before God, saying to the sixth angel which had the trumpet, "Sound the warning that the four angels which are still bound in the bottomless pit which is near unto the great river Euphrates shall be loose."

And the key was given to the sixth angel to loose the four angels bound in the bottomless pit; which were prepared for an hour, and a day, and a month, and a year, for to slay the third part of men. And the number of the army of the horsemen were two hundred thousand thousand, and their end I could not see. But I heard the number of them. And thus, I saw the horses in the vision. And them that sat on them rode thereupon, having breastplates of fire and of jacinth and brimstone. And the heads of the horses were as the heads of lions; and out of their mouths issued fire and smoke and brimstone. By these three, was the third part of men killed: by the fire and by the smoke and by the brimstone, which issued out of their mouths. For their power is in their mouth, and in their tails. For their tails were like unto serpents, and each of their tails had heads, and with them they do hurt.

And the rest of the men which were not killed by these plagues still did not repent of the works of their hands; that they should not worship devils, and idols of gold and silver and brass and stone, and of wood; which neither can see, nor hear, nor walk. Neither did they repent of their murders, nor of their sorceries, nor of their fornication, nor of their thefts.

And I saw another mighty angel come down from heaven, clothed as it were with a cloud in the day of rain. And he appeared as if he were covered that all upon the earth could not see his face. And a rainbow shown from the crown which was upon his head, and his face was as it were the sun, and his feet as pillars of fire. And from his countenance came forth a great light upon the earth. And he had in his hand a little book open, which contained that which was sealed from the foundation of the earth. And he set his right foot upon the sea, and his left foot on the earth; even that his whole countenance did fill the earth, even that there was not a part thereof that was not filled with his light.

And he opened the seventh seal and cried with a loud voice, as when a lion roareth and maketh all afraid. And when he had cried, it was as if seven thunders uttered their voices. And when the seven thunders had uttered their voices, I was about to write that which they spoke. And I heard a voice from heaven saying unto me, "Seal up those things which the seven thunders uttered, and write them not, for these things shall not come forth unto the children of men until the end of times."

And the mighty angel which I saw stand upon the sea and upon the earth, lifted up his hand to heaven, and sware by Him that liveth for ever and ever (who created heaven, and the things that therein are, and the earth, and the things that therein are, and the sea, and the things which are therein), that there should be time no longer, for the time, times, and half of time have passed. And thus, I heard the voice of the seventh thunder speak. But in the days of the voice of the seventh trumpet, when it shall begin to sound, then shall the mystery of God be revealed, as he hath declared to his servants the prophets.

And the voice which I heard from heaven spake unto me again, and said, "Go and take the little book which was sealed with the seven seals and is now open in the hand of the angel which standeth upon the sea and upon the earth."

And I went unto the angel, and said unto him, "Give me the little book."

And he said unto me, "Take it, and eat it up. And it shall make thy belly bitter, but it shall be in thy mouth sweet as honey."

And I took the little book out of the angel's hand, and ate it up. And it was in my mouth sweet as honey, for that which I read brought much joy to my soul. But as soon as I had eaten it, my belly was bitter. And he said unto me, "Thou must prophesy again, before many peoples and nations and tongues and kings."

And the angel gave me a reed like unto a rod, and said unto me, "Rise, and measure the temple of God, and the altar, and them that worship therein. But the court which is without the temple, leave out, and measure it not; for it is given unto the Gentiles to measure. And when they measure it, they shall tread the holy city under foot forty and two months. And I have given power unto my two witnesses that they may prophesy. But during the thousand two hundred and threescore days, they shall prophesy clothed in sackcloth."

These witnesses are the two olive trees, and the two candlesticks standing before the altar of God upon the earth. And if any man will hurt them, fire proceedeth out of their mouth, and devoureth their enemies. And if any man will hurt them, he must in this manner be killed. These witnesses have power to shut heaven, that it rain not in the days of their prophecy. And they have power over the waters to turn them to blood; and to smite the earth with all plagues, as often as they will.

And when they shall give their testimony, the beast that ascendeth out of the bottomless pit shall make war against them, and shall overcome them, and kill them. And their dead bodies shall lie in the street of the great city, which spiritually is called Sodom and Egypt, where also our Lord was crucified. And they of the people and kindreds and tongues and nations of the earth shall see their dead bodies three days and an half, and shall not suffer their dead bodies to be put in graves. And they that dwell upon the earth shall rejoice over them, and make merry, and shall send gifts one to another, because these two prophets are dead which tormented them that dwelt on the earth.

And after three days and an half, the Spirit of life from God entered into them, and they stood upon their feet; and great fear fell upon them which saw them. And they which saw them heard a great voice from heaven saying unto the two witnesses, "Come up hither."

And they ascended up to heaven in a cloud; and their enemies beheld them. And the same hour was there a great earthquake, and the tenth part of the city fell in the earthquake. And there were saved of men seven thousand. And this remnant was affrighted, and gave glory to the God of heaven.

The second woe is past; and behold, the third woe cometh quickly. And when the seventh angel sounded, there were great voices in heaven, saying, "The kingdoms of this world are become the kingdoms of our God, and of his Christ; and he shall reign for ever and ever."

And the four and twenty elders, which sat before God on their seats, fell upon their faces, and worshipped God, saying, "We give thee thanks, O Lord God Almighty—which art, and wast, and art to come; because thou hast taken to thee thy great power, and hast sent thy Christ to reign upon the earth. And the nations were angry because thou hast come. And the time of the dead hast come, that they should be judged as the living. And that thou shouldest give reward unto thy servants the prophets, and to the saints, and them that reverence thy name, both small and great; and shouldest destroy the power of them who destroy the earth.

And the temple of God was opened in heaven, and there was seen in his temple, the ark of his testament. And there were lightnings and voices and thunderings, and an earthquake, and great hail.

And there appeared a great sign in heaven showing those things as they are upon the earth. And I saw a woman clothed in a robe as if it were the sun; and the moon under her feet, and upon her head there was a crown of twelve stars. And the woman was with child, and was crying and travailing in birth, being pained to be delivered. And there appeared before my eyes another sign given in heaven in likeness of things upon the earth.

And I beheld a great red dragon, which was the serpent which I saw that had power over the bottomless pit. And the serpent had seven heads and ten horns, and seven crowns upon his heads. And with his tail, he drew after him the third part of the stars, which were upon the crown worn by the woman. And the dragon took the crown from the woman and cast it to the earth. And the dragon stood before the woman, who was ready to be delivered, to devour her child after it was born.

And she brought forth a man child, who was to rule all nations with a rod of iron. And before the dragon could devour the child, it was caught up, and taken unto God, and to His throne. And the woman fled into the wilderness, where there was a place prepared by God for her. And I saw the four and twenty elders and the four beasts standing before the woman, and it was given them that they should feed her there a thousand two hundred and threescore days.

And there appeared another sign in heaven in the likeness of a war being waged both in heaven and upon the earth. And Michael and his angels fought against the dragon; and the dragon and his angels fought against Michael. And at the end of the battle, the dragon and his angels prevailed not against Michael or the child or the woman. And the place which had been given to the dragon and his angels was not found any more in heaven or on earth. And the great dragon was cast out, that old serpent, called Lucifer, the Devil, who is also called Satan, which deceiveth the whole world. He was cast out of heaven and also out of the earth, and his angels were cast out with him.

And I heard a loud voice saying in heaven, "Now is come salvation, and strength, and the kingdom of our God, and the power of his Christ to the earth. For the accuser of men is cast out, which caused them to accuse him before our God day and night. For they have gained victory, and overcome him by the blood of the Lamb, and by the word of their testimony which they have borne. For they loved not their own lives, but kept the testimony of the word even unto death. Rejoice, ye that dwell in the heavens and upon the earth!"

And after I had beheld these things, I heard another voice saying, "The time of rejoicing is not yet, because the devil still reigneth upon the earth. Therefore, woe to the inhabiters of the earth and they who dwell upon the islands of the sea! For the devil is come down unto you, having great wrath; because he knoweth he shall be conquered, and that he hath but a short time."

And when the dragon saw that he was to be overcome and cast out of the earth, he pursued the woman which brought forth the man child, to torment her. Therefore, the elders and the beasts which stood before the woman gave her two wings of a great eagle that she might fly into the wilderness, into a place prepared for her, where she is nourished for a time, and times, and half a time, safe from the face of the serpent. And the serpent cast out of his mouth water as a great river after the woman, that he might cause her to be carried away because of the flood. And the earth helped the woman, and the earth opened her mouth, and swallowed up the flood which the dragon cast out of his mouth. And because the earth helped the woman, the dragon was wroth with her, and went to make war with the remnant of her seed who were not drowned in the flood, and who keep the commandments of God, and have the testimony of Jesus Christ.

And I saw another sign in heaven in likeness of the kingdoms of the earth. And I saw a beast rise up out of the sea and stand upon the sand of the sea, having seven heads and ten horns; and upon his horns ten crowns, and upon his heads the name of blasphemy. And the beast which I saw was like unto a leopard, and his feet were as the feet of a bear, and his mouth as the mouth of a lion. And the dragon gave him his power, and his seat, and great authority.

And I saw one of his heads as if it were wounded even unto death; but his deadly wound was healed. And all the world wondered after the beast and bowed down before him. And they worshipped the dragon which gave power unto the beast. And they praised the beast, saying, "Who is like unto the beast? Who is able to make war with him?"

And there was given unto him a mouth speaking great things and blasphemies. And power was given unto him to continue forty and two months. And he opened his mouth in blasphemy against God, to blaspheme His name, and His tabernacle, and them that dwell in heaven. And it was given unto him to make war with the saints, and to overcome them. And power was given him over all kindreds and tongues and nations. And all that dwell upon the earth shall worship him, whose names are not written in the Book of Life of the Lamb slain from the foundation of the world. If any man have an ear, let him hear: He that leadeth into captivity shall go into captivity. He that killeth with the sword must be killed with the sword. Here is the patience and the faith of the saints.

And I beheld another beast coming up out of the earth. And he had two horns like a lamb, and he spake as a dragon. And he exerciseth all the power of the first beast before him, and causeth the earth and them which dwell therein to worship the first beast, whose deadly wound was healed. And he doeth great wonders, so that he maketh fire come down from heaven on the earth in the sight of the beast. And them that dwell on the earth are deceived by the means of those miracles which he had power to do in the sight of the beast; by saying to them that dwell on the earth that they should make an image to the beast, which had the wound by a sword, and did live.

And he had power to give life unto the image of the beast, that the image of the beast should both speak, and cause that as many as would not worship the image of the beast, should be killed. And he causeth all, both righteous and wicked, small and great, rich and poor, free and bond, to receive a mark in their right hand, or in their foreheads; and that no man might buy or sell, save he that had the mark, or the name of the beast, or the number of his name. Here is wisdom. Let him that hath understanding count the number of the beast: for it is the number of a man. And his number is Six hundred threescore and six.

And I looked, and lo, in the midst of this beast, I saw as it were a Lamb that stood on the mount Zion. And with him were those of the hundred forty and four thousand, having his Father's name written in their foreheads. And I heard a voice as if it came from heaven, even as the voice of many waters, and also the voice of a great thunder. And the sounds I heard were like unto the voice of harpers harping with their harps. And they sung as it were a new song to them; but before the throne, and before the four beasts, and the four and twenty elders, the song was not new. And no man could learn that song but those of the hundred and forty and four thousand, which were redeemed from the earth.

These are they which were not defiled with the woman who sits upon the beast. For they remain as virgins, committing no fornication with her. These are they which follow the Lamb whithersoever he goeth. These are the redeemed from among men, and are the firstfruits unto God and to the Lamb. And in their mouth was found no guile, for they are without fault before the throne of God.

And I saw an angel fly in the midst of heaven, having the everlasting gospel to preach unto them that dwell on the earth: to every nation and kindred and tongue and people; saying with a loud voice, "Behold those who fear God and give glory to him. For the hour of your judgment is come. For ye worship not him that made heaven and earth, and the sea, and the fountains of waters."

And there followed another angel, saying, "Babylon is falling, is falling; even that great city, because she makes all nations that partake of her fornication drink of the wine of the wrath of God."

And the third angel followed them, saying with a loud voice, "If any man worship the beast and his image, and receive his mark in his forehead, or in his hand, the same shall drink from a cup of wine, which is a mixture of the wrath of God and His indignation, which is poured out upon the earth. And he who shall drink thereof shall be tormented with fire and brimstone in the presence of the holy angels, and in the presence of the Lamb. And the smoke of their torment shall ascend up before God for ever and ever. And they shall have no rest day nor night, who worship the beast and his image, and whosoever receiveth the mark of his name."

And I heard a voice from heaven saying unto me, "Write: Here is the patience of the saints. Here are they that keep the commandments of God, and the faith of Jesus. Blessed are the dead which die in the Lord from henceforth. Yea," saith the Spirit, "because they shall rest from their labours because their works follow them."

And I looked, and behold, a white cloud. And upon the cloud one sat like unto the Son of man, having on his head a golden crown, and in his hand a sharp sickle.

And another angel came out of the temple, crying with a loud voice to him that sat on the cloud, "Thrust in thy sickle, and reap: for the time is come for thee to reap; for the harvest of the earth is ripe."

And he that sat on the cloud thrust in his sickle on the earth, and began to reap the earth. And when he stopped reaping for a season, another angel came out of the temple which is in heaven, he also having a sharp sickle like unto the first. And another angel came out from the altar, which had power over fire, and cried with a loud cry to the first that had the sharp sickle, saying, "Thrust in thy sharp sickle, and gather the clusters of the vine of the earth; for her grapes are fully ripe."

And the one like unto the son of Man thrust in his sickle into the earth, and gathered the vine of the earth, and cast it into the great winepress of the wrath of God. And the winepress was trodden without the holy city, and blood came out of the winepress, even unto the horse bridles, by the space of a thousand and six hundred furlongs.

And after these things, I saw another sign in heaven in the likeness of those things upon the earth. And great and marvelous were these things. And I beheld as it were, seven servants having power over the seven last plagues; for in them is filled up the wrath of God. And I saw as it were a sea of glass mingled with fire, and upon it stood those seven servants who had gotten the victory over the beast, and over his image, and over his mark, and over the number of his name. And as they played their harps, they sang the song of God.

And they sing the song of Moses, the servant of God, which is the song of the Lamb, saying, "Great and marvelous are thy works, Lord God Almighty; just and true are thy ways, thou King of saints. For we shall not fear thee, O Lord, and shall glorify thy name with our song. For thou art holy, and all nations shall come and worship before thee. For thy judgments are made manifest unto us."

And after I had beheld these things, I looked, and behold, inside the temple in heaven, the tabernacle of the testimony was opened. And the seven servants came out of the temple, having power over the seven plagues, clothed in pure and white linen, and having their breasts girded with golden girdles.

And one of the four beasts gave unto the seven servants seven golden vials full of the wrath of God, who liveth for ever and ever. And the temple was filled with smoke, and all were blinded from the glory of God, and from his power. And no man was able to enter into the temple because of the smoke till the seven plagues of the seven servants were fulfilled. And I heard a great voice out of the temple saying to the seven servants, "Go your ways, and pour out the vials of the wrath of God upon the earth."

And the first went his way, and poured out his vial upon the earth. And there fell noisome and grievous sores upon the men which had the mark of the beast, and upon them which worshipped his image. And the second servant poured out his vial upon the sea; and it became as the blood of a dead man. And every living soul died in the sea. And the third servant poured out his vial upon the rivers and fountains of waters. And they also became as the blood of a dead man. And I heard the servant who poured out his vial upon these waters say, "Thou art righteous, O Lord, which art, and wast, and shalt be, because thou hast judged them by their works. For they have shed the blood of saints and prophets, and thou hast given them blood to drink—for they are worthy."

And I heard another voice out of the altar say, "Even so, Lord God Almighty, true and righteous are thy judgments."

And the fourth servant poured out his vial upon the sun; and power was given unto him to scorch men with fire. And men were scorched with great heat, and blasphemed the name of God who hath power over these plagues; but they repented not to give him glory. And the fifth servant poured out his vial upon the seat of the beast. And his kingdom was full of darkness. And they gnawed their tongues for pain, and blasphemed the God of heaven because of their pains and their sores; but still they repented not of their deeds.

And the sixth servant poured out his vial upon the great river Euphrates. And the water thereof was dried up, that the way of the kings of the east might be prepared. And because the water was dried up, I saw three unclean spirits like unto frogs, come out of the mouth of the dragon, and out of the mouth of the beast, and out of the mouth of the false prophet.

For they are the spirits of devils, which work miracles, and go forth unto the kings of the earth and of the whole world, gathering them for the battle of that great day of God Almighty.

If any man have an ear, let him hear what the spirit sayeth: "Behold, I come as a thief. Blessed is he that watcheth, and keepeth his garments upon him, lest he walk naked and see his own shame."

And they were gathered together into a place called in the Hebrew tongue *Armageddon*. And the seventh servant poured out his vial into the air. And there fell upon men a great hail out of heaven, every stone about the weight of a talent. And men blasphemed God because of the plague of the hail. For the plague thereof was exceeding great.

And after the seven plagues of the seven servants were fulfilled, I heard great voices and thunders and lightnings coming out of the temple of heaven from the throne, saying, "It is done." And there was a great earthquake, such as was not since men were upon the earth; so mighty an earthquake, and so great. And the great city was divided into three parts, and the cities of the nations fell. And great Babylon came in remembrance before God, to give unto her the cup of the wine of the fierceness of his wrath. And every mountain fled away, and the islands were not found.

And there came one of the four beasts which had the seven vials which were given to the seven servants, and talked with me, saying unto me, "Come hither. I will show unto thee the judgment of the great whore that sitteth upon many waters, with whom the kings of the earth have committed fornication, who are the inhabitants of the earth who have been made drunk with the wine of the cup of her fornication."

So he carried me away in the spirit into the wilderness, where I saw a woman sit upon a scarlet coloured beast, full of names of blasphemy, having seven heads with seven crowns and ten horns. And the woman was arrayed in purple and scarlet colour, and decked with gold and precious stones and pearls, having a golden cup in her hand full of abominations and the filthiness of her fornication. And upon her forehead was a name written: MYSTERY, BABYLON THE GREAT, THE MOTHER OF HARLOTS AND ABOMINATIONS OF THE EARTH.

And I saw the woman drunken with the blood of the saints, who are the martyrs of Jesus. And when I saw her, I wondered with great admiration because of her glory and her beauty. And the angel said unto me, "Wherefore didst thou marvel? Thou knowest not the mystery of the woman, and of the beast that carrieth her, which hath the seven heads with crowns and ten horns. Behold, I will tell thee: the beast that thou sawest was, and is not; and shall ascend out of the bottomless pit, and go into perdition. And they that dwell on the earth shall wonder after the beast (whose names were not written in the Book of Life from the foundation of the world) when they behold the beast that was, and is not, and yet is.

"And here is the mind which hath wisdom and understanding: The seven heads are seven mountains, on which the woman sitteth. And the seven crowns are seven kings: five are fallen, and one is, and the other is not yet come; and when he cometh, he must continue a short space. And the eighth is of the seventh, and receives its power from the beast that was, and is not, and yet is, and which goeth into perdition. And the ten horns which thou sawest are ten kings, which have received no kingdom as yet, but receive power from the beast as kings for the last hour with the eighth. These all have one mind, and shall give their power and strength unto the beast. These shall make war with those who follow the Lamb, and those who follow the Lamb shall overcome them; for they know the Lamb is Lord of lords, and King of kings. And they that follow him are called and chosen and faithful."

And he saith unto me, "The waters which thou sawest, where the whore sitteth, are peoples and multitudes and nations and tongues. And the ten horns which thou sawest upon the beast, these shall cause the peoples and multitudes and nations and tongues to hate the whore. And they shall make her desolate and naked, and shall eat her flesh; and they shall burn her with fire. For the beast hath put in their hearts to fulfill his will. And these agree with the eighth, and give their kingdom unto him, until the words of God shall be fulfilled. And the woman which thou sawest is that great city, which reigneth over all the kings of the earth."

And after these things, I saw another angel come down from heaven, having great power over fire; that by the flame of his fire, the earth might be lightened with the glory of God. And he cried mightily with a strong voice, saying, "Babylon the great is fallen, is fallen, and is become the habitation of devils, and the hold of every foul spirit, and a cage of every unclean and hateful bird. For all nations have drunk of the wine of the wrath of her fornication, and the kings of the earth have committed fornication with her, and the merchants of the earth are waxed rich through the abundance of her delicacies."

And I heard another voice as if it came from heaven, saying, "Come out of her my people, that ye be not partakers of her sins, and that ye receive not of her plagues. For her sins have reached even unto the God of heaven; and she shall remember her iniquities in the Day of Judgment. For when the Lamb cometh, he shall reward her even as she rewarded you, and recompense double unto her according to her works; in the cup which she hath filled, it shall be filled to her double.

"How much she hath glorified herself, and lived deliciously, so much torment and sorrow give her. For she saith in her heart, I sit a queen, and am no widow, and shall see no sorrow. Therefore, shall her plagues be manifested in the day of the Lord: death, and mourning, and famine. And she shall be utterly burned with fire. For strong is the Lord God who judgeth her. And the kings of the earth, who have committed fornication and lived deliciously with her, shall bewail her, and lament for her, when they shall see the smoke of her burning. And these shall stand afar off fearing her torment, saying, 'Alas, alas that great city Babylon, that mighty city! For in one day is thy judgment come.'

"And the merchants of the earth shall weep and mourn over her. For no man buyeth their merchandise any more: the merchandise of gold and silver and precious stones, and of pearls and fine linen, and purple and silk and scarlet, and all thyine wood, and all manner vessels of ivory, and all manner vessels of most precious wood, and of brass and iron and marble, and cinnamon and odours and ointments, and frankincense and wine and oil, and fine flour and wheat, and beasts and sheep and horses, and chariots and slaves and souls of men. And the fruits that thy soul lusted after are departed from thee, and all things which were dainty and goodly are departed from thee; and thou shalt find them no more at all.

"The merchants of these things, which were made rich by her, shall stand afar off for the fear of her torment, weeping and wailing, and saying, 'Alas, alas, that great harlot that was clothed in fine linen, and purple and scarlet, and decked with gold and precious stones and pearls; yea, even that great city which reigneth over the kings of the earth. For in one day, so great riches is come to nought.'

"And every shipmaster, and all the company in ships and sailors, and as many as trade by sea, stood afar off, and cried when they saw the smoke of her burning, saying, 'What city is like unto this great city!' And they cast dust on their heads, and cried, weeping and wailing, saying, 'Alas, alas, that great city, wherein were made rich all that had ships in the sea by reason of her costliness! For in one day is she made desolate.'"

And I saw in the likeness of things upon earth, a mighty angel in heaven take up a stone like a great millstone, and hang it about her neck; and cast her into the sea, saying, "Because of her violence shall that great city Babylon be thrown down, and shall be found no more at all. And the voice of harpers, and musicians, and of pipers, and trumpeters, shall be heard no more at all in thee. And no craftsman, of whatsoever craft he be, shall be found any more in thee. And the sound of a millstone shall be heard no more at all in thee. And the light of a candle shall shine no more at all in thee. And the voice of the bridegroom and of the bride shall be heard no more at all in thee, for thy merchants were the great men of the earth; for by thy sorceries were all nations deceived. And in her was found the blood of prophets and of saints, and of all that were slain upon the earth. Rejoice over her, all ye who are in heaven, and all ye upon the earth who have heeded the words of the holy apostles and prophets, for God shall avenge you on her."

And after these things, I heard as it were the voice of a great multitude in heaven, saying, "Alleluia! Salvation and glory and honour and power, unto the Lord our God!"

And the Lamb slain from the foundation of the world stood before the throne with the Book of Life in his right hand. And the Lamb said, "True and righteous are thy judgments O Lord God Almighty. For thou hast judged the great whore, which did corrupt the earth with her fornication; and now thou must avenge the blood of thy servants at her hand."

And again, the voice of a great multitude said, "Alleluia and Amen!"

And the smoke of her torment rose up for ever and ever. And the four and twenty elders and the four beasts and the Lamb fell down and worshipped God that sat on the throne, saying, "Alleluia and Amen!"

And the voice of the Lamb came out of the throne, saying, "Praise our God, all ye his servants, and ye that fear him not, both small and great."

And I heard the voice of a great multitude, and as the voice of many waters, and also as the voice of mighty thunderings, saying, "Alleluia and Amen: for the Lord God omnipotent reigneth! Let us be glad and rejoice, and give honour to him. For the marriage of the Lamb is come, and his wife hath made herself ready. Behold, I am the bridegroom prepared for my wife."

And to those bidden to the marriage was granted that they should be arrayed in fine linen, clean and white. For the fine linen is the righteousness of saints.

And he which spoke saith unto me, "Write these truths, for blessed are they which are called unto the marriage supper of the Lamb."

And he saith unto me, "These shall know the true sayings of God which he has hidden from them from the foundation of the world."

And then I knew with whom I spoke, and I fell at his feet to worship him. And he said unto me, "See thou do it not. I am thy fellowservant, and of thy brethren that have the testimony which I gave unto you in the flesh as the man Jesus. Worship God for that which He hath given you through me; for he who hath a testimony of that which I did as the man Jesus in the flesh, hath the spirit of prophecy."

And I saw heaven opened, and behold, a white horse; and he that rode had a book in his right hand, which had the seven seals: six already open and one left. And he that spoke with me sat there upon, and was called Faithful and True. And in righteousness he doth judge and make war. His eyes are as a flame of fire, and on his head are many crowns. And he has a name written, that no man knows, but he himself. And he is clothed with a vesture dipped in his own blood and the blood of those who were killed upon the altar; and his name is called The Word of God.

And the armies, which are in heaven, followed him upon white horses, clothed in fine linen, white and clean. And out of his mouth goeth a sharp sword, even The Word of God, that with it he should smite the nations. And he shall rule them with a rod of iron. And he treadeth the fruit of the vine with fierceness, which is in the winepress of wrath of Almighty God. And he hath on his vesture and under his thigh, a name written: KING OF KINGS, AND LORD OF LORDS.

And I saw an angel standing in the sun. And he cried with a loud voice, saying to all the fowls of the air, "Come and gather yourselves together unto the supper of the great God and eat the flesh of the Lamb which was slain for you. That ye no longer eat the flesh of kings, and the flesh of captains, and the flesh of mighty men, and the flesh of horses, and of them that sit on them; nor the flesh of any man, free or bond, small or great."

And I saw the beast, and the kings of the earth, and their captains and their mighty men and their armies, gathered together to make war against him that sat on the horse, and against his army. And when he had opened the seventh seal, the beast was taken, and with him the false prophet that wrought miracles before him, with which the beast deceived them that had received his mark, and them that worshipped his image. These both were cast alive into a lake of fire burning with brimstone. And the remnant of the beast and the false prophet, even all those from whose flesh the fowls of the air were filled, were slain with the sword of him that sat upon the horse, which sword proceeded out of his mouth.

And in the likeness of things upon the earth, I saw an angel come down from heaven having a great chain in his hand. And he took the key to the bottomless pit from the star which had fallen unto the earth, which is the Devil, and Satan. And he laid hold on the dragon, that old serpent, and bound him with the great chain for a thousand years. And cast him into the bottomless pit and locked it up, and set a seal upon it that the dragon should deceive the nations no more, till the thousand years should be fulfilled; but after that, he must be loosed a little season.

And I saw the dead upon the earth, and the souls of them that were beheaded for the witness of Jesus, and for the word of God, and who had chosen not to worship the beast, neither his image, neither receive his mark upon their foreheads, or in their hands; and they lived and reign with Christ a thousand years. And I saw as it were, thrones, which were given them of Christ. And they sat upon them; and judgment was given unto the world because of them. And the dead were raised by the power of the Lamb. But the rest of the dead, who were the remnant that chose to continue to worship the beast and his image and his mark, will not live again until the thousand years are finished. This is the first death. Blessed and holy is he that hath part in the first resurrection, for on such the second death shall have no power; but they shall be priests of God and his Christ, and shall reign with him a thousand years.

And when the thousand years are expired, the dragon shall be loosed out of his prison with those who followed him. And they are as Gog and Magog, and shall go out again to deceive the nations which are in the four quarters of the earth. And all the inhabitants of the earth, the number of which is as the sand of the sea, shall be gathered together to battle. And the armies of Gog shall go up on the breadth of the earth, and compass the camp of the saints about, and the beloved city. And I saw fire come down from God out of heaven, and devour them who fought against the Lamb. And the Devil, who is the dragon that deceived them, was cast into the lake of fire and brimstone, where the beast and the false prophet are, who are tormented day and night for ever and ever.

And I saw a great white throne; and him that sat on it, from whose face the earth fled away. And the veil that covered the host of heaven dissolved, and heaven was rolled together as a scroll. And there was found no place for those who had been cast into the lake of fire and brimstone. And I saw the quick and the dead, small and great, stand before the Lamb of God. And the books were opened; and another book was opened, which is the Book of Life. And all were judged out of those things which were written in the books, according to their works. And the sea gave up the quick which were in it; and death and hell delivered up the dead which were in them. And all were judged, every man according to their works. And whosoever was not found written in the Book of Life was cast into the lake of fire. This is the second death. And then are death and hell cast into the lake of fire.

I saw as it were a new heaven and a new earth, because the first heaven and the first earth were passed away. For the earth had fled, and the mountains thereof, and there were no more isles of the sea. And I John, saw in the heavens a likeness of the holy city, a new Jerusalem, coming down from God out of heaven; prepared as a bride adorned for her husband. And I heard a great voice out of heaven saying, "Behold, the marriage is complete. The tabernacle of God is now with men, and the Lamb will dwell with them; and they shall be his people, and his Word shall be with them and be their God instead of wood and stone. And God shall wipe away all tears from their eyes. And there shall be no more death, neither sorrow nor crying.

Neither shall there be any more pain. For the former things are passed away, and all things have become new: even new heavens and a new earth."

And he that stood before the throne said, "Behold, I make all things new by the Word of God."

And he said unto me, "Write: This Word is true and faithful."

And he said unto me, "It is done. I am the Christ, Alpha and Omega, the beginning and the end. I will give unto him that is athirst, of the fountain of the water of life, freely. He that overcometh this world shall inherit all things; and I will make him a son of God. But those who are the fearful and unbelieving, and the abominable and murderers, and whoremongers and sorcerers and idolaters, and all liars who shall not forsake these things, shall have their part in the lake which burneth with fire and brimstone, and upon whom the second death will have power."

And there came unto me one of the four beasts (which had the seven vials which were given to the seven servants who had power over the seven last plagues), and talked with me, saying, "Come hither. I will shew thee the bride, who is now the Lamb's wife."

And he carried me away in the spirit to a great and high mountain; and shewed me that great city, the holy Jerusalem, descending out of heaven from God, having the glory of God. And her light was like unto a stone most precious: even like a jasper stone, clear as crystal; and had a wall great and high, and had twelve gates. And at the gates, twelve cherubim by which all must pass whose names are written thereon, which are the names of the twelve tribes of the children of Israel: on the east three gates, on the north three gates, on the south three gates, and on the west three gates. And the wall of the city had twelve foundations, and in them the names of the twelve apostles of the Lamb.

And he that talked with me had a golden reed to measure the city, and the gates thereof, and the wall thereof. And the city lieth foursquare; and the length is as large as the breadth. And he measured the city with the reed, twelve thousand furlongs. The length and the breadth and the height of it are equal. And he measured the wall thereof, an hundred and forty and four thousand cubits, according to the measure of a man's arm that is, and not of the golden reed of the angel. And the building of the wall of it was done of jasper and emerald. And the city was overlaid with pure gold, the streets like unto clear glass. And the foundations of the wall of the city were garnished with all manner of precious stones. The first to garnish the foundations was jasper; the second, onyx; the third, a beryl; the fourth, an amethyst; the fifth, agate; the sixth, ligure; the seventh, diamond; the eighth, sapphire; the ninth, an emerald; the tenth, a carbuncle; the eleventh, a topaz; the twelfth, a sardius. And the twelve gates were as twelve pearls; each of the gates was of one pearl. And the street of the city was pure gold, as it were transparent glass.

And I saw no temple therein: for the Lord God Almighty and the Lamb are the temple of it. And there was found no darkness in the city, and it had no need of the moon to shine in it and reflect the light of the sun. For the glory of God did lighten it, and the Lamb is the light thereof. And the nations of them which are saved shall walk in the light of it. And no longer shall the kings of the earth bring their glory and honour into it. But they which are saved shall bring the glory and honour of all nations into it. And the gates of it shall not be shut at all by day, and there shall be no night there. And there shall in no wise enter into it any thing that defileth, neither whatsoever worketh abomination, or maketh a lie; but only they whose names are written in the Lamb's Book of Life.

And the Son of man appeared before me, and he shewed me a pure river of the water of life, clear as crystal, proceeding out of the kingdom of God and of the Lamb. In the midst of the street of it, and on either side of the river, was there the tree of life, which bare twelve manner of fruits, and yielded her fruit every month according to it seasons; and the leaves of the tree were for the healing of the nations. And there shall be no more curse because of that which was hidden. But the throne of God and of the Lamb shall be in it where God shall reign in truth and righteous. And his servants shall serve Him, who have overcome the world. And they shall see His face and know Him; and His name shall be in their foreheads, because their works have been His works. And there shall be no night there. And they need no candle, neither the light of the moon. For the sun, who is the Lord God, giveth them light according to their works. And they shall reign in His kingdom for ever and ever.

And he said unto me, "These sayings are faithful and true, and have been hidden from the foundation of the world because of the wickedness of men. But the Lord God who called the holy prophets, and who sent His angels to shew unto his servants all things which must shortly come to pass, hath commanded His prophets to write these things and seal them up until the last days before I come again into the world. Behold, I am Jesus Christ, the Son of God, and I come quickly. Therefore, blessed is he that keepeth the sayings of the prophets who have sealed up the prophecy of this book."

And I John saw these things, and heard them. And when I had heard and seen, I fell down to worship before the feet of him who shewed me these things.

Then saith he unto me, "See thou do it not, but worship God who hath sent me; for I am thy fellowservant, and of thy brethren the prophets, and of them which keep the sayings of this book. And this book doth not teach a man to fall down and worship another, but it teacheth a man to worship God and keep His commandments in all things; and these are those things which have been sealed up to come forth unto the children of men."

And he saith unto me, "Therefore, seal not the sayings of the prophecy of this book any longer, for the time is at hand when it shall come to pass that kings shall shut their mouths. For that which had not been told them shall they see, and that which they had not heard shall they consider. And these things shall be preached upon the housetops to all the people. And there shall be no more excuse for the wickedness of a man.

"And he that is unjust, let him be unjust still in that which he believeth. And he which is filthy, let him be filthy still in those works which he doeth. And he that is righteous, let him be righteous still in the works that he hath chosen for himself to do. And he that is holy, let him be holy still, and stand in a holy place and wait for me to come. And behold, I come quickly; and my reward is with me, to give every man according as his work shall be.

"I am Alpha and Omega, the beginning and the end, the first and the last, and have revealed all things unto my servants, the prophets, that they might preach repentance and teach men the commandments of God.

"Blessed are they that do His commandments, that they may have right to the tree of life, and may enter in through the gates into the holy city, which is the kingdom of God. For without, are those men who are like dogs, who ceaselessly bark unto others of their own; and sorcerers who deceive others and set themselves up as a source of light, and whoremongers, who are led by the lusts of their hearts, and also the murderers, and idolaters, and whosoever loveth and maketh a lie.

"I Jesus have been sent by God to send forth mine servants to testify of these things in the churches that have been set up among men. And this have I commanded them to testify unto the people, that I am the root and the offspring of David, and the bright and morning star. I am he who hath sent forth the word of God by my own mouth and by the power of the Spirit, and who hath come to prepare the bride for the wedding; and who saith, 'Come unto me.' And to him that heareth I say, 'Come and partake of the living waters, which are the words that I have spoken and given unto the world. And let him that is athirst come. And whosoever will, let him come also and take the water of life freely so that he shall never thirst.'

For I testify unto every man that heareth the words of life given in the words of prophecy of this book: If any man shall add unto these things, God shall add unto him the plagues that are written in this book. For in these things which are written, ye shall know of that which must surely come to pass upon the earth. And if any man shall take away from the words of life given in the book of this prophecy, God shall take away his part out of the Book of Life; and he shall be kept out of the holy city, and from the holy things which are written in this book."

He which hath testified of these things, saith, "Surely I come quickly. Amen."

Even so, come, Lord Jesus.

Tasharrafna Ismi J.

APPENDIX 2

SCRIPTURE REFERENCES

Scripture quotations from King James translation (other than Revelation)

Old Testament

Genesis	Page
1:26-27	63
1:28	140
3:5	63
3:19	256
6:5,12	181
7:24	181
8:2-3	181
9:13	181
22:17	246
22:18	219
24:2,9	341
41:27	155
47:29	341

Exodus	
4:2-4	275
9:18	192
10:4-5	207
10:13	173
14:10	350
15:6	128
19:4-5	289
19:17	343
24:12	343
24:13-31	343
25:11	360
26:31	378
28:15-21*	111, 448

Exodus	
28:30	113
28:39-40	345
31:18	343
32:15-16	343
32:18	274
34:1	344

Leviticus	
20:3	122

Deuteronomy	
4:10-13	197
4:28	198

*(NOTE) An asterisk by the reference indicates there is another reference within that range. For example, Matthew 7:24-27 also includes a reference in Matthew 7:26-27 on a different page.

28:58-59   349
29:17-18   437

Joshua
14:10   279

Judges
10:9   350
15:18   351

1 Samuel
16:14-17   257
16:23   257
17:43-46   337

2 Samuel
18:2   162
18:18*   91, 101

1 Kings
10:14   315
19:18   266

2 Kings
18:18   96
18:26   97
18:37   97
19:1-2   97
19:18*   226, 437

2 Chronicles
9:13   315
16:9   137
23:3-6   194

Ezra
9:8   98

Nehemiah
1:9-10   227
9:19-21*   278, 280

Job
4:9-10   212
15:2-3   174
18:5-7   405
25:4-5   163

30:29-31   273
37:15-18   121
38:4-7   133

Psalms
2:9   418
16:8   129
19:7-11   192
42:9-11   342
43:1-5   157
48:1-2   318
48:7   197
51:5-12   171
55:23   204
57:4-6*   204, 213
90:4   185
90:16   352
147:18-19   172

Proverbs
5:1-14   199
22:12   136
23:1-8   399
24:20   405

Ecclesiastes
1:2   381
1:13-15   381
4:1-2   438

The Song of Solomon
5:4-16   105-107

Isaiah
1:4-6   143
1:10-17*   244, 257
1:15-20*   143, 244
2:2-5   444
3:8-9   257
5:30   358
6:9-10   140
7:4   207
8:19-22   359
9:4-7*   369, 420
9:19-20*   385, 422
10:17-19   193

11:5   74
13:10-13*   161, 201
14:12-21*   204, 244
14:25   244
17:7-8   158
19:3   257
22:20-25   98
23:14   197
24:16-17   204
24:18-23   162
25:7-9   271
26:5-6   244
27:5-8   176
29:10*   325, 357
29:13   325
30:1-3   193
30:27   164
34:4   433
34:11-15   273
35:10   321
36:3   96
36:11   97
36:22   97
37:1-2   193
37:27   193
37:29   378
38:17   205
40:2   392
40:6-8   193
40:23-24   192
41:1   167
42:13-16   436
45:23-24   228
48:13   129
49:10   357
49:26   385
50:2-3   163
52:7   318
58:1   70
59:2-10   167
59:17*   167, 213
59:18   167
63:1-6   129
63:9-12*   129, 171
64:10-11   278
65:16-18*   436, 438

19:30	449	1:17	441	4:1-7	68
23:2-7	364	2:15-16	215	4:7-9	62
23:12	119	3:3-6	430	5:14	450
24:27	174	3:15	443		
24:31	176	4:14*	183,188, 331, 353	**Ephesians**	
24:42-44*	226, 367	5:17	133	4:14	174
24:50-51	121	5:30	415		
25:1-13*	121, 347	6:32-35*	134, 182, 279	**1 Timothy**	
25:14-30	373	6:51-57*	87, 406, 422	1:4	441
25:31-40*	129, 373	6:54-58	87		
25:41-42	129	8:19	134	**2 Timothy**	
26:41	255	10:16*	248, 276	3:7	99
		10:18	134	4:1	433
Mark		10:31-38	61	4:3-4	176
4:11	181	12:28	325		
4:30-32	420	12:31	188	**Titus**	
9:41	355	14:2-3	135	1:14	440
10:14	181	14:7-12	135	1:15-16	443
16:19	62	14:14-17	188		
		14:26	112	**To the**	
Luke		15:9-12	135	**Hebrews**	
2:42	262	17:4*	94, 326	9:1-2	73
3:9-11	429	20:17	62	9:14	352
3:16-17	332	20:29	239	10:26-27	442
4:15-21	82	21:20-25*	53, 246		
4:28-29	82			**The Epistle**	
4:43	182	**The Acts**		**of James**	
6:21	182	1:9-11	62	1:12-22	323
6:25-26	183	2:1-4	172	2:8	103
8:1	182	10:34-37*	181, 447	2:19-20	92
8:11-15	440			4:1	255
9:46-48	415	**The Epistle to**			
10:18-19	203	**the Romans**		**1 Peter**	
13:6-9	164	6:12-21	256	1:7-12	240
13:29-30*	446, 449	8:13-14	442	1:18-19	352
14:11-14	399	8:16-17	144	2:6-8	133
16:19-31	403			2:11	255
17:1-2	404	**1 Corinthians**		2:21-22	324
17:20-21*	101, 182	8:5-6	61		
18:24-25	403	11:4-5	212	**2 Peter**	
19:11-27	373	13:3	296	1:16	268
22:24-27	132			3:7-9	185
24:44	340	**2 Corinthians**			
24:51	62	4:6	445	**1 John**	
				2:15-16	343
John		**Galatians**		3:15	443
1:1-14*	65, 102, 416	3:28-29	145		

INDEX

A

Aaron, 113, 128, 345
Abaddon, 214, 215
abomination of desolation, 154, 165, 261, 326
abortion, 329
Abraham, 145, 247, 263–4, 270, 402–3, 419
academia, 205, 223
Adam, fall of, 152, 216   (*see also* Eden)
adultery, 99, 199
advanced Being   (*see* beings)
advanced technology, 127, 135, 348, 409, 413, 434
adversity, 159
affliction/afflicted, 171, 253, 259, 365, 369, 426
African slaves, 383
afterlife, 238, 309   (*see also* eternal)
agency   (*see* free agency)
aging, 46, 54
alcohol, 45

alien   (*see* being, alien)
Allah, 326
Alleluia, and amen, 119, 408, 409
Alpha and Omega
  beginning and the end, 68, 70, 439, 458
  first and the last, 70, 46
altar
  angel came out from, 241, 334
  Antipas burned in, 85
  candlesticks, 73, 268
  Christ slain upon, 146
  dimensions specified, 158, 217
  figurative, 241, 247
  fire from, 191
  four corners of, 216
  golden, 190–1, 216, 472
  symbolism, 216–17, 242
  those slain/sacrificed/killed/blood spilt upon, 129, 156–7, 159, 416

two witnesses, standing before,
247, 268
works, 158, 243, 355, 343
Amen   (*see also* Alleluia)
affirmation by, 147, 179, 408–9
Hebrew meaning, 408
America   (*see* United States of America)
American Dream
ability to attain/realize, 310, 360
ancient version of, 361
enemy comes to destroy, 366
illusory/illusion of, 380, 432
image of the beast, 295, 316
lust after, 357, 365
promise eaten up, 387
world organizations promoting, 384
American lifestyle, 254, 308, 311, 313–14,
394, 403
Ancient of days, 74
angel(s)   (*see also* servant)
ascending (from the east), 172, 471
cherubim, 116, 123, 148, 445–6
description of, 117–18
directing prophets, 234, 238, 300, 334
exalted human beings
(*see* beings, exalted)
four, 117, 218, 376, 409, 444
help in the universe, 130, 326
holding incense, 190–1
holding little book, 234–5
holding vials, 334, 345–6
Jesus Christ, 64, 66, 235, 238
mighty, 225, 226, 228,230, 401
of devil, 477
of dragon, 280
of God, 452
straight feet of, 117
travel, 119, 122
trumpeting/rejoicing, 131, 189, 346
unseen, 10, 289, 409
voice of (see voice)
wings, 117–18, 124, 289
withholding God's intervention, 177,
336, 354
anger
against truth, 59

Ephesus, 78
for enemies, 80
of the LORD, 161, 196
animal(s)   (*see also* names of individual
animals)
and natural law, 2, 4, 16, 19
food chain, 28
human   (*see* wise ones)
instincts, 1–2, 28, 69, 319
sacrificed, 146
animal kingdom, 3, 5–6, 16, 18, 115
anointed, 82, 113, 301, 409, 446
Anointed One, 113
(see also Jesus Christ; Millennial
Reign two; edged sword)
brings peace through love, 302
follows book of life, 137, 407, 409
holds the Holy Grail, 454
one per solar system, 63
oversees our solar system, 63, 68, 313
prepared so he could not fail, 133
Second Coming of, 216, 232, 267,
283, 395
serves all equally, 44, 268
teaches us how to live, 127, 216, 226,
394, 431, 439
unanimously sustained, 268
unification with five virgins, 120
we fight against, 366
Anti–Christ, 366
Antipas, 79, 85
anxiety, 195, 210, 358
Apocalypse, 394–5
Apollyon, 214–15
apostasy, 289
apostle
John, 55, 65
of the Lamb, 79–80, 446
twelve, 363, 446
appetite
bottomless, 154
of the flesh, 81, 83, 308
worldly, 79, 95   (*see also* gluttony)
Ark of his testament/the Covenant
(*see also* Moses)
in the tabernacle/temple, 269, 344, 430

C

clothed with, 209, 225–6
covers sun, 163, 202, 226, 277
of darkness, 54–5, 197, 290
in formation of hail, 372
prophet sitting on, 331–3, 389
pillar of, 277–8
coals, burning, 118, 192
coat(s), 105, 288, 359, 429
college, 7, 33, 423
colonies, American, 26, 76, 304–5, 309
Comforter, 112, 188, 438
    (*see also* Holy Ghost)
commerce, 154, 307, 361
common sense, 30, 62, 160
computer, 112, 221, 309, 364
Confucius, 248
Conscience, 258, 352, 370–1, 431, 443
consequence(s), 5, 18, 28–31, 76, 219, 373
    (*see also* plagues)
continent(s)
    American, 306, 310
    churches represent, 72
    dragon has power over, 273
    John aware of, 65
    loud voice heard throughout, 228
    seven rays, 310
    seven, 307, 337
    (*see also* seven heads)
cornerstone, 132
court(s) of law, 288, 306–7, 311
covenant
    everlasting, 71, 73, 462
    God's *c.* of peace and happiness, 197,
      226, 231–2, 238, 454
    shown by the bow, 210
    under his thigh, 419
    with Abraham, 263–4
    with Assyrians, 174
    with the king, 193
creation(s)
    blueprints of, 128
    measure of, 34, 231, 325, 381
    of a solar system, 139
    of God, 31, 59, 72, 102, 118, 238, 467
    of our spirits, 145
    of sun, 55

of earth, 147
One oversees, 130
Quantum, 149
Creator, 441
    abide by eternal laws, 137
    angels work for, 130
    bow before, 147
    comes from another galaxy, 179
    consider us gold, 138
    covenant of, 454
    created/programmed Christ, 63, 133,
      137
    creates us in His image/to have joy,
      102–3
    does not get angry, 167, 327
    eternal plan of, 341, 418
    expects us to work, 310,
    follows Book of Life to create solar
      systems, 126–128
    have always been, 124
    is not sadistic, 413
    laid out earth according to laws of
      nature, 217
    not a respecter of persons, 398
    of all things, 150
    power and authority of, 432
    prepared everything to bring us
      happiness, 146
    presented plan of happiness for us,
      146, 319
    purpose is to provides happiness for
      His creations, 31
    unification with, 437
    universal organizers of life, 135
    we become like, 60
    withheld power until latter days, 219
crime, 210, 387
criminal, 23, 43, 297
cross, 94, 285, 303, 416–17
crown
    golden, 210, 331–2, 481
    of life, 84, 322, 463
    of power, 152, 469
    of the earth, 84
    symbolic of, 101
crucifixion   (*see* Christ, crucifixion of)

bowing down, 138, 147
clothed in white raiment/robes, 114,
   159, 180, 331
crying to God, 158
four and twenty
   (*see topics in this heading*)
John as, 180
message of, 115, 177
represent prophets, 114–5, 122, 125,
   289, 319, 321, 409
speaking to John, 132
stand before the woman, 276, 288
with golden vials, 137–8, 147, 346
with harps, 137–8
worship God, 268, 332, 409
elect, the, 65, 72, 80, 115, 240
   follow His guidance, 178
   gathered from four winds, 176
   not affected, 177, 334
electricity, 149, 309, 355
element(s)
   basic, 396
   body, 195
   dark matter, 59
   first estate, 126
   forced from natural state, 395
   impurity of, 169
   natural world, 149
   obey eternal laws, 60
   purest, 74
   refined, 169
   spirit, 126, 166, 319
   spiritual, 112
Elijah, 339
elite, 37, 153, 222, 297
emerald, 113, 448–9
emperor, 298, 307
empire (*see also* Rome, Empire)
   Babylon, 218
   British, 382
   Byzantine, 299
   Great, 155, 298
employee, 386
employment, 7, 39, 259, 392, 403
End of Times, 249, 370
Endowment, John's, 184

enemy/enemies, 32, 35, 128
   anger for (*see* anger)
   Christ conquers, 421
   love for, 144, 360, 364
   of God, 216, 275
   of peace and happiness, 216, 267
   of the Holy Scriptures, 253
   of truth, 215
energy, 355
   heat, 396
   in thunderheads, 372
   kinetic, 308
   nuclear, 149, 221
   to save lives, 41
   to sustain plants and animals, 4
English, 305–6, 358, 383, 395, 402
   (*see also* ten kings)
entertainment, 223, 259, 364–5
enticement(s), 256
   of the flesh, 203, 205, 282
   of human nature, 272
   of spiritual nature, 216
environment, 320
   adapting to, 2, 282
   control over, 4, 167, 327
   destroyed, 356, 393
   of peace and happiness, 127, 208,
      231, 283
   proper, 231
envy, 78–9, 86, 99, 109
Ephesus, 71, 78–80
Ephraim, 174, 350
equality, 9, 294, 320, 398, 449
   absolute, 178
   assured to all (by the Lord), 44, 49
   Doing Unto Others, 156, 218, 265, 431
   desolate of, 154
   established by the Word of God, 256,
      373, 442
   expressed in thirds/three parts,
      195–6, 200–1, 374, 446
   in society, 196, 212
   taught by Christ, 271, 298, 329, 357
   peer groups of, 33
   restored to earth, 212, 324, 404
   worldwide, 49, 398

eternal, 164, 179, 323, 452
    laws, 60, 63, 68–9, 84–5, 128, 130, 137,
        326
    perspective, 338, 341, 346–7, 352,
        415, 445, 449
eternal plan
    all creations agree to support, 118
    angels serve purpose of, 130
    is forever and ever right, 409
    of happiness overseen, 131, 150
    of salvation, 138–9, 150
    prophets understand, 236
eternal life
    exist forever in happiness, 95, 127,
        144, 283
    immortality and, 137
    live on one of planets, 139
    no murderer hath, 443
    purpose of all things, 60
    requirements for, 88
    resurrection unto, 91
    those who receive manna, 87
    through Jesus Christ, 127, 406, 422
    through living the gospel, 301, 352
    way to *e.l.* embedded in our souls,
        454
    works can give, 92
eternity, 423, 432
Euphrates River, 218–19, 290, 360–1, 474
Europe, 297–8, 304–7, 383–4
Evangelist, 341, 353
Eve (*see* Adam, fall of)
evil
    from thy flesh, 201
    spirit, 284, 320–1
    they make good, 81, 393
    works, 79, 409, 432
evolution, Theory of, 2–3, 5–6
exactness, 241, 260
exercise (physical), 17
expectation(s)
    educational, 24
    family, 7
    golden vial full of the smoke of
        incense, 139
    of God, 146

    of happiness, 138
    of others, 43
    of the world, 47, 52, 197
    prayers, 138
    set to guarantee agency, 48
    we cannot set, 47
explorer, 19, 302
extraterrestrial   (*see* beings)
eyesalve, 103–4
eyes
    being opened, 61
    of the Lord, 136–7
    shut, 71, 96, 140
    that see, 71, 144, 264, 316, 370
Ezekiel, 75, 116, 158, 175, 196, 431
        (*see also* Appendix 2)
Ezra, 98 (*see also* Appendix 2)

F

fables, 176, 440
faces
    four, 115–23,
    calf, 122–3,
    eagle, 118, 122–3
    lion, 123, 468
    man, 124, 468
    of men, 211, 473
    of the poor, 310–11, 401–2
    shall gather blackness, 417
    symbolism of four, 118
faith
    and support, 10
    charity, service, patience, 88, 302
    in an unseen God, 309
    Jewish, 263
    organized, 59, 83, 90, 120, 135, 176,
        250, 266, 363, 398
    tribulation, 83
    without works, 92
fall of Adam, 152, 216
fallen star, 203
false doctrine, 164, 173, 175–6, 193, 210,
       290 (*see also* doctrine)
familiar spirits, 257, 359, 362
family (*see also* marriage, species)

ancestry, 177
prayer, 259
unit, 33, 198, 299, 367, 397
wealth, 297, 311
famine, 173, 194, 291, 394
fashion, 41, 217
father   (*see also* family; parent)
and/or mother, 7, 285
children, 29–30
in heaven, 61–2, 66–8, 73, 87
in wilderness, 464
fear/fearful, God, 75, 325–6, 341–3
feast(s), 244, 421, 414
feeling(s)
fuzzy, 87
of confusion, 320
of pride and vanity, 112
of superiority, 45
of remorse and embarrassment, 216, 267, 391
secure, 34
feet
of a bear, 295, 478
burned in a furnace, 74, 462
of a calf, 117
fell at *f.*, 76, 234, 414
like fine brass, 88
moon under her *f.*, 270
as pillars of fire, 108, 225, 227, 474
of the poor, 244
straight, 117
washed my *f.*, 105
fellowservant, 139, 234, 414, 457
female, 1–3, 6, 61, 145, 236
field, 24, 39–41, 193, 333, 339
Christ in, 398
beasts of, 373, 379, 420–1
fig tree, 163–5, 433
final battle (*see* Armageddon)
financial independence, 39, 310–11, 337, 384
fine linen, 345, 397, 400, 402, 412–13, 417
fire
and brimstone, 193, 222, 328, 424, 432, 442
appearance, 113–14

burning, 54, 74–5, 115, 118–19, 221, 425
devour, 196, 211, 417
everlasting, 129, 329, 423
from heaven, 197, 308–10, 324, 432
from the altar, 191–2
mingled with hail, 192
refiners, 169, 195
first
begotten, 66, 113
estate, 126
resurrection, 66
shall be last, 279, 298, 311, 449, 458
firstborn, 113, 279
firstfruits, 322–3
five months, 208–9, 214, 292
flag, 23, 26, 76
flood(s)
came, 88, 173, 242
of Egypt, 291
Great Flood, 210, 226, 292
mind, 290, 292
food, 6, 18, 278, 311
chain, 28
clothing, shelter, and health care, 38, 48–9, 223
of the kings, 79, 83–4
and wine, 88, 424
foot, 66, 73, 350
calf's, 117
left, 227–8
right, 129, 227–8
travel by, 17–18
tread under, 243–5, 247, 278
forehead
mark in (*see* mark)
seal in   (*see* seal in the forehead)
forgive/forgiveness, 338, 341, 364
brings happiness, 370
ignored, 327
less than any other time in history, 303
solution to problems found in, 360
unconditional, 362
vs. preaching, 93
fornication, 224, 376
commit, 86, 89, 90, 321–2, 376, 390, 395

looking, 121
sea of g. mingled with fire, 338, 341, 345–7
glory
   of God, 67–8, 116, 348, 373, 389, 408, 445, 451
   to God, 146, 204, 265, 267, 325, 356, 407
   worldly, 364, 366, 431
gluttony, 78–9, 109
gnawed tongues, 357–8, 365
goal(s), 20
   personal, 8, 18, 19, 25, 46
   worldly, 197, 292, 322, 437
God, pick a page
Gods, 137
   advanced human beings, 60–2
   have always been, 124, 150, 356
   idols are her *g.*, 89
   of wood and stone, 437
   prophets called by, 235
   scientists, 150
   unseen, 10, 398
   Gog and Magog, 431
gold, 42, 108, 304
   Breastplate of Judgment encased in, 448–9
   city/Ark overlaid with, 448, 450
   considered *g.* to our Creators, 138
   crowns of *g.*, 210–11, 331
   idols, 37, 213, 342, 344
   more precious than, 161, 201
   pure, 448, 450
   raw, 104
   refined/purified/purged, 104, 169, 195
   shall be removed, 168, 397
   should not worship, 223
   Solomon's, 315
   woman decked with, 294, 378, 400
Golden Rule, 447
Gomorrah, 200, 243, 257
good and evil, 61, 127, 209
good works, 61, 161
   are done in vain, 87–9
   let your light shine, 72, 325, 341, 389
   taking care of the needy, 143

were evil, 432
goodness, 29, 31, 109
gospel
   of the Father, 246, 264
   everlasting, 281, 324, 342
   of Jesus Christ
      (*see* Jesus Christ, gospel of)
   of John, 65
government(s), 16, 218, 422
   (*see also* Antipas)
   Christ's 91, 98, 284
   corruption of, 297
   democracies/powers, 294–5
   established to protect, 23, 273
   greed and profit, 302, 305, 386
   masses hate, 386
   overthrown at Christ's coming, 273
   policy, 387
   promote selfish desires, 16
   protected by locusts, 211
   Roman, 297–8
   saints stand up against, 85
   shall be upon his shoulder, 369, 420
   systems of, 298–9, 302, 304
   ten horns, 273
   United States, 304–7, 311
grace, 98, 239
   and truth, 416, 437, 441
   be unto you, 65, 460
   in thy sight, 419, 441
   of Lord, 98, 459
   under, 256
grain, 11, 420
grapes, 165, 334
grass, 208
   burnt, 191, 193
   green, 192, 210, 287
grasshoppers, 211
graves, 257–8, 282
graven image, 273, 310, 316
gravity, 18
Great Britain, 305
Great Flood, 210, 226, 292
Great Minds, 309, 355
greed, 42, 47, 78, 104, 109
   corporate, 47

government, 297, 302, 386
Greek(s), 85, 101, 233, 248
grind the face of the poor, 310, 392
grinding wheel, 311, 402
ground, 36, 397, 440
guile, 323–4

H

hail/hailstones, 191–2, 207, 269, 371–3
hair, 74, 160, 162, 211–12
half a time, 245, 260, 288–9
half an hour
    Daniel vision, 189
    of God's time, 185
    of silence, 184, 188, 348
hand(s), 106
    clean, 169
    full of blood, 142, 244
    left, 128–30, 310, 329, 385, 423
    of the angels, 124–5, 235
    of a man, 116–17
    of a potter, 91
    right   (*see* right hand)
happiness
    bring, 9, 30, 362, 441
    eternal, 60, 62, 77, 81, 116, 139, 449
    experience, 127, 132, 281, 348, 381,
        407, 450
    on earth, 437
Har Megido, 268
harlot
    and abominations, 294, 371, 379
    mother of *h.*, 294, 371, 379
    great *h.*, 400
harps/harpers, 138, 157, 273, 319–321, 338
hate
    against the homosexuals,
        non–Christians…, 326
    and persecute, 79, 330
    one another, 359
    others, 365, 443
    the system, 386
    the whore, 385
haughty/haughtiness, 37, 161, 201
he that hath an ear, 91, 95, 102, 108

healed (deadly wound), 296, 298, 302,
    304, 306
health, 18, 157
health care, 48–9, 223, 399
heart, 180, 423
    and contrite spirit, 189, 237–8
    clean, 171
    of the children, 339
    own, 199–200
    song of, 312
heat, 182, 396, 408, 454
    burned with, 356–7
    elements of earth refined with, 169
heathen, 199, 335, 380, 387, 437
heavenly Being, 332
Hebrew   (*see also* Appendix 2 for OT
    Hebrews)
    Paul's writings to, 73
    midwives, 289
    words, 113, 214, 367–8, 402, 408
heir of God, 61, 145
hell, 402
    brought down to, 204–5, 281
        (*see also* bottomless pit)
    chains of, 234
    Death and Hell, 155–6
    destruction and, 214–15
    emotional, 205, 215
    fire, and damnation, 119, 341, 394
    free from, 77, 160, 434
    keys of, 76
    upon earth, 381, 383, 434
    we create, 31, 56, 205, 239, 284, 444
helmet of salvation, 213
herbs, 192, 304, 420, 436
Herod   (*see* king, Herod)
hidden, 55, 138
    because of wickedness, 234, 250, 457
    John's words, 184, 189, 240, 395, 456
    manna, 86–7
    mysteries, 275
    technology, 308–9
    things will be known, 414
    truth, 95
high priests, 410
higher law, 213, 342

of Jacob, 70, 318, 444
of Joseph, 200
of the LORD, 97, 194, 335, 404
of a stranger, 199
to be broken up, 226, 367
household
man's foes shall be of own *h.*, 285
those of same *h.* invited to wedding,
410
housetops, 83, 192, 302, 457
human being, 54, 39–40, 203, 392
6 billion plus on earth, 36
actions of, 28
balance/happiness, 150, 282
driven by lusts and desires, 216
free agency of, 116
isolated, 299
killing another, 33, 222, 360
provided free food, clothing, shelter,
and health care, 223, 380
smile of, 19
successful, 367
unstable/unhappy, 8, 47
human nature, 149
controls the works of all people,
214–15
creates hell, 215
effects of, 218
enemy of peace and happiness, 216
flesh, 66–7, 219
lusts of, 205, 223, 286, 376
must overcome, 95
prince of the kings of the earth, 67,
187, 255
rejects gospel, 256
Satan/Lucifer, 153 205–6, 255, 284
struggles of, 109
subdued by the royal law, 428
supports governments, 16, 294
witnessed by John, 52–3, 58
humanity/humankind
can fail but Christ cannot, 69
civilized *h.*, 5
equally, 119
in this solar system, 139, 146
is oblivious, 259

is under condemnation, 193
the effects of their works, 291
represent, 149, 164, 170
humble
himself before God, 237
himself shall be exalted, 119, 399
prophets humbled, 237
hundred forty and four thousand
(144,000), 115, 177, 317, 319, 448
hunger, 182, 278
hungered, 129, 329, 424
hurt
by "wind" of truth, 177
earth and the sea, 172–3
grass of the earth, 208
instead of kill, 222
men five months, 214
not the earth neither the sea, 175
not the oil and the wine, 153
of second death, 84
the word of God, 252
husband, 12, 253, 436
hypocrites, 92, 120, 253
hyssop, 171

I

idol(s)
calf, 213, 342
gold and silver, 38, 223
golden, 342, 344
of men, 37
people worshipped instead of the
Lord, 437
therefore will I lay desolate, 273
wood and stone, 198
idolaters, 442–3, 458
illegal alien, 374, 403
illusion, 27
abstract, 380, 383
created to support personal agendas,
10–11, 24
hopeless, 21, 25
of a magician, 71
of American Dream, 432
of human achievement, 27

of success, 383, 387
the image
American dream, 316
of the beast, 331, 313–14, 316, 365, 348, 380, 384, 432   (*see also* dream)
of God, 61
of human perfection, 46
for the little girl, 20
and the mark, 44
of the established measure, 223
in a mirror, 52
becomes a reality, 21
self, 10, 20
of worldly success, 362
immigrant (workers), 386
incense
an abomination, 244
burned, 139, 190
the prayers of saints, 137, 346
the golden censer, 190
individuality, 7, 10, 49
maintain, 6, 10, 32
protect, 45, 48
inequality
no escape from, 36
poverty, 49, 56, 223, 380, 396, 415, 428
misery and sorrow, 441
inherit
all things, 441
the earth, 182   (*see also* Beatitudes)
the kingdom of God, 144, 403
the kingdom prepared for you, 129, 426
iniquity, 123, 391, 417
innate desires, 5, 8, 27, 282
inner conflict, 32, 39
inspiration from God, 211–12
instinct(s), 1, 28
intelligence, 5, 8, 16–17, 367
intent
Christ–like, 87–8, 90, 115, 118, 122
John's, 54, 190, 371, 437
intentions, 87, 115, 118, 123
intervention   (*see* wrath of God)
inventors, 19, 218
iron

breastplate,   (*see also* breastplate)
fourth Kingdom, 418
merchandise, 397
represents, 418
rod of, 276–7, 418–19
teeth, 295
Isaiah   (*see* Appendix 2)
isles/islands
of the sea, 37, 286, 372
were not found, 374, 435
Israel
shall blossom and bud, 176
land of promise, 278–9
mountains of, 167, 379
tribes, 114, 152, 227, 266, 270, 446
Israelite(s)
in the wilderness, 87, 165, 174, 279, 289–90
Lost the Ark of the Covenant, 261

J

jacinth, 220–1
Jacob, 172, 176, 291, 385, 387
house of, 70, 318, 444
jasper, 445
last stone in Breastplate of Judgment, 113, 449
used in the city, 448–9
Jebusites, 317   (*see also* Zion)
Jerusalem, 392, 317–18
(*see also* mount Sion/Zion)
Christ visits temple in, 278
daughters of, 107–8
foundation of peace, 318, 436
Lord shall reign in, 162
Lord utter voice from, 335
measure, 243
New, 101, 245, 318, 436, 444, 452
prophets of, 200
ruined/desolate, 257, 278
set in the midst of the nations, 194
voice ceases from, 258–9
wisemen from the east visit, 362
Jesus Christ   (*see also* Lamb; Second Coming; Bethlehem; crucifixion;

K

eat the flesh of the *k.*, 414, 422
Herod, 361, 429
hid themselves in rocks,167
James version/translation, 63, 80,
248, 338, 401
marriage of son, 410–12
of Babylon, 123, 405
of beasts (lion) 212
of Kings, 384, 419, 484, 487
of the earth, 390, 395, 400, 406, 451
of the east, 361
prince of the *k.* of the earth, 66–8, 187
receives power as we give it to him,
376, 395
seven, 382
Solomon, 266
ten, 383–4, 387
who rules over them, 214–15, 243,
255, 361, 387
King's Highway, 360–1
kingdom
eternal, 68–9, 135, 144, 231, 260
of heaven, 120, 329, 340, 370, 410, 450
kingdom of God,
"a child is delivered," 271
"A sure place," 98–9
build, 241–4, 263
establish, 247, 263, 300, 423, 447–8
experience, 286
foundations, 132
heirs of, 68
holy/beloved city, 432, 458
inherit the kingdom of, 144, 403
John gets excited relating the
wonderful promise, 286
Lamb's bride, 412
mystery of, 181–3
saved in the *k.*, 180
Understand, 284, 353
Upon earth, 144, 432, 447
knees, 168, 186, 266
knowledge, 9–11, 100, 119, 372–3
great, 125, 128, 357
pretended, 79, 198, 232, 355
pure, 107, 348, 389
sure, 238–9

L

labor/laborer, 402, 425
and are heavy laden, 136, 160, 214,
331
desire to be free from, 310
hot sun all day, 40, 403
menial, 383, 24
replaced with machines, 360, 387
survival, 24, 26, 47, 155, 386
value placed on, 397
lake of fire, 424–5, 432, 434
lamb(s), 44, 136–7, 244, 310–11, 379
beast presented as, 310–11
government presented as, 302
prepared to be slain, 139, 352
two horns like, 303–6
Lamb   (*see also* Christ)
blood of, 159, 180–1, 285–6
church of, 68, 83, 102
flesh of, 414, 420
of God, 69, 304, 433
marriage of, 75, 408, 410
specific to this solar system, 179
wife of, 412, 444
wrath of, 167, 330   (*see also* wrath)
lamentations, 166, 196, 236, 291, 396, 401
lamp, 55, 118, 121, 197, 347
John's, 55–6
seven burning, 115, 119, 198
star burning as a *l.*, 197–8
ten virgins, 119–21, 347
land
borders drawn, 208
defiled, 392–3
desolate, 201, 258, 291, 405
of promise, 277–9, 289, 440–1
ownership of, 20, 25–6, 305
to water ratio, 195
Lao Tse, 248
last/latter days, 309, 370, 444
Revelation unfolded in, 72, 66, 77,
186–7, 240, 389
sins in, 78, 339, 391, 422
technological advances, 100, 219–20,
309, 372

full of, 216
money and substance, 252
not the world, 215
of neighbor, 103, 303, 360, 368, 431,
    450
one another, 135, 144, 189, 352, 357,
    370, 372
our enemies, 79–80, 300, 330, 340,
    360, 370
peace, harmony (balance), 93, 109,
    181–3, 346
the poor and needy, 252
universal teaching, 325
lower law, 213, 239
Lucifer (*see also* human nature)
    "fallen star," 203
    human nature, 66–7, 95, 153, 187, 216
    overcomes the "name" of Christ, 93
    Prince of the Kingdom of Persia,
        186–7
    "Satan," "the devil," 66, 203, 281–2,
        284, 441
    sins of the flesh, 76
    son of the morning, 66, 204, 281
    "the accuser of men," 283
    the dragon, 273, 275, 280–1
    the prince of the kings of the earth,
        66, 187
    the prince of the world, 250
lukewarm, 103
lust(s), 109, 255, 219, 255–7
    (*see also* Thyatira)
    brimstone, 221
    caused by leaders' example, 363
    commandment against, 340
    conceiving sin, 322
    desires, 205, 370
    driven by, 216, 256, 298
    for ease and comfort, 309
    for material things, 205, 290, 294,
        298, 365
    gospel helps to overcome, 378
    government, 302, 307
    of human nature, 223, 356, 383, 428,
        453
    of the flesh (Sodom), 79, 203, 215,

286, 296, 442
    of the heart, 443, 458
    of the world, 291, 215, 268
    provided by the beast, 294
    righteous do not participate in, 292
    rule over them, 376, 395
    satisfied by locusts, 232
    sexual desire, 376
    war against the soul, 255
luxury/luxuries, 303

M

magic(ian), 71, 140–1
Magog, 431
majority, 22, 43, 155
    desolate of happiness, 154
    exploited, 45, 304, 307
    lead by a few, 208
    must unite, 49
    survival of, 36
male, 145, 289
    alpha, 1, 3, 7
    and female Gods, 61
    partnerships, 6–7
    prophets, 236
manna, 86–8, 278
mansions, 128, 132, 134
the mark, 23–7, 35, 44, 328
    (*see also* dragon; materialism)
    in right hand or forehead, 51, 56,
        313–15, 326, 328
    left after accomplishment or
        experience, 313
    of beast, 350–1, 380, 384, 424, 429
    of his name, 328
    upon all human kind, 31
    victory over, 331, 338, 428
market, 305, 327, 359, 364, 384
marriage (*see also* unification; ten virgins)
    of the Lamb, 75, 408, 410
    of the King's son, 410, 414
    saving oneself for *m.*, 408
    supper, 53, 413–14
Mary Magdalene, 392
materialism, 371, 382

of beast (speaking great things),
299–301, 306, 311, 362
bitter taste in, 29–30
blasphemed God, 300
of Christ, 171–2, 174, 196, 200, 288,
439, 458
of dragon/serpent, 290–1, 362, 364
draw near with, 190, 325
of false prophet, 362
fire and smoke, 220–1, 251
no guile found in, 323–4
kings shall shut their *m.*, 457
of a lion, 295–6
of the original author himself, 240, 394
power in, 221–3
of religious and political leaders, 290,
362, 365
spued out of, 103
sweet as honey, 235–6, 238
sword of   (*see* two–edged sword)
movie stars, 398
multitude(s), 179, 335
and nations and tongues, 170, 385
give unified consent, 118
spoken to by Christ, 94, 174
stood before throne, 159, 178–9
voice of great, 75, 119, 407–9
murder(s)/murderers, 272, 411, 442–3, 458
of Christ, 67
repent not of, 223–4
music, 138, 312, 321, 338, 364–6
musicians, 19, 404
Muslims, 326   (*see also* Mohammed)
mystery/mysteries, 309
Christ's knowledge of, 333
given in the latter days, 372
hidden/sealed, 59, 75, 110, 132, 140,
240, 348, 377
inability to know, 277, 328, 354–5, 414
invented, 232
name written on woman's forehead,
379–80
of God, 58–9, 62, 99, 101, 120, 124,
232–4, 276
of life, 233, 453
of the kingdom of God, 181

overcome Lucifer to understand, 189
prophet's understanding of, 110, 125,
180, 187, 229, 334
revealed by Christ, 275–6
revealed, 226, 354, 373
seven stars, 77
spiritual make up, 166
understanding of, 175, 208, 239, 308,
347, 356
unsealed, 54, 59, 63, 96, 276, 301

N

nail, fastened in a sure place, 98–9
naked/nakedness, 95, 103–4, 387, 426
pass by you, 253, 259, 329, 424
whore, 385
name
of the beast,   (*see* beast, name of)
of blasphemy, 293–4, 356
of Christ, 79, 92–3, 253, 269, 329, 334
new, 87–8, 101–2
of Father written in their foreheads,
177, 317–18
written, King of Kings, 419
written, Mystery, Babylon…, 294, 379
nation(s), 10, 155, 302, 358
(*see also* candlestick; Babylon;
United States of America)
all *n.* shall flow unto it, 444
allegiance to, 34, 301, 313
deceived, 404, 431
destruction among, 202
do not provide for masses, 385
fell, 374
gathered, 425
healing of, 456
law of, 297
lead away from Royal Law, 168
of world prominence, 155–6
overrun other lands, 153, 300, 302–4
ruled with a rod of iron, 276–7, 418
seven, 77
those sealed among, 177
warring, 33
wealth of, 305

P

pain(s), 312, 417
  caused by us, 214, 392, 454
  gnawed tongues for *p.*, 357–9
  of hunger, 278
  over at death, 225
  relieved, 271, 438
pale horse (*see* horse)
Palestine, 73
palm(s)
  in hands, 159, 178–9, 186
  leaf, 179
  tree, 165
parable(s), 181, 421
  bride/the lamb's wife, 410–12
  marriage of the King's son, 410–12
  mustard seed, 439
  rich man/Lazarus, 402–3
  talents, 373
  ten virgins, 119, 347
  thief, 226
parent(s) 7, 10, 24, 33, 205, 319
pastor, 159, 278, 353
patience, 79, 88–9, 100
  of Christ, 69
  fruits of, 429, 440
  of God, 104
  of the saints, 32–5, 44, 302, 330–1, 216
Patmos, 69
patriotism, 392
  allegiance to nation, 34
  duty to support nation, 301
  emotional security from, 15
  leads to isolation, 299
  rhetoric of "new kings," 26, 305
  used to pacify followers, 222
Paul (apostle), 73, 87, 94
peace (*see also* happiness, balance)
  another beast, 302
  balance, 47–8, 181–2, 281, 304, 390–1
  breast plate of cloth, 24, 47–9, 54,
    231–2
  create/establish *p.* without, within,
    34, 48, 222, 284, 354, 384, 437
  destroy/opposite, 48, 93, 153, 166,

    222–3, 232, 331
  enemy of, 216, 267, 317, 371–3
  foundation of *p.* (see Jerusalem)
  from the earth, 152–3
  fruit of the spirit, 109
  guarantee, 24, 208
  harmony, 91, 93, 127, 153, 183, 320
  harp, 330
  of human kind, 48
  key to, 395
  on planets, 135, 302
  p. and equality, 304, 324, 384
  peace on earth, 285, 366
  place of peace, 280
  prince of, 366–9, 420
  promised, 102, 106, 180, 232, 269
  righteous and *p.*, 275, 318
  "rock," 309
  salvation, 283, 288
  serenity, 112
pearl(s), 397
  of great price, 450
  twelve, 450
  woman decked with, 294, 400
peers/peer groups, 20, 33
Pentecost, 172
perdition, 185, 380–1, 383
Pergamos, 71, 78–9, 85
persecution, 326, 330
Persia, 382
  prince of the kingdom of, 186–8
  prophets of, 248
personal revelation, 390, 420
pestilence, 194, 351–2
Pharaoh, 191, 257, 350
Pharisees, 180, 340, 363, 410
Philadelphia, 71, 78–9, 95
Philosophy, 218
physical body, 45–7, 127–8
physical strength, 22, 43, 213
picket fence, 338, 356–7, 366, 374, 397
pilgrims, 255, 309
pillar
  of cloud, 227, 277–8
  of fire, feet, 108, 225, 227–8
  in the temple, 101

pit of destruction, 204
plague(s), 206
  added to man, 251, 454, 459
  brought upon by words of Christ,
    253–4
  of hail, 371, 373
  manifested in day of the Lord, 394
  power over, 356–7, 385, 444
  prophet during final, 355
  relief from, 385, 390–1
  seven, 334, 337, 344–9, 373
  smite the earth, 253
  temporary relief from, 364
  threatening human race, 223
plan of salvation, 128, 130, 135, 138–9,
    150, 410
planet(s), 3, 131–2, 149, 160
    (*see also* solar system, Universe)
  angels sent to earth, 114, 119, 122,
    124, 324
  Christ oversees, 136, 139, 226
  eternal, 84–5, 95, 127, 135, 139, 164
  best suited for each of us, 144, 281
  earth at second coming, 228, 302
  inhabited, 111
  natural laws of, 16, 47
  of our solar system, 131–2
  of God, 112–13
  prepared by Creator, 52, 126
  where Christ lives, 49, 62–3, 113
pleasure, 6, 125, 201, 322, 326, 333, 366
plowshares, 49, 334, 444–5
poison rain, 290
policy/policies
  United States, 296, 306, 311, 384, 387
  Roman, 154–6, 298
  rule the world, 296
  of the world, 154, 386
political parties, 34, 155
politicians, 86, 222, 267, 290, 305
politics, 210, 294, 298–9, 301–3, 307
poor (the), 37, 103–4, 210
  affected by others, 393–4
  become poorer, 380
  exploited, 153, 304, 386, 402, 425
  forgotten, 290

giving to, 87
gospel preached to, 82
grind at the wheel, 310, 392, 397, 402
invite to dinner, 399
love churches more than, 253
masses, 155, 304, 311
receive mark, 313
rejoice, 212
shall inherit the kingdom of God, 403
popes, 54, 207, 353
poverty, 83, 210
  attempts to eliminate, 49
  caused from war, 155
  eliminated by living Royal Law, 223
  ignoring, 39, 223
  increasing, 380, 387
  perpetuated by monetary system, 56
  poor laboring class, 155
praise, worldly, 253, 364
prayer(s), 123, 237, 259
  of the saints, 137–9, 190, 346
  will not be heard, 142, 244
precepts, 183
  accepted as truth, 59, 192–3, 198, 232
  cannot change eternal truth, 418
  learned from birth, 99
  of religion, 90, 176, 290, 342, 363
  of God, 76
  of men, 85, 173, 208, 210, 253, 325,
    330, 333
  of the gospel/Royal Law, 159, 389,
    413
  of world, 164, 307
  shaken, 265
predestined, 124
presidents, 21, 207, 300, 305
pride, 49, 78–9, 81, 109, 373
  and authority, 256–7
  burn from, 74, 396
  corrupts knowledge, 198
  destroyed, 175, 367
  erase, 112
  of your hearts, 252
  results of, 156, 166, 168
priest(s), 213, 445
    (*see also* locust; religious leader)

becomes universal law, 374, 396
Do Unto Others, 404
human interactions in relation to, 394
law of the gospel, 408
lead away from, 168
living without, 155, 327–8, 168, 407–8
love another as yourself, 139, 156, 383
of the Father, 103
opposed by guile, 323
results of following, 208
those living, 144, 177, 385

S

of stumbling, 133
tables of, 197, 343
tablets, 274, 342, 344
twelve, 152, 445, 448
white, 87
stranger(s), 393
and pilgrims, 255
house of a *s.*, 199
pass through her, 335
ye took me in, 129, 329, 424, 426
street(s)
caused me to sleep in *s.*, 424
like unto clear glass, 448–9
tree of life in midst of the *s.*, 456
dead bodies shall lie in, 256, 259, 261, 263
Christ walked, 318
pure gold, 450
lay/lie dead in the *s.*, 259, 261, 263
stress
anxiety/worry, 354, 358
emotional, 21, 215, 324, 391
level of *s.*, 385
of existence, 210
and torment, 215
stumbling block(s), 86, 94, 123, 140–1, 168
suicide, 239
sun, 258
burning fire, 75, 123
clothed, 270
cover the *s.* with a cloud, 55, 163, 202
darkened, 161, 168, 201, 206, 291, 327, 335, 417
done under the *s.*, 381, 438
light of, 40, 55, 113, 226, 270, 277, 290, 333
Lord/God, 457
pour from vial upon the *s.*, 355
represents, 227, 300, 356
rise on the evil and good, 300
that gives life, 55, 63
third part of, 200
warmth from, 162
word of God, 164
supernatural, 10, 283
supper

call not thy friends, 399
marriage *s.*, 413–14
of the Lamb, 53, 414, 420
of the great god, 420–2
of the kings son, 414
sweat
and blood, 139, 141–2
stings the eyes, 40
and tears, 141–2
and toil, 40
face(s), 310
of the brow, 41, 402
sword, 303, 421
not lift up s. against nation, 444
cuts both ways, 36–37
two–edged, 44, 75–6, 199
of him that sat upon the horse, 425
into plowshares, 49, 335, 444–5
not peace but a *s.*, 285, 366
proceeding from my mouth, 76, 86, 90, 143, 365–6, 370, 425
third part shall fall, 194
of truth, 36–7, 90, 415
sharp, 85, 204, 213, 252, 418
of vengeance, 253
words of Christ, 76
wound by a *s.* and did live, 309, 311, 313, 365, 417
synagogue, 82, 99

T

tabernacle, 73, 397, 405
(*see also* Ark of the Covenant)
blasphemed, 300
opened, 342
portable temple, 343–5
veil in, 430
with men, 436
table
rich man's, 402–3
of stone, 197, 343–4
spread with fruits of truth, 404
tail(s), 223
also have mouths, 222
dragon, 274–5

after righteousness, 182
shall never *t.*, 134, 182–3, 279, 353,
    357, 458
for knowledge, 198, 353–4
temporarily appeased, 353, 355
dieth of, 351
for happiness, 454
for money, 337
quenched, 430
sore *athirst*, 350–1
ye gave me no drink, 129, 329, 424
unquenchable, 453–4
thorns, 193, 207, 235, 272, 440
thought(s), 331, 354, 384, 386, 438, 443
three and a half years (3 1/2 years), 245
three days and an half (3 1/2 days), 249,
    257–60, 264, 279
throne   (*see also* thunder, from throne)
    about the *t.*, 121, 145, 179
    altar before, 190
    child taken to, 276
    beasts (four) about, 115
    given to Christ, 71
    given to the elect, 428–9
    Lamb before, 182, 407, 439
    multitude stood before, 159, 178
    of God, 65, 124, 126, 137, 146, 179,
        181, 323, 456
    rainbow round about, 113–14
    sea of glass before, 121
    sitting on, 111–14, 167, 181, 190
    spirits about, 145
    twenty–four elders in midst of, 114,
        136
    voice coming from, 75, 153, 409
    white, 432
    worshiping before, 179, 268, 332, 409
thrust in sickle, 333–4, 390
thunder/thunderings, 269
    coming out of lamps, 115
    coming out of temple, 373
    filled the censer, 191
    from throne, 118
    God's power and will, 118, 148
    noise, 148
    seven, 184, 187, 228–9

seventh, 230
storms, 372
upon Egypt, 192
voice of, 75, 119, 319, 321, 409
Thyatira, 71, 78–9, 88, 90
time, times, and an half, 230–1, 245,
    260–5, 279, 288–9
timetable(s)
    used by prophets, 185
    Daniel's, 231, 245, 261
    established, 231
    exact, 245
    John's, 260–4, 300
    of God, 185, 248
tithes (and offerings), 303, 329
Titus, 440, 443
tolerance (other's beliefs), 93, 223, 341
tongue(s)
    as fire, 196,
    kindred, *t.*, and people, 139, 159, 170,
        178, 324
    speak lies, 358, 386
    hate the whore, 385
    against the Lord, 257
    speak in *t.*, 172
    as a sharp sword, 204, 213
    other, (i.e., languages), 214, 367–8
torment(s), 328, 392   (*see also* tribulation)
    emotional, 209, 216
    fear of, 399
    endless, 205, 210, 225
    from scorpion, 208–10, 214
    we create, 215
    of locusts, 211, 427
    ends at death, 225
    of prophets' dead bodies, 259
    the woman, 287–8
    learning from, 209
    of the flesh, 195
    plagues, 349
    relief from, 209–10
    smoke of, 328, 396, 408, 427
tradition
    of parents/fathers, 10, 352
    of men, 132
    of Gentiles, 244

U

flag of, 76
government of, 311
great beast, 51
history of, 297, 305–6, 313
influence of, 327
intervention by, 305, 313, 384
laws, 311
people under darkness, 76
seat of the beast, 296
standard of living, 311, 313
waste in, 380
works of pale horse & rider, 156
Universe, 15, 63, 75, 30–1
angel's help in, 130, 326
balance in, 77
has always been, 60
humans in, 149
instructions in Book of Life, 326, 434
laws of, 326, 432–4
matter of, 59–60
not alone, 283
part of, under Christ's direction, 63, 68, 135, 139
seen in vision, 75, 111
updraft, 372
urban sprawl, 20 (*see also* Babylon)
Urim and Thummim, 113, 121

V

values (monetary), 42, 48, 153–4, 208, 443
placed on individuals, 11, 41
system, 299, 314
value(s), 16, 18, 397,400
abstract, 7
American, 383–4
eternal, 396
family, 363, 383
conscience vs. beast, 370
taken away, 396–8, 374, 451
that sustain happiness, 31
set by others, 43, 208
human, 43, 153, 397–8, 418
lead people… away from Royal Law, 208, 383
individual, 8, 23–4, 27, 47

presented by organized religion, 363
self–worth, 32–3
based on standards set, 38, 46, 299
of others, 273
vanity, 112, 192, 201, 386, 393
all is *v.*, 381
in false beliefs, 173
truth destroys, 175
veil, 107
ark (*see* Ark of the Covenant)
fleshly brain, 236
inability to know all of the mysteries, 277
reason for, 236, 238
removed, 106, 237–8, 432–3
seeing through, 344, 377
vengeance, 143, 213, 253
vessels, 91, 98, 119, 138, 397
Via Maris, 369–70
our own, 370
Way of the Sea, 361
vial(s)
golden, 137–9, 147, 190, 345–6
in servants' hands, 189, 346
poured out, 189, 334, 346–7, 349, 350–3, 355–7, 360, 371, 373
human wickedness, 189, 346
filled with wrath of God, 345–7, 349, 447
seven, 375, 444
victory, 285
over the beast, 338, 347, 351
palm leaf, 179
swallow up death in *v.*, 271, 438
video games, 364–5
vine (*see also* winepress)
fruit of, 175, 418
in thy blood, 277
dried up, 165
leaf falleth from, 164, 433
natural, 55
of the earth, 334–5
virgin(s)
remain as, 321–2
ten, 119–20, 347
vision, 72, 149, 272–3

recorded, 165, 433
tie flesh and spirit together, 73
unrighteous, 95, 142–3, 310, 434
vain, 87,190, 396
World Bank, 384
World War I and II, 398
Worldwide United Foundation (WUF), 49
wormwood, 198–200
worry/worries, 351, 391
    block understanding, 354
    past, present and future, 112
    victory over, 112, 337–8, 354
worth, 45
    eternal, 396
    individual, 23, 33–4, 38, 41, 46–8
    material, 153–4, 397
    monetary, 42
    self   (*see* self–worth)
worthy, 24, 254–5, 285
    called by my name, 93
    cause, 381
    Lamb to be slain, 145
    of power and authority, 117, 128, 136
    prove yourself, 160
    to open the book, 113, 130, 139
    to oversee work of Father, 131, 135
wound(s)/wounded, 106
    by the sword, 309, 311, 313, 365
    first beast, 302, 304, 311
    Great Roman Empire, 298
    healed, 296, 302, 306
    policies and laws, 298
    unto death, 296, 478
    watchmen, 106
wrath, 82, 201, 286–7, 323, 393
    non–intervention, 31, 168, 360, 373, 418, 444
    of God, 35, 44, 334, 336–8, 345–6, 349, 418
    of her fornication, 390
    of the Lamb, 167, 330, 385
    of the Lord, 161, 168, 422
    pouring out, 346, 349, 354–7
    wine of, 326–8, 374, 376

Y

Yeshua, 278
yoke
    broken the *y.* of his burden, 369, 419
    depart from off them, 244
    is easy, 136, 160, 214, 331, 338
youth, 201

Z

zeal
    of the Lord, 369, 420
    tread with *z.*, 418
Zebulun, land of, 369
Zechariah, prophet, 243
Zion, 318, 335, 444
    fortress of the Jebusites called *Z.*, 317
    is a wilderness, 278
    Mount Zion, 162, 317–18
    songs and everlasting joy, 321

From Section 9—page 49

Religious prophets and social pundits have made various attempts throughout human history to eliminate poverty and inequality. There is only one human organization that has ever been founded on the premise of worldwide equality and the guarantee of food, shelter, clothing, and health care to **all** *"wise ones."* This organization has the proper formula needed to succeed:

The Worldwide United Foundation

This united effort is the last chance for the species of *"wise ones"* to stop their decline and spiral into chaos, turmoil, and emotional and physical destruction. United, the people of the earth *can* solve their own problems and reinstate the preamble of their existence: We are free-willed beings with the ability to reason and use our free agency to establish our own individuality.

Worldwide United
FOUNDATION

www.WWUNITED.org
1.888.499.9666

ONE world
ONE solution
ONE people
ONE DAY!

2303 Sherwood Drive • Lemon Grove, California, USA • 91945

AUTHOR'S BIO:

Christopher (last name concealed for his personal protection) was born on December 2, 1961. Though raised in a very large religious family, his pursuit of truth led him to question the validity of organized religion and the effect it has on the world. By no choice of his own, he was chosen by others to bring to the world the true meaning hidden in the Apostle John's Revelation. Unlike those who set themselves up as leaders and spiritual guides to others, Christopher believes in only one universal mandate: Do unto others what you would have them do unto you—nothing more, nothing less. His life experience is vast, but his gentle love for humankind remains unaffected by his many personal tragedies. He is unlike those of similar goals who seek to profit monetarily or in popularity from their works. He has contracted all profits, royalties, and earnings from his writings, to the establishment of The Worldwide United Foundation (wwunited.org), an organization dedicated to the elimination of poverty and inequality throughout the world. Though very personable, approachable, and amiable to all, Christopher chooses to live as the "least among us," having few possessions and no worldly aspirations. He is best described as the one inferred by the popular song,

The Impossible Dream:

"To dream the impossible dream
To fight the unbeatable foe
To bear with unbearable sorrow
To run where the brave dare not go

To right the unrightable wrong
To love pure and chaste from afar
To try when your arms are too weary
To reach the unreachable star

This is my quest
To follow that star
No matter how hopeless
No matter how far

To fight for the right
Without question or pause
To be willing to march into Hell
For a heavenly cause

And I know if I'll only be true
To this glorious quest
That my heart will lie peaceful and calm
When I'm laid to my rest

And the world will be better for this
That one man, scorned and covered with scars
Still strove with his last ounce of courage
To reach the unreachable star."